Inspiration
& Reality

Inspiration & Reality

The First Fifty Years of the
Scott Bader Commonwealth

Robert Oakeshott

MICHAEL RUSSELL

To John Leyland and Andrew Gunn,
two distinguished Quaker members of
the Scott Bader Commonwealth,
whose commitment to Quaker idealism in business
has been made that much more effective by
a lively sense of the realities

The right of Robert Oakeshott to be identified
as the author of this work has been asserted by him
in accordance with the Copyright, Designs
and Patents Act, 1988

First published in Great Britain 2001
by Michael Russell (Publishing) Ltd
Wilby Hall, Wilby, Norwich NR16 2JP

Typeset in Sabon by Waveney Typesetters
Wymondham, Norfolk
Printed and bound in Great Britain
by Biddles Ltd, Guildford and King's Lynn

Contents

Contents

Foreword

There is a growing perception across the world that the Anglo-American model of capitalism, with its heavy emphasis on shareholder value, is becoming an inescapable global norm. Allowing employees a formal role in corporate governance is, by the same token, increasingly seen as inhibiting the ability of firms to restructure in response to the pressures of global competition. This new conventional wisdom, which is largely a response to the resurgence of US corporations against German and Japanese competition in the 1990s, raises difficult questions for alternative forms of ownership. If shareholder value is a key to international competitiveness, where does that leave those corporate forms that eliminate shareholder capital?

The history of Scott Bader, with its system of common ownership and co-determination, provides helpful clues, many of them far from discouraging. The mere fact of the company's profitable survival in the highly competitive international market for polyester resins and speciality polymers suggests that the lack of conventional shareholders may be less of a handicap than appears at first sight.

Profit maximisation, it should be emphasised at the outset, was never the goal. The vision of founder Ernest Bader was, as Robert Oakeshott reminds us in this study of the first 50 years of the Scott Bader Commonwealth, one of a democratic working community aiming for the minimum growth compatible with the expression of Christian social values and economic survival. By the standards of other such ventures the Scott Bader agenda was particularly challenging, with its aspiration to replace commercial values with Christian values, its commitment to pacifism and to high levels of charitable giving.

That said, it has to be asked why there are not more Scott Baders; why the hopes invested in common ownership and other cooperative forms of corporate organisation in recent decades have not been fulfilled on the scale that many expected. The combination of shared ownership, co-determination and labour-friendly welfare does, after all, appear to hold out the promise of greatly improved industrial relations. If workers are given a real sense of a stake in the business and a genuine say in the operations of the workplace, there ought surely to be less alienation and higher labour productivity.

There are many possible explanations, starting with the difficulties inherent in the initial legacy of such ventures. In the US and the UK many cooperatives have been born of financial crises in times of recession. Under the British Labour governments of 1974–79 some enjoyed a degree of political support and subsidy which was not justified by the prospects of the underlying businesses. The outcome was disastrous in terms of the message it conveyed about the effectiveness of employee ownership. In the US there were many more successful examples of employee equity involvement in the restructuring of ailing businesses. This reflected, among other things, a greater readiness on the part of American workers to accept large pay cuts as a quid pro quo for ownership and continuing employment. But even in the US, employee ownership and involvement in governance could not always provide a durable solution in many mature industries where US labour was trying to compete with low pay rates in the developing world.

Another important aspect of the initial legacy concerns the personality and aspirations of the founder of the non-conventionally-owned business. In many cases, as at Scott Bader, there is a powerful element of paternalism in the motives and attitudes that lead to the transfer of ownership. The transfer of control rights to employees may also occur at a slower pace than the transfer of ownership. The risk is that the processes of co-determination may not be sufficient, whether in design or implementation, to break down a 'them-and-us' culture. Without a serious cooperative effort by management and employees to achieve productivity improvements common ownership cannot deliver on its promise.

Then there is the question of labour costs and incentives. There is always a risk with businesses that are committed to non-profit-maximising values that labour will become uncompetitive and that management remuneration will depart so far from market rates that it becomes difficult to recruit and retain people. On this score, Scott Bader's experience demonstrates that flexibility is possible within the common ownership framework. Despite a commitment in the constitutional documents to reducing pay rather than making people redundant, the community has voted in favour of voluntary redundancies with generous compensation on three separate occasions. In the case of an ill-judged acquisition that threatened the viability of the group, agreement was even reached on compulsory redundancies. As for management remuneration, the original arrangement in 1951 stipulated a specific maximum differential of 6 to 1 for pay levels within the group. This was cancelled in 1990 in favour of a general injunction that the differential should not be excessive.

Such potential conflicts between social values and competitiveness do not arise exclusively from the labour side of the equation. From the outset the Scott Bader constitution imposed a duty to have regard to the interests of the local community and the environment. Clearly there is a balance to be struck between such duties and the requirements of financial viability. The problem is not, incidentally, confined to common ownership corporations. In Germany some Mittelstand companies – owner-managed small and medium-sized firms – often have a deep commitment to the local community. Some have foundered because they have been reluctant to close uncompetitive plants in the home town and re-establish their operations in eastern Europe or other parts of the world where unit labour costs are much lower.

Perhaps the most difficult questions of all concern access to capital and corporate governance. When confronting the challenge of maintaining a significant share of a global market, internal financing carries risks. It is noteworthy, for example, that the Baxi Partnership – once regarded as an exemplary model of British common ownership – overstretched itself through debt-financed acquisitions. It was left with no alternative but to sell the business. Scott Bader's expansion has been more judicious, partly because it has consciously aimed for the smallest size compatible with sustainability. After initial financial strains, its moves into France, South Africa, Dubai and Croatia were accomplished without damaging the balance sheet. If there is a question about its growth, it relates to the return on capital rather than the serviceability of debt.

The return on capital at Scott Bader is undeniably low by the standards of its competitors. If it were a quoted company, it would almost certainly have attracted takeover interest by now from a potential predator. As long as it retains a strong balance sheet and remains immune from shocks, it can survive for the foreseeable future. The very difficult challenge for management, working within a unique and somewhat ambiguous system of corporate governance, is to find an alternative to genteel relative decline.

It would be easy at this point to offer a pessimistic prognosis. Yet the striking thing about the corporate governance debate is how it is moving in the direction of many of the original Scott Bader values.

There is a growing recognition that corporate success now depends heavily on sound management of stakeholder relations, including those with employees, suppliers, the community and the environment. That is implicit in the definition of directors' duties proposed by the UK Company Law Review. It is also acknowledged by many large companies in the Anglo-American corporate world.

With human capital becoming increasingly important for competitive advantage, the idea of the shareholder as the residual risk-taker in the capitalist system, enjoying all the rights to the profit after other claims on the business have been met, looks anachronistic. In many companies employees have more at risk, and less ability to diversify that risk, than big institutional investors. The dividing line between human capital and shareholder capital is thus becoming blurred. It follows that alternative approaches to equity ownership and employee involvement are likely to be the subject of wider interest in future.

Whether they follow a Scott Bader-type model of common ownership, a stock option model or some other ownership format is less important than the values embedded in their constitutions or governance arrangements. It seems probable that those values will be closer to many of the values in the Scott Bader constitution than to the anachronistic shareholder-oriented 19th century liberal model. Ernest Bader often employed the phrase 'responsible ownership' in explaining his goals. Today politicians, businessmen and institutional investors are beginning to use that same phrase and to interpret it, albeit in a secular way, along similar lines to the founder of the Scott Bader Commonwealth. That, in the end, is a more important legacy than the survival of the Scott Bader business itself – a tribute to the extraordinary vision of an extraordinary man.

JOHN PLENDER

John Plender is a senior editorial writer and commentator for the Financial Times. *He served on the steering group of the UK Company Law Review from 1998 to 2001.*

Author's Preface

I hope that this history of the first 50 years of the Scott Bader Commonwealth will be of interest and just possibly of some use to two distinct, if partially overlapping, groups of readers. At the centre of the first group are those who either are or have been actual members of the Commonwealth during the last half century and are now either still working for the business or have moved on, whether into retirement or otherwise.

The second group whose attention I am hoping to attract is more diffuse. At its maximum, it includes all those who are interested in those businesses which have chosen to adopt corporate government and ownership forms which are as democratic and broadly based as is consistent with reasonable and sustainable business success. Partly because there is much variation in their detailed arrangements, there is no description of them which is both short and generally accepted. So those who write about this subject must choose their descriptions with some care. Even within Scott Bader there is a continuing – and often quite bracing – debate about whether the business should be characterised as a 'common ownership' or, alternatively, as a 'trusteeship' firm. Twenty-five years ago in 1976, when, quite largely as a result of Scott Bader's inspiration, an Industrial Common Ownership Act was passed by the British Parliament, this whole field was to some extent occupied by competing and more or less exclusive sects: for example those who favoured the much older corporate form of the production co-ops, those who favoured 'common ownership' on Scott Bader lines, and thirdly those who preferred to talk about a less ideologically constrained 'employee ownership', initially based on American models.

Those days of competing sects and exclusivity are now mercifully almost over. It is true that my friend Godric Bader, since 1990 Scott Bader's life president, is still inclined to respond with a shudder when *employee* ownership is mentioned. It is also true that there is still something of a gulf or barrier – what has indeed sometimes been a chasm – between the generally much older production co-ops and all the others. But however that may be, it is people involved in what has lately become a broad church of these businesses who form my second target group of readers.

Though the interests of the two groups overlap, they are far from identical. Readers from the first group will have to put up with – or skip – material which may not be narrowly relevant to Scott Bader's half century of Commonwealth history; and the same applies to those in the second group. There are details, for example about the evolution of Scott Bader's institutional arrangements, which they may have either to read right on through – even if found fairly boring – or pass over.

But where, I have reasonably been asked, does the author fit in with this background? At the end of the preface I will formally declare an interest in the shape of debts which I owe to Scott Bader, both financial and otherwise. More generally I should make clear that I worked more or less full time in this field for the 30 years which ended with my retirement in the autumn of 1999. That work has been of different kinds, ranging from employment in an actual building co-op, through research and writing, to consulting and advocacy. The longest continuous spell was 20 years, starting in 1979, as executive director of Job Ownership Ltd (JOL). As its name implies, JOL was set up to promote the ownership of businesses by the people who worked in them, and not by either faraway absentee private shareholders or the state. About corporate structures to fit such ownership arrangements JOL has always been pluralistic and pragmatic: given that the 'insider' ownership and associated employee participation in decision-making must be broadly based and fair, then whatever works well is right.

On the other hand, as I have tried to show in my *Jobs and Fairness: the Logic and Experience of Employee Ownership* (Michael Russell, 2000), some of the ventures which fall into this general category have been more and others less successful; and many have failed. That is a sufficient explanation, or so it seems to me, of the sometimes critical stance which I have adopted in tracing the history of Scott Bader over the last 50 years. One source of my critical attitude is the belief that, over the last 50 years, ideas and practices within the broad church of these enterprises have moved on, and that some examples of potentially universalisable best practice have begun to emerge. Another is the hypothesis that, in this sphere as in may others, the best, perhaps defined as the most idealistically ambitious, may be the enemy of the good. Like his father Ernest, the founder of both the Scott Bader business and the Commonwealth, Godric Bader is a tireless advocate of arrangements which can be presented as 'transcending ownership', and thus, at least in theory, make possible the emergence of people with quite different values working in industry. Well, my own response would be, 'Perhaps *just* possibly, and if those who are to work in such environments are pre-selected.' In this context I would also be inclined to draw readers' attention to a passage in a speech addressed by Ken Clarke to the Tory Reform Group in 1986, shortly after his return from a visit to the Mondragon Co-operatives in the Basque Provinces of Spain: 'I have increasingly come to believe that one of the worst things that Tony Benn ever did was to give co-operatives a bad name. He linked co-operatives in the public mind with left-wing politics, loss-making production, and endless taxpayers' subsidy.'

And that brings me on to a second issue about which I have been asked to clarify my position: the Christian religion. In the second chapter I argue that the single most important driver behind Ernest Bader's decision to set up the Commonwealth in 1951 – and then to pass over to it in stages the ownership and control of the business – was the idea of a social Christianity, or of what has sometimes been called the social gospel. Despite the fact that there were other sources, for example the teachings of Gandhi, there is no serious doubt that Christian social teaching, and perhaps within that Quaker teachings and the traditions of Quaker businesses, was the main one.

However, it does not follow at all, or so it seems to me, that efforts to propagate explicit Christian teaching or even Christian morality and values among Commonwealth members – or other Scott Bader employees – necessarily make good sense. Indeed there are two cases, in the 50-year history which follows, of Christian professionals who argued in effect, even if for rather different reasons, that it was a mistake to attempt any such thing. One was the former full-time Baptist minister, Gwen Veale, who was the first head, in the 1950s and early 1960s, of what was then the personnel department at Scott Bader; and the second was an Anglican priest, the Revd Bruce Reed. The latter undertook an important consultancy for the business in 1969 when he was head of the prestigious Grubb Institute in London. The result was the seminal Reed report which had wide-ranging consequences.

I define my own position in relation to the Christian religion with some reluctance because I have come to think that for non-professionals this is something which can reasonably be kept within the private domain. With that disclaimer, I would describe myself as an Anglican agnostic. I attend a local church quite regularly but not as a communicant. My position is perhaps a little like those of parents who want their children to attend a Christian school but are not themselves full believers. I also like to associate myself with the person who said that he supported the church 'like a buttress from outside but not like a pillar from inside'.

I hope it is not unacceptably self-serving to offer an anecdote at this point which has some bearing on both my commitment to employee ownership and my position in relation to the Christian religion. The scene at which the encounter which generated the anecdote took place was the grounds of Wollaston Hall. The date was 28 April of this year. The event was a celebration of the Commonwealth's 50th birthday, including a number of speeches and the planting of a tree. One of the speakers came up to me after the tree-planting was over and introduced himself at the development manager of Industrial Common Ownership Finance (ICOF), about which see later in chapter 11. Imagine my feelings, dear readers, when Andrew Hibbert then told me that two books with which I have been associated – *The Case for Workers Co-ops* (as sole author) and *The Christian Response to Industrial Capitalism* (as one of three joint authors) – were substantially influential in his decision to make a knight's move in the late 1980s: out of an Anglican theological college and into a local co-operative development agency.

That is something of a digression. But now, having offered some response to questions about where I come from, I need to say something about the 'editorial limits' within which I have written this book which was, of course, commissioned by Scott Bader.

The logic of these editorial limits is really a judgement about how best, given the constraints of space, the public interest is served. Within the public interest rubric, account is also taken of the fact that some of the excluded material is at least partly private. The writing and publication of this book may not be a sufficient reason for shifting much of that into the public domain.

What follows, in line with this editorial judgement, is first that we have left out many of the things which the Founder, Ernest Bader, got up to between his retirement and his death in 1982.

Readers may be interested to know that, after his death, colleagues and friends of the founder of the John Lewis Partnership put together a fine celebratory and commemorative publication, *John Spedan Lewis 1885–1963*. He had retired in 1955 and left London to live in the country near Stockbridge in Hampshire.

Thus Spedan Lewis survived in retirement for no more than eight years, a significantly shorter period than that enjoyed by Ernest Bader. Unlike Ernest he also took himself right away from head office. By contrast, as readers in my first target group and many others will already know, Ernest and Dora Bader went on living 'above the shop' at Wollaston Hall until they died. Of Spedan's retirement years, his successor as partnership chairman, Sir Bernard Miller, wrote in the book which commemorates and celebrates his life:

> I think by that time he had lost his judgement. ... He started a campaign to get the Central Council to say ... that certain things could not be done without his agreement. Of course it wasn't on at all. ... It really was a very difficult time for me trying to stop the partnership at large, through its communication media, from being more beastly to him than they wanted to be. I kept having to remind them that what they'd got was because of what the founder had done for them.

Among the various things which Ernest Bader 'got up to' in his retirement was the burning of the portrait bust in polyester resin with which he had been presented to mark his 90th birthday, and the theatrical aftermath of that *événement*. Both because it is already in the public domain and because it is a good story that is in. Most of what else Ernest got up to during those years, some of it potentially damaging to the business as well as hurtful to individuals, has been left out.

Secondly, we have in fact thought it reasonable to exclude so far as possible disputes, conflicts and 'difficulties' between the holders of Scott Bader's two 'apex positions' since these were split when Godric Bader stood down from the position of managing director but retained the chairmanship in the early 1970s. Those in my first target group of readers will already know or have access to information about 'turbulence' of this kind. For those in the second group I would say that to give emphasis to such personal conflicts very often misses the main point: namely that the 'system' of having *two* apex positions with inadequately defined roles may well be as much the source of trouble as the personalities.

Likewise, we have decided not to ventilate charges of behaviour unacceptably biased against people of a particular race, political party, gender or sexual orientation. Once again insiders either already know or can find out all there is to know under these headings. Once again too, careful research will often suggest that supposed examples of unacceptable bias of these kinds can as well be explained in other ways.

Next a point of clarification about Scott Bader and the Third World. Readers of Susanna Hoe's biography will remember that this became an important interest of Ernest Bader, that he financed the setting up of a Third World aid-dispensing charity called STRIVE (The Society for Training Rural Industries and Village Enterprises) which in turn was one of the forerunners of Dr Schumacher's Intermediate Technology Development Group (ITDG). The latter has, of course, been tremendously influential and has now survived – as a key source of both new thinking and new projects in its field – for more than 40 years. It is true that what has continued at Scott Bader is an important Third World focus in its charitable giving. It is also true and is properly covered in this book that in the closing years of the apartheid regime in South Africa, all company profits from its operations in that country were deflected into a charitable fund and applied to finance educational projects for black Africans, especially in Natal. However, in the case of the ITDG an editorial judgement has been made to the effect that partly because it is already the subject of an immense and growing literature, it should not be allocated space in what follows here. And that judgement has been extended to cover STRIVE. They are referred to in the text but not discussed.

I have explained and agreed these limits with my two Scott Bader 'minders' – Andrew Gunn, Scott Bader's head of finance since 1982 and also company secretary since 1989, and Brian Elgood. Brian Elgood retired from a senior management position with Scott Bader in 1997 and has made a huge contribution to the research that has gone into this book, after some 35 years as a company employee and Commonwealth member.

Before closing this preface I must say a word about an important but fundamentally melancholy recent event in the still small world of Britain's employee ownership of which Scott Bader is a key and contributory member, even if one with its own highly idiosyncratic and sometimes dissenting approach. I refer to the sale to a venture capital group in the late autumn of 2000 – and while this book was being written – of the previously employee-owned Baxi Partnership.

Many readers, both outside and inside the Scott Bader community, will remember that in early 1983, and in what was in many ways an exemplary transaction, Baxi's family owners – that is Philip Baxendale and his cousin Mrs Castleton – sold the business to an employee trust.

The price at which it was sold was rather over £5m. The *Daily Tele-graph* suggested at the time that if Baxi had been offered on the stock exchange it would have fetched between £40m and £50m.

This is not the place for detailed account of the events leading up to the sale of the same business to a venture capital group towards the end of 2000. Perhaps it is most easily understood as having been, at least in part, the result of the clash between two conflicting goals: that of seeking to ensure the survival of the business, its jobs and incomes over the very long term, and that of preserving its employee ownership. The latter, for those who don't know, had always been substantially Trust Ownership with only a small minority of shares owned by employees as individuals. There were those, including the top management team of the business, who had been arguing for some time that if Baxi was to have any real chance of long-term survival in a European market dominated by mega-groups, it must itself adopt a policy of rapid expansion by acquisition. A first step down that road was taken in 1998 with an acquisition which effectively doubled the asset base of the enlarged business. But that, or so it was argued by the top management group, was not sufficient. They subsequently proposed a second acquisition which, if completed, would have increased the asset base of the re-enlarged business to roughly *six times* its original size. To cut a long story short, the same top management eventually persuaded those responsible for voting the employee trust shares that the acquisition could be made without putting Baxi's employee ownership at serious risk. Several hundred millions of pounds were duly borrowed to finance the deal. But it had already become clear within a matter of months that Baxi could not meet the interest charges on those borrowings. In the end those who voted the employee trust's shareholding were probably relieved to reach a deal with the venture capitalists by which the latter acquired the by then much reduced equity capital of the business for approximately £20m. The individual employee shareholders had, of course, no choice but to accept that deal.

For the purposes of this preface just one final point is worth appending to this saga. The point is that, contrary to an opinion widely held and voiced at Wollaston, Scott Bader, despite the ownership of its share capital by a charity, is in principle just as vulnerable as Baxi was to being confronted by a choice of this same kind: between seeking to sustain the company's jobs and incomes on the one hand, or seeking to sustain its special ownership and co-determinational arrangements on the other. To ask how the general meeting of members would actually vote if they genuinely believed that they were faced with such a choice is, of course, an entirely separate question.

Finally I have two quite specific financial debts to Scott Bader which must constitute an interest that needs to be declared. There was first, in the 1970s, financial assistance – in the form of a subscription for loan stock – from what was then called the Commonwealth Development Fund (CDF) to the building co-operative, Sunderlandia, for which I was then working. The Fund kindly agreed to write that off when Sunderlandia went into voluntary liquidation in 1979.

Second, with a start during the 1990s and continuing into the present, both the Scott Bader company and the Commonwealth have contributed recurrent and non-repayable financial support to my most recent employer, Job Ownership Ltd; and to its charitable half sister. I also have a less palpable debt – both to Scott Bader and to individuals working for it over at least 30 years – for stimulus, friendliness and moral support.

Be warned readers. I am not unbiased.

Acknowledgements

First I need to thank all those who have made written contributions to the book either in the main text or following the end of the final chapter. Godric, for his Afterword, heads this list. But I would also like to offer my thanks to others: to Barry Sauntson for his contributions about Texipols and 'closed mould forming' and to Tony Lovell for his account of the development of a special kind of polyurethane, for use in the manufacture of boots and shoes and in other important applications; to John Raymond for what he has written about Crystic Systems; to Don Wildman for his epic narrative about the building of the first reinforced plastics plant in China in the middle of the 'great cultural revolution' in 1965; to Les Norwood for his account of Scott Bader and defence industry contracts; to Brian Elgood for his account of the experience with SRL on Merseyside, but also for his memories of Ralph Woolf's management innovations and about Canon Scuffham's 'values workshops' in the 1970s; and to Bob Bridgeford for a series of most helpful points of detail about how the Wollaston business was basically sustained by its polymers in the 1940s and 1950s when 'unsaturated polyesters' were still little more than a gleam in Brian Parkyn's eye.

To Alan Green, John Leyland, Roger Sawtell, Roger Scott and Austin Shelton my thanks are due for their invaluable contributions at the end of the book, and to John Plender for his masterly Foreword at the start.

For published and pre-publication written material my two big debts are to Susanna Hoe – for quotations from her biography of Ernest Bader – and to Brian Parkyn for allowing me pre-publication access to selected chapters from his autobiography. For material from which I have borrowed extensively in chapter 12 on the local community of Wollaston village, I must acknowledge a big debt to David Hall's *Wollaston, Portrait of a Village*, and also to Eric Stockwell, himself one of Scott Bader's original Commonwealth members, for use of his unpublished Wollaston-focused dissertation, 'Breaking with Tradition'. A second unpublished local source from which I have been pleased to quote is an essay written by Diana Green in 1964, 'The Effects of Industry on Wollaston'. For pointing me to John Ruskin's *The Bible of*

Amiens, to which I refer in the chapter (8) devoted to Scott Bader France, I have to thank his biographer John Bachelor. The subtitle of his book, *No Wealth but Life*, should commend it to Godric and, indeed, to the shade of his father, Ernest.

In a special category of those whose published and unpublished work I have extensively relied upon is the late Professor Roger Hadley. Scott Bader was the subject of the doctoral thesis which he wrote at the LSE in the 1960s. In the 1990s he co-authored, with Dr Maurice Gold-smith, an article about the company, which was published in the presti-gious international journal *Economics and Industrial Democracy*. In between, he had spells conducting a survey on employee participation and employee attitudes at Wollaston and actually worked there in the industrial relations management team for a number of years. Of the academics who have studied Scott Bader, his, in my opinion, was the sharpest eye and his feet were most firmly on the ground. In July of last year I spent a most stimulating and enlightening two hours with him in the village to which he had retired in North Wales. Early in the New Year I telephoned to arrange a second meeting. Alas, I found that he had died of cancer ten days before.

Among the staff at Scott Bader's headquarters at Wollaston Hall my list of acknowledgements would be unacceptably long if I named all those who have helped me. But there are those to whom my special thanks are due. They start with Stuart Reeves, whose name will soon become familiar to readers as the co-author of the semi-official Traxton/Reeves *Scott Bader Diary*. It starts in the 1920s and runs on to the 1990s. It has proved a most valuable source. One of Stuart's present jobs is that of archivist. In that capacity he has been unfailingly helpful and friendly to me. So has his assistant, Valerie Busby, who lent me her own copy of *Wollaston, Portrait of a Village*, once it became clear that the archive copy has disappeared. For detailed information about per-sonnel and about engineering matters, I have to thank Helen Dollimore and Chris Webb. Others at Wollaston Hall whom I would like to men-tion by name start with Denise Sayer, the Commonwealth Secretary, who has helped me to avoid what would otherwise have been serious mistakes about tricky constitutional details, and her assistant Hayley Sutherland; not to forget Denise's now retired predecessor as Com-monwealth Secretary, Mick Jones. For taking over responsibility for the pictures and for advice and help in other ways I must thank Tracy Smeathers; for her sustained administrative and secretarial support, Carol Kennedy; and finally for computer wizardry, Chris Tucker. I must acknowledge an important debt to Austin Shelton (also now retired but living, like Bob Bridgeword, at Wollaston) and to his wife Marie.

In a rather different way, my thanks are due at Wollaston Hall to the three women who control the reception desk and the switchboard, Suzanne Berry, Deana Horne and Sue McDonald. The telephone arrangements are almost old-fashioned in the best sense and most reassuring. You are answered by a real speaking voice and not by a recording. Moreover those women start to recognise *your* voice after the second or third call and from then answer you by name. In consequence a call to the Hall switchboard comes close to being a real pleasure rather than a potential source of telephone rage.

Finally, for help from the start to the finish of this whole substantial labour, easily my most important debt has been to Brian Elgood for truly heroic amounts of work, and to his wife Margaret for her great forbearance. I very much hope that my new friendship with them can survive.

I

The Two Foundations of Independent Survival

Appearance and the reality behind it are often rather different. The first sighting of Scott Bader to greet the visitor is of a fine early Georgian manor house surrounded by a small estate in rural Northamptonshire. The unexpected reality is that this also happens to be the headquarters of a medium-sized, unusual, multinational business specialising in synthetic resins. The manor house, which is built in the warm-coloured local Northamptonshire stone, would offer an appropriate setting for one of those romantic and critically acclaimed costume pictures made by the Merchant-Ivory film production team in the 1990s. The first sight of it, as normally approached along the short drive which winds up through a gate from Wollaston, flanked by the churchyard wall and leaving the parish church behind it to the left, can hardly fail to lift the spirit. An accountant who worked there for more than 25 years went so far as to tell me that the sight of the manor house – Wollaston Hall – was a source of daily aesthetic uplift to him as he came to work each morning. Using this way of approach, the plant and factory buildings are screened from view. There is a large and splendid lawn to the side of the manor house and a row of adjacent garden seats on which employees can relax and take it easy during their breaks when the weather is fine. A woman now in early middle age who has worked for Scott Bader for many years told me that to take a break sitting out on one of those seats is for her one the greatest attractions the company has to offer.

The business is not only unusual because of the architecture and landscaping of its headquarters site. As many readers will know, it is exceptional – if not quite unique – in the arrangements by which it is owned and controlled. Sometimes these are described as constituting 'common ownership'. Others prefer to call them 'a trusteeship'. Much has been written both about those arrangements and how they may

best be described. We shall discuss their origin and some of their more
salient features – as one of the two main starting points of the company's history over the last 50 years – in a moment. Here it is sufficient
to say that the Scott Bader business is owned by a charity – the Scott
Bader Commonwealth – and that all those in the UK who work for the
business are eligible to become members of the Commonwealth, and
thus to share in the ultimate control of the business undertaking.

The products manufactured by Scott Bader on the Wollaston Hall
estate and elsewhere – and sold worldwide – are concentrated in a fairly
narrow range and have complicated semi-technical names, like unsaturated polyester resins (or just polyesters), inverse polymer emulsions,
and alkyds, which are almost certainly unknown to non-chemists. The
products are characteristically manufactured in large, tall, cylindrical
vessels which are called reactors and which have capacities of tens of
tons of chemical inputs. What goes on inside those reactors is, of
course, a set of controlled chemical reactions. In more homely language, the processes that go on inside the reactors are those of mixing,
cooking, and making compounds of the various chemical ingredients
which go into them. Both by weight and by value the most important
products manufactured and sold by Scott Bader at the end of the 20th
century and the start of the 21st are those polyester resins which, when
moulded with glass fibre or other stiffening material, become reinforced
plastics.

The company's second most important product line is a range of special polymers. These are chemical molecules of a particular type which,
with just one exception, emerge from the company's reactor vessels in
liquid form and are used mainly by the manufacturers of paints, adhesives, and other surface coatings. Throughout most of this Scott Bader
story of the last 50 years, we shall find that these 'speciality polymers'
have been less important to it – both technically and commercially –
than those polyester resins which are the key ingredients of reinforced
plastics. But here we need to underline that that was not always so.
Down to the mid-1950s it was these speciality polymers which
accounted for almost all of both the company's output and its profits. It
needs also be understood that both these product lines – the speciality
polymers as well as the polyester resins – fall within what for some purposes should be treated as a single industry: that of synthetic resins, as
opposed essentially to the natural resins, like rubber and shellac and
amber.

The only further point to make about these speciality polymers in this opening snapshot of the company taken at the turn of the century is that Scott Bader's management announced, in March 2000, a £6m investment programme to replace and renew its existing 'speciality polymer' capacity. It is true that in today's international chemical business an investment of £6m is hardly even peanuts. But for Scott Bader, with worldwide sales of rather less than £100m in 1999 and a worldwide workforce of some 680 at the start of the new century, it amounts to a large investment. As such, it is good evidence of the management's commitment to and confidence in the company's future. Construction work got underway in late July 2001.

A PRIVATE COMPANY OF MODEST SIZE IN AN INDUSTRY OF GIANTS

This brings us to a second surprising reality behind Scott Bader at the present time. The manufacturers of polyester resins and special polymers in today's world are characteristically huge undertakings. They are also, typically, quoted companies, with shares traded on international stock exchanges. Most of them employ tens of thousands of people and make annual sales in £ billions. In comparison with its peers Scott Bader is small, even very small, and its shares, as a consequence of its unusual ownership arrangements, may not be traded at all. But the main point to underline here is about its relatively small size. Indeed in the mid-1990s it became one of the proudest boasts of Ian Henderson, its then chief executive, that Scott Bader was Europe's only surviving polyester resin and special polymer manufacturer employing less than 1,000 people.

As we shall see in more detail later, there is an ideological thrust behind the small size of the business as indeed behind a number of its other features, including its already mentioned ownership and control arrangements. Its present size is not simply the outcome of a long series of commercial decisions. The economist Fritz Schumacher, who made his name with a book with an almost uniquely famous title – *Small Is Beautiful* – became closely associated with Scott Bader in the 1960s. But in fact the company's commitment to relatively small size predates its connection with Schumacher and has survived it. In effect the size which the company seems to have aimed at during most of the 50 years between 1950 and the end of the century reflects whatever is the smallest scale compatible with sustainability into the future. In earlier years numerical limits were set, but that has not happened since about 1980.

The visual contrast between the rural 18th-century architecture of Wollaston Hall and the industrial reality of today's polyester resin manufacturer is mainly the result of a lucky find in wartime and a worldwide lead in the manufacture of those resins achieved by the company in the1940s and early 1950s. The ideological thrust which partly explains Scott Bader's small size in today's world of giant chemical companies is directly attributable to the non-commercial ideas and actions of the company's founder, Ernest Bader. Those, as we shall see, would have been quite unusual in an ordinary person. They were highly exceptional for a successful businessman. But if we are to understand today's Scott Bader and see a coherence behind the company's detailed record over the last 50 years, we must look first at not just one, but two distinct and exceptional starting points. Both can be linked to 1951. One is about cumulative technological discovery and innovation. The other is about the ownership and control arrangements, and various other ideas, applied to a business operating in a competitive market by Ernest Bader.

STARTING POINT ONE

The company which has been engaged in the manufacture of various industrial chemical products since between the wars and which, since 1940, has the been mainly located in Wollaston, first became known to a wider public in 1951. In April of that year, it attracted considerable attention and publicity because of a distinctly unusual, even if not quite unique, change of ownership. The then principal family owners of the business, Ernest Bader and his wife Dora (née Scott), their son Godric, and their nephew Brian Parkyn, gave away for nothing 90% of its shares. They gave them to a new entity, the Scott Bader Commonwealth, which has already been mentioned, and which had been set up as a charity precisely for the purpose of receiving the shares and holding onto them. Twelve years later, in 1963, the ownership transfer was completed: the remaining 10% of the share capital was passed to the Commonwealth.

The business in 1951 was not a really large one, anyway by today's standards. But nor was it really small. Total workforce numbers were approximately 150. Moreover it was making profits which were respectable even if not breathtaking. So the gift of ownership was universally seen – and rightly seen – as an act of most notable and selfless benefaction. By the stroke of the signing over of the shares in April

1951, the company and its founder and former main shareholder, Ernest Bader, by then a man in his early 60s, became famous. But what the Bader family bequeathed to the company and the new Commonwealth in 1951 was more than just their shares. A whole constitution and set of rules for governing and guiding the business was laid down. Not least important among the latter, as already noted, was a prescribed limit on the numbers to be employed. That was initially set at 250. Later it was increased. Though a numerical limit was eventually abandoned, an ideological preference in favour of small size has remained.

As for the constitution – as used here an umbrella term intended to embrace aspirational as well as legal and other more down-to-earth documents – we will find in what follows that it has been changed several times. For better or worse, we shall also find that it has never been far from the centre of the company's life. We will find too that it is unusually complicated – some would argue problematic – to the extent that we shall need to devote an extended discussion to it later. Here it is sufficient to make just five points:

1 The constitution reflects the key fact that since the family gift of that 90% shareholding in 1951, there have been two corporate and legal entities not just one, namely:
   a) The Scott Bader Commonwealth Ltd.
   b) The Scott Bader Company Ltd.
2 Partly to express the social purpose of the undertaking, the Commonwealth is a registered charity and holds all the shares in the company, and thus legally controls it.
3 The company is the business and, by virtue of its ownership by the Commonwealth, is not subject to takeover.
4 Subject to modest age and length of service qualifications, and to showing an understanding of Scott Bader's principles, all the company's employees in the United Kingdom – and since 1999 some of those overseas – are eligible to take up Commonwealth membership. But membership does not involve individually held shares, since Commonwealth members' liability is limited by guarantee and not by shares. The shares in the company are all held collectively, or 'in trusteeship'.
5 At least as a first approximation, we can say that the design logic behind these arrangements is that the company – and in effect its top management – should be 'controlled' by the whole body of the workforce (including management-grade employees) on a democratic, one member/one vote, basis.

Yet possibly more important than any of the above – the gift of the shares, the constitutional rules, or the ideological prescription in favour of no more than moderate size – was a set of something like moral imperatives enjoined upon the Commonwealth's members: perhaps above all that, in some sense in return for the gift of the shares to the Commonwealth, employees should commit themselves to behave 'responsibly' and in line with a number of high-minded principles of Christian morality, including, at least in some measure, principles of pacifism and charitable giving. True, the obligation to behave in these ways is not presented precisely or in the language of a bargain or contract in the constitutional documents associated with the setting up of the new Commonwealth and the receipt by it of the family shares. On the other hand I do not myself believe that we can make much sense of Scott Bader's subsequent history unless we take some such implied contract or bargain into account.

Moreover, linked to the high moral principles with which the new Commonwealth was endowed at its birth was a related idea that has continued to be of great significance ever since, at least in Scott Bader's self-presentation. This is the idea that what was being established was an almost entirely new species of business undertaking, viz. a *democratic working community* in industry. At one level the phrase seems entirely acceptable and in line with Japanese business ideas, where, for example, managers are often presented – to borrow the language of Professor Ronald Dore – not as the paid agents of capitalist share-holders but as the trusted elders of a working community. Or, and equally acceptable, the phrase may be taken to imply a set of arrange-ments, as exemplified in Britain by, for example, the John Lewis Partnership, where the management is democratically accountable for its actions to the non-managers or rank-and-file partners. It is also true that there are indeed major differences between the ways of working in Scott Bader's industrial community and what goes on in many con-ventional capitalist businesses in today's Britain. We will be faced with a most compelling example of those differences when we come to examine Scott Bader's takeover of a conventional capitalist business on Merseyside in the 1980s and its sequel, the close-down of the latter with a high percentage of compulsory redundancies. The differences which lay behind the inability of Scott Bader's democratic working community to digest its short-lived Merseyside subsidiary must be acknowledged. In some sense they are both its defining characteristics and its glory. But that very phrase, 'democratic working community', may be liable to lose touch with reality if it gives rise to expectations of an entirely new social order at people's work places, once the ownership of equity capital by private individuals has been extinguished. Such ownership of equity capital was, of course, extinguished at Scott Bader after the completion of the ownership transfer to the Commonwealth in 1963.

We shall find numerous expressions or expectations of this idea – of an entirely new social order – as we trace the post-1951 history of the business. As late as the 1980s we find Professor Fred Blum, an academic sociologist and a truly committed believer in, and publiciser of, the Scott Bader model and its virtues, putting forward a proposal for a 'New Era Centre' to be built on the estate at Wollaston Hall. Readers will have to decide for themselves whether the proposal may have been somewhat premature, and whether before proposing such a centre it would be prudent to make sure that a new era has indeed been ushered in. More generally, it is probably wise to be cautious about assuming that, with the extinction of capital owned by private individuals, as in the Scott Bader model, all conflicts of interest between management and non-management employees will just disappear. The history of state-owned businesses, whether in the UK or elsewhere, must surely have taught us to be sceptical about that assumption. True, there is an obvious difference between state ownership and common or trustee ownership without the state, as at Scott Bader. Yet in what is perhaps Europe's outstanding example of the latter – the great Zeiss undertaking in Germany – there was evidence of lively conflict between management and non-management staff in the 1980s. Clearly this is a topic which we will have to explore closely in what follows. It was still the subject of lively debate at Wollaston when this was being written in the second half of the year 2000 and the first six months of 2001.

STARTING POINT TWO

I move on now to what I see as the second starting point which lies behind Scott Bader's experience over the last 50 years. It is less well known than the gift of shares and other bequests to the Commonwealth in 1951, but arguably at least as important for its future as a business. This second starting point is quintessentially technical. By a fortuitous synchronism, it was in that same year, 1951, that Scott Bader took a big step towards establishing itself as the British and European –

even perhaps for some years, as the world's – leader in what became in effect a new industry and one which has been growing steadily ever since. The industry has been and continues to be variously described: as Glass Reinforced Plastics, as Reinforced Plastics, as Plastics Composites, and as simply Composites. More colloquially, and to the irritation of the chemical manufacturers responsible for the plastics component of what is in effect a new material, it is sometimes known simply as Fibreglass, as when people talk of fibreglass boats. In what follows, and after a brief later explanation, I shall use any one of the first four descriptions indiscriminately.

The specific step taken by Scott Bader in 1951, on the road to leadership in the then emerging new industry of plastic composites, was the lodging, for subsequent full registration and protection, of a key patent. The patent and its antecedents will be described in more detail later. It is enough to say here that it protected a way of ensuring that the new plastics composite material emerged from its moulding process with a smooth hard surface rather than a tacky one. It is probably fair to claim that, taken together with the earlier discovery by the laboratory staff of a method of 'cold curing' the new plastic composite material, the 1951 technical breakthrough created the conditions for the emergence of a really substantial new industry and one which – to repeat – has been continuously growing ever since.

Before those two discoveries were made, the costs of the new material were such that it could only be used economically in the construction of very high value items, like the wing tips or nose cones of aeroplanes. Thereafter, and once the separate problem of reducing the costs of the necessary stiffening or reinforcing material had been solved, its uses and applications became almost limitless. In the early years it probably became most famous for its use by the builders of sailing dinghies, yachts and of other pleasure boats, and later of trawlers for fishing fleets and even naval ships. But uses across the whole of the surface transport industry, for car and bus bodies, lorry cabs, railway carriages, and even for train sets, soon followed. More or less concurrently, and starting from roof sheeting, it spread out all over the construction industry and has even been used to build a bridge. Measured in tonnes the market in Britain has grown from less than 10,000 in the late 1950s to upwards of 80,000 in the late 1990s. The European market into which Scott Bader now sells, both by direct exports from Wollaston and through sales by manufacturing subsidiaries in France and Croatia, is proportionately almost as large, and Europe's total market is widely expected to reach a minimum of 500,000 tonnes over the next 10 years. There are similar growth prospects worldwide, and Scott Bader is also in a position to take advantage of them, both by direct export from Wollaston, and by sales from a cluster of overseas subsidiaries. These now include manufacturing units in South Africa and Dubai as well as the two on the European mainland mentioned above. Moreover industry optimists foresee many decades of growth as plastic composites continue to replace metals and other materials because of a combination of cost and lightness.

CONNECTIONS BETWEEN THE TWO STARTING POINTS

Brian Parkyn has already been mentioned as the nephew of the founder of the business, Ernest Bader, and, alongside his first cousin Godric Bader, as one of the two second-generation family shareholders, when 90% of the share capital of the original Scott Bader company was given to the new Commonwealth in 1951. In 1947, at the invitation of his uncle Ernest but against the advice, as he writes in his forthcoming biography, of most other members of his family and friends, Brian Parkyn had accepted a position as head of the company's polyester laboratory. He would himself acknowledge that discoveries made in chemical laboratories larger than one-man bands are always to some extent discoveries made by teams. Nevertheless there is no doubt at all that, both as the man in charge and in terms of direct personal responsibility, Brian must be assigned the main credit for solving the 'tackiness' problem of polyester resins which I have just presented as one of the two great starting points for the subsequent half century of Scott Bader history. Readers who are professional chemists will apply a more technical description to it and call it the 'air inhibition' problem. But however described, its solution in Scott Bader's laboratory was a crucial step in the sequence of events that gave the company its lead in the manufacture of a more or less entirely new material: low-cost reinforced plastics. Brian Parkyn indeed has been publicly described many times as the 'father of reinforced plastics'. As we will see later, when we cover that whole extraordinary story, he has both accepted the title and demurred. He has demurred by saying that the industry has two fathers and not one, the late Kurt Joseph of Fibreglass Ltd, as well as himself. But he would not, I think, want to contest the view that it was his vision of the potential of the new material, more than anyone else's, which was one of the key factors which drove it forward in the 1950s and 1960s.

Here it seems worth suggesting that my two starting points are linked in the person of Brian Parkyn. He was a family shareholder when the shares were first given to the Commonwealth in 1951 and, without him, it seems most improbable that Scott Bader would have established its lead in the new industry of reinforced plastics in the early 1950s. Together they have underpinned Scott Bader's business prosperity and independence over the last 50 years. Though propositions of this kind can never be proved, it is most improbable that an independent Scott Bader could have survived until the end of the century in the absence of either one. Without the gift of the shares and the setting up of the Commonwealth as a charitable entity, more or less protected from takeover, to hold them, the business would surely have been acquired sooner rather than later in the half century by a big competitor. Without its lead in reinforced plastics, it seems highly improbable that its activities in the manufacture of specialist polymers could have been viable for long as a business on their own, even if they had enjoyed the takeover protection afforded by the Commonwealth. That at least seems probable although it is also true that the polymers were profitable before the polyesters, and thus supported the cost of polyester development.

FAST FORWARD THROUGH THE BUSINESS RECORD:
1951–2000

1 *Numbers employed* From the viewpoint of those who live in Wollaston and in those surrounding villages and small towns which fall into the 'travel to work' area from which Scott Bader draws its workforce, it is, of course, the number of jobs and the value of the incomes generated by them which are its most important contributions to their well-being. The company's records show that its total United Kingdom workforce in 1951, the year of my two starting points, was 161. Though there was still at that date a small sales office in London, almost all of those people must have been employed in Wollaston. Excluding temporary staff, the corresponding figure for the company's UK employees at the beginning of 2000 was approximately 360. Despite a network of regional sales and distribution centres, the great bulk of those people were again employed in Wollaston.

At the far end of our 50-year period, on the other hand, Scott Bader had become a multinational, with three established and majority- or wholly-owned manufacturing subsidiaries – in France (with two separate sites), South Africa and at Dubai in the Persian Gulf – and a fourth, on the way to becoming majority-owned, in Croatia. Together, those four businesses employed just over 300 people in the year 2000. We will postpone till later a discussion of their contribution to the parent business. It is enough to say here that, with the exception of the French subsidiary, they are Scott Bader children – and its children by acquisition – of the 1990s.

Employment in Britain's manufacturing industry has, of course, sharply declined, both in absolute numbers and as a percent of the workforce over the last 50 years. Admittedly the evolution of the chemicals – and especially of the plastics – industry has been rather different. Indeed a learned publication of the early 1960s (*The First Century of Plastics, Celluloid and Its Sequel*, by M. Kaufman, The Plastics Institute, 1963) refers to a post-war 'cataract of plastics', which many of the now older generation can vouch for.

In round numbers, and ignoring those employed overseas, we can say that Scott Bader's UK workforce increased by just over 100% during the 50 years starting 1951, or by an average of between two and three jobs each year. But in fact the number of these jobs has moved down as well as up during the half century; the increase of rather over 100% is a net figure. The UK workforce has experienced three episodes of voluntary redundancies – in 1978, 1980 and 1994. Taking the two earlier episodes of voluntary de-manning together, the numbers employed in the UK were reduced by about one-third. The corresponding reduction in 1995 was that much smaller: by about 40 in number and something over 10%. In all these three cases Scott Bader's working community voted to accept voluntary redundancy, with generous compensation terms. By doing so, it chose to set aside the formal guidance which has featured in the constitutional documents since the early 1950s, and is still operational at least on paper in the year 2000: that in cases of this kind there should be agreed all-round pay cuts rather than any actual redundancies. As it turned out, and doubtless partly because of the relative generosity of the redundancy terms, more employees than could be spared volunteered to become redundant in each of the three cases, though there was also at least one 'refusenik' among those whose actual positions in the business ceased to exist. He changed his occupation but stayed on.

But, as noted briefly above, there has also been one case in the UK during the 50 years involving compulsory redundancies. This last was associated with the close down of Synthetic Resins Ltd (SRL) at Speke on Merseyside in 1985. The business had been acquired from Unilever three years before. It is not too much to say that this whole sequence of events on Merseyside – the acquisition of SRL, the attempt to make a success of running it, the closure decision, and the compulsory redundancies when that attempt failed – was probably the most traumatic experience in the whole post-1951 Scott Bader story. Because it put the spotlight on a huge difference of 'industrial culture', between Scott Bader's ways of working at Wollaston and SRL's at Speke, it is also highly instructive. A quite detailed discussion will be necessary when we get on to it in the narrative. At the end of an extended struggle against heavy odds, a total of about 100 employees, though qualifying for redundancy payments similar to those agreed with the Wollaston workforce shortly before, were faced with compulsory redundancy.

We can probably follow the 50-year evolution of Scott Bader's employment numbers most clearly by taking a succession of five-year averages.

Numbers Employed by Scott Bader Group
Averages 1951/55 to 1996/2000

1951/55	150
1956/60	194
1961/65	275
1966/70	343
1971/75	413
1976/80	501
1981/85	510
1986/90	454
1991/96	550
1996/2000	661

We already know that the company's total workforce in the UK in the year 2000 was just 360. We also know that it had remained at approximately that level since the redundancies of the mid-1990s. It follows that over the 4 years 1996 to 1999 the company was employing an average of about 300 people at its overseas subsidiaries. A discussion of the business logic behind the huge 1990s expansion in the overseas employment will come in a moment.

Here our main interest is in the numbers of jobs created by Scott Bader in the UK since 1951. If we subtract from the totals in the table the new overseas jobs in the 1990s, and then make slight adjustments to the numbers in earlier years – to exclude those employed by Scott Bader France (who figure in the total from the late 1960s) – we find:

Average annual Scott Bader employment numbers in the UK

1951–1975   270
1976–2000   420

Thus the approximate annual average over 50 years is 340 jobs. Put differently, Scott Bader has been responsible for not much less than 17,000 man-years of work in the UK since 1951. What's more, of that total not much less than 15,000, at an annual average of about 300, will have been in Wollaston. By a huge measure, those jobs, and the incomes (and pensions) associated with them, are the biggest benefit contributed by Scott Bader to Wollaston and its neighbouring travel-to-work area over the half century from 1951 to the present. There is also the added benefit that, at least for its non-management staff, the rates of pay and other conditions at Scott Bader have been consistently ahead of those on offer from other local employers.

This 'fast forward' exercise through the employment numbers at Scott Bader over the last half century may be concluded by anticipating a question: given the so-called 'cataract of plastics' in post-war Britain, and the lead established by the company in the late 1940s and early 1950s in the specialised new field of reinforced plastics, why was its employment growth not more substantial and faster? The main answer becomes apparent after no more than a moment's reflection: the company's commitment to an ideology of 'small is beautiful' and its resulting business aim, to keep its workforce numbers down to the minimum size compatible with long-term survival. But perhaps, as Godric Bader suggests, the company had no real choice, since it was in no position to raise new capital from outside shareholders.

2 *The growth of sales* At the price level in the Festival of Britain year (1951) Scott Bader achieved total sales of £634,000. The corresponding figure at the end of our period and in the prices of 2000 was £90.5m, an increase of well over 100 times before inflation is taken into account. However, we will only have a proper understanding of what has happened if we adjust those numbers for inflation. Andrew Gunn, head of finance and systems at Scott Bader since the early 1980s, and whom we shall meet again in these pages, has kindly done the necessary work for me. He has contributed the discussions which

follow about the evolution of the company's inflation-adjusted sales, and of its productivity and profitability. He writes:

> Over the period from its formation as a Commonwealth to 2000, the inflation-adjusted value of sales has grown at an annual average rate of 4.15%, slightly faster than the increase in UK GDP over the same period. By the end of the period 56% of these total sales revenues were earned outside of the UK and Eire. From the 1970s onwards the year-by-year numbers – and chart A below – suggest a 10-year cycle in turnover with the low point of the cycle being in the early years of each decade. These low points coincide with economic recessions in the UK in the early 1970s, 1980s and 1990s. The sales revenues also reflect the effect of acquisitions: for example Strand Glassfibre in 1978, Synthetic Resins Ltd in 1982, Scott Bader Middle East and Scott Bader Proprietary Ltd in South Africa in 1993, NCI in the US in 1996, and Chromos Tvornica Smola dd in Croatia in 1999. If the effects of acquisitions are eliminated, the 'Wollaston' rate of sales growth would be less than that of UK GDP.

3 Productivity The inflation-adjusted value of sales in 2000 was just over seven times that in 1951, whereas the number of people employed had only increased four times, indicating an approximate doubling of sales per person over the period. This corresponds to an

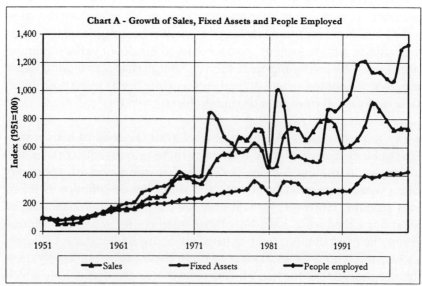

Chart A - Growth of Sales, Fixed Assets and People Employed

average increase of constant value sales per person of around 1.1%, which is less than the real value of the increase in pay. On the other hand, but also suggesting some lack of dynamism, the inflation-adjusted investment in fixed assets over the same period increased by 13 times (an average annual constant value increase of 5.41%), indicating an approximate halving of the sales productivity of fixed asset investment.

Productivity is also measured in terms of *value added*. Chart B shows that over the 20-year period since 1980 the inflation-adjusted value added has fluctuated between a low of £12.6m (1983) and a high of £24.7m (1996) and is now only 17% greater than it was 20 years ago. Value added, expressed as a percentage of sales, has also fluctuated between a low of 16.3% (1983) and a high of 24.2% (1991 and 1999) and is now 19.8%. As a proportion of value added, however, pay has also fluctuated sharply over the period from a low of 53% (1987) and a high of just over 76% (2000). These fluctuations in the percentage of pay to value added mirror the movements of the inflation-adjusted value added i.e. when the real value of value added reduces, either because of decreases in volumes or decreases in input costs (and therefore margins, assuming a similar reduction in output values), pay (which follows a more stable upward movement) increases as a percentage of value added. The contrary applies when sales volumes increase and/or raw material costs also increase (and therefore margins

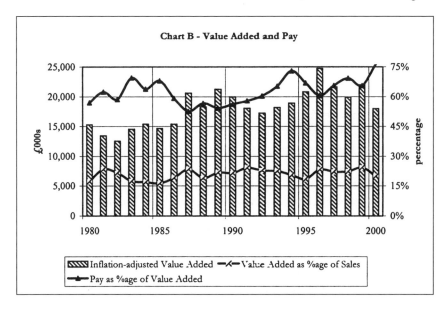

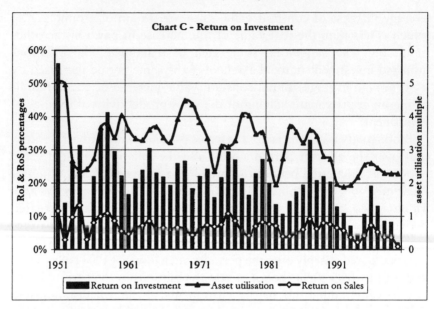

Chart C – Return on Investment

Return on Investment ▬▬ Asset utilisation ▬▲▬ Return on Sales ▬◇▬

increase, assuming output prices increase at the same rate as raw material price increases). Productivity has also improved following the voluntary redundancy programmes in 1978, 1980 and 1994, and the closure of SRL in 1985.

4 Profitability Chart C traces the return on investment over the whole period and shows that the return on investment (RoI) has fallen over the decades from a high during the 1950s of 28.4% to the level achieved in the 1990s, which was 9.6%. Over the same period the return on sales has fallen but much less sharply: from 8.4% in the 1950s to 6.5% in the 1980s and 4.3% in the 1990s. The reason for the discrepancy between these two trends is as indicated above: the productivity of fixed asset investment has fallen over the period. This is also apparent if we look at the so-called asset utilisation multiple. It fell from 3.5% in the 1950s to 2.2% in the 1990s.

We should probably also emphasise here at the outset that the whole employment regime at Scott Bader, at least for those outside the ranks of top management, has been and continues to be associated with an unusually labour-friendly set of welfare arrangements, generous pensions, good sickness benefits, holidays of above average length and a one-off tax-free travel grant with associated sabbatical leave for those who complete 25 years of service. Partly as a consequence labour turnover is low. It may be argued that these labour-friendly conditions may well partly explain and indeed partly justify – because of a hypothesis of quality of life advantages – the comparatively low rate of its productivity growth and the other measures of no better than moderate economic performance which Andrew Gunn has just reviewed There is also to be kept in mind, as always, the company's commitment to the 'small is beautiful' philosophy. All the same it would be wrong not to highlight Scott Bader's comparatively low score by the measure of long-term productivity growth. Those who argue for forms of ownership in market economies other than conventional capitalist ones have increasingly come to do so by pointing to positive statistical evidence about the performance of these businesses, especially in relation to labour productivity improvement. On the face of it Scott Bader's unconventional ownership (or trusteeship) arrangements cannot be persuasively advocated on precisely those grounds. It may be possible to argue for them convincingly on other grounds, for example because of the higher quality of life enjoyed by people who work there or, alternatively perhaps, because of the virtues of experiment. At a different level it has sometimes been argued that Scott Bader's experience has placed unusual emphasis on customer service and so, perhaps, has allowed it to sustain itself with lower rates of productivity growth than would otherwise have proved necessary. These are clearly issues which will merit further attention later on.

The 50-year downward trend in Scott Bader's return on its investments and in its profit margins on sales must most fundamentally reflect growing competition in its markets, and especially of those for its 'flagship' products: the polyester resins used to make reinforced plastics. As we have seen, the company grabbed a lead in the development and marketing of this range of products in the 1950s, and was a world market leader in them for upwards of two decades. In some sectors of the market, especially in the use of reinforced plastics for marine applications, in the building of boats and ships, it retained an important if not perhaps quite a world leader's position at the start of the new century. Pioneers of anything successful will almost always suffer the fate of being caught up. Scott Bader has nothing for which to reproach itself in this respect. Given its now small size in relation to its competitors, what may be most remarkable, as the former chief executive Ian Henderson argued forcefully in the mid-1990s, is that Scott Bader has managed to survive in these markets at all.

5 Scott Bader's performance compared with others in the industry An authoritative case study of Scott Bader was prepared in 1977 by the School of Management at the then Cranfield Institute of Technology, and later published in the institute's journal. The authors were two business academics, R. W. Wagstaff and Professor C. J. Constable. From 1951, the date of our two starting points, down to 1976, it supplies an extended range of year-by-year financial and other business performance data. It also describes the company's constitutional arrangements, and the two gift transfers of shares from the family to the Commonwealth in 1951 and 1963.

But for our purposes here, what is most interesting and important in this Cranfield study comes when it focuses not on Scott Bader alone but on how it compares with four companies prominent in the chemical and plastics industries: Albright & Wilson (UK), Ciba Geigy (UK) Ltd, ICI (UK), and Laporte Industries (Holdings Ltd).

The study offers its readers comparative performance data about Scott Bader and these four companies over a six-year period, 1971–6. It is true that the authors introduce an important caveat. Having pointed out that 'most [of the companies with which Scott Bader's performance is compared] were subsidiaries or divisions of major chemical companies with a wide range of other interests', they go on, 'Direct financial comparison is not therefore possible.' Nevertheless, despite this caveat, the authors proceed to publish the information as if it had some comparative validity. What's more, judgements based on these comparisons have been regularly offered by company spokesmen ever since.

To begin with, by setting out the numbers employed, the data shows just how small was – and indeed still is – Scott Bader's business compared with those of its then competitors. Over the six-year period Scott Bader's employment numbers reached a peak of 429 in 1974. The corresponding numbers of the other four companies in that year were:

Laporte Industries	5,100
Ciba Geigy	7,800
Albright & Wilson	7,600
ICI	132,000

The data then moves on to set out the comparative position of the five businesses under five headings: sales per employee, pre-tax profit per employee, labour cost per employee, net assets per employee, and return on net assets %.

By the measure of sales per employee Scott Bader comes first in every year by a large margin. By the measure of pre-tax profit per employee it comes first in three years, second in one year and third in two years – an average position just above second. In the case of labour costs per employee, its position over the six years averages out at just above the middle.

All those are direct measures of comparative performance. Scott Bader also scores better than average, in fact brilliantly well, by the measure of net assets per employee. Its number by this measure is easily the lowest. In other words, Scott Bader during these years was achieving the highest level of sales per employee from the base of the lowest net capital invested per employee, a notable triumph one might think.

By the final comparative measure in the Cranfield study, namely the percentage return on net assets, Scott Bader again has the best score in each of the six years, 1971 to 1976, and by a large margin.

On the face of it, only the most granite-hearted zealot for conventional capitalism could deny that these comparative measures of performance between 1971 and 1976 – assuming they have any comparative validity at all – add up to a brilliant result for Scott Bader. And yet, the evidence of the third measure – labour costs per employee – may offer some grounds for anxiety, especially in the light of the company's later propensity to experience an increase in the percentage of its value added which is absorbed by employee costs. As noted earlier, this propensity was especially marked at Scott Bader during the early 1990s, perhaps in part because of the introduction of profit-related pay. However, and at least for the moment, we can treat this point as no more than a minimal qualification to a truly brilliant result.

Looking backwards into the 1960s from the years covered by the Cranfield study, it must be a racing certainty that any comparative data would show that Scott Bader had been outperforming its competitors from the moment – perhaps in the late 1950s or in the early 1960s – when it had firmly established its lead in the production and sale of those polyester resins, or composites, which are the key components of reinforced plastics. But when we look forwards over the quarter century from 1976 onwards, the company's comparative position vis-à-vis its competitors cannot simply be deduced from its initial lead. At the time when this was written, in the summer of the year 2000, there was one piece of specific comparative evidence that was generally taken to be reliable. It is a report prepared and published by Schooner Direct Marketing and later included in the 1999 edition of the Business Ratio

Report for the Industrial Chemical Manufacturers. The comparative data set out in the report mainly covers the performance of companies in 1998. In the case of Scott Bader, the data is taken from its financial year ending 2 January 1998.

The results from nearly 100 companies figure in the survey. But many of these are not really comparable with Scott Bader. So, following the example of Andrew Gunn, the comparison here is made with the results of a smaller group of 17 companies. He selected those on the basis that they were 'either direct competitors ... or they seek to be specialist chemical manufacturers (serving niche markets) rather than "commodity" chemical manufacturers'. He also pointed out in his paper to the board that 'with the exception of DSM Resins, none of the companies in the sample has a composites business comparable to Scott Bader'. And he explained the reason for this, namely that Scott Bader's 'competitors in the composites business are now major multinational companies domiciled outside of the UK'.

For our purposes here, it is sufficient to select just a few highlights from these comparative results.

First, about profitability: the data shows that Scott Bader's fell 'below the median of both the whole survey and also the sample'. For what it's worth, Andrew Gunn adds the comment that Scott Bader's 'pre-interest profit margin of 4.5% is below our target of 8%'.

Also worth highlighting is what Andrew deduced from a comparison with the small sample of companies about wages and productivity. He wrote that Scott Bader's rate of sales per person was 'close to the lower quartile' but that its pay to sales ratio was 'above the median'. And he went on, 'The rate of pay to value added is the fourth highest in the sample.' An easily understood analogy would be one of those states in the US where teachers' pay is relatively high but the students' test scores are relatively low.

It is true that by measures of financial strength, for example indebtedness, Scott Bader emerges from comparisons with the sample companies with a high ranking. Nevertheless what is surely most striking about this comparative data from the late 1990s is how it contrasts with what we looked at earlier for the years 1971–6. In effect, by a number of measures of business performance, Scott Bader fell from having the highest ranking position in that earlier comparison to one well below the middle at the end of the 1990s. Comparative data for the years in between would presumably track the decline between the two.

About this decline in the company's comparative business performance, two points may be worth underlining at this stage. The first is that the relative decline in the company's business performance over the second half of its 50 years 'in trusteeship' is neither more nor less than one of the facts of its history. But that that should have happened does not necessarily imply policy choices over those 25 years which were either irrational or discreditable. We know that competition in the main – and indeed the subsidiary – markets supplied by Scott Bader has been growing continuously since it established its lead in the new field of polyester resins in the early 1950s. We also know that a policy of going for a huge expansion – to keep up with the 'big boys' – was never really a starter. Quite apart from the ideology of 'small is beautiful', we must also take into account the 'trusteeship' character of Scott Bader's ownership and thus its inability to raise equity capital on the stock market. In these circumstances a policy decision to go for a business with the smallest size compatible with its sustainability may well have been the most rational choice. Similarly, and in view of its special commitment to employee security and employee welfare, the company may well have accepted as its profits target not a percentage at the top of the range but, once again, whatever figure, however small, that could be defended as compatible with survival in the present and sustainability in the future. Such a policy might also be defended, more or less persuasively, with the argument that companies get into real crises not because of low profits but because they run out of cash. Given its strong balance sheet no one has so far suggested that Scott Bader is close to running a risk of the latter.

6 *Acquisitions, 1951–2000* Before concluding this 'fast forward' through Scott Bader's business history from 1951 to 2000, it is worth having on record the main facts of its acquisitions over these years. The main events in chronological order have been:

> 1966 First stage in creation of Scott Bader, France. Tripartite new venture at Amiens with two French partners initially. After withdrawal of French partners (in 1967 and 1974), this became wholly owned as Scott Bader SA in 1974.
> 1968 Acquisition of Artrite Resins Ltd in UK.*
> 1978 Acquisition of polyester businesses of Bakelite Xylonite Ltd (BXL) in UK.*

1978 Acquisition of Strand Glassfibre UK and Strand SA in France: distribution and stockist business.

1982 Acquisition of Synthetic Resins Ltd on Merseyside. Close-down in 1985. Its polyester resin and alkyd manufacture shifted to Wollaston.

1993 Start-up of Scott Bader Middle East Ltd in Dubai. Mainly polyester resin manufacture.

1993 Acquisition of South Africa business which becomes SB (Proprietary) Ltd. Mainly polyester resin manufacture.

1994 Acquisition of technology and business from Convert SA*†

1996 Acquisition of National Composites Inc in the US. Close-down in 1998. Mainly polyester compounds.

1997 Acquisition of emulsion polymer business of Arizona Chemical SA*†

1999 First stage in acquisition of Chromos Tvornica Smola dd in Croatia. Mainly polyester resin manufacture.

* These acquisitions covered customer lists and technologies only.
† These acquisitions were acquired by Scott Bader SA, rather than by the Scott Bader parent company in the UK.

As already noted, the numbers employed outside the UK in what had by then become the Scott Bader Group had reached some 300, out of around 687 in 2000. Moreover, by that same date well over half of the group's total sales (56%) were made outside the UK and the Republic of Ireland taken together. Within that 56% total roughly 9% was accounted for by overseas exports manufactured in Wollaston.

In effect, starting from the beginnings of what later became Scott Bader SA in Amiens, in 1966, but then with a pause of more than 25 years down to the early 1990s, Scott Bader switched from making money overseas mainly through a combination of direct exports and licence fees to doing so mainly through sales by overseas manufacturing subsidiaries. The value added by the latter was evidently greater than the earlier combination, and that by a significant margin. Indeed it must be doubtful, even if it cannot be formally proved, whether the business overheads at Wollaston, and especially its research and development overheads, could have been sustained much longer than they were without the contributions of the overseas subsidiaries. That was the logic behind the drive under Ian Henderson in the 1990s to establish new overseas subsidiaries outside Western Europe. It was a bold and substantially new strategy and one which, at least down to mid-2000, had been more justified than not by its results. In respect of the speciality polymers a rather specific, but easy to understand, technical point is worth adding. With many of them, and in particular the water-based emulsion polymers supplied mainly to customers in the paint industry, half the weight of what is supplied by Scott Bader is typically just water. Given transport costs to markets outside the UK, it is easy to see that the returns from manufacturing closer to those markets may be significantly more favourable than those which result when the material is directly exported from Wollaston.

ACCEPTING LOWER GROWTH AS A COST OF SUSTAINING LABOUR-FRIENDLY POLICIES

This is not the place for an extended review of what I have called Scott Bader's 'labour-friendly' policies – policies which are part of the company's ethos – and what I suggest may perhaps, at least over the last 20 years of its first half century of trusteeship and in today's world, may be both its main glory and its defining characteristic. But at the end of this 'fast forward' project through the company's business record, it may be worth highlighting the main elements in those policies and reflecting about – without any attempt at quantification for the moment – their likely expense. There are perhaps four outstanding elements in the mix of these policies:

1 The rule that in normal circumstances – with the Merseyside close-down in 1984 not counting as normal – there will be no compulsory redundancies, taken together with generous redundancy terms for those who agree to go voluntarily.
2 The company's quite unusually generous pension arrangements: in return for no more than a 3.5% contribution from their salaries, those with 37 years' service qualify for a pension at the Inland Revenue limit, namely two-thirds of final salaries.
3 The award of a substantial tax-free grant of after 25 years' service, to be spent on a sabbatical; to be devoted to either overseas travel or study.
4 The fact that pay increases, at least over the last 20 years, have been only loosely linked to increases in productivity and have frequently run ahead of them.

At this stage it will be enough to make just three points about the above. The first is that such a mix of policies – and especially 1 and 4 – are bound, in the absence of windfall advantages from outside the company, to have a negative effect on the rate of profit and thus of potential growth. But second, given its continuing commitment to 'small is beautiful', Scott Bader's long-term objective is not growth maximisation but the minimum growth rate compatible with survival. Third, and at least up to the end of the century, Scott Bader's ability to survive in the market had not been seriously threatened. Furthermore, those in the company best placed to judge these matters tend to assert that if such a threat was ever to appear, then the working community could be relied upon to take the steps necessary to stave it off.

2
Where the Commonwealth Came From

Not for us content, and quiet and peace of mind,
For we are seeking a city we shall never find.
The Revd Reginald Lord Sorensen, 'A Backbencher's Pilgrimage'
(unpublished autobiography), 1968

THE IDEAS OF A SOCIAL CHRISTIANITY

Reg Sorensen was a friend of Dora and Ernest Bader from as early as
their courting days before the First World War and at least down to
Ernest's 80th birthday in 1970. By then a life peer as well as an
ordained Nonconformist clergyman, he was the main speaker at a Wollaston Hall ceremony to mark the occasion. He had represented the
Labour Party in the House of Commons as MP for West Layton from
1929 to 1950, with a short break of just four years between 1931 and
1935. Within the Labour's Parliamentary Party he was one of a small
group who won seats at Westminster from backgrounds in the world
of 'social Christianity', which flourished quite widely in working-class
neighbourhoods before and after the First World War, and survived,
albeit precariously, until shortly after the end of the Second. At this
stage I shall simply state my opinion that, together with Wilfred
Wellock – with whom the Baders first made contact 30 years later,
during the Second World War – Sorensen was one of three key direct
and personal influences on the Baders when it came to the ownership
and related changes of 1951. Wellock, like Sorensen, was mainly driven
in his politics by the ideas of a social Christianity, and was even briefly
an elected MP at Westminster for the Independent Labour Party
between the wars. My opinion about their influence on the Baders is
based partly on the premise that Dora and Ernest were themselves
driven by what they mainly saw as the imperatives of a similar social
Christianity. And the same applies, broadly if also with some differences, to the third person whom I see as personally and directly influential in the thinking of the Baders in relation to the 1951 changes: the
industrialist and would-be company law reformer George Goyder.

As a footnote to this hypothesis about the centrality of social Christianity in the relevant thinking of Ernest Bader and his wife, I need to add that it came to include, at least in Ernest's case, a marked millennial, or Kingdom-of-God-Building, component. There is a sense in which, in creating and then sustaining the Scott Bader Commonwealth, the Baders came to think of themselves as aiming to do good deal more than to construct a business model that improved on its conventional counterparts by being more labour-friendly and more committed to the expression of Christian values. They wanted to do more. Part of their disappointment towards the end of their lives may be explained perhaps by their feeling that they had failed to reach that higher objective: of building a radically different human nature.

The ideas of a social Christianity, or perhaps more accurately of a social Christianity applied to the business world, were the central drivers which led on eventually to the setting up of the Commonwealth in 1951. They also lay behind, and formed the starting point for what was contributed to that whole process by Sorensen, Wellock and Goyder. What's more, and especially as applied to business, they may be seen as being closely related to important ideas of the Quakers: a Nonconformist Christian denomination which was joined by Ernest and Dora Bader during the Second World War, and imbued with the high-minded business traditions with which they sought to identify the company. But, central as these ideas were, they were not the only ones that played a part. It is also true that in Wellock's case they came to be overlaid by a kind of Mahatma Gandhi gospel of the virtues of small-scale village communities and, more generally, of the simple, low-tech life. We also need to recognise at this early stage that the ideas of Robert Owen, the Welsh industrialist and social reformer, contributed to the process we are trying to understand. It need hardly be said that Gandhi was not a Christian. Nor, for that matter, was Owen. But that, of course, in no way tells against the enlightenment and humanity of their social and business thinking.

If only for the avoidance of doubt, I should make clear at this stage too that pacifism – which is at least analytically separate from social Christianity – also came to be included in the mix of principles on which the Commonwealth was constructed. As most readers will know, the Quakers have been pacifists ever since they were founded by George Fox in the 17th century. On the other hand, as we shall see in more detail in a moment, Ernest and Dora became pacifists in 1915, much earlier than they became Quakers.

In fact, when asked about the influential sages whose ideas lay behind the Scott Bader Commonwealth – to which, as we know, he and his family gave away 90% of the share capital of the Scott Bader company in 1951 – Ernest Bader invoked different names at different times. For example, in a television programme in 1976, as reported by Susanna Hoe in her biography of Ernest Bader (*The Man Who Gave His Company Away*, Heinemann, 1978), he blandly told the interviewer that the Commonwealth and his gift of the business to it 'was not my idea because Robert Owen and Gandhi thought of it before' (p 108). Then, in a piece specially written as an appendix for Susanna Hoe's book, Robert Owen is invoked again but coupled not with Gandhi but with Rousseau and Ruskin. Partly because of the choice of the word 'Commonwealth' to describe the new entity set up in 1951, the names of Gerrard Winstanley and Peter Cornelius Plockhoy, from the pioneering days of the Diggers and the Levellers of the 1640s and 1650s, are often also included in an extended family tree of Scott Bader's ownership arrangements, stretching back all the way to those early Christian communities mentioned by the authors of the Acts of the Apostles in the New Testament as having 'held everything in common'.

There will, no doubt, be many for whom this prestigious ancestry adds lustre to Scott Bader's Commonwealth. Some striking parallels of detail can be identified. Scholarly research projects might well be promoted to explore them further. However, for our purposes here it seems sufficient to do no more than identify the more remote forerunners and to move on to more recent and direct influences. On the other hand, at the proper place and later, we shall need to say something of substance about the influence of both Owen and Gandhi.

Two footnotes are needed to complete this introductory discussion. First we need to acknowledge that the relationship between Christianity and social projects which may flow from it will not necessarily be unproblematic. Apart from anything else the benefits of charitable giving may reduce the commitment to greater social justice on the part of those involved in it. Secondly, we need to recognise that in the background to projects like the Scott Bader Commonwealth there may be influences which are not altogether rational and perhaps not altogether attractive. Readers when they come on to it shortly may think that in this case the influence of the writings of the British novelist Marie Corelli (1855–1924) may fall into that category.

INFLUENCES IN THE FAMILY AND RELATED BACKGROUNDS
OF ERNEST BADER AND DORA SCOTT

Ernest Bader's invocation of Rousseau serves to remind us of his birth and upbringing in Switzerland, even if in a German-speaking canton rather than in Geneva. Presumably the main point of the reference is to imply a parallel between what Rousseau saw as the political oppression of ordinary people under Europe's pre-democratic authoritarian regimes, and what Ernest saw as its counterpart for ordinary employees under the regimes of conventional capitalism. But Ernest Bader may also have wished to suggest that his own and Rousseau's love of freedom was grounded in the centuries-old democratic – even if men-only democratic – arrangements of the Swiss cantons.

However, or so it seems to me, the main influences which he brought to England in 1912 from the first 22 years of his life in Switzerland were rather different. For the purposes of understanding 'where the Commonwealth came from', they were – or so Susanna Hoe persuasively argues (p 16) – primarily religious:

> It was his mother and his Christian upbringing which formed the most important foundation of his future. God was all around in the beauty of nature and the light of the distant mountains; more particularly, He was in the chapel to which Ernest's mother led him by the hand. His father was a deacon in the local Protestant church but his mother preferred the intimacy of the chapel. Here, under the guidance of Father Zeller, Ernest learnt what Christianity meant: it meant loving one another, loving the poor, loving one's neighbour

The importance for Ernest Bader of 'God ... in the beauty of nature and the light of the distant mountains' had been briefly anticipated by Susanna (p 16) in an earlier passage where, writing of his 'attachment to nature', she tells her readers that it 'was to expand in three directions: the growth of plants and living things would become symbolic; the towering beauty of his native Switzerland was also to mean its freedom – and therefore freedom itself – and a relationship with God; gardens and gardening were to prove almost his only relaxation.'

About his mother, Susanna Hoe also tells us that she wanted him to be a minister of the church (p 20). And she uses language which suggests that it may have been his mother who first put into his head the idea that he might be destined to do great things: '"Ernestle, Ernestle," she used to say to him, "think of what you might be."' During their courtship Dora was to be more explicit. 'What I feel about you', she told him at least once (p 29), 'is that God wants you for some special purpose.' It seems entirely plausible to suppose that not later than from his early manhood, and influenced first by his mother and then even more so by his wife, Ernest Bader may well have thought of himself as in some way marked out for the possibility of a 'high calling', and one with a substantial Christian content.

His years in Switzerland down to 1912 may also, Susanna Hoe argues, have influenced his attitudes to business in ways that can be detected both in his later business practice in the UK and in the design of the Scott Bader Commonwealth. Her main point is that his Swiss father's experience in borrowing from Zurich bankers to finance a project, and then going into their debt when it failed, gave Ernest a real horror of credit finance. She goes further and suggests (p 21) that for Ernest later in life, '*usury* and *interest* became synonymous with *exploitation of labour, unemployment, capitalism* and *war* [emphasis original]'. Formulated precisely in that way, with a postulated identity between usury and interest on the one hand and exploitation of labour, unemployment, capitalism and war on the other, the proposition may seem a little far-fetched as an expression of the view of someone who became a notably successful businessman. But it can scarcely be denied that conventional capitalism a) relies substantially on credit for its dynamism and b) has frequently been associated with levels of unemployment which seem to many to be unacceptably high. Nor is it at all far-fetched to see the design and setting-up of the Scott Bader Commonwealth – endowed with a strong balance sheet and a collective form of ownership, and offering a 'mutual' protection against compulsory redundancy – as having been planned, among other things, to overcome unemployment and the exploitation of labour, and to be largely released from the need for credit finance.

At a level closer to the day-to-day realities of business, Susanna Hoe suggests, with a charming tale of practical instruction from his early childhood, that 'the Swiss sense of orderliness' may have been one of the items which Ernest had to declare to Customs officials when he first arrived in Britain:

[Sometimes] ... his father led him round the farm explaining about life from practical examples. Walking through the village his father might say, 'Look, my boy, can you see, this farmer has got his heap of manure in front of his barn neatly piled and sprayed with gypsum. He is a good man. [But] that farmer there, he is just a mess.'

Though there is nothing in the constitutional documents of either the Scott Bader Commonwealth or of the company which says so, there is plenty of evidence that Ernest was totally opposed to anything which involved non-management employees in management tasks, though not, it must be emphasised, in management oversight. Perhaps the anecdote about those two manure heaps points to the source of what some recall as an almost pathological hostility to anything which smacked of 'workers' management'.

That is a hypothesis of detail. When we come on to what Dora Scott brought from her family background to the marriage and so, over time, to the ideas on which the Commonwealth came to be based, we get back to what I have suggested may be the central driving concept – a 'social Christianity': that is a Christianity which emphasised the imperatives of working for higher levels of social justice than those which prevailed under the regimes of late 19th and early 20th-century capitalism.

Apart from the evidence of her later actions with Ernest, like their membership of the Fellowship of Reconciliation during the First World War, and their later adhesion to the Religious Society of Friends – that is to the Quakers – my main evidence for putting forward a hypothesis about the commitment of Dora Scott to social Christianity is admittedly indirect. We know to begin with that the Scott family were Baptists. We know too that that Dora's brother, Tom Scott, was a sufficiently committed Baptist to make a major career change in middle life; from being a successful, and presumably quite well-paid, engineer and business manager, to being an ordained Baptist minister with, or so I would presume, a distinctly lower stipend. And we know that Dora's own religious sentiments were strong. Susanna Hoe (p 29) goes so far as to suggest that she took a pledge to abstain totally from alcohol at the tender age of seven. It is, of course, one of the defining characteristics of Baptists that they are only admitted into membership of the denomination, by baptism, when they are old enough to profess the faith. It seems entirely possible that for young Dora Scott her profession of the faith and her pledge to abstain from alcohol roughly coincided in time, when she was 7 years old. Her father died when she was only 12, and we must suppose she was a rather serious child.

The British Baptists date their origins to the early years of the 17th century. Among the country's Puritan or Dissenting denominations – which only became the Nonconformists as recently in the 19th century – they have the longest continuous history. Moreover, since these Dissenting Christian groups started to align themselves along a left-to-right political spectrum, the Baptists have tended to place themselves to the left of centre, far to the left of the mainstream of followers of John Wesley, though a good deal less left-leaning than the so-called Primitive Methodists. It is also true that the Baptists were the first of Britain's Dissenting denominations to embark on major missionary programmes in what we now call the Third World. At home they were strongly committed to good works, were apparently the builders of 'adult schools' and focused their activities primarily in working-class and lower-middle-class neighbourhoods. Their Christianity, we may say, has been more a matter of action, and especially social action, than of meditation.

REG SORENSEN, THE FELLOWSHIP OF RECONCILIATION, AND MARIE CORELLI

On his arrival in London in September 1912, Ernest Bader took a room as a lodger in the terraced house of a widow in Harringay, about half a mile west and slightly north of Finsbury Park. The widow was a Mrs Scott, and her two unmarried daughters, Dora and Gwen, were living with her. Dora, the elder, was already 28 and worked as a babies' nurse and as a midwife at Queen Charlotte's Hospital. Membership of their local Baptist church was a salient feature of the Scott family life. According to Susanna Hoe (p 26), the normal Sunday routine involved three church visits and three sermons. Ernest was evidently a very willing participant.

He returned to Switzerland when war broke out in August 1914, to be called up into the Swiss Army in line with his citizen's obligations. However, during his stay of just less than two years as a lodger in the house of Mrs Scott and her daughters, he became engaged to Dora and, along with Dora, fell very much under the influence of the young Reg Sorensen. The latter was only 19 when the three of them first met. Given how events unfolded, it is not too much to say that those months in London before the First War were probably as seminal as any which Ernest Bader ever spent, if what we are looking for are the sources of his future thinking about the Commonwealth. In so far as they had separate views when they became husband and wife, Dora was surely the most important source. Despite his much later advice against the act of benefaction to the Commonwealth – in the shape of the gift of the family shares – Reg Sorensen was, after Dora, the second most important.

Susanna Hoe offers her readers a striking account of the first meeting with Reg Sorensen (p 30). It follows a discussion of Ernest's passionate nature and the way in which enthusiasms of the moment often took hold of him. That first meeting took place in Finsbury Park: 'A dark-haired young man of 19 with a mellifluous voice was standing on a soapbox holding the crowd before him spellbound. At the end Ernest went up to him and told him ... how impressed he had been. Ernest Bader and Reg Sorensen ... became firm friends for life.'

About Sorensen we learn in the next paragraph about both his denominational and his political affiliation. He 'ran his own Free Church' and had 'been a pupil of R. J. Campbell and the New Theology'. The chief tenet of the latter, Susanna Hoe tells her readers, was a demand for 'a social application of the Christian ethic'. Sorensen's church building was a 'tin hut near a street market in Walthamstow'. Apparently he couldn't use the regular church hall because it was needed by the Independent Labour Party, a political party with close links to his church and to R. J. Campbell.

After describing that first meeting in Finsbury Park, Susanna Hoe writes (pp 30, 31):

> Ernest and Dora often went to listen to him ... and Ernest began to think for himself about Christianity in practical terms. Sorensen was talking about the dignity – or rather indignity – of labour and the influence of economic pressure on human behaviour. He spoke from personal experience for his background had been similar in some respects to that of Ernest Bader. His father, in his eyes, had been meanly rewarded for a lifetime of labour. He himself had been an errand boy, an office boy, and a clerk. He worked for a company dealing with South America and saw how workers were exploited for the benefit of shareholders. By 1914, with war clouds lowering over Europe, he spoke too about the incompatibility of war and the Christian faith.

Ernest Bader was required as a citizen to undertake military service in Switzerland after the outbreak of war in August 1914. But this spell in military uniform lasted only a matter of months. Moreover, he was given leave in early 1915 to visit his fiancée, Dora Scott, in London. In effect, while on that visit to London, he went what the British Army calls AWOL (absent without leave). By the time of his next visit home, in 1924, he was a naturalised British subject.

It seems that during that short spell of Swiss military service Ernest Bader became a pacifist. Reg Sorensen's pre-war speeches may well have had something to do with that. Susanna Hoe also identifies some persuasive literature mailed out by the Swiss Jehovah's Witnesses as what chiefly convinced him (p 32). But she also cites a second source, the Swiss theologian and pacifist Leonhard Ragaz. The point to stress here is the ideological commitment which came to underpin his own and Dora's association with a new pacifist body – the Fellowship of Reconciliation (FOR) – which they seem to have joined shortly after Ernest had returned to England in early 1915. Reg Sorensen was one of this group's leading lights. He has apparently described it as 'troubled group of Christians and Quakers' who first came together in December 1914. I am not quite clear why the Quakers are classified separately from the Christians.

Susanna Hoe reproduces a brief but also in some sense comprehensive statement of the Fellowship's central beliefs. The commitment it demands from its members is notably unqualified and uncompromising:

> Love, as revealed and interpreted in the life and death of Jesus Christ ... is the only power by which evil can be overcome ... that, therefore, as Christians, we are forbidden to wage war... that our loyalty to Jesus Christ calls us instead to a life of service for the enthronement of love in personal, social, commercial, and business life.

In the jingoistic atmosphere of Britain in 1915, it must have taken considerable courage to get up and advocate such a set of beliefs to the public in the street. The FOR, Susanna Hoe tells us (p 34), used to hold open-air meetings, and she quotes a Sorensen memory of them with which it is hard not to sympathise:

> I confess I shrank from my task of holding those meetings yet I believed I must do so, and therefore in trepidation for a few weeks after Sunday evening services, I went with a group of young people to face hostile crowds ... Those meetings deteriorated into an orgy of abuse and threatened assaults.

Ernest and Dora attended these meetings. Given their uncompromising temperaments, it is a fair bet that the hostility they faced served only
to increase their commitment. And the effect on Reg Sorensen was no
doubt similar. It is true that in the unpublished autobiography which he
wrote in the 1960s Sorensen questioned the FOR's pacifism as open to
a charge of oversimplifying the issues. It is also true that in 1950 he
advised Ernest and Dora *against* giving the family's shares to the Scott
Bader Commonwealth. On the other hand, his commitment to pacifism
still had a number of years to run, and it seems doubtful whether he
ever discarded his general dedication to social Christianity.

Earlier in this discussion I mentioned the late Victorian British novelist Marie Corelli as having been an important influence on the lives of
Ernest Bader and Dora Scott during their younger days, and very likely
too as they got older. Corelli's main output consisted of romantic moral
tales mostly played out against a background of more or less directly
specified religious and semi-philopsophical beliefs.

Susanna Hoe draws that influence strongly to the attention of her
readers (pp 27, 28). Part of the writer's message as a romantic novelist
was about the need for 'love ... to compass life, perfect it, complete it
and carry it on to eternal happiness'. This passage had been underlined,
Ms Hoe tells us, in the Baders' copy. The next two sentences, also
underlined, are: 'But please bear in mind that I am speaking of real love
– not mere physical attraction. The two things are as light from darkness.'

That message is no doubt more directly related to their 60 years of
married life together than to anything about the Commonwealth. But it
must be doubtful whether, without the great strength of their together-
ness as well as their shared Christian beliefs, the Commonwealth would
ever have been born.

But I also agree with Susanna Hoe that the writings of Marie Corelli
may have been important in other ways as well to that young courting
couple in the two years before the First World War. Like Ernest, Corelli
has a tendency to see the forces of nature as in some way associated
with the power of God, and as such as a source of 'radiant energy'.
Susanna Hoe quotes a sentence from Corelli's *The Life Everlasting* in
which she asserts that '*Electricity* is all things and all things are *Electricity* [emphasis original].' From the same novel she also cites the
author's pronouncement to the effect that 'there is an ever living spirit
within each of us'.

Much of what Marie Corelli wrote in the prologues or prefaces that introduced many of her moral and romantic novels would now be regarded as cranky to say the least. Her biographer, Eileen Bigland (*Marie Corelli*, 1953), cites a telling passage from a review of the first novel, *A Romance of Two Worlds*, when it first appeared in 1886: 'Taken as a pure romance, a romance of electricity we may call it – the book is a tolerable thing enough. If the writer intends us to take it seriously – as her preface seems half to suggest – it is pure bosh.' It doesn't seem all that far-fetched to suppose that neither Ernest Bader nor Dora Scott, anyway in the days when they were reading Marie Corelli's romantic novels before the First World War, had developed their 'bosh detection equipment' to especially high levels of sensitivity. But in a general way, it seems best to see the writings of Marie Corelli as having in the main supplied a kind of inspirational reinforcement to the Baders' life projects before as well as after they had become man and wife. Godric Bader thinks that these writings may also have helped his parents to become man and wife 'mystically'.

However, and especially for the benefit of those who have simply read Susanna Hoe on the subject of Marie Corelli's influence, a cautionary note must finally be added. As others have done, Susanna Hoe cites a famous and apparently pacifism-endorsing Corelli pronouncement: 'Patriotism is understood to be the virtue which consists in serving one's country; but in what way is … this country served by slaying its able bodied men in thousands?'

But she does not go on to tell her readers, presumably because she didn't know (which implies that the Baders didn't either), what Eileen Bigland in her biography moves on to share with *her* readers immediately after quoting that same 'pacifist' pronouncement: 'Yet, no sooner did the First World War break out, than she was filled with such jingoistic fervour that she spoke on recruiting platforms, wrote countless articles, offered [her home] as a military hospital and gave white feathers to young men still in civilian clothes.'

REG SORENSEN, THE MOORE PLACE COMMUNITY AT STANFORD-LE-HOPE, AND ROBERT OWEN

There was widespread optimism in Britain and France after the outbreak of the First World War in August 1914, about how long it would last. According to a popular and journalistic view, it would all be over by Christmas. Consequently there was no rush to introduce conscription. In fact it was not introduced until 1916, when a military service law was passed through Parliament by the Asquith government. For pacifists and others with conscientious objections to fighting on whatever grounds, that raised the question of exemptions. Those in various occupations, for example those working on the land, and ordained clergymen of the Anglican and some other Churches, were exempted from the provisions of the law. There were also procedures under which bona fide conscientious objectors could put their case for exemption to local tribunals not normally notable for their progressive views. A minority of prominent conscientious objectors who put their case for exemption to one of those tribunals were given the thumbs down and went to prison instead. That was what happened, for example, to the then leader of the Parliamentary Labour Party, Ramsay MacDonald, and also to the already quite famous philosopher, Bertrand Russell. Nearer to home, at what was to become Scott Bader, it also happened to Brian Parkyn's father Leslie, who spent many months in Wormwood Scrubs.

I am not clear whether the Free Church, of which he was ordained a minister in 1917, was sufficiently 'respectable' for Reg Sorensen to have obtained exemption as an ordained clergyman. In any case what he chose to do was rather different. Somehow he got his hands on the resources necessary to acquire a lease on a small farm called Moore Place outside the village of Stanford-le-Hope in Essex. There, with his wife Muriel, he set up what was essentially an agricultural co-operative community. All or most of its members were conscientious objectors of one kind and another. Because they were working on the land they enjoyed automatic exemption from the military service law. The member workers were evidently not required to make any financial contribution to the capital base of what quickly became the Moore Place community. Susanna Hoe offers her readers this account of how Ernest and Dora came to be linked to it as sympathetic neighbours:

> The Baders came down for an occasional weekend and found the spirit of the enterprise compatible with their own thinking and the area itself attractive. One weekend they came down to be shown an empty house nearby. It had four bedrooms and a large sitting room ... and three acres of land. They had no money but, with the help of Mrs Scott and an acquaintance of the Sorensens, they could just about manage to take out a lease on the house and they became the Sorensen's neighbours. They were to live in Stanford-le-Hope for the next 23 years.

In fact until they moved to Wollaston Hall in 1940.

However the fortunes of the Moore Place community had evolved, Susanna Hoe is surely right in her judgement that it could not have offered a possible long-term programme for Ernest Bader (p 38): 'They [the Baders] were naturally interested in the Sorensen community experiment next door, but Ernest was beginning to realise that he was not a man to join someone else's venture: he wanted to create his own.'

Not long after their move to Stanford-le-Hope and for essentially high-minded reasons, having pledged themselves to chastity in marriage for the duration, the Baders adopted three children in quick time. About the same time, Ernest planted an orchard of 'sweet-smelling apple trees' on their three acres of land. It was not a commercial success. Then, Susanna Hoe tells us (p 41): 'In 1920 Ernest rented an office and set up shop as an import agent. In the end it was to be the company Scott Bader Ltd which ... was to grow into a highly successful chemical and synthetic resin-manufacturing company.'

We will later track the highlights of that business over its first 30-odd years, down to the formation of the Commonwealth in 1951. There is no case for anticipating that story here. On the other hand there can be little doubt that the Moore Place co-operative community was an important and specific source behind some of the thinking on which the Commonwealth was eventually established. We must go back to its story.

It seems that the community itself, though not the Sorensens' involvement with it, managed astonishingly to soldier on until 1939. In the unpublished autobiography which he wrote in the 1960s, Sorensen writes no more about its end than that 'after the armistice the Moore Place community was beset by acute financial and human strains'.

We are not told exactly when the Sorensens decided to leave. But it must have been soon after the armistice in November 1918. Though it does not say so in as many words, Sorensen's autobiography leaves the impression that he was greatly disillusioned by what happened, and critical of his own action in promoting the venture in the first place. Here is how, more than 40 years later, he explained and also criticised his part in the whole undertaking in his 'A Backbencher's Pilgrimage':

I believed profoundly that the only fundamental justification for not participating in the war was the dedication of a totally new way of life which would, to use the Quaker phrase, take away the occasion for war. With superheated altruism I believed that an example of this could be given by founding a local community embodying fraternal principles in the tradition of the early Christians and discussed in the visionary writings of More's *Utopia*, Edward Bellamy's *Looking Backward* and William Morris' *News from Nowhere*.

Already in 1921 Sorensen was fighting his first political election, for a seat on the Walthamstow Urban District Council. As we know, he was a Labour MP with only one quite short break between 1929 and 1964, when he was persuaded to accept a life peerage by Harold Wilson so that the latter's cabinet colleague, Patrick Gordon Walker, could have a by-election run at what was thought to be the safe labour seat of Leyton. It wasn't – but that is quite another story. For our purposes here the main point is that, though he and his wife remained close friends of the Baders, Reg Sorensen played no further part in the Scott Bader story, except on just two occasions. First in 1950 or 1951, and in response to a request for advice from Ernest Bader about the soon-to be-born Commonwealth project, he wrote a long letter. Susanna Hoe tells her readers that it ran to seven pages. As we know, the thrust of his advice was 'don't go down that road'. Susanna Hoe cites a passage from his autobiography where he reflects about his Moore Place experience:

> The inherent problem was one of many arising in our venture that demonstrated how biological and psychological facts can frustrate intellectual theories and economic plans alike in microcosmic communities and in society as a whole. It began to dawn on me that voluntary communism could be incompatible with individual freedom and that social idealism is prone to sad deception.

Sorensen's last direct involvement with Scott Bader was when he was the main speaker at the celebrations to mark Ernest's 80th birthday. But here, in concluding this discussion of the influence of Reg Sorensen on the thinking of Dora and Ernest Bader on the long road which was to end with the establishment of the Commonwealth in 1951, we must not overlook the likely influence of the whole Moore Place community project, however semi-detached they were from it and however equivocal its outcome. It is impossible to believe that when the Baders and the Sorensens discussed the progress (or otherwise) of the community, that could have happened without reference being made quite early on to Robert Owen and his so-called villages of co-operation. As most readers will know, none of these ventures, neither those like New Harmony in the US nor those like that on Hampshire's Queenwood agricultural estate in Britain, achieved sustainable business success. None in fact survived for more than a few years. Between them they absorbed the whole of the fortune which Owen had accumulated in his younger days as highly successful progressive businessman and in particular at the famous New Lanark cotton mills in Scotland. Nevertheless these villages of co-operation must surely have come to be seen by Ernest as offering some sort of model for a self-governing business. In fact we know from Susanna Hoe's book that the conversion of Scott Bader into a co-operative type of legal entity was one of the various possibilities which he considered in the late 1940s.

Here it is worth suggesting that Reg Sorensen and the Moore Place community may have done more than suggest those Owenite villages of co-operation as possible models for what eventually became the rather different Scott Bader Commonwealth. Into Ernest's subconscious, if not his conscious, mind there may well have been planted the idea of Owen as a personal role model. It would be wrong to put this suggestion forward as more than a quite speculative hypothesis, even if it gains some support from his proselytising activities after his retirement.

To pursue Robert Owen much further would take us beyond the limits of this book. But for readers with a not yet fully satisfied interest in the great man, may I take the opportunity of recommending the chapter about him by Ernest Bader's nephew, Brian Parkyn, in *Democracy, Accountability and Participation in Industry* (MCB Publications Ltd, 1979). The treatment of the subject is as strong for Owen's career as a progressive businessman as it is for his later years on a wider stage. I found myself particularly struck by two sentences which relate to Owen's first job as a textile mill manager when he was still only 20: 'He found himself responsible for about 500 workpeople and a great deal of modern plant and machinery. It was here that he learnt that the workers in a factory would repay careful treatment and upkeep just as much as the machines.' Owen was to put that lesson into effect on a much larger scale when he moved into Scotland in 1798 and became the manager and part owner, with his father-in-law David Dale, of a complex of textile mills in New Lanark. The success of his progressive and humane policies in that new and enlarged setting made him – and those Lanark mills – world famous. It is an astonishing story of business virtue rewarded by outstanding business success. Little wonder that in both his career as a captain of industry and later as a promoter of (admittedly unsuccessful) villages of co-operation Owen was an inspiration to Ernest Bader as to many others.

WILFRED WELLOCK AND MAHATMA GANDHI

Among the godparents of the 'Commonwealth' set up in 1951 to hold the shares in a synthetic resin business, with a prospective world lead in the manufacture of reinforced plastics, Wilfred Wellock and Mahatma Gandhi seem the most unlikely. Yet, as was noted earlier, Gandhi was named alongside Robert Owen by Ernest Bader in a 1976 TV interview as having had 'the idea' (that is of common ownership) before him. And Susanna Hoe, Bader's biographer, was clearly speaking for many when she wrote (p 163) that Gandhi 'contributed so much to his ideas'. It is not immediately obvious that a man whose great achievement was to mobilise the Indian peasantry into a mass movement of non-violence against the British Raj could have had much to contribute to the ownership and other governing principles of a synthetic resin business. However, a case is made forcefully by Godric Bader that Gandhi's commitment to the imperative of all-pervasive non-violence and his emphasis on the concept of 'trustee ownership' and/or just 'trusteeship' are key features of the Scott Bader model and have so been since the Commonwealth first came into existence in 1951.

Wilfred Wellock may quite well have refocused Ernest Bader's attention on Gandhi as a possible source of inspiration. But if so, given the timing of what was apparently his first visit to Scott Bader, in 1946, the original inspiration seems unquestionably to have come earlier. Brian Parkyn remembers that the Mahatma's official visit to the UK in 1931, when he chose to stay during his days in London not in a hotel at the expense of the government, but in at a Quaker settlement in the East End, was much discussed in pacifist circles. It is also true, as Brian also suggests, that Gandhi's vegetarianism and his commitment to indefinite periods of 'chastity in marriage', which were also well known by the 1930s, are bound to have had inherent appeal to Ernest and Dora. Still, 1946 was the year before India's independence and the partition of the subcontinent in 1947, and it coincided with the high point of British interest in Gandhi. So it would not be surprising if the new contact with Wellock managed to reignite what had been an earlier flame in Ernest's and Dora's minds. On Wellock's side his autobiography suggests that India – and thus Gandhi – became of overriding interest to him following the end of the Second World War.

More generally, for Wilfred Wellock, as for Reg Sorensen, Christianity with a social purpose, learnt in their Nonconformist chapels, was the starting point from which his thinking, his politics and the main projects of his life all stemmed. Wellock, like Sorensen, was elected to the House of Commons but for the duration of less than one parliament, and not for Britain's mainstream Labour Party but for its less worldly, more 'spiritual' (in his own words), and much less politically successful half sister, the Independent Labour Party. Sorensen seems to have come to think of himself at least in the second half of his life as primarily a politician. Wellock never did. He says of himself that he was an 'experimenter in the art of living'. In his autobiography *Off the Beaten Track,* published by an Indian publisher, Sarvodaya Pracuralaya, in 1961, he singles out John Ruskin as one of the seminal influences upon him, and quotes a famous passage from the latter's *Unto This Last, Four Essays in Political Economy,* (Smith Elder and Co, London, 1862, p 156):

> There is no wealth but life – life including all its powers of love, of joy and of admiration ... That country is richest which nourishes the greatest numbers of noble and happy human beings; that man is richest who, having perfected the functions of his own life to the utmost, has also the widest influence, both personal and by means of his possessions, over the lives of others.

More directly relevant, perhaps, to the day-to-day concerns of people working at the manufacture of synthetic resins, was the subject Wellock chose to talk about when invited to address them on the occasion of the company's 25th birthday in 1946. Susanna Hoe writes (p 109) that he spoke mainly about the way in which 'the quality of people's lives was decided largely by the work they did', and went on to argue about the 'tragedy of the modern world' in that respect, that 'labour was becoming less interesting and so failed to satisfy the needs of the human spirit'. We are not told what remedies, if any, he proposed.

Among Wellock's publications there is a pamphlet, dated 1949, with the title *Gandhi as a Social Revolutionary.* We may reasonably assume that two of the pamphlet's main points of emphasis deal with the value assigned by Gandhi to small-scale, preferably village, communities, and to low-technology systems of manufacture. Gandhi's simple lifestyle and his commitment to a vegetarian diet must surely also have been commended, and the whole package was surely presented as a 'social revolutionary' set of moves against the forces of mechanisation, large-scale urbanisation and luxury living. Wellock, it must be acknowledged, was a living exemplar of what he advocated. A vegetarian like Ghandhi, he spun wool, collected from the hedgerows, and then knitted it into jerseys for himself and his wife to wear. Moreover, as his extreme gesture in support of the simple life, he never allowed his income to rise above the threshold at which income tax became payable. Wellock must have been one of those quite rare people who are genuinely content with a truly modest standard of material living. The second paragraph of the preface he wrote to his autobiography *Off the Beaten Track* begins with a pronouncement which will surely come as a surprise to many readers as it has to me: 'Current Western civilisation is unique in that it exhibits for the first time in history an *affluent* proletariat [emphasis added].'

But perhaps, on second thoughts, the remark should not be seen as all that surprising. After all, Harold Macmillan had won the general election of two years before, in 1959, with his famous slogan 'You've never had it so good'.

However, to return to Gandhi, an excellent source covering Gandhi and Scott Bader is a chapter written by Godric Bader himself in a book entitled *Gandhi and the Contemporary World*. Called 'Gandhi on Trusteeship, a Transforming Ethic', the chapter was reprinted in *World Business Academy Perspectives,* vol 9, no 4, 1995 (pp 41–50). For me, this 1995 review of Gandhi's ideas on trusteeship contains some of the more persuasive arguments for recommending the Scott Bader business model in the 21st century. Godric, who is the only non-adopted son of Ernest and Dora, has held the post of Scott Bader's Life President since his retirement from the chairmanship of the business in 1990. So he has had some time for reading and reflection. Here I will highlight some of the main points in Godric's chapter, which begins with two linked propositions:

a) Gandhi's basic commitment to non-violence ... extended well beyond direct conflict resolution to the very root causes of violence.
b) [The latter are] inherent and endemic in our present economic, social and industrial systems.

Readers will remember what Susanna Hoe writes (p 21) about Ernest Bader's views on a contiguous set of issues, that once 'he could afford the luxury of altogether eschewing borrowing, *usury* and *interest* became synonymous with *exploitation of labour, unemployment, capitalism* and *war* [emphasis original].' This surely tells us that the pacifist founder of the Scott Bader Commonwealth would have been quite at home with Gandhi's notion that violence is 'endemic' in the capitalist system. Whether he took that idea from the Mahatma or arrived at it independently, is, of course, another matter.

What about trustee ownership or, in the language of the Godric Bader's chapter, 'trusteeship'? Godric tells his readers that 'Gandhi believed that change should and would be brought about through the application of his concept of trusteeship.'

He goes on to offer a definition: 'Trusteeship essentially means having faith and confidence in a process of taking responsibility for assets and social values, and administering their rightful and creative usage for the benefit of others – now and in coming generations.'

This seems to me to be an excellent account of the ownership arrangements as they have evolved at Scott Bader since the setting up of the Commonwealth in 1951. Members are indeed enjoined to act as trustees in line with the meaning defined by Godric Bader for the word 'trusteeship'.

So it seems that about trusteeship the views of the founder of the Scott Bader Commonwealth and of Mahatma Gandhi were for practical purposes identical. What I don't know is whether the former came to the idea of trusteeship independently of Gandhi or what part, if any, may have been played by Wilfred Wellock as an intermediary.

At this stage there are a number of further points that need to be made about Godric Bader's 1995 article 'Gandhi on Trusteeship'. First I want to highlight the dimension of *time* in the notion of trusteeship. Lawyers will know that there are specific provisions in the laws of England and Wales to prevent what is called the 'perpetuity of trusts'. However since the Scott Bader Commonwealth is not, in law, a trust but a company limited by guarantee with charitable status, we may simply make a note of that and pass on. The more important related point is that in his definition of trusteeship Godric rightly includes a time dimension, by referring to 'coming generations'. In effect one of the aims of the trusteeship notion at Scott Bader is that the arrangements by which it is set up should continue indefinitely. We may be sure that *that* particular aim goes back to Godric's father. Whether it figures either explicitly or implicitly in the trusteeship writings of Mahatma Gandhi, I do not know.

The final point is about the duty of care, enjoined upon the members – and *de facto* trustees – of the Scott Bader Commonwealth, in relation to the physical environment *in* which, and the physical materials *with* which, they are working. In so far as they are working with non-renewable resources – which account in fact for most of the raw materials used in the manufacture of synthetic resins – this duty of care will presumably become more urgent as time passes. Its emphasis among the principles which are supposed to guide the Commonwealth must raise questions about the policies of the Scott Bader business in relation to growth. It is a principle which is entirely compatible with what in later years has become Scott Bader's growth policy: namely the minimum needed to ensure survival and future sustainability in the synthetic resin industry.

In relation to this last point, the duty of care towards the material environment, we can say quite categorically that it is a value or duty which emerged independently in the thinking of both Ernest Bader and Gandhi. As we shall see, it became much later, in 1972, one of obligations in the code of conduct then adopted by and for Commonwealth members. On the other hand Gandhi's commitment in this respect may well have strengthened that of Ernest Bader – especially given that it will have been reinforced by Wilfred Wellock.

A point of overlap of a rather different order in the thinking behind the Scott Bader Commonwealth and the teaching of Mahatma Gandhi is emphasised in Godric Bader's 1995 chapter and must also be noted here. In this case it seems best to quote almost a whole paragraph from that article. I do so without comment except to say that the Baders' views in this respect, that is both father and son, are almost bound to have been reinforced by Gandhi's:

> For our further evolution we have an essential need to release the divine spirit and purpose. Gandhi yearned to provide an environment in which this could be achieved. Influenced by his time and education in the UK, he gradually developed his ideas of trusteeship. The primary inspiration for this concept was the unfailing source to which his inner spirituality continually led him back, namely the Bhagavad Gita. He understood the Gita teaching of non-possession to mean that those who desire salvation should act like the trustee who, 'though having control over great possessions, regards not an iota of them as his own'.

A similar point is made in an *Anthology of Gandiji's Thoughts on Trusteeship Management* (Shri Vijay Merchant, Bombay, 1969), to which Brian Parkyn has kindly drawn my attention: 'He said … that everything belonged to God and was from God. Therefore it was for His people as a whole not for a particular individual. When an individual had more than a proportionate portion, he became a trustee of that portion for God's people.'

The same anthology also and rather differently derives Gandhi's idea of trusteeship from his ideas of economic justice and equality:

> Flowing from the concept of economic justice or equality, Gandhiji deduced the theory of trusteeship … he did not tolerate the idea of the inevitability of class conflict and the indispensability of strikes and lock-outs. He thought that if employers and industrialists treated themselves as trustees, the problem of evolving industrial harmony and making economic justice a reality could be solved non-violently on the strength of the doctrine of love.

The conclusion of this discussion must be that to the sources of the Scott Bader Commonwealth, Gandhi's ideas need to be added to those of social Christianity. No doubt there is a large overlap between the two. But the values of small scale, of working *communities*, and of trusteeship (including a duty of care towards the physical environment), have at least as much of a Gandhi provenance as a social Christian one, and perhaps more.

QUAKER VALUES AND THE QUAKER BUSINESS TRADITION

There is a justly famous passage in Adam Smith's *The Wealth of Nations* (University Paperback Edition, edited by Edward Cannan, 1961, vol 1, p 412) in which Scotland's great economist offers a wonderfully tart comment on a decision taken a few years before by the Quakers in Pennsylvania to free their slaves:

> The late resolution of the Quakers in Pennsylvania to set at liberty all their Negro slaves, must satisfy us that their number cannot be very great. Had they made any considerable part of their property, such a resolution could never have been agreed to.

It is also true that on close study the record of Britain's Quaker businessmen, in the debates about and struggles over child labour in the new factories over the first half of the 19th century, is by no means shiningly progressive. It seems that as many, or almost as many, Quaker industrialists were opposed to Lord Shaftesbury's efforts to limit abuses with his factory legislation as supported him. I suppose there must always have been some tensions in the thought processes of those Quakers – and they were a surprisingly large number – who became captains of business and industry in the 18th and 19th centuries: tensions between the imperatives of business success and the claims of charity and philanthropy. Their successes were surely due in the main to a combination of fair dealing, frugal living, and attention to detail. In some respects, most notably perhaps in relation to the position of women and women's education, they were almost universally progressive. On issues like employee housing their record was notably good. On child labour, on the other hand, it was at best mixed. It would be unrealistic to expect that the typical Quaker businessman of the late 18th and 19th century could have been a bold and pioneering visionary on the model of Robert Owen during his days at New Lanark.

However, despite these qualifications, it remains true that alone among the sects of Protestant Christians who emerged in Britain in the 17th century, the Quakers established a tradition in the 18th and 19th century of building and then sustaining successful businesses with a marked social conscience. That tradition was still very much alive and well when Ernest Bader arrived in Britain in 1912. We must remember too that from their earliest beginnings in the 17th century they had renounced violence and embraced pacifism. So it should not be a matter of any surprise that the Fellowship of Reconciliation (FOR) at the start of the First World War should have included Quakers as well as other Christians.

However, in terms of its influence on the thinking of Ernest Bader, it was an initiative by Britain's Quakers at the end of the First World War which seems to have proved especially important. What then happened was the publication and official adoption, with the authority of the British Quakers' so-called Yearly Meeting, of the 'Eight Foundations of a True Social Order'.

Susanna Hoe (p 217) reproduces the whole text of the document in an Appendix where it can be studied in detail. By her account the starting point of the Foundations was a question raised by the famous and evidently saintlike 18th-century American Quaker, John Woolman, about the possibility of some link between people's 'possessions,' on the one hand, and 'the seeds of war' on the other; and specifically about whether the latter 'have nourishment' in the former.

In response to the question, and apparently after three years' 'exercise of mind', the Eight Foundations were laid down '*not ... as rules of life but [as] an attempt to set forth ideals that are aspects of eternal truth and the direct outcome of our Quaker testimony to the individual worth of the human soul* [original emphasis]'.

In effect the first of the Eight Foundations enjoins a duty to base the 'true social order' on 'brotherhood', and derives that imperative from the 'fatherhood of God as revealed by Jesus Christ'. The last, which has been the most widely quoted, lays down the criterion on which to base 'ownership', namely whatever will 'best minister to the need and development of man'. Wisely it chooses *not* to prescribe any owner-ship template which would meet the criterion. It is essentially a second-order Foundation.

Foundations Two to Seven are something of a mixed bag, but there is little doubt that Ernest and Dora Bader would have ticked them all in their personal copy. The need to transcend material ends and material things is one of the points in both Foundation Two and Foundation Four. Instead the aim should be 'the growth of personality truly related to God and Man', or as amplified in Foundation Three, the 'full devel-opment, physical moral and spiritual, should be assured to every member of the community, man, woman, and child'.

Another theme which crops up in both Foundation Three and Four is that no 'excessive burdens shall be put on labour', and that 'the devel-opment of man's full personality should not be hampered by unjust conditions nor crushed by economic pressure'. Similarly in Foundation Six 'methods of outward domination and of the appeal to force' are rejected not only in 'international affairs' but also in relation to the 'whole problem of industrial control'. Instead, Quakers are enjoined to focus on the 'spiritual force of righteousness, loving kindness and trust' on the grounds that they appeal 'to the best in everyman and when applied to industrial relations [achieve] great things'. Finally Founda-tion Seven lays down that 'mutual service should be the principle on which life is organised', and Quakers are reminded that that service, not private gain, should be 'the motive for all work'.

There is no need to labour the point. These Foundations seem to offer almost a 'designer' set of principles to suit the thinking of Ernest and Dora Bader as it evolved during the First World War; and much later to supply at least one of the starting points of reference when it came to laying down the principles on which the Scott Bader Common-wealth was to be based. There are certainly echoes of the language of the Eight Foundations in the Commonwealth's constitutional docu-ments. It is hard not to believe that, for the Baders, this correspondence

of language with a celebrated Quaker original offered an extra legitimacy to the constitutional principles with which the Commonwealth
was endowed.

Ernest and Dora Bader joined the Quakers, by being admitted to
membership of the Wellingborough meeting, only in 1943. But according to Susanna Hoe Ernest had already been attending Quaker meetings, though less formally, for some years. Moreover Godric had been
sent to the independent Friends School in Saffron Waldon – what we
would loosely call a public school – in 1935, and had been admitted to
the Friends in 1942. He seems to have enjoyed himself at the school,
and felt comfortable with both the Quaker principles and the competitive games. Evidently he was delighted as well as surprised by being
made captain of the school's football team in his last year.

The occasion for the Baders' formal admission to the Society of
Friends in 1943 is explained by Susanna Hoe as having followed a
change of minister at the Baptist chapel in Wollaston which they had
previously attended. David Oliver, the minister when they first started
going to the chapel and whom they liked, was called up as a chaplain to
the armed forces. His successor, a Reverend Harris, was described by
Dora as a 'proper warmonger'. We don't know whether he was an ex-
Army chaplain. But given the Baders' pacifist views, a switch to the
Wellingborough Quakers made obvious sense. Both of them, and their
daughter Erica, are buried in the burial ground of the town's Meeting
House. Very near the end of her biography (p 209), Susanna Hoe tells
her readers that 'Ernest had hoped to have the concept [of the Scott
Bader Commonwealth] adopted as a Quaker plank in line with their
Eight Points on social reform of 1918'. Earlier (p 78) and in her discussion about the origins of the Scott Bader Fellowship, a kind of half-way
house on the road to the Commonwealth that we will come onto in the
next section, she wrote: 'As for the Quaker Eight Point testimony ...
Ernest was to spend the next 30 years [i.e. 1945 to 1975] trying to
persuade – or compel – the Society of Friends to do something constructive in industry with their Eight Points.' But, dealing at the end of
the book with the same issue, she writes simply that the effort to persuade them 'fizzled out'. Given the way the Quakers work, not to
mention the vested interests of what were still through much of the
20th century privately-held Quaker family firms, it was surely unrealistic on Ernest Bader's part to expect that such an initiative could have
had a really positive ending. Yet it is surely also true that he greatly
valued the high-minded tradition of Quaker business ethics and saw the

Commonwealth as a beneficiary of that. There was also, although Ernest did not live to know about it, a kind of posthumous consolation prize: in the 1995 edition of the so-called Quaker Book of Discipline, known officially as *Quaker Faith and Morals*, in the chapter on social testimony, Scott Bader's constitution is cited and to that extent recommended.

Ernest Bader died in February 1982, more than a year into his tenth decade. On 21 September 1997, over 15 years later, the *Financial Times* published a piece by Richard Wolffe which was centred around Scott Bader, and included an interview with Godric. The headline was 'Quaker spirit on the wane', and the main thrust of the piece was summarised by a cross headline: 'Most Quaker-founded companies have few qualms about shaking off the past.'

Wolffe amplified the point, writing that 'most of the best-known businesses founded by Quakers lost almost all trace of their religious roots decades ago as the companies were expanded or taken over. From Lloyds and Barclays Banks to Rowntree and Cadbury the chocolate-makers, the Quaker influence in business stretched far wider than their numbers – estimated at about 20,000 at the peak at the start of the century.'

Arguing that Ernest Bader took seriously those Eight Foundations that we have just considered, the writer of the piece went on: 'In a monumental gift in 1951, he placed the entire company in the hands of a charitable trust, known as the Scott Bader Commonwealth. Unlike other Quaker companies, he ensured it would never be bought or sold.'

Though he does not say so in his interview for this piece in the *Financial Times*, Godric Bader has argued forcefully to me more than once that Scott Bader and its fidelity to true Quaker principles has been badly let down both by the Quaker community and by the few other surviving Quaker family businesses over the last 50 years. I feel entitled to be sure that his father frequently argued in the same way over the 30-odd years which elapsed between the founding of the Commonwealth and his death.

This is not the place to discuss in any detail either why, in the words of the *Financial Times* headline, the 'Quaker spirit' has been 'on the wane', or why the Scott Bader model does not seem to have been followed by any other Quaker family businesses at all. But one very general point is obvious enough: namely the accelerating secularisation of almost all aspects of life in the West, at least since the Second World War. Even the most successful and committed of the production co-operatives of mainland Western Europe – whether those in the social Catholic tradition of the Mondragon Group in the Basque Provinces of Spain, or in the very different and left radical tradition of the Imola co-operatives in Italy – have been effected by it. Co-operative forms may remain the same but their content has been everywhere, as the Italians say, laicised. As for the specific point about why the Scott Bader model has not been followed by other Quaker-owned family businesses, a rather specific answer is available. With the exception of C. & J. Clark of Street in Somerset, all or almost all of them had become public companies before 1951 and some, for example what was originally Joseph Rowntree and Co, even before those Quaker Foundations were published in 1918. For the record, it is also worth noting that in the Rowntree case the family, before giving up control, endowed three trusts with substantial capital sums to enable them to finance good works of one kind and another.

THE SCOTT BADER FELLOWSHIP 1946–7

Rightly in my view, given the man who is her subject, Susanna Hoe devotes a full chapter (pp 74–89) to the Scott Bader Fellowship. This was the halfway-house forerunner of the Commonwealth and had a formal, though no legal, existence during parts of 1946 and 1947. It had evidently also been the subject of extensive discussion with the staff during 1945 after the Second World War ended. Ernest Bader's biographer implies without saying so in as many words that there was a kind of three-stage dialectical relationship between, first, the Fellowship, its formation and subsequent wind-up; second, a strike in 1948 – the only one in the company's history – together with how it was settled; and third, a discussion about possible long-term future structures for the business which was eventually completed with the setting up of the Commonwealth in 1951. As we shall see, Brian Parkyn is almost explicit about a dialectical connection between these events, with frustrations over the wind-up of the Fellowship as a factor behind the 1948 strike, and with an understanding about a long-term co-operative type structure as a key component in the settlement with the Chemical Workers' Union which brought the strike to an end.

Susanna Hoe starts her chapter with a discussion of the background to the Fellowship and the thinkers who influenced its formation. There is a big overlap between the latter and what we have been reviewing as the sources of the 1951 Commonwealth. For example, she reproduces an extended quotation from the famous 1659 pamphlet in which Peter Cornelius Plokhoy sets out the rationale of his co-operative society or Little Commonwealth. The Quakers and their Eight Foundations duly appear, and so do Wilfred Wellock and Rousseau. It is to Rousseau rather than to Fritz Schumacher – who appeared on the Scott Bader scene only in the 1960s – that she attributes (p 80) an implicit view about optimum business *size* which Ernest Bader put on paper during the run-up to the Fellowship: 'Businesses might be sub-divided for social ends into small groups of say 30 to 100.'

It is in this discussion of the thinkers behind the Fellowship that Susanna Hoe offers (p 78) something of substance about the Swiss pacifist theologian Leonhard Ragaz. Readers may remember that he was just introduced much earlier in her story, as someone whose writing, together with a Jehovah's Witness pamphlet, had influenced Ernest Bader to embrace a full-blooded pacifism during his brief period of citizen's military service in Switzerland in 1914. Here we learn that:

> He was a rebel, a revolutionary and an unorthodox, anti-establishment Christian propounding what has been described as a 'Kingdom of God theology which was a society criticising theology'. The goal he put forward was to transform earthly conditions towards the will of God and to take the words of the Sermon on the Mount and the promises of the Gospels seriously. He saw in the Gospels hope for the future, as the relationship of God to man and man to God and to brother. The latter was important because there could be no true relationship with God without a proper relationship with one's neighbour.

There were two other essential corollaries: the defeat of capitalism and the establishment of peace.

Given these views, what seems extraordinary is that this Swiss theologian, when consulted much later, in 1950, about the Bader family's proposal to give away 90% of their shareholding for nothing, advised *against it*. But about his project for 'the defeat of capitalism and the establishment of peace' as a necessary precondition of better things, I suspect that most ordinary people will respond to this kind of thing, whether propounded by a Swiss theologian or anyone else, by saying something like: 'Quite so. But ...' *But*, of course, Ernest Bader was *not* an ordinary person. We have evidence of that later in the same chapter (p 86) when his biographer aptly quotes a passage which begins with an Ernest Bader description of himself as a mystic and ends with what may well remind many readers of the fascination which Marie Correlli's radiation and electricity had had for Ernest Bader and Dora Scott during their younger, courting, days:

> In a way I imagine one might say I'm more a mystic than an intellectual. It's the consciousness of being surrounded by a kind of spirit, if you like – lively action growing round in everything you see. It's an alive world. You are in the middle of it. You are part of it. You are trying to find your friends – those who are nearest in your thinking. It's shuffling about in a sea as if you were a drop which had consciousness and you tried to get other drops thinking like you.

So what about the content of the Fellowship? Brian Parkyn has preserved a letter written to him by his 'Onkel Ernst', and dated 4 December 1945:

> I think you will be interested to have a copy of our latest ideas on the S.B. Fellowship with regard to the basic principles, objects, and constitution, and I am therefore enclosing a copy, together with two charts which show the organisation in outline. Besides this, there is of course a the letter which I propose to send to the Fellowship to be read at its first meeting, containing the terms of what I intend to do, i.e. put about 85% of the shares at the disposal of the Fellowship.

By itself, the phrase about 'putting the shares at the disposal of the Fellowship' is perhaps a little elusive. Susanna Hoe (p 81) supplies the relevant specifics from a Fellowship booklet published in 1946:

> To encourage a spirit of goodwill and sacrifice on which the success of the Fellowship will depend, Mr and Mrs Bader have decided to hand over to the Fellowship Fund *dividends* [emphasis added] they receive on the capital represented by their shares in the company which amount to 85% of the total.

We may note that what are being passed to the Fellowship fund are the dividends on the Bader's capital and not the shares themselves. More importantly, I should explain that notwithstanding the booklet and, no doubt, other printed material, neither the Fellowship nor the fund were ever incorporated in law. They were simply grace and favour or ex gratia phenomena initiated by Ernest Bader. That becomes clear beyond all possibility of doubt when we read the final short paragraph (p 89) of Susanna Hoe's Fellowship chapter: 'So he wound up *his* [emphasis added] Fellowship, because, after all, "I was the initiator of the idea and it had to go my way not the other way. That's simple."' I may add that the issue which caused Ernest Bader to kill off the Fellowship had nothing directly to do either with its place in the Scott Bader business or with the business itself. It was wound up by its initiator on the issue of pacifism. Members were asked to pledge themselves 'not to serve in the army'. The date was 1947. It was only two years after the end of what had been essentially a defensive war against Hitler's Germany and one in which for more than a year Britain had stood alone. In the circumstances it was surely absurd to expect many members of the Fellowship to sign such a pledge.

Earlier in her Fellowship chapter (p 83) Susanna Hoe wrote that 'the most outward sign of the Fellowship to most employees of Scott Bader was the half-hour prayer meeting on Saturday morning'. Brian Parkyn goes a good deal further and has argued that the fellowship was 'little more than a set of simplistic Christian platitudes which Ernest hoped would bind employees more closely together'.

Brian Parkyn has also explained why he chose *not* to join the Fellowship, the membership of which was voluntary but involved 'signing and approving a list of Christian principles':

> About two-thirds of all the employees were members, but the firm was so paternal in those days that most would have been afraid of losing their jobs if they had not joined. In spite of considerable pressure from Ernest I refused to join. I did not object to the platitudes as such, but the fact that they were worded in such a way as to make them seem exclusively Christian ... Apart from a handful of genuine agnostics, there were two or three Jewish employees in the firm. One of them, Horst Behmak, a refugee from Germany who had lost his parents in Buchenwald, worked in the laboratory and was a close friend of mine.

But to be fair, though it existed on no more than a grace and favour basis, there was to the Fellowship during the period of its formal existence some more or less real content as well as those dividends on the Baders' shares, the Christian principles, and the half-hour prayer meeting on Saturday mornings. According to Susanna Hoe (p 82) there was a semi-elected Fellowship committee and, for at least some months, a part-time Fellowship secretary and a Fellowship publication, called *The Catalyst*.

In any event, leaving out the Christianity, it seems that the Fellow-ship gave rise to ideas and expectations of possible moves by Ernest Bader towards a greater accountability for his actions to the workforce. Brian Parkyn has pointed out that his uncle was 'almost pathologically opposed to trade unions and refused to recognise them in the com-pany'. In the circumstances, he has further explained that 'a small group of us, six in all, and all members of the Wollaston Labour Party ... wanted to establish a democratically elected workers' council along the lines of Wilfred Brown's works council at the Glacier Metal Co ... We called ourselves the *vigilantes* and had our first meeting in March (1948).' In other words early in the year following the close-down of the Fellowship. The strike came in November of that same year.

THE 1948 STRIKE AND THE INVOLVEMENT
OF BOB EDWARDS

Whatever may have been the indirect and dialectical connection between the strike in November 1948 and the expectations frustrated when the Fellowship was wound up in the previous year, both Susanna Hoe and Brian Parkyn anchor its direct cause in the dire commercial conditions which the company was having to face at the time, and in Ernest Bader's response to them. Susanna Hoe quotes from a circular sent out by Ernest Bader at the end of October:

> Notice is hereby given ... that with great regret the directors have decided that in view of the present slackness in trade, the produc-tion bonus [then paid monthly] is to be suspended.

Worse was to follow, and almost at once. In November, according to Brian Parkyn, 'Ernest decided that there should be a 10% reduction in the entire workforce'. According to Susanna Hoe, 'half a dozen men were sacked', a good deal less than 10% at that time. No matter. What is important is what happened next. Here is Brian Parkyn's account of it:

> The *vigilantes* then set up a workers' council to look after the interest of all employees, but Ernest refused to negotiate with it. As a result, the *vigilantes* decided at a meeting that I attended to take strike action so as to get recognition for the workers' council. I disagreed with the decision to strike and left the meeting.

Susanna Hoe quotes from the *Northamptonshire Evening Telegraph* of 11 November to tell her readers what happened next. Under the headline 'Resin workers come out on strike', the paper reported:

> Nearly 70 workers at a Wollaston firm came out on strike today following the suspension of two members of staff. The managing director of the firm, Scott Bader and Co Ltd, referred to the walk-out of his employees as a 'communist attempt to get hold of factory control'. He added, 'It was the best thing that could have happened. It will clear out the dissatisfaction instigated over the past month by the ringleaders.'

Predictably, Ernest Bader refused to negotiate with the strike committee as he had earlier with the workers' council. However, in Brian Parkyn's words, he was finally persuaded 'to accept Bob Edwards, the general secretary of the Chemical Workers' Union as a mediator'.

For the final stage in the story of the 1948 strike and its settlement – and for a key episode and very likely a turning point in the much longer story of the formation of the Scott Bader Commonwealth – I can do no better than quote a paragraph from Brian Parkyn's autobiography:

> The following day, I met Bob at Wellingborough station and drove him back to Wollaston Hall. It was with considerable trepidation that I introduced him to Ernest. His first words to Ernest were, 'Who the hell do you think you are, Jesus Christ?' I kept quiet and waited for the Old Man to explode, but surprisingly he responded warmly to Bob and instantly liked him. As well as representing the Chemical Workers' Union he was also a member of the Co-operative Party and a pacifist. He proposed that the company should be turned into a co-operative trust. This was agreed and the strike was called off after two days. It was the start of a long series of discussions which finally led to the foundation of the Scott Bader Commonwealth in 1951.

As many readers will know, Bob Edwards was elected as a Labour MP in 1955 and chosen to be one of the first of the external trustees of the Scott Bader Commonwealth in 1963. Some may feel that the opening gambit with which he accosted Ernest Bader is evidence of a surprisingly high level of briefing by his union's research department. Those who think in the language of Providence may well see his involvement in the settlement of the 1948 strike as providential: only a small minority of senior trade union officials have been either members of the Co-operative Party or pacifists – at least since the war – and only a *tiny* minority have been both. And that remains true, notwithstanding the fact that, so Brian Parkyn tells us, Bob Edwards fought with the International Brigade in the Spanish Civil War. From an obituary published shortly after his death in the mid-1980s, we learn that his 'forebears helped to establish the first co-operative bakery in Lancashire 100 years before'. The same obituary is surely right when it argues that the setting up of the Commonwealth in 1951 'needed the support of the shop floor and the trade unions'. Bob Edwards, it tells us, was 'instrumental in securing both'.

THE SCOTT BADER OWNERSHIP AND CO-DETERMINATION
MODEL AND ITS SOURCES

Godric Bader has kept a letter written to him by George Goyder in the closing week of 1990. With that letter was enclosed a copy of an article by Goyder entitled 'Socialism and Private Industry – A New Approach', and published by *Fabian News* in November 1949. The letter goes on to report an evidently important point that Ernest Bader had made to him, Goyder, in the presence of a named witness (Mr Norman Lowe) in 1977. It even specifies the actual date, 8 March, when the point had been made. It had been to the effect that the Goyder *Fabian News* article had first suggested to him the idea of giving away his company. For what it's worth, I would not myself see a conflict of evidence between this letter and the one written by Ernest in 1945 to his nephew Brian Parkyn and quoted above, about his ideas for the proposed Scott Bader Fellowship. It seems unlikely in view of what subsequently happened that Ernest ever planned to give actual family shares, as opposed to dividends on them, to the Fellowship.

Among other things Goyder's 1949 article in *Fabian News* draws his reader's attention to important features in the statutes of the Carl-Zeiss Foundation in Germany. There are a number of points in the Zeiss statutes – and in the Zeiss set-up more generally – which find echoes in the constitutional documents of the Scott Bader Commonwealth in 1951. At the lunch in Cambridge in April 1951 at which 90% of the Bader family shares were signed over, and the foundation of the Commonwealth was celebrated, George Goyder was the main speaker. When he wrote his *Fabian News* piece in 1949 he evidently did not know that Zeiss had been reborn at Oberkocken in West Germany in 1948. But he must have learnt that soon afterwards for he actually visited the reborn successor to the original Jena business in Oberkocken in May 1950. We know from Susanna Hoe (p 113) that he 'helped Ernest to work out a legal scheme', and though no actual dates are specified, the context points clearly to the second half of 1950, in other words soon after his return from visiting the reborn Zeiss in West Germany. However, there is one curious feature about the Goyder article on the one hand and the claim made in his end-1990 letter on the other: though the article's praise for the Zeiss arrangements is quite unqualified, the fact that the business was *given away* in 1896 to the Zeiss Foundation or *Stiftung* is not mentioned at all.

We will come back shortly to the hypothesis that the constitutional arrangements with which the binary system of the new Scott Bader Commonwealth and the old Scott Bader company were endowed in 1951 were significantly in line with a Zeiss original. But before that it makes sense to discuss what other models were available at the time which were in effect rejected by the choice of following Zeiss, anyway in broad outline.

To begin with and at least in theory, once the Bader family had chosen to give away its shares, the recipient could have been a co-operative society rather than, as was the case, a company limited by guarantee with charitable status and called the Scott Bader Commonwealth. Indeed, if Brian Parkyn, is right about what had been agreed between Ernest Bader and Bob Edwards as a settlement of the 1948 strike, a co-operative or co-operative type solution was originally very much on the cards. True Brian Parkyn writes not of a co-operative society but a 'co-operative trust' whatever that may be. Moreover, in 1951 the number of surviving production co-operatives in Britain was still well into double figures. Even more interestingly, one of them, NPS Shoes, and perhaps the oldest since it dates from 1872, *must* have been known to Ernest. Its Wollaston factory is scarcely 200 yards from the front gates of Wollaston Hall, with its name and date of birth carved above the front door. Most notably, as a small independent shoemaking operation it is still very much in business in 2001.

It is true that there may well have been commercial advice between 1948 and 1950 against going for a solution such that the word 'co-operative' would have come to feature in the SB name. It is also true that Ernest may have had objections to a regime, as would have happened in a co-operative, where final decisions were taken by a directly elected board. As we shall see later, that is mainly *not* the position in today's Scott Bader. Ernest may quite well also have rejected a co-operative solution because he was uneasy about co-operative society shares which are often held individually. Nevertheless I was truly astonished to learn from Godric Bader that in 60 years at Wollaston he had never paid a visit to NPS Shoes and that, so far as he knew, the same was true of his father and mother during their lifetime. It is perhaps worth adding, for the benefit of specialist readers, that one of the outstanding businesses within Italy's much larger contemporary population of production co-ops, La Ceramica, was in fact *given* to its then workforce by its previous owners, the Bucci family, in 1874. The gift was in fact a quite exceptional transaction in that it included a provision for the receiving back of the business by the family from the co-operative if the latter proved unable to cope with it. In a country which is easily the world's largest manufacturer of ceramic wall tiles, La Ceramica figured as the third most important in the late 1990s.

It is not clear to me how seriously a co-operative society solution was actually considered by Ernest Bader and his family before the decision was taken to go for an ownership arrangement which was 100% collective (or, in the language later favoured by Fritz Schumacher, extinguished) and for an entity registered under the Company's Acts rather than those of the Industrial and Provident Societies. About what might be called the John Lewis model Susanna Hoe (p 111) tells her readers that it was 'another inspiration', and then adds that the Scott Bader ownership 'was to be neutralised in a rather different manner'. My own view is that the differences between Scott Bader and John Lewis have a good deal more to do with corporate government or co-determination in the first place and with the nature of the ownership transfer in the second place, than with their respective arrangements of 'extinguished ownership'. Apart from anything else the John Lewis business was not *given* by Spedan Lewis to the trust, which has now owned it since 1929. It was sold, albeit at a substantial discount, and with a loan from the former owner to enable the sale and purchase to happen. By contrast, and as we know, the Scott Bader business was given by the family to the Commonwealth for no financial consideration at all in 1951.

It may be worth noticing here that significant private companies in the UK which have chosen to embrace 100% employee and/or charitable ownership over the last 20 years – like, for example, Tullis Russell, the manufacturer of quality paper based in Fife – have chosen to go for a mixture of individual and collective employee ownership. This has come to be regarded as the best way of maximising sustainability on the one hand and incentives for improved employee performance on the other. Such a mix would have been entirely feasible in Scott Bader's case notwithstanding the give-away character of the ownership transfer. But it is notable that the word 'incentive' simply does not figure in Susanna Hoe's index, nor, I think, anywhere in her book .

What then of the similarities between the Scott Bader that was born with the establishment of the Commonwealth in 1951, and the gift of shares to it, and the German undertaking Carl Zeiss which was so strongly commended by George Goyder in his end-1949 article in *Fabian News*? To begin with there is charitable ownership in both cases. As we have seen, the legal character of the Scott Bader Commonwealth is that of a company limited by guarantee with approved charitable status. In the case of Carl Zeiss, the ownership of the business is vested in what the Germans call a *Stiftung*, or charitable foundation. Secondly, in both cases the ownership of the business was transferred to the charity by the previous owners, by the Bader family and by Dr Ernst Abbe, as a free gift. Thirdly, and as a direct consequence of the businesses being owned by charities, there are no individual shareholders. So far as I know there are no other examples anywhere of *businesses* of any size with precisely these ownership arrangements. I have deliberately emphasised the word *businesses* because there are certainly other *institutions* with the same or very similar ownership arrangements. The colleges at Oxford and Cambridge are good examples of that in the UK. Whether the university presses at Oxford and Cambridge, which have a similar corporate structure, should be regarded as businesses is an interesting question but one which cannot be taken further here.

Thirdly, both Scott Bader and Zeiss are required by their relevant statutes to concern themselves with technical education and research, especially in areas of study on which their own business activities are focused. In the case of Scott Bader, this duty is laid down in article 42 of the operating company which sets out the company's 'principles': 'To conduct research and to provide technical education mainly in Synthetic Resins and their applications in the paints plastics and allied industries.'

For comparison at Zeiss, the owning *Stiftung* is enjoined: 'To promote study in the natural and mathematical sciences both as regards research and teaching.'

Fourthly, in each case a duty is laid down to the effect that the business and the charity which owns it must have a proper regard for the interests of the local community.

This is not the place for a detailed account of either Carl Zeiss as a business or of the *Stiftung* which owns it. They figure prominently in three books by George Goyder, namely *The Future of Private Enterprise* (1951), *The Responsible Company* (1961), and *The Just Enterprise* (1987). In a campaign which stretched over five decades until his death in 1997, he sought to persuade successive British Governments to introduce radical changes in company law. Many of his proposed reforms reflected originals in the statutes of the Carl-Zeiss *Stiftung*. I have already cited Susanna Hoe for the help which George Goyder gave Ernest Bader with what she calls a 'legal scheme'. There can be no serious doubt that much, perhaps most, of Goyder's advice in this respect came from his knowledge of and admiration for Zeiss.

I also believe that both Ernest Bader and George Goyder were attracted to Ernst Abbe, who had set up the *Stiftung* in 1896 and then transferred the shares in the business to it as a free gift, because his thinking on at least two key issues was very similar to their own. First, he was distinctly unenthusiastic about trade unions. Secondly, he believed that professional managers should be free to manage. Indeed in this second respect his solution was that much more conservative than Scott Bader's. At Scott Bader the professional management is at least accountable to the non-management employees and the latter must at minimum consent to the top managerial appointments. In the case of Zeiss that is not so. The top professional managers form in effect a self-perpetuating oligarchy. It is also true that at Scott Bader the final say about matters of employee discipline rests with representatives of the community and not with management, even if – as we shall see – it proved necessary to force a test case against management to establish this in the early days.

But it would be wrong to omit from this discussion of the Scott Bader model, or perhaps more precisely the constitutional documents associated with it, two features which seem to me to be quite unusually exceptional, if not unique. First, as I will argue at greater length later, the preamble to the 1951 constitution of the Scott Bader Commonwealth is not simply concerned with its own life, those of its members and that of the business of which it has become a trustee. In effect a duty is laid upon both the Commonwealth and its members to 'change the world' and to work to replace commercial values with more Christian ones. In the language of an earlier generation, it calls for a project of world amendment.

What is more, this implied duty is made unequivocally specific in at least one respect in the objects clause of the Commonwealth's memorandum of association, in its 1951 version. So far as I know this was not reproduced by Susanna Hoe in her book. The substance of the opening paragraph deserves to be quoted in full:

> The objects for which the Commonwealth is established are *the promotion of the Christian ethics* [emphasis added] and the encouragement of Christian principles in industry with a view to ensuring good relations between management and labour in industry and the discharge by persons engaged in industry and in particular in the paint and plastics trades of their social obligations to the community ...

As we shall see, this clause was perhaps the key feature of the Commonwealth's constitutional arrangements which was successfully challenged by the Charity Commission in the 1960s as being out of line, or even in conflict, with charitable principles. More about that when we come to it in the historical narrative.

The final point to be flagged up here does not figure explicitly in either the memorandum or the articles of association of the Scott Bader Commonwealth, as these were originally registered in 1951. Instead it forms a sentence in clause 4 of the so-called 'preamble to the constitution'. The clause begins by asserting that 'by common ownership in industry we mean such a fundamental reconstruction so that undertakings are communally owned and co-operatively run, and show that teamwork which is neither collectivism or individualism, depending on leadership founded on approval rather than dictation within a framework of freedom of conscience and obedience to God.' It then goes on:

> This involves a self-divestment of privilege and power on the part of present employers and shareholders, and *on the part of the employees the acceptance of their full share of responsibility for the policy, efficiency and general welfare of the undertaking* [emphasis added].

The suggestion seems to be that because the former owners have divested themselves of their former privileges, the employees are obliged to assume a new duty of accepting their full share of responsibility for the policy etc. of the company.

For the rest, there are various specifics of Scott Bader's 1951 binary constitution – that is the statutes of the two separate entities, the

Commonwealth and the company – and of the other constitutional documents associated with it, which will come up again, and sometimes more than once, when we reach in the narrative the 1963 constitutional changes and later those which followed it. Some are indeed live issues and even problematic ones today. It makes sense to introduce the main ones here.

To begin with there are three important prescriptions which relate to manpower, its numbers and its security, and to maximum differentials of pay between the highest and the lowest paid employees. In 1951, the maximum workforce number was set, in the Constitution, at 250, and the maximum pay differential, *de facto* if not on paper, at 6:1 before tax. As for security of employment, it was laid down that, in the event of a recession of trade, there would be no compulsory redundancy. Instead, pay would be reduced all round but with the size of the cuts being graduated in line with pay levels. This particular arrangement was in fact embodied in a formal document issued to all Commonwealth members and called a Certificate of Mutual Security. As we shall see, it has since proved necessary to adjust each of these three specific prescriptions to bring them into line with the realities of the company's experience.

What is also in part a manpower issue – but of a very different kind – is about the qualifications for Commonwealth membership, a formal status which is voluntary but which can be revoked on disciplinary grounds. Age and length of service conditions of a basically 'open door' character were laid down in 1951 and have been revised on the margin from time to time. But at least for the first 50 years of the Commonwealth's life, these membership rights were restricted – *de facto* if not *de jure* – to the company's employees in the UK and the Republic of Ireland. A resolution to open up membership to employees of Scott Bader outside the British Isles was in fact passed by a general meeting of its members in April 2000, but only by the most narrow of margins. It is a matter to which we will need to come back.

A specific manpower issue which is different again is about the power to dismiss employees and/or Commonwealth members on disciplinary grounds. As we shall see it surfaced quite soon after 1951.

A second category of specifics relates to responsibilities enjoined upon the company and/or the Commonwealth in their dealings with 'the world'. These can best be understood as three duties: a) a duty of corporate charitable giving; b) a duty to refrain from the manufacture and sale of weapons of war; c) a duty of what might be called eco-friendly behaviour.

Unlike the constitutional specifics relating to manpower, these duties have not required revision during the first half century of the Commonwealth's life. On the other hand there have been tricky questions of interpretation in relation to b). Do minesweepers, for example, count as weapons of war? But what is perhaps especially notable is that by a resolution passed by Commonwealth members as early as 1953, the duty of corporate charitable giving was made more generous. From being limited to 5%, it was required to be not less than any bonus paid to employees out of profits with a maximum of 20%.

There is a third and perhaps most problematic category of constitutional specifics: about the membership, powers and methods of appointment (or election) of the important governing bodies recognised in the constitution – for example of the company and Commonwealth boards and, since 1963, of the so-called trustees of the constitution – and of the relationships between these and other recognised bodies. Given that they define where control lies for various different purposes it is scarcely surprising that these particular specifics have proved to be the most problematic and the subject of virtually continuous debate. Here I will do no more than identify two fundamentals which can provide us with a starting point from which to discuss the first set of constitutional changes, in 1963:

a) The 10% of the share capital which the Bader family held on to between 1951 and 1963 enjoyed special powers which meant that for those dozen years they retained an overriding control.

b) Ignoring those retained family shares, the basic logic of the binary arrangement put in place in 1951 was that the operating Scott Bader company should be accountable to the Scott Bader Commonwealth by virtue of the latter's shareholding. But there is a problem with both that logic and that language. It implies but does not lay down that in the last resort the company and its directors are constitutionally subordinate to the Commonwealth.

Finally, the binary character of the organisation as a whole has itself also been the subject of almost continuous debate. Of the two separate entities – the company and the Commonwealth – the former must devote itself to commercial and technical tasks, as distinguished in the 1969 Bruce Reed report which will come up later. Similarly, the special responsibilities of the Commonwealth relate mainly to the organisation's charitable (social) and political tasks, as also distinguished in the Reed report. Alternatively, we can say that the company is concerned with earning a living and the Commonwealth with 'doing good', e.g.

by charitable giving. For the employed trustee owner, confusion about his or her role may arise at any moment: 'In making this decision am I acting as an employee or as a trustee owner?'

Attempts to resolve these difficulties have run on two lines. First, there has been an emphasis on Commonwealth *education* exemplfied by the Commonwealth 'values workshops', and the proposals for what eventually became the Learning Centre (about which more later). Secondly, there have been a series of attempts to reform the binary structure itself, usually in the direction of a single non-binary arrangement (while respecting the charitable nature of the Commonwealth). We shall come across numerous instances of these endeavours in what follows.

3
How a Lead Was Grabbed in Reinforced Plastics

SYNTHETIC RESINS, PLASTICS AND SURFACE COATINGS

Before attempting to trace the emergence of either reinforced plastics as a new material in the world, or of Scott Bader as a world leader in the early stages of its technical development and manufacture, a word needs to be said about two possible linguistic confusions. The first is between resins and plastics At least since the war and in particular since two seminal visits paid to the US in 1945 and 1946 by its then technical director, John Hand, the principal manufacturing activity at Scott Bader has been – to repeat – the production of synthetic resins.

On the other hand, at least since the middle or late 1950s, the company's most important single group of products has been those polyester resins which, when combined with glass fibre or other stiffening material, become reinforced plastics. In other words this language suggests, what seems on the face of it perverse, that once the resin is stiffened it becomes a plastic. That is on the face of it perverse because the defining characteristic of a plastic is supposed to be that it can be bent or moulded. However, with a grateful acknowledgement to Brian Parkyn, I am happy to share with readers an understanding of this difficulty and how the apparent perversity of the language can be resolved. This is done if we distinguish plastics (plural), a noun, from plastic (singular), an adjective. Only the adjective, and not the noun, carries the familiar meaning of susceptibility to moulding.

There is a second possible confusion in the language used to describe the products manufactured by Scott Bader. It is pointed to in a sentence used by Brian Parkyn in his forthcoming autobiography. He is describing what he set himself as his priority task when he started to work in Scott Bader's laboratory in January 1947: 'My first task was to learn what I could about polyester resins. These syrup-like liquids had been developed in the United States for use in paints and lacquer, and also as casting resins.'

In ordinary language, materials used in paints, lacquers and other surface coatings are not among the things which would be called 'plastics'. On the other hand it seems that in contexts relevant to this study Brian Parkyn uses language differently. The evidence is in a public lecture which he delivered at the Royal Society of Arts on 12 December 1962 under the title 'Glass Fibre Reinforced Plastics'. Early on in that lecture he argues that the plastics industry had by then reached 'such a size and complexity that it is convenient to subdivide it into five main sections.' It will come as no surprise that the one which interests him most and to which he devotes the remainder of the lecture is 'Reinforced Plastics'. But the important point here is that, included among his other four sections are 'Surface coating and electrical insulation varnishes'.

For Brian Parkyn it seems that each of the two main branches of manufacturing activity at Scott Bader over the last 50 years – the reinforced polyester resins and all or most of the speciality polymers – may be classified as falling within the family of the plastics industry. The former may be so classified because when combined with glass fibre or other stiffening material, they become, as we have seen, reinforced *plastics*. As for the latter, their classification as plastics follows from the fact that the main use for most of them is in connection with paints, lacquers and other surface coatings. It seems that when, for those purposes, these synthetic resins are dried or cured to a hard finish, they may, permissibly, be classified as plastics. That the two main manufacturing activities at Scott Bader over the last 50 years – the polyester resins and the speciality polymers – are closely linked within the overall 'plastics family' will help us to understand how it was possible for Scott Bader to choose to move into a new dominant direction when it grabbed a world lead in the development of reinforced plastics in the 1950s.

THE PREHISTORY OF REINFORCED PLASTICS AND THEIR
EMERGENCE IN THE US IN THE SECOND WORLD WAR

Some authorities, like Dr M. Kaufman, author of *The First Century of Plastics, Celluloid and Its Sequel,* trace the origins of plastics back to what was defined in the 1930 edition of *Encyclopaedia Britannica* as an 'artificial substance, known also as artificial ivory and xylonite [which] is a compressed, solid solution of nitrated cellulose in camphor or a camphor substitute'. Those of us who were born before the war will remember celluloid as the material out of which were made a wide range of familiar articles, from the common comb and toothbrush handle to the schoolroom geometry protractor. In her biography of Ernest Bader, *The Man Who Gave His Company Away*, Susanna Hoe tells us that in the late 1920s and 1930s Scott Bader was an importer of that then popular material, and supplied it to a firm in Leicester to make 'penny windmills'. Celluloid is an artificial, or semi-synthetic, substance. It figures both in the wider history of the plastics industry and in the narrower story of Scott Bader.

Other authorities, like the author of the first essay in *The Development of Plastics* (Royal Society of Chemistry, 1994), start from a stage further back, from *natural* rather than *artificial* plastics materials. The essay suggests horn as an example and its author offers his readers a fascinating account of 18th- and 19th-century snuffboxes moulded out of horn. Indeed he offers much else besides, like the assumed horn content of the windows of the earliest lanterns. Tempting as it may be to follow him into areas like snuffboxes, we will not ourselves trace the origins of plastics and other synthetic resins further back than to celluloid. In this respect we are following the example not only of Dr Kaufman, but also of Brian Parkyn in his just quoted 1962 lecture to the Royal Society of Arts (RSA).

Celluloid articles were first produced by the British inventor Alexander Parkes, and were first publicly displayed by him in London's second great International Exhibition in 1862. According to Brian Parkyn, these articles included 'knife handles, buttons, pens and imitation tortoiseshell combs'. Parkes gave the name 'Parkesine' to his new material, but it did not survive for long. The actual word 'celluloid' was coined by an American, John Wesley Hyatt, in 1869. He was the first person to exploit its commercial possibilities to a significant extent.

Having a tensile strength of 10,000–12,000 lb per sq inch, celluloid was at that time one of the strongest of artificial materials. Moreover, if raised to the boiling point of water, it can be easily moulded into an almost limitless range of useful shapes. On the other hand it has a serious drawback, and one which has increased as governments and the public have become more and more conscious of the need to avoid accidents at work: it is highly inflammable.

There is a reference in the article on celluloid in the 1930 edition of *Encyclopaedia Britannica* to the search for a 'non-inflammable celluloid', and it goes on to claim that this has been 'to some extent successful'. However, the subsequent record suggests that that success was at best partial. In effect the post-1900 history of what was only much later designated as the 'plastics' industry was driven, at least to a significant extent, by the search for a non-inflammable substitute for celluloid. (Only, it seems, in the rather special case of what came to be called non-flam film was a cellulose-based material, precisely a cellulose acetate, developed which was also largely non-inflammable.) Later generations have seen the success of that search and its main results in the so-called 'cascade' of plastics which followed the Second World War.

Within that cascade are the plastics which have now become familiar not only in the West but throughout the world, for example the polyethylene which constitutes the main raw material for plastic bags, the PVC which is now used almost everywhere for water and sewage pipes, the polypropylene which finds its way, among other things, into lightweight moulded tables and chairs, and the polystyrene which we use as a packing material to protect fragile objects. These articles in mass consumption reflect outputs of their constituent plastics running into many millions of tons. It need hardly be said that these are areas of manufacturing into which Scott Bader, with its commitment to 'small is beautiful', has never ventured. Nevertheless it remains true that, if we also take into account a highly special set of essentially military needs which emerged in the Second World War, we can locate the development of Scott Bader's key polyesters within this same overall process which began with celluloid: the process of creating new materials based on new chemical compounds. In chemical terms polyesters result from the reaction between certain alcohols and certain acids.

THE WARTIME ORIGINS OF REINFORCED PLASTICS

The need for special materials with which to build non-metallic housings in combat aircraft – for the protection of the apparatus from which radar waves were beamed – seems to offer the best explanation of why glass-fibre-reinforced plastics were first developed and applied outside the world of laboratories. Radar had been invented shortly before the war. By sending out short-band radio waves it became possible to bounce them off objects like ships and aircraft, which would then reflect those same waves back. In this way it became possible to plot their positions and directions of movement. A very high-strength non-metallic material was needed for housing the new radar apparatus for two reasons: first, so that the radio waves could easily pass through it on their outward and return journeys; and secondly to be a weather-resistant housing which could form part of the fuselage, generally in the nose of the aircraft. The material therefore needed to be lightweight, strong, and as minimally inflammable as possible. Furthermore, so the professionals say, the material needed to have exceptionally low dielectric loss characteristics. Unsaturated polyester resins have outstanding dielectric properties.

For the non-specialist reader a word of explanation about these important *dielectric* properties is in order. We need first to understand that most plastics materials are electrical insulators. On the other hand, in the presence of the very high frequency radio waves used in radar and, for example, in television, many of them absorb the electrical energy and convert it into heat. The dielectric properties of unsaturated polyester prevent that loss of energy.

This is one of two important properties that made possible the use of unsaturated polyester resins in connection with radar. The other is that they were the first synthetic resins which – unlike bakelite, for example – could be cured without the use of great pressure, and thus the first resins that could be reinforced with glass fibre. For this reason unsaturated polyester resins have also been called *low-pressure* resins.

In any event, the resulting radar apparatus housings were given the name of 'radomes'. They were normally fitted into the nose cones of military aircraft. They came to be made out of polyester resins reinforced by glass fibre *woven into cloth*. It makes sense to italicise the phrase 'woven into cloth' in this context because, when in the 1950s glass fibre came to be used to reinforce polyester resins to make glass-reinforced plastics for use in a great range of new applications, the glass fibre was not woven into cloth but simply combined, in an unwoven 'mat' form, with the resin. Up to the end of the war the necessary polyester resins were not produced in this country. The key material for making radomes had to be imported from America.

SCOTT BADER'S EARLY LEAD IN GLASS-REINFORCED PLASTICS AND ITS BACKGROUND

Two events may be isolated as the immediate driving causes behind the lead which, by the early 1950s, Scott Bader had established for itself in the development, manufacture and commercial exploitation of glass-reinforced plastics (GRP). The first was the pair of visits made to America in 1945 and 1946 by John Hand, then the company's technical director. The second was the research initiated by Brian Parkyn when he started to work in its laboratories in January 1947. Both have already been mentioned. The first was a necessary condition of the second. But readers are likely to judge that the work of Brian Parkyn and his laboratory colleagues was the key *technical* contribution – something to be distinguished sharply from the winning of its acceptance – to the whole development. However, before focusing on either John Hand's American visits or the laboratory work of Brian Parkyn and his team, we need another fast-forward exercise through the history of the Scott Bader business down to 1945.

1 Background between the wars A most valuable 80-year diary of salient events in Scott Bader's history, first compiled by Mike Traxton and maintained by the company's current archivist, Stewart Reeves, has as its first commercial listing, in long ago 1920, the acquisition of a sole agency for importing into Britain the products of what must then have been a fairly new business in the country of Ernest Bader's birth. The name of the company is Swiss Celluloid SA. It was presumably from that source that the raw materials mentioned by Susanna Hoe as having been supplied to a factory in Leicester – for making up into celluloid windmills – originated.

The private limited company – Scott Bader and Co Ltd – was not in fact registered until 1923. Before that, Ernest worked first with one partner and then a second. Given the driving side of his character, much in evidence throughout both his long business career and afterwards, it is not altogether surprising that neither of those two partners stayed with him for any length of time. In its earlier, pre-corporate, incarnations the business had been named, first, as E. Scott Bader, and then E Scott Bader and Co. Much later, apparently in the late 1960s, the corporate name of the business was shortened and became simply Scott Bader Company Ltd, with the elimination of the 'and' which was deemed to have become redundant.

The next two commercial events recorded in the Traxton/Reeves diary are at least as indicative of what lay in the future as the celluloid import licence of 1920. Both relate to the import of specialist materials which were then sold on to the paint and lacquer industries. And both reflect a switch away from linseed oil and into various synthetic compounds by the paint and lacquer manufacturers in the period between the wars. The first is described by Susanna Hoe (p 43), as 'low viscosity nitro-cellulose', or in other words a cellulose lacquer, imported from a German manufacturer called Wasag. The second was a sole licence to import so-called Albertols into this country. They are described, both by Susanna Hoe (p 44) and in the Traxton/Reeves diary, as 'the first oil-soluble synthetic resins' and had been invented in Germany by a Dr Kurt Albert. Susanna Hoe suggests that these were to become the 'cornerstone' of Scott Bader's business relationship with the paint industry until the war came. In effect they were the first of the oil-derived synthetic resins which began to replace the non-synthetic linseed oil as the favoured base material for the paint and lacquer industries.

There is no need to multiply examples. It is enough to say that in its role as a trading company down to 1939, Scott Bader's business had two dominating characteristics: its main suppliers were in Switzerland, where Ernest had come from, and above all in Germany; and its main customers were in Britain's linked industries of paints, lacquers and other surface coatings, and it was in relation to their needs that the company built its most valuable base of knowledge and experience. In particular it had gained a pioneer's knowledge and experience in the importing and handling of 'oil-soluble synthetic resins'. What's more, it had become a buyer and seller of celluloid, the synthetic material widely considered to have been the starting point of the modern plastics industry and thus of reinforced plastics.

About the company's business experience before the war, two further key points need to be mentioned even in this most summary record. The first is that in 1932 manufacturing was added to Scott Bader's trading activities. A larger site, at Stratford in East London, was acquired to make that possible. In view of its new expertise readers will not be surprised by what the company decided to manufacture as a first step. It began with a range of pigment pastes. Then, shortly before the war, in 1938, there was a significant new development. Having previously distributed and sold as Crestanol to the paint and lacquer industries what were in fact modified phenolic resins, Scott Bader bought a licence from Crestanol's parent company and started to manufacture the resin itself. About the same time it hired – or rather, according to Susanna Hoe, poached from a competitor – its first professional chemist: Courtney Bryson. He left soon after the end of the war, apparently after a row with Ernest Bader, and well before the Commonwealth was established in 1951. However, his contribution was highly regarded by the founder, anyway in retrospect. One of the most important early post-war new buildings on the Wollaston Hall estate is named after him.

Secondly and more so, it seems, than in the years after 1951, the commercial and financial success of the business depended very much during the pre-war period and indeed for some little time later, on three remarkable women: Josephine Potter, Betty Turner and Sarah Gaetsky. Sadly, I am not in a position to offer any distinctive appreciations of their work or characters. But without the sure business foundations that they helped to build, it is doubtful whether Scott Bader could have grown and flourished later in the way it did.

2 *Background during the war years* Despite having its two London premises – its stores in Stratford and its offices in Kingsway – bombed out in German air raids in 1941, and suffering a fire at Wollaston which burned down one of its first factory buildings there in the same year, it is not too much to claim that the Scott Bader business had a 'good war'. Looking back after an interval of nearly 60 years, Godric Bader told me in the summer of 2000 that in his view the key change which the war permitted was the expansion of the company's manufacturing base. I would add that, partly in consequence, it was during the war that Scott Bader began to strengthen its technical and scientific capability. Courtney Bryson, as we have seen, joined just before it in 1938. John Hand was the next big name. He joined in 1940. Both, according to Susanna Hoe, were pacifists. Ernest Bader had become one as far back as 1915.

But about Scott Bader's experience during the war years, what must seize the imagination of most readers is the move of its main operations out of London's East End and into rural Northamptonshire on the estate of Wollaston Hall. Unquestionably what precipitated the move out of London in 1940 was the threat of German bombs, which became all too real in the following year. The story of how Wollaston Hall was actually found is a good one. Susanna Hoe tells it in the words of a much later company publication, written by Brian Parkyn and entitled *A Kind of Alchemy*:

> The search for a suitable place was not easy. It was decided that Ernest Bader should go west and Courtney Bryson, the chief chemist, should go north. Each weekend these two went exploring and they compared notes with each other when they returned on Monday mornings. Nothing looked more incongruous than Courtney Bryson, dressed in a dirty dilapidated pair of shorts and an old anorak, bearing a large bulging rucksack and wheeling a truly veteran bicycle. After some months of combing the country-side Ernest Bader found a beautiful building in the Cotswolds the same weekend that Courtney Bryson found a manor house in an almost forgotten village in Northamptonshire called Wollaston.

The Northamptonshire property was chosen and soon bought, and during the autumn of that year the stores and machinery were moved lock, stock, and barrel, to the quiet and peace of Wollaston.

The main point to underline is about the change of location from the East End of London to rural Northamptonshire, and from quite ordinary urban/industrial factory buildings of the early 1900s to fine Georgian ones in an almost park-like setting. It is impossible to resist the hypothesis that the company's experience after the war, and especially perhaps after the formation of the Commonwealth in 1951, would have been very different had there been no war, and had it remained in London. It may indeed be suggested that the chemical industry's trade union in London would have resisted the Commonwealth's establishment, rather than accepting it and agreeing to work with it very much on Ernest Bader's terms, as happened in Northamptonshire. It may also be questioned whether even a minority of those working in the Commonwealth during the days of its highest morale – say from the mid-1950s to the mid-1970s – would have felt the same about it had the experience been transposed from Wollaston, in rural Northamptonshire, to Stratford in London's East End.

More generally it may be argued that without the magic of the Wollaston Hall setting, the idea of the Commonwealth and of a 'new social order' in industry might never have materialised. This is one of those issues which it would be a mistake not to mention but which inescapably cannot be settled.

But to return to the business. The total number of the staff working at Wollaston after the move in 1940 was 30. By the end of the war, the corresponding figure was about 70. The main sales office remained in London throughout the war and indeed for some years afterwards. At Wollaston as well as the manufacturing operations there were the stores. Two product lines were added to the pigment pastes and other products which had been made in the Stratford factory. These were Texyn resins made, as Bob Bridgeford points out, with 'materials which were available at the time – mainly rosin modified with vegetable oils and maleic anhydride', and the Texylon range of water emulsions. These products were designed for buyers in the company's then major market of surface coatings.

To fill a gap opened up by the wartime shortages of rubber, the company manufactured a special adhesive paste for selling on as a material for sealing up bags of sugar and similar commodities. The essential manufacturing process was to put waste rubber products – like old tyres which had come to the end of their useful lives – through grinding mills. Another wartime product manufactured at Wollaston was Rubbone, a special coating material with some of the properties of liquid rubber.

So during the war, with the complete switch-off of imports from its former suppliers in Germany and Switzerland, Scott Bader changed. Before it had essentially been a trading company though with the manufacture of pigment pastes – and later Albertols and nitrocellulose lacquers – added as sidelines in the 1930s. What it changed into was essentially a manufacturing company.

Then, as it became clear in late 1944 and early 1945 that the war with Germany was coming to an end, and that some little time would be needed before pre-war German sources of resin supply could be re-opened, the company started to think about finding a post-war role for itself. Without its old suppliers in Germany, Scott Bader would have had real difficulty rebuilding a trading role for itself. On the other hand, if it decided to build on its new manufacturing base – and to secure its future and its independence in that way – there was really nowhere to look but to the US.

But that indeed was not at all a bad place to look, for during the war years the American industries of synthetic resins had overtaken not only Germany's but all others, and by 1945 effectively led the world. Against this background, in early 1945, Ernest Bader made what was without any real doubt the most consequential business decision of his life. He sent his technical director, John Hand, on a first reconnaissance visit to America to see what he could find in the world of America's synthetic resins industries. The success of that first reconnaissance mission was completed by a second – and essentially licence-signing – visit by John Hand in 1946. From that second visit he brought back a set of licences which were to enable suitable newly developed American products to be manufactured in Wollaston.

Evidently a most engaging and talented Irishman, John Hand was normally known at Scott Bader as Johnny or Jack. As we have seen, he shared a pacifism with Ernest Bader. But he was far from sharing his superior's hostility to alcohol. Apparently because of his drinking habits, he had to leave Scott Bader soon after returning from his second visit to America. And yet his talents as a chemist and a businessman were such that the company could not afford to be without him for too long, and he accepted an invitation to come back at the end of the

1940s. But the apex of his achievement was undoubtedly that pair of visits to America in 1945 and 1946.

3 What John Hand brought back from America From his second American visit in 1946, John Hand brought back four licences. The most consequential of these in the long run related, as we have seen, to reinforced plastics, and was a necessary condition of the company's later worldwide lead in their technical and commercial development. However, it was not until the mid-1950s that Scott Bader started to make any significant profits from that new material. We shall look in a moment at the particular licence which made it possible, but in the meantime we need to give some attention to the three other licences brought back by John Hand. For without the cash flow and profits that they generated, it is doubtful whether the company could have survived to reap the later harvest of its pioneering work in those reinforced plastics.

By the criterion of its contribution to Scott Bader's early post-war profits and cash flow, it was almost certainly the licence which John Hand secured from the American Polymer Corporation which was the most important. This allowed the manufacture at Wollaston of vinyl and acrylic polymer emulsions. For non-specialists, like the writer, it may be helpful to explain that these are 'water-based emulsions'. As such they need to be distinguished from the 'oil soluble synthetic resins' which Scott Bader had imported from Germany before the war. Paint and lacquer manufacturers, and those of some other surface coatings, normally need one or the other – either a water-based polymer emulsion or an oil-based synthetic resin – to combine with ground-up pigments to make their final products.

As it so happened, another of the licences which John Hand brought back from America covered the manufacture at Wollaston of a special kind of 'oil soluble synthetic resin', namely alkyds. Substantial development went on into alkyds in the labs, and a range of branded Crestalkyds was developed. These products, having quicker drying and better weathering properties than the competition, were sold into the surface coatings market.

As we shall see later, Scott Bader discontinued this alkyd manufacture in the late 1960s, but their manufacture was restarted in the mid-1980s. Because they are the source of solvent emissions when the paints with which they have been mixed dry out, they have become progressively more unpopular as environmental sensitivity has increased since the war.

But their manufacture at Wollaston has always been a useful, even if quite modest, source of jobs and incomes. The fact that their inputs from the petrochemical industry substantially overlap with those of the polyester resins which go into reinforced plastics may perhaps partly explain why Scott Bader started to manufacture them again in the 1980s.

The third paint-industry-related licence which John Hand brought back to Wollaston permitted Scott Bader to manufacture a special kind of paint drier called Nuodex, derived from metal salts and naphthenic acid. By an extraordinary chance Nuodex is also important in Scott Bader's story for an essentially contingent reason. It played more than a bit part in the discovery, in Brian Parkyn's laboratory in 1947, of a method for the so-called cold curing of unsaturated polyester resins. More about that shortly.

And that brings us on to the fourth and last – and in the long run most consequential – of the licences brought back from America after the war by John Hand. Precisely, it permitted the manufacture at Wollaston of just those unsaturated polyester resins which were to be the starting point from which Scott Bader later established a world lead in the making of glass-reinforced plastics. The company which sold the licence to John Hand was called Marco Chemicals Inc, located in the small New Jersey town of Sewaren. The licence specified the company's 'Marco resins' as what the licensee was permitted to manufacture. Its president was a chemist called Dr Irving Muskat. Later, in 1950, Brian Parkyn, during a visit to America, challenged Dr Muskat to his face about the legitimacy of the patents on which the licence rested. On the basis of that challenge Scott Bader had in fact stopped making its royalty payments some little time before. Threats of legal retaliation by Dr Muskat were never brought to court action, so Brian Parkyn's challenge may well have been soundly based. But it remains true that the licence, however problematic its basis, was the starting point for Scott Bader's work on reinforced plastics and it must be rather improbable that the relevant work would have happened without it.

Taking the four together, it seems fair to claim that John Hand's two post-war visits to America and his success in negotiating licences amounted to a genuine triumph. It should, however, be acknowledged that credit for its success should be shared with a third party as well as between Ernest Bader and John Hand. In his choice of which synthetic resin companies to visit, John Hand greatly benefited from the advice of John Breskin, the then editor of the American magazine *Modern Plastics*.

Given what had happened before and what was to happen soon after, it also makes sense to underline a rather general point. It is that all four of the licences had to do with what Scott Bader was already to a degree manufacturing and supplying to Britain's paint and related industries. There was only one, that from Marco Chemicals Inc, which could also, when reinforced by glass fibres, be used to make glass-reinforced plastics. In this latter case, there was, of course, not yet any manufacture at Wollaston. Moreover, five years later, in 1950, Scott Bader sold no more than just 15 tons of Marco resins. It is also true that most of that was not sold to be combined with reinforcement to make glass-reinforced plastics, but for casting purposes and for electrical, wood and plaster impregnation.

But we must now turn our attention to the research efforts which had been necessary to secure even a modest output tonnage. As we shall see, the work, though already marked by valuable progress, was still unfinished by 1950.

BRIAN PARKYN AND THE DEVELOPMENT OF GLASS-REINFORCED PLASTICS: 1947–60

In his forthcoming autobiography, *A Kind of Alchemy*, Brian Parkyn writes:

So here I was one very cold morning in January 1947 at Wollaston. I had a laboratory of my own and two or three assistants, entrusted by Ernest '*to develop polyester resins, the new wonder material that will transform the company*'. In time it did, but not as Ernest intended. His whole business life had been involved with Celluloid, paints and lacquers. He knew the industry through and through and wanted me to find some way of using polyester resins to develop a solventless lacquer of outstanding durability and performance. On the other hand I saw the possibility of using polyester resins reinforced with glass fibres to make vast structures of incredible strength and lightness; in fact to complete the work that I had started in the research laboratory at Micanite in 1941. I was determined to resolve the problem that I had dreamed about ever since those days when I had been trying to make an aircraft radome. For me, therefore, the birth of Reinforced Plastics really began in 1941. Fortunately Ernest had little technical knowledge and left me largely free to do whatever I wanted.

After that high-flying opening paragraph to chapter 7 of his auto-biography, Brian Parkyn gets down without further ado to what then became the top priority on his agenda: 'My first task was to learn as much as I could about polyester resins.'

We shall come back to that in its proper place later. But first we must understand how it was that Brian Parkyn came to be in that Wollaston laboratory in January 1947 at all.

1 *Do-it-yourself schoolboy experiments* In an unpublished paper, 'Reinforced Plastics: A brief history of my involvement at the beginning and how it all started', Brian Parkyn describes his work at Micanite and Insulators Ltd in 1940 and 1941, and how it related to his subsequent research work at Wollaston. He also traces even further back, to the pre-war childhood which he partly shared with his cousin Godric Bader at Stanford-le-Hope in Essex, his own – and indeed Godric's – early interest in things scientific. In particular, he clearly enjoys writing about their do-it-yourself approach to scientific experiment, something which seems to have started at an early age. In the midwifing of that interest and that approach, the key figure was a maternal uncle whom they shared, Tom Scott. He was the brother of the two Scott sisters who had married Ernest Bader and Leslie Parkyn at what was an unusual event even in the austere and money-scarce days of October 1915 – a double wedding.

The range of Tom Scott's professional activities suggest that his was almost a 'Renaissance career'. He worked with Guglielmo Marconi on the development of wireless before the first world war. But in 1912 he accepted a post with the then Anglo-Indian Telegraph Company and was apparently responsible for the submarine cable from Karachi to Basra. In the 1930s he made what was up to then his biggest career move. Returning from India he became a minister in the Baptist Church. But later, at the outbreak of the Second World War, and under regulations governing the compulsory recruitment of senior scientific personnel, he was ordered to join the Admiralty Mines Counter-Measures Establishment at Longtown near Gretna Green in Scotland. There he became responsible for its counter-mines development programme.

Young Parkyn's interest in science and in a do-it-yourself approach to scientific experiment was first stimulated by his Uncle Tom when he had only just passed his fourth birthday. The latter, on leave from the East, came on a short visit to Brian and his parents in 1927 and brought with him a home-made crystal set. With the precocity of a child with a marked genetic orientation towards things scientific, Parkyn can still remember important details about both the visit and the set. Later, in the 1930s and 'starting with the building of simple crystal sets',

> I tried out many types of crystal in addition to the usual galena. Then I moved on to thermionic valves, triodes, tetrodes, pentodes. I even made an illegal transmitter. Finally in 1939 I built a remarkable single-valve 'super-regenerative' receiver, running on only 9 volts, that could pick up signals under favourable conditions world wide.

I could go on about Brian Parkyn's happy times between the wars, doing experiments with his crystal sets and then with those valve-based wirelesses of which I have myself a rather dim memory. But space is limited and I can do no more than record Godric's clear memory that it was he, not Brian, who made the first 'super-regenerative receiver'.

However, and providentially, some might argue, from the viewpoint of the development of Scott Bader's business after 1947, this particular do-it-yourself interest began to be supplemented, from about the mid-1930s onwards, not indeed by the kind of specialist-do-it-yourself chemistry experiments which could have led directly to unsaturated polyester resins, but by what amounted perhaps to a first set of steps in that general direction.

As he puts it in his unpublished paper on the origins of reinforced plastics, Brian Parkyn as a schoolboy 'was fortunate in having access to many exciting materials not available to other boys'. He goes on to explain how that was, taking as his point of departure something which we already know:

> My mother's sister Dora had married a Swiss, Ernest Bader... He started a chemical company in 1920 which became Scott Bader Company Ltd. They manufactured cellulose lacquers and were agents for a wide range of materials including fluorescent and luminous powders.
>
> During the long school holidays I would stay with my cousin Godric Bader at his house in Stanford-Le-Hope. Since he was about my age and had similar interests we could do our 'pottering about with natural objects' together. We were also provided with a wooden shed in the garden which was called the House of Inventions. Of course like many boys at that time we made gunpowder

and coloured fireworks and sparklers, but what was different was that we had a plentiful supply of Celluloid (cellulose nitrate) and collodion cotton.

Now collodion cotton is gun cotton ...

It is tempting to pursue this account of those two schoolboy cousins, Brian Parkyn and Godric Bader, 'pottering about with natural objects', like cellulose nitrate and gun cotton, in their shared summer holidays at Stanford-le-Hope during the late 1930s. Especially in a company history like this one, I cannot resist sharing with readers how together they made 'gigantic jumping crackers':

> These were three feet long. With a fuse of over 30 feet made by putting hundreds of celluloid strips end to end, the crackers would jump as high as the house, greatly impressing our sisters.

But enough! The main point for our purposes is that those two boy cousins, Brian Parkyn and Godric Bader, had already by 1939, when the Second World War came, developed a taste for the practice of do-it-yourself experiments, especially in the adjacent fields of cellulose nitrate and gun cotton. During 1940 and 1941, when he worked for Micanite and Insulators Ltd, Brian Parkyn (who was the older by a few months) was able to take specific advantage of the time spent jointly with his cousin Godric Bader on those do-it-yourself chemistry experiments.

In normal contexts the French word *bricolage* can be translated as 'do-it-yourself activity'. It is so defined in the latest edition of the French *Larousse* dictionary and illustrated by the phrase '*Aimer la bricolage*: to love doing-it-yourself'. Closer to its use in this context, *Collins Dictionary* suggests that 'tinkering about' is an appropriate translation. However, following the *Times* journalist Philip Howard, Brian Parkyn both in his forthcoming autobiography and in his unpublished 'Reinforced Plastics' paper, endows it with a more sophisticated meaning. Howard in a piece quoted by Parkyn as the epigraph of his 'Reinforced Plastics' cites the French anthropologist Claude Levi-Strauss, as having 'coined "bricolage" as a model for the way all humans build scientific theories by *pottering around with natural objects* [emphasis added] in various combinations'.

2 *Bricolage on the job at Micanite and Insulators Ltd, 1940–1* Brian Parkyn wrote his school certificate papers in the summer term of 1939 with results which would have qualified him for entry into university if

he had decided at a later stage to go for a university degree. Partly perhaps because the war came, he never did so. He went back to school to do sixth form work but stayed only for one term. Early in 1940 he moved to London and was soon afterwards recruited as a laboratory assistant by a company called Micanite and Insulators Ltd. By an extraordinary chance, the company was already engaged in the manufacture of 'Paxolin' laminates, described in 'Reinforced Plastics' as being 'made by consolidating under great pressure and heat hundreds of sheets of paper or cotton fabric impregnated with a Bakelite type of synthetic resin'. In the next sentence we learn that, in turn, 'Bakelite is a brittle plastics material, but *when it is reinforced in this way with cellulose fibres, the final laminate has very considerable strength* [emphasis added].' Even readers with a zero education in chemistry will surely grasp that bakelite resin reinforced with cellulose fibres is a fairly close relative of polyester resin reinforced with glass fibre. Only just out of school, Brian Parkyn had parachuted himself onto one of the roads, perhaps the main road in the UK, which would lead to reinforced plastics. Let me reproduce by direct quotation from 'Reinforced Plastics', where that road lead on to next:

> Early in 1941 a special 'secret' laboratory was set up in the company to develop an aircraft nose fairing to protect some new type of radio equipment. I was excited when I was told I was to be transferred to this work. I did not know at the time that the new equipment was radar, and that the nose cone fairing was what we would now call a 'radome'.
>
> The fairing needed to be mechanically strong yet transparent to radio and so it had to be non-metallic. The cellulose fibres of paper and cotton were not found to be strong enough as reinforcement for the resin laminate. It was therefore decided to use glass fibre, at that time the strongest of all known materials. It was my first experience with this remarkable product: glass fibres woven to form a fabric.

Later in the same year Brian Parkyn received his call-up papers and spent until December 1946 working within a special agricultural programme for conscientious objectors in mid-Wales. But we cannot leave what was for him clearly a seminal experience with Micanite and Insulators without quoting two further short passages from 'Reinforced Plastics'. The first is about how he searched in that 'secret' laboratory to find an appropriate material for the Radome fairing:

> I was now engaged in *'bricolage'* to my hearts content, and being
> paid for it as well. We tried this resin and that resin, and all the
> latest plastics materials ... but try as we might we could never get
> the glass cloth to reinforce the resin satisfactorily.

The second is more visionary: 'In this environment it was hardly surprising that I became fascinated with the possibility of making high-
strength non-metallic materials which might in time rival the strength
of metals.'

Brian Parkyn had found his mission when he was still someway short
of his 20th birthday.

3 Bricolage at Wollaston from 1947 Brian Parkyn was released from
his wartime conscientious objectors' work programme in mid-Wales in
December 1946. Almost at once thereafter he was telephoned by his
uncle Ernest Bader who 'pressed me hard to join his company as a
research chemist'. All his close relatives and friends advised him not to
accept the offer. But as we know, he chose to say yes. Given what he
had already identified as his mission, it would surely have been surprising if he had done otherwise. For in pressing his nephew to join him at
Wollaston, Ernest Bader had in effect offered him a way forward by
which that mission just might be accomplished:

> He told me that he had recently made an agreement with an
> American company to manufacture under licence a remarkable
> new resin with a vast and almost unlimited potential. It was an
> unsaturated polyester resin. I would be given a laboratory to
> myself with the necessary supporting staff of assistants and I
> would be responsible for this new product.

Elsewhere, as quoted above, Ernest Bader was said to have wanted a
'solventless lacquer' to be developed from the polyester resin and that
was contrasted with Brian Parkyn's hopes for it. Both men no doubt
hoped that the outcome would favour their preference. It was those of
the latter which substantially prevailed, at least after a number of years
– an outcome which was surely far and away the best possible one for
the business. Albeit for a maximum of no more than about two
decades, Scott Bader became a world leader in the production of a new
material, reinforced plastics. What's more, as we argued at the start,
that early lead has sustained the business down to the present day. It
seems improbable almost to the point of impossibility that a business

based on a new 'solventless lacquer' could have achieved a similar success. If that is so, it seems right to applaud Brian Parkyn's decision to accept his uncle's offer of a job in 1947.

But that cannot have seemed anything like a certainty in January 1947. In any case the first priority of the new head in the Wollaston polyester laboratory was 'to learn as much as I could about polyester resins'. What is rather surprising is just how quickly the first research breakthrough was achieved. As we shall see, it was a most notable advertisement for the positive possibilities of *bricolage*.

But before we look at exactly what happened in Brian Parkyn's laboratory in early 1947, we need to put on record his own much later assessment of the relative value of that research work. In a letter to me, dated 6 June 2000, he wrote:

> On the larger picture of the history of reinforced plastics it is important to understand that my main contribution was not cold-cure and the elimination of air inhibition, important as these developments were. It was my belief that immensely strong mouldings of unlimited complexity and size could be made with what I first called *reinforced plastics,* a dream I had had since my days on the research laboratory at Micanite ... It was the cold-cure and finally the elimination of air inhibition which made this all become a reality.

Well, perhaps. What is being claimed is that the 'vision' was more important as a contribution than the actual developments impelled by it. Again – well, perhaps. On the other hand, it surely cannot be denied that in the absence of the actual developments in the laboratory, the vision by itself would have had an almost zero value. It would have been worth almost nothing either to Brian Parkyn or to Scott Bader. But perhaps in these sorts of cases it is a mistake to try to assign relative positions on a scale of importance to the concept on the one hand and that actual developments which flowed from it on the other. Perhaps we should think of them as indissolubly linked in one overall contribution. A possible parallel suggests itself in a bizarrely different field of post-war development: not in reinforced plastics but high-jumping, About the famous 'Fosbury flop', would it make sense to argue about the relative importance of the initial abstract concept or vision, on the one hand, and its successful execution on the other?

My own view is that it doesn't make much sense to ask such a question in either of the two cases. But I must leave it to readers to decide the issue for themselves. I will now move on to what happened in that Wollaston laboratory with, first, the discovery of how to 'cold cure' polyester resins in 1947, and then subsequently in 1951, when it was discovered how they could be cured in such a way as to come out of the process with a smooth and solid surface and not a tacky one. Both these breakthroughs may be reasonably classified as examples of the success of *bricolage*.

We may begin by recalling that what Brian Parkyn and his team worked on in 1947 were the unsaturated polyester resins which John Hand had brought back – with a licence allowing Scott Bader to manufacture them at Wollaston – from Marco Chemicals Inc in New Jersey after the war. Susanna Hoe (p 75) rightly highlights their defining characteristic as the fact that in order to be moulded into a solid material, they did not need to be put under pressure. In slightly more technical language they were 'low-pressure' synthetic resins. On the other hand to become solid in form they had to be heated up, hence the search for a 'cold cure'. Furthermore, and as we saw near the start of this study, the polyesters from Marco Chemicals suffered from a second and perhaps especially unsatisfactory defect: unless protected from contact with the air by a cellophane wrap, their surfaces at the end of the reinforcing process were tacky rather than solid and smooth. This was designated the problem of 'air inhibition'. In the Wollaston laboratory, while attempting to solve the air inhibition problem a cold cure was found: a truly exemplary success for a *bricolage* approach.

'Paints dry', Brian Parkyn has explained to me in a special note about the *bricolage* work which went on in the Wollaston laboratory in early 1947, 'through oxidation with the atmosphere, and in order to increase the rate of drying it is customary for paints to contain additives called driers. These are mainly naphthenates of zinc, cobalt or manganese.'

On the basis of what happens in the case of paints, the laboratory team at Wollaston worked briefly on the hypothesis that the 'tacky' surface of the reinforced polyester resins might be overcome by using a suitably modified paint drier. Readers will remember that a naphthenite-based paint drier called Nuodex was among the four American products which Scott Bader had become licensed to manufacture as a result of John Hand's two post-war visits. In a neighbouring laboratory to that for polyester resins, other members of the company's research staff were in fact working at that very time on the development of improved paint driers. So Brian Parkyn and his team had no difficulty in securing the necessary ingredients. For readers who are specialist chemists it may be helpful to know that what was added to the polyester resins in an attempt to smooth their tacky surfaces was a combination of 'various naphthenates' not with 'benzoyl peroxide', as originally thought (but which, when tried, failed to produce the desired result), but with a totally new type of catalyst called HCH. By an extraordinary *bricolage* type of happy chance, it was discovered that, given an admixture of this new catalyst, the reinforced plastic could be cured cold and did not need to be heated up.

Two points are worth adding to this story of a notable research success in the discovery of a practical way of cold-curing the unsaturated polyester resins imported to Wollaston from Marco Chemicals. The first is that soon after this discovery Brian Parkyn learnt that a slightly different method of cold-curing, using a different combination of chemicals, had been developed in America and was being marketed in liquid form, with the brand name Accelerator 1000. Samples were obtained from America and these were successfully analysed and reproduced. To cut a longer story short, by midsummer 1947 Brian Parkyn and his team in their Wollaston laboratory had become masters of *two* slightly different ways of curing unsaturated polyester resins at room temperature.

If only for the record, a second point should be added to complete this story. A patent application, or more precisely two patent applications, were duly filed. But when, a year later, a decision had to be made about whether to go through the much more expensive process of patent registration, it was decided not to. The cost was an important consideration. But there was also some doubt about the patent position in America and a persuasive judgement that Scott Bader might well get involved in costly litigation. When, much later, the American patent position was explored, it was found that the filing of each of Scott Bader's two patent applications had priority in time over the corresponding moves in America. It need hardly be said that that was a source of considerable pride. It could also provide a solid defence if Scott Bader's rights to its cold-curing processes should ever be challenged.

A solution to the problem of the tacky surface of the reinforced polyester resins – the so-called problem of air inhibition – was also found in that same Wollaston laboratory, but not before 1951 and then by the kind of lucky accident which even those most committed to a *bricolage* approach can only realistically expect to happen about once in a lifetime. In this case I can do no better than quote verbatim from Brian Parkyn's account in 'Reinforced Plastics':

One of my laboratory assistants, Don Wildman, needed to mix some polyester resin, catalyst and accelerator together. This was usually carried out in small aluminium cups, but because he could not find one he used instead one of the waxed paper cups we used in the laboratory for our tea and coffee. He noticed that when the resin had cured, the surface was not tacky but hard and glossy. He immediately showed it to me and there was no doubt that the resin was not air-inhibited. It had to be the wax from the paper carton, but we both knew that for years we had carried out countless experiments with wax to overcome air inhibition, and they had all proved unsuccessful. We had used every known type of wax in every amount from 0.1% upwards. I said that we should repeat the experiments but in amounts of 0.1% *downwards*. In a very short time we discovered that the amount of wax added to the resin, and its precise melting point were very critical. When it is exactly right, the resin is not air-inhibited. I immediately applied for a patent to cover this important breakthrough, but until it was published we decided that for commercial security, the new additive which was to be incorporated in the resin during manufacture should not be referred to by name. It was called 'additive 12351', from the date of our discovery.

Less than two months later, on 28 April, the documents were signed at a ceremony in Cambridge by which Scott Bader's family shareholders transferred 90% of the share capital of the business to the newly created Scott Bader Commonwealth. I have already highlighted the astonishingly close synchronism between these two seminal events: the discovery of 'air inhibition' and the foundation of the Commonwealth, endowed with its 90% shareholding. The first was the final milestone along the path pioneered by Scott Bader by which it established its initial big lead in the manufacture of the new 'wonder material', reinforced plastics. The second, among many other things, offered the company a secure – at least secure for its first 50 years – defence against takeover. But both have been adequately discussed in the first chapter. There is no need to go over the same ground again here.

Of course it is true, as Brian Parkyn and others have always insisted, that to have a technical lead in the development of a new product is not the same as winning its widespread acceptance and thus creating a market for it. All or most of the latter work remained to be done. It will be properly discussed when we look at the company's business record during the first 10 years or so of its life after those to seminal events of spring 1951.

On the other hand, since the relevant process started in 1948 – well before the watershed year of 1951 – it is worth recording at this stage the start of something else which was clearly going to be critical if glass-fibre-reinforced plastics were ever to be sold in markets other than highly specialist ones. For the sale of material to be used to construct radomes and other small but much-needed parts of military and other aircraft, cost and price were clearly secondary considerations. But if, as Brian Parkyn had already started dreaming, the new material was to be successfully offered to those who would need much larger quantities, boat-builders and even ship-builders, for example, then big cost reductions would have to be found. It seems that the key breakthrough in relation to cost had to do not so much with the plastics but the glass fibre component of the material and was essentially conceptual in character. It stemmed, as we already know, from collaboration between Brian Parkyn at Scott Bader and Dr Kurt Joseph, a German refugee working with the Pilkington subsidiary, Fibreglass Ltd, in St Helens. It was conversations between them that eventually resulted in the replacement of woven glass fibres by glass fibres in a crude mat form as the normal reinforcement for reinforced plastics – with huge consequential cost reductions.

A non-chemist before the Second War could scarcely have conceived that unsaturated polyester resins, reinforced with glass fibres, were going to become a material in the post-war world which threatened steel and other metals in many of their traditional markets. Very few, including the writer, would even have known what was meant by unsaturated polyester resins. I hope I have now passed on an adequate understanding of polyester resins. As for the meaning of unsaturated in this context it apparently distinguishes those polyester resins we are talking about from those others which form the raw material for the artificial fibre polyester.

Equally, no one but the most committed believer in the potential benefits of *bricolage*-type research could have foreseen that in the manufacture of the new material an initial lead was going to be grabbed by a small, family-owned, manufacturer of chemical resins in an almost unknown village in rural Northamptonshire. But that, as we shall see more clearly when we start looking at Scott Bader's record from 1951 onwards, was what happened. Finally, however, we need to highlight a rather different point. It has already been made but perhaps with insufficient emphasis. It is that a decade, or even slightly more time, elapsed between when Brian Parkyn and his team started working towards reinforced plastics in 1947 and when that side of the business became profitable. As Bob Bridgeford, who worked on polyesters and alkyds (among many other things), points out, 'The major selling lines well into the 1950s were the alkyds and driers and the emulsion-based products manufactured at Wollaston'. For all of those years the reinforced plastics work was only possible because of the profits earned by the less glamorous division of the business devoted to meeting the needs of the paint, lacquer and surface coatings industries. It is also true that until he took over from his father as Scott Bader's managing director in 1957, it was Godric Bader, Brian Parkyn's first cousin, who had managerial responsibility for that side of the business.

Partly because of Scott Bader's quite separate commitment to pacifism and a linked belief in abstaining so far as possible from all things associated with waging war, it is important here to rescue from otherwise almost certain oblivion a 'war reparations' benefit enjoyed by Scott Bader in the early years of peace and one which was especially helpful to the polymer division of which Godric was then in charge, and to the later development of plasticisers in Wollaston. I am greatly indebted for this information to Brian Parkyn. He tells us what happened in his own words:

> At the end of the war, in fact in 1947, key German scientists were *required* to be seconded to British and American firms and research establishments to give us the benefit of their knowledge, experience and research during the war under the Reparations Agreement. We received Dr Kraus, Germany's leading authority on plasticisers, and Dr Lendle, their leading authority on polymer emulsions. They remained working in the laboratory at Wollaston until the early 1950s. Their great contribution enabling Scott Bader to move into the plasticiser and emulsion fields cannot be exaggerated. Furthermore, since they were both quite eminent scientists, they trained many of our otherwise untrained laboratory staff to adopt *for the first time* clear scientific principles in their research. They both remained working at Wollaston for (I think) about six years before they were allowed to return to Germany.

To repeat: it seems salutary to highlight the post-war contribution to the ideologically pacifist Scott Bader of these two 'Reparation scientists' from Germany. I should only add that Godric Bader's memoir of their area of specialist knowledge differs from that of his cousin Brian Parkyn. Godric thinks that the specialist knowledge of both Kraus and Lendle was in the field of nitrocellulose.

4

Growth, Market Success and Constitutional Changes: Mid-1950s to Early 1970s

The Traxton/Reeves company diary opens its record for the year 1979 with two rather different items:

> 22nd January, Scott Bader Social Club opened in 'The Hill'.
> 31st January, 93 people left under the voluntary redundancy scheme.

The year 1979 was also the first of three consecutive years in which the company distributed no dividends. More precisely, annual payments out of profits a) to charity and b) as a bonus to employees, two distributions which had been required to be equal since 1953, were both fixed at zero. This was the first time since the start of the Commonwealth in 1951 that these so-called dividends had been passed. The 1979 decision clearly reflected the difficult times which the company had experienced in the recent past. And so, it need hardly be said, did those relating to the 93 voluntary redundancies of 31 January which the diary records.

The difficulties in its main markets encountered by Scott Bader at the end of the 1970s are reflected, if anything more sharply, if we compare the output and sales of its main products in home markets for the years 1979 and 1980:

Output and Sales: 1979 and 1980 (tonnes)

	Polyesters	Polymers	Plasticisers	Total
1979	16,274	10,831	4,667	31,772
1980	11,36	7,132	3,764	23,225

Thus, in round figures and measured by weight, production and sales to the home market fell by 25% between 1979 and 1980, essentially because of the effects of a combination of the new economic policies launched by Mrs Thatcher's first government and the second oil price shock. But of course the 1979 redundancy scheme reflected events *before* the sharp fall off in output and sales as between that year and 1980. The troubles of 1980 were reflected in a second voluntary redundancy in 1981. We shall deal with each in turn in chapter 6.

Here we need to do no more than acknowledge that the four years 1978–81, with their two separate episodes of voluntary redundancies, marked perhaps the single most dramatic break point in the 50-year history of the Scott Bader Commonwealth from 1951 down to the start of the 21st century. The two redundancies were also both traumatic and precedent-setting. About the latter we can say that, at least for Commonwealth members within the group's workforce, the rules, procedures and generous compensation payments of the first voluntary redundancy set a pattern which has been fairly closely maintained down to the present day. For non-Commonwealth members or, perhaps more precisely, those employed in what may be called the group's 'outer circle', the story, as we shall see later, is rather different.

As for the trauma associated with the first schemes of voluntary redundancy among Commonwealth members, I can do no better than cite a point made by Godric Bader to the Canadian academic and employee ownership specialist, Professor Jack Quarter, in the mid-1990s:

> Common ownership didn't matter that much to employees. What did matter is that they couldn't be chucked out. They had what's called a certificate of mutual security which is more important than money. That they did understand: if they were accepted as Commonwealth members, they would have a job for life.

Nevertheless, despite the reality and the pain of this 1978–81 break point, and especially if we are talking about the company's single most important market – that for unsaturated polyester resins – the fundamental change of trend clearly preceded those two voluntary redundancies by a number of years. The 'draft Scott Bader Polyester Plan, 1980–1985', an internal company planning document devoted to the output and sales of its unsaturated polyester resins, and dated 1980, distinguishes between two phases in the growth of their UK market:

The market grew from about 10,000 tonnes in 1960 to 70,000 in 1973: approximately 14% annually.

Following the oil crisis the market entered a second phase in which growth was much slower.

For the purposes of this book we will break the narrative in the early 1970s rather than at the end of the decade, closing the first narrative chapter in 1971. As we shall see, that was the year in which, following a recommendation in an important advisory report prepared by the Revd Bruce Reed of London's Grubb Institute of Behavioural Studies, the posts of chairman and managing director were split. Since his father's retirement from the chairmanship in 1966, Godric Bader had held both positions. In 1971, while he remained non-executive chairman, Nick Broome was brought in from outside as managing director. For the first time in the history of a business which was already by then 50 years old, a member of the Bader family did not hold the position of chief executive.

Any business history covering half a century needs to be broken up into shorter periods, divided – as it may well be – both by sharp break points and lesser ones. Faced with Scott Bader's half century from 1951 to 2000, anyone who looks at the evidence is, I think, bound to put the big break in the 1970s. There can be arguments about which actual year should be identified as the watershed, and whether it should fall towards the beginning or at the end of the decade. However, it seems reasonable in this case to go for the earlier year. Scott Bader's 'flight path' between the early 1970s and the end of the decade was like that of an aircraft which, after climbing steeply, more or less levels out at its cruising altitude. From about 1955 and down to the early 1970s its climb – buoyed onward and upward by the extraordinary annual growth rates in the market for unsaturated polyester resins – was steep and fast. Some of the year-on-year statistics of market growth may be a little problematic, and there are also classification problems, like whether gelcoats (which we shall explain shortly and which Scott Bader seems to have started manufacturing in 1961) should be classified within the general category of polyester resins or separately. On the other hand there can be no real question about either the speed or size of the growth in the company's output and sales of polyester resins during that earlier period, from perhaps 1,000 tonnes of output and sales in the later 1950s to rather over 15,000 tonnes (albeit including gelcoats) in 1972. By contrast, between 1972 and 1979 annual output and sales of the same product moved within a quite narrow range. Compared with that figure of rather over 15,000 in 1972, the corresponding total was rather over 16,000 in 1979. In between there had been highs of somewhat over 17,000 tonnes in 1973 and 1977. There is nothing seriously problematic about these 1970s numbers. Their source is a set of company records that have been carefully preserved in the archives.

So in the section which follows about Scott Bader as a *business*, we shall be concerned essentially with the extraordinarily rapid growth in its output and sales of unsaturated polyester resins during the 1950s and 1960s, and with a climb in the tonnages up to what became, more or less, its 'cruising altitude' in the 1970s; and, for that matter, to a substantial extent beyond.

THE GLASS-REINFORCED PLASTICS MARKET AND SCOTT BADER'S SPECIAL FOCUS ON MARINE BUYERS

It may have become a cliché, but it is still, I think, more true than untrue that the British in the 20th century, while sustaining their genius for inventing new products, became progressively less successful at bringing those to the market. Scott Bader can reasonably claim that its own success over the 1950s and 1960s in bringing to the market the newly invented material of glass-reinforced plastics (GRP) should be counted as an exception. According to Brian Parkyn, as was noted earlier, the company manufactured and sold perhaps 10 tons of unsaturated polyester resins in 1950, much of it not to be reinforced but sold to be cast into objects like buttons and knife handles which do not need to be especially strong. As we have seen, a series of company tonnage numbers provide us quite precise total tonnage data for 1972: 15,120 tonnes of unsaturated polyester resins including gelcoats, with well over three-quarters of that being sold to customers who mixed it with glass fibre to make GRP. If the gelcoat tonnage is kept separate, the adjusted polyester number becomes 10,605.

For the years 1980–5 that same 'draft Scott Bader Polyester Plan, 1980–1985', mentioned above, offers a breakdown of the market for these polyester resins by a classification of the buyers. Both in 1980 and throughout the six years 1980 to 1985, and indeed still today, the total tonnage of this new material sold to boat-builders and ship-builders – so-called marine users – was larger than any other. They accounted for roughly one-fifth of the total tonnage of unsaturated polyester resins then projected to be sold by Scott Bader and its competitors. For reasons which will become clear in a moment, Scott Bader has from the outset paid special attention to marine buyers. Starting from a first entry in 1950, the company diary features a succession of boats of increasing sizes of which the hulls had been built out of the new GRP material.

Brian Parkyn's 1961 lecture to the Royal Society of Arts (RSA) in December 1962, entitled 'Glass Fibre Reinforced Plastics', has already been mentioned. The version printed in the RSA *Journal* in February 1962 contains a number of photographs, one of which shows an unusual fishing boat called a curragh. These boats have been built and used by Irish fishermen of the Aran Islands in the Atlantic Ocean, off Ireland's west coast in Galway Bay, for very many years. They are presented as an early and quite specific example of boats constructed – in this case out of a tar-like substance and sacking, stretched over a wooden framework – using a method of contact moulding, about which more in a moment. Brian Parkyn does not say in so many words that it was the contact moulding of these curraghs which first suggested to him that he should focus especially on boat hulls as a market for the new GRP material. But the discovery of a successful application of this method can scarcely have discouraged him from looking in that direction.

What may well have been a both a more specific and influential prompt came from work carried out by the Winner Manufacturing Company of Trenton, New Jersey in 1947. Brian Parkyn has written about it in the chapter on 'Fibre-reinforced composites' which appears in a book entitled *The Development of Plastics*, published by the Royal Society of Chemistry in 1994. The company, according to Parkyn, attempted 'to mould a 28 ft-boat for the US Navy using the vacuum impregnation process'. After explaining what that process is Parkyn goes on:

Even after several attempts, considerable difficulty was experienced in getting all the reinforcement evenly impregnated ... leaving large areas of dry reinforcement. Although some of the first GRP boats ever to be made were finally achieved using this system, it appeared to the author at the time that this was not a practical way to make a GRP boat. It seemed obvious that the boat hulls should be made in the same way as the moulds had been made, that is by *wet hand lay-up* [emphasis added].

For those like the present writer who are new to the world of using GRP material for building boat hulls – or indeed anything else – a word of explanation about the phrase 'wet hand lay-up' may be helpful. It is perhaps most easily understood if we start from a picture of the mould to which the GRP material is applied. What we are talking about is a female mould, like for example a jelly mould, to the inside of which the GRP material is, as it were, 'painted on' in successive layers of resin and glass fibre 'mat'. The operation is performed by hand when the poly-ester resin is still liquid and the glass fibre 'mat' is laid on top of it. There are, in effect, alternate layers of resin and glass fibre which bond together. To achieve the best result, the operation is usually performed with a roller. It is that operational process which is called 'wet hand lay-up'. The adjective 'wet' attaches to the whole phrase 'hand lay-up' and not to the word 'hand' by itself.

Because the material has come to be specially associated with the process of building GRP hulls in the marine market – hulls whether for pleasure boats or working boats or small ships – this is probably the best place to say a word about gelcoats. These are unsaturated poly-ester resins but they are not reinforced either with glass fibre or any other stiffening material. Instead they are typically reacted with various special chemicals which give them special qualities: for example resis-tance to blistering. When applied in the process of building GRP boat hulls they are also typically mixed with pigments and thus become coloured. They are applied in that process by the same method of wet hand lay-up that is used in the case of the GRP itself. In other words they are normally painted on with a brush or roller. In a development which the Traxton/ Reeves diary notes as having taken place in 1973, a special gelcoat resin, Crystic Gelcoat 68PA, for application by spray gun was, however, put onto the market as a new product. Rather later, spray-gun gelcoats became important sources of income for Scott Bader SA, the company's subsidiary in France. But the builders of GRP boat hulls in Britain have mainly continued to favour the traditional method of application by wet hand lay-up. The gelcoat is the first layer to be painted on to the surface of the female mould. Thus when the mould is eventually removed, it becomes the surface coating of the GRP hull in the water.

The word 'gelcoat' is a Scott Bader coinage though it is now used throughout the industry. According to Brian Parkyn it was coined by a member of his laboratory staff, John Emms, in 1954 and first used in print in the 1955 edition of the company's *Polyester Handbook*. The first reference in the company archives to its production at Wollaston is in 1961 when the resin, with the brand name of 'Crystic gelcoat 33', was first sold to customers in the marine market. It appears that before the development of this and other gelcoats Scott Bader sometimes supplied its GRP customers in the marine industry with a so-called 'pre-gel' material, while in others boat-building customers developed this material themselves, in line with technical advice and specifications contained in the *Polyester Handbook*.

About gelcoats it only remains to add that commercially speaking, measured by the margins at which they can be sold, they have been among Scott Bader's most successful products over the last 40 years. They have been constantly developed and improved to meet customers' special needs. And they are a substantial part of what explains the company's continued pre-eminence in this sub-segment of the GRP market.

That is something of a digression. Here we must ask how it was that, having focused on the marine and more particularly the boat-building market as probably the most promising source of demand for the new material, Brian Parkyn managed to gain his first foothold in it. In his forthcoming autobiography he tells us, to begin with, of an extended but abortive sales and marketing journey which he undertook as early as 1948, that is after the discovery of cold-curing but before the problem of air inhibition had been successfully solved. Setting out from Maldon in Essex, he drove his motor bike all the way up the east coast of England as far as Whitby in Yorkshire. He had in his pocket a 12″ model of a GRP boat which he had himself moulded earlier in the year in his Wollaston laboratory and which he had called *Red Biddy*. But he had no luck at all. He reports, 'Every boat-builder I visited said the same thing: "Boats have always been made of wood and always will be."'

It was not until 1950, two years later, that Brian Parkyn made his first GRP sale to a boat-builder. As he tells the story, it was a close-run thing that his own and his team's work on unsaturated polyester resins survived at Wollaston that long:

In May 1950, shortly after my Easter holidays, Ernest asked me to see him. We had a long discussion about the problems of the company. Although it was a little healthier [than it had been in 1948], it was clear to us both that my department of polyester resins was a major drain on the firm's resources. ... We had developed resins suitable for the manufacture of radomes and other parts of aircraft, and were selling several tons for these applications to at least half a dozen aircraft firms. We were also supplying resin for making corrugated roof sheeting, electronic potting and embedding, and a little for the manufacture of knife handles. Nevertheless the total cost of my laboratory staff and overheads far exceeded the small surplus we were making, and this was well known in other departments of the company. They felt strongly that I was a major drain on the firm and that if I had not been Ernest's nephew polyester resins would have been abandoned long ago. I therefore felt vulnerable, although I personally never doubted that polyester resins would eventually have a great and profitable future.

Next we are told what Ernest Bader thought of all this and what his decision was:

Ernest totally supported me and trusted my judgement, but in view of the general concern in the company, he considered that an independent external consultant should be brought in to assess the whole situation. So he engaged a well-known financial expert ... John Edwards MP, who had been financial secretary to the Treasury ... under Attlee. ... He produced his report on 21 July 1950.

In effect the Edwards report strongly vindicated Brian Parkyn and his judgement:

The situation as he saw it 'was not as black as he had been led to believe', indeed he forecast that by 1952 we should be breaking even. Thereafter polyester resins should be making an increasing, and indeed substantial profit.

To make more comprehensible what happened next, I need to explain that, earlier in 1950, Brian Parkyn had written his first two in a long series of articles on reinforced plastics in the technical press. One was entitled 'Low-pressure Resins' and the other 'Boat Hulls by Low-pressure Lamination'. They were published in the journal *Plastics* and the journal *British Plastics* respectively. Let Brian Parkyn now take up the story again:

A few days after the Edwards report I received an extraordinary telephone call. It was from an ex-naval officer called Geoffrey

Lord, a professional naval architect and marine engineer. Apparently with two other ex-naval officer engineers he had set up a small boat-building company in Blyth, Northumberland. 'Look,' he said, 'I have just read your article on boat-building. I believe in fast cars, fast living and fast women, and I intend to build the fastest sailing dinghy in the world. I want you to help me build a plastic boat.'

Even on the roads of the 1940s, Blyth in Northumberland cannot be much more than 90 minutes on a motor bike from Whitby in Yorkshire. But this was not the time for extended reflection and regrets. Events moved on rapidly:

> I was on the train to Newcastle the next day. Lord met me at the station in an open bright red *souped-up* sports car, and took me at an incredible speed through the streets of Newcastle and on to Blyth. They already made a range of sailing dinghies by the then unconventional method of moulding them in plywood. Now they intended to build a 16-ft centreboard sailing dinghy in GRP.
>
> After a long discussion I returned to Wollaston and arranged for them to have the necessary materials without delay. Three weeks later I returned to Blyth and the four of us worked all through the night. As dawn was breaking over the North Sea we took out of the mould the first GRP boat to be made by *wet hand lay-up* [emphasis original] using a cold setting polyester resin.

Given the imperative of marketing GRP boat hulls to potential buyers, the sequel was almost equally important and could hardly have been bettered:

> Several weeks later, after a mast and sails had been fitted, Lord, who was an experienced yachtsman, went on to win every sailing race in the country. His exploits received wide-scale publicity, not only in the yachting journals and other technical press, but also in mainstream newspapers such as *The Times* ...This single event was to lead to a dramatic diversification and expansion of GRP over the next few years.

The Traxton/Reeves diary comes in here with valuable corroborative evidence. For the year 1950 it names a number of other boats, as well as

Wildfire, built with GRP hulls. Its items for 1951 include: '*Tod 12*, one of the first GRP production series boats, made by W & J Tod.'

Then, in 1952, the diary's final item is evidence of diversification that GRP was becoming accepted in other markets: 'World's first complete GRP car body. Singer Motor Co.'

Perhaps most consequential of all, because it marks the start of a commercial/partnership link which has remained important to both companies to this day, is an item recorded in the Traxton/Reeves diary for 1954: '*Perpetua*, the first large 48ft 8in ocean-going GRP boat, made by Halmatic in Crystic 189. Also the first fitted with diesel engines.'

'Crystic 189' is a Scott Bader brand name which has since been used without interruption to describe the unsaturated polyester resins which it supplies to its marine sector and some other customers. Brian Parkyn explains the genesis of Crystic – though not of 189:

> At first I considered calling the resins *Glastic*, from 'glass' and 'plastic' but the patent office informed me that this was already registered in the United States. So I decided to replace it with crystal, and coined the word *Crystic*. In due course this was registered at the Patent Office and our polyester resins were thereafter called Crystic Resins.

The building of the 48ft 8in hull of the *Perpetua* for Halmatic in 1954 was not unproblematic. Partly because it involved the solution of an important technical problem, the story of what happened is worth re-telling here. When GRP was used for the first time to build the hull of a boat of that much larger size than a 16ft dinghy, a problem arose in the wet hand lay-up process which has already been described. When first attempted the moulding was found, in Brian Parkyn's words, to be 'severely damaged by internal delamination and was totally unusable'. He goes on to explain why: 'Nothing so large ... had ever been made of GRP before, so that each layer of glass fibre and resin had cured too hard for the subsequent layers to bond together effectively.'

A full house, assembled at the Halmatic boatyard in Havant to observe the opening of the mould, watched this disaster happen. It included the Halmatic chairman, Patrick de Laszlo, as well as Halmatic staff, Brian Parkyn and members of his Scott Bader team. De Laszlo confronted Parkyn and asked him to explain what had gone wrong. Providentially he was able to come up with the above answer, which soon was found to be right. De Laszlo was told, as Brian Parkyn writes in his autobiography, that Scott Bader would 'need to develop a new special polyester resin with a much longer *green life* [emphasis original], suitable for building very large GRP boats'. '"Alright, Parkyn," he said to me, "I will give you three weeks to do this, but this will be your last chance. If that fails I shall be finished with you and Scott Bader for ever."'

The story has a happy ending which includes glasses of champagne all round. About how that was achieved, it is worth quoting at some length from Brian Parkyn not only because it involves the solution of a technical problem. It is also striking because it conveys something of the excitement generated at Scott Bader in Wollaston's early pioneering days. And at least in Parkyn's view it was immensely consequential. My guess is that by the measure of the number of annual man years of work at Scott Bader, the few man weeks at Wollaston devoted to working on a replacement resin for the *Perpetua* in 1954 were almost certainly the most fruitful in the company's history.

> On returning to Wollaston, I brought all my laboratory staff together with Bob Bridgeford, our best resin chemist. I explained what had happened and told them to drop whatever other work they were doing and concentrate on resolving this problem. Over the next two weeks, often working late into the night, Bob made a dozen or more experimental batches of resin, each with a different formulation. Each was then carefully tested for *green life* by making small experimental laminates of considerable thickness. Water resistance and other properties were also evaluated.
>
> This critical work was carried out by Don Wildman, and I trusted his judgement absolutely. He had joined me in the laboratory straight from school in 1947, and apart from his absence on National Service, he remained in the firm until retirement. He was an intuitive *bricoleur* and this was *bricolage* with a vengeance.
>
> At least one of the formulations looked promising, and since it was now the start of the third week, we decided to make a full-scale batch of the new resin without further delay. This was immediately despatched to Halmatic, and we desperately hoped that it would resolve the problem. Looking back I am surprised at the great gamble we took.
>
> I returned to Havant and we moulded another hull over the next two or three days. The resin performed perfectly. De Laszlo

was there again as we opened the two giant moulds with a crane. It was a moment I shall never forget. A perfect 45ft boat hull emerged, the largest GRP moulding in the world. Everyone clapped their hands and cheered, and after a brief speech by de Laszlo, we were all served with glasses of champagne.

The boat was named *Perpetua*, and I decided to call the new polyester resin *Crystic 189*. Eventually, after the boat had been fitted out and the engines installed, it went to the Persian Gulf. We publicised both the resin and the boat very widely, and never looked back after that. Reinforced Plastics had really arrived.

Brian Parkyn concludes this story with some specifics about GRP successes in the marine market over the next few years, and some remarks about Scott Bader's and his own longer-term links with Halmatic:

Soon, Halmatic was to build a 54-footer and then a 67-footer, and within five years 80% of all the boats at the London boat show were manufactured of GRP using *Crystic 189* polyester resin.

Halmatic remained totally loyal to Scott Bader and refused to use any resins from our rivals even when lower prices were offered. In 1979 I was invited to become a non-executive director of Halmatic, and I continued to serve as a director of Halmatic until I retired.

At least to the non-specialist reader – if the writer is a typical example – the 'boat show' may well suggest pleasure-boating. But I should make clear that what Halmatic builds and sells are mainly working boats. Indeed towards the end of the 1990s it was bought by the Southampton shipbuilder Vosper Thorneycroft.

But here, to reinforce the point that the marine market into which Scott Bader sells GRP includes builders of working boats as well as pleasure craft, it is worth reproducing five items from the Traxton/Reeves diary of the 1950s and 1960s, together with a final one from Brian Parkyn:

1956 World's first GRP lifeboats [built] by Viking Marine, using *Crystic 189*.
1964 First all-GRP fishing fleet, 74ft and 83ft. [built in] Cape Town, South Africa.
1966 Maritime Industries, Cape Town, start production of series GRP trawlers over 70 feet in length

1967 Hovercraft, HM2, first GRP passenger carrying craft, designed by Hovermarine Ltd. 50ft/16m in length.
1968 World's Largest GRP Hovercraft, 165 tons and 130 feet, RSN 4 launched at Cowes.
1969 The world's first series of purse-seine 100ft trawlers built in Lima, Peru, using *Crystic 189*.

It is developments of the above kind which seem to suggest that, particularly after the 1954 success with the *Perpetua*, there may be some justification for characterising this period as one of 'sunshine years'. We must now turn to additional supporting evidence: from the growth of Scott Bader's output of unsaturated polyester resins, from its success in selling GRP to non-marine customers, and from the licensing arrangements which it agreed with resin manufacturers in other countries. Overseas licensing began – as the Traxton/Reeves diary tells us – with an agreement signed with the Swedish Company, Syntes, in 1953.

THE GROWTH OF POLYESTER PRODUCTION DOWN TO 1972, NON-MARINE MARKETS AND LICENCE INCOME

I have already referred to Scott Bader's 'draft Polyester Plan, 1980–1985' and cited some data from it. Included are estimates of both the total British market for unsaturated polyester resins at various dates and of Scott Bader's contribution to it. Tiresomely, some of the estimates are presented in graph form only – without the associated actual numbers – and the latter are therefore more rough and ready than exact. I must also acknowledge that Brian Parkyn is unhappy about some of the estimates of total UK market size which he thinks are mainly too high. On the other hand, the compiler of the draft plan must surely have had access to Scott Bader's actual records for its own output. I therefore assume that those are as close to the truth as we are now likely to get, given all the intervening years. If Brian Parkyn's mainly lower figures for total market size are closer to the truth than those in the draft plan, then Scott Bader's percentage contribution to that total becomes that much larger. I suspect myself that much of the difference between the Parkyn estimates and those in the draft plan may have arisen because of uncertainties about the size of the defence industries markets in the UK. What is certain is that down to the mid-1980s Scott Bader imposed on itself, for pacifist reasons, a nearly complete self-denial in those markets. The sacrifice was considerable in both tonnage and market share terms.

Estimates of total polyester market size and of Scott Bader's contribution to it: 1962–72

Units are 000s of tonnes except for percentages in Column 2

	(1)	(2)	(3)
1962	11	20.0	2.2
1963	15	18.0	2.7
1964	18	17.5	3.1
1965	25	16.5	4.1
1966	26	14.5	3.7
1967	27.5	17.0	4.7
1968	35	20.0	7.0
1972	50	31.0	15.5

Notes: (1) Market size estimates from draft plan . (2) and (3) Draft plan's estimates of Scott Bader's percentage market share and corresponding tonnage.

Another graph in the same draft polyester plan is headed 'Polyester resins margin (1960–1979)' in £ per tonne. The margins are expressed in 1979 prices and those in earlier years have been adjusted for inflation. What the graph shows is that, with the inflation adjustment, Scott Bader's margin per tonne in 1979 prices fell from £600 in 1960 to no more than £220 in 1972. The adjusted price for 1962 is shown to be £450. Thus on the basis of these data we can say that Scott Bader will have made a total margin of £990,000 (in 1979 prices) on its sales of polyester resins in 1962, and rather over £3m in the same prices in 1972. Sellers are rarely pleased by falling prices. Nevertheless we must assume that for the period as a whole this polyester margin record was judged to be at least satisfactory.

To understand fully the Scott Bader numbers in 1972, as presented in the table, an important footnote point must be added. Down to 1968 the growth in the company's output tonnage and market share was entirely a matter of organic growth at Wollaston. However in 1968, while Godric Bader was still managing director as well as chairman, he launched a policy of growth by acquisition which was to be followed in turn by each of his first four successors as chief executive. What he acquired in 1968 was Artrite Resins, the polyester division of Turner and Newall. That was the single most important factor behind the upward shift of the company's market share by more than half – from 20% to 31% – between 1968 and 1971. As in the case of many, though not all, of the company's subsequent acquisitions, what was acquired in this transaction was essentially Artrite's customer list and its in-house technology. It was not bought as a going concern and no plant or machinery was shipped to Wollaston, though a small number of key technical people came across.

When we turn next to the non-marine markets which Scott Bader's GRP had started to penetrate during the years down to 1968, it is worth noting, to begin with, that among the photographs in the printed version of Brian Parkyn's 1961 RSA lecture is one of a bus and another of a road tanker. The caption under the first reads, 'Bus body entirely built in glass fibre-reinforced polyester resin (by courtesy of Eastern Coachworks Ltd).' That for the second reads, 'Road tanker for chemicals. Wound from glass fibre filaments impregnated with polyester resin (by courtesy of ABR, Familleureux, Belgium).'

Perhaps more glamorous than either of those two references to non-marine applications of GRP is the item which appears in the Traxton/Reeves diary which I cited earlier, and which dates all the way back to 1952: 'World's first complete GRP car body (Singer Motor Co).'

Even those, and Brian Parkyn is probably foremost among them, who are most optimistic about the potential of GRP are not prepared to wager real money on it replacing sheet steel as the normal material for the car bodies of models with mass-production runs. The existing investments are too large to be at all easily replaced, and 'wet hand lay-up' does not sound like a plausible method when it comes to motorcar assembly. Still, those considerations do not apply with anything like the same force when we are talking about models, like those of Singer, which were and are assembled on a batch and not a mass-production basis. Another example is Lotus, a company with which Scott Bader was later to form a joint venture to explore the feasibility of a 'closed mould' rather than a wet hand lay-up system of applying GRP. We shall come on to that later in the narrative.

Here it makes sense to highlight the fact that for long stretches of years since it first grabbed a lead in the market for unsaturated polyester resins, and especially for GRP, the land transport market has been, for Scott Bader, the second most important. As well as being used for coach and tanker bodies and widely for the cabs of road haulage vehicles, GRP started to be sold to British Railways at an early date. For passenger rolling stock on the railways, Brian Parkyn mentions its use, among other things, for seats and window surrounds and doors. Later it began to be used as the main material for the bodies of big new railway locomotives.

In line with the relative importance of this land transport market, a table towards the end of the draft Scott Bader Polyester Plan, 1980–5, projects a breakdown by market segment of the company's sales between those two dates. It shows that sales to land transport industries were then expected to increase compared with those to buyers in the marine category, from roughly one quarter in 1980 to approximately one third in 1985. The optimism may well have been significantly based on a prospective sales to British Rail. If that targeted growth was in fact achieved – something which cannot now be established – then buyers for land transport businesses would have become, if we exclude sales to 'stockists' , the third most important group of buyers of SB's GRP material, after those classified as marine and as building materials. The market breakdown numbers given in the 1980 draft plan are worth making more accessible here:

Scott Bader polyester: projected sales tonnages by market segment, 1980 and 1985. Units 1,000 tonnes.

	1980	1985
Building materials	1.6	2.2
Tanks, containers & pipes	0.6	0.6
Industrial equipment	1.0	0.8
Marine	3.5	3.6
Land transport	0.9	1.2
Stockists	5.0	6.6
Non-reinforced	2.0	1.8
Total	14.5	16.7

Stockists only began to become really important for Scott Bader as sales outlets for GRP, based on its unsaturated polyester resins, when Strand Glassfibre was acquired in 1978. In this discussion, on the other hand, our special focus has been on sales to businesses in the land transport industries. Before leaving that sector, I can't resist reproducing an anecdote from Brian Parkyn's autobiography about an unexpected application of GRP within it. My excuse is that it was evidently the source of quite excellent publicity for the new 'wonder material' of reinforced plastics. The date is 1952. The words are Brian Parkyn's:

An ex-racing driver called Spike Rhiando built himself a motor scooter and decided to attempt to break the London to Cape Town land speed record. After 14 days of battling across the Sahara his engine seized up and the pistons were ruined. For five days and nights he lay in a dried-up river bed, burned by the heat of the sun by day, and tortured by cold at night. By the fifth day, with all his food and drink gone, Spike gave himself 12 hours to live. Fortunately at that moment of despair a plane spotted the bizarre bright colours of his scooter, and in the nick of time a party of French geologists was sent to rescue him ... The real significance of Spike's adventure is that nearly all the national newspapers carried the story, not just *The Times,* but also the *Daily Express* and *Daily Mail.* GRP was now being talked about not only in Fleet Street, but even in the comfort of the best London clubs.

As we have seen, users of Scott Bader's polyester resins in the UK's building materials sector were projected as to be the second most important customers of its GRP-linked polyester sales in both 1980 and 1985. Perhaps surprisingly, I can find only four items which reflect this in the Traxton/Reeves diary down to 1971:

> 1966 Hemel Hempstead Pavilion built with 134 GRP domes moulded in Crystic Resin by Sindall Concrete, designed by Clifford Culpin.
> 1967 Scott Bader Services launched with John West Design Group to advise on feasibility of GRP for structures.
> 1968 Scott Bader Services build their first GRP structure, a swimming pool at Lincoln.
> 1971 New airport terminal at Dubai built by Mickleover in Crystic resin.

But, of course, the diary was not designed to tell us directly what are the main uses to which Scott Bader-linked GRP material has been applied by buyers of building materials. However it seems that corrugated roof sheeting and external cladding were the most important of those. Somewhere on the borderline between the market segments of 'building materials' and of 'tanks, containers and pipes' comes its use in sewage systems, which was important from a quite early date and apparently remains considerable.

On the other hand the Traxton/Reeves diary gives useful, but almost inescapably incomplete coverage to 'polyester technology' licensing agreements with businesses in foreign countries which Scott Bader started to negotiate as early as 1953. For the 20 years from 1953 to 1972, Brian Parkyn has kindly supplied me with a complete list of countries and dates. There are 16 in all, or just less than an average of one negotiated each year over the 20-year period:

1953	Sweden	1963	South Africa
1955	Switzerland	1965	China
1958	Australia	1966	Colombia
1959	Austria	1968	Turkey
1959	Brazil	1970	India
1959	Argentina	1970	France
1960	Italy	1970	Spain
1962	Israel	1972	Mexico

About the life span of these agreements, Brian Parkyn explains that they ran initially for a 10-year period at the end of which the licensees could choose whether or not to extend their association with Scott Bader. It seems that in the above list of 16 countries, licensees in a total of 7 chose to negotiate an extension when the 10 years were up. The countries in which they did so were Sweden, Switzerland, Brazil, Argentina, Australia, Italy and South Africa. Brian Parkyn makes no secret of his judgement about the importance of polyester licence fees to the success of the business in the 1950s and 1960s, and points out that the only costs to be set against royalty income were 'administrative, some laboratory costs, and travel costs'. No data about licence fee income is available for the period down to 1972 on which we are directly focusing. However, the draft Scott Bader Polyester Plan, 1980–1985, projects the gross and net income from these polyester technology royalties for each of those six years. The gross annual income is projected to rise from just under £250,000 to some £340,000 between the first and last of those six years. Net of expenses, the corresponding projected numbers show an increase from £156,000 in 1980 to £200,000 in 1985. The company's actual profits before tax averaged just over £1m for each of those six years. So, on the assumption that the projections were more or less in line with what later actually happened, we can say that net of expenses these royalties probably contributed between 15% and 20% of pre-tax profits over the first half of the 1980s. Given that many more licensing agreements were operational during the earlier period down to

1972, it must be a fair bet that these royalties were then contributing a higher profit percentage.

In two of the 16 countries listed in Brian Parkyn's table, France and China, special features require some special attention. In France, the 1970 agreement was with a company in which Scott Bader already held a 50% interest. In 1973 it bought out its partner and became the 100% owner of what then changed its name to Scott Bader SA. Beyond noting that this French venture was initiated in 1966 when Godric Bader was managing director – and was to enjoy steady growth from the middle 1970s onwards – we shall postpone the main discussion until chapter 8.

The 1965 agreement with China was in fact negotiated by Brian Parkyn himself, and he needed two visits to do the job. It was unusual in two main respects. First, it provided that Scott Bader should be paid not through an arrangement of annual royalties but in a single upfront payment. Secondly, the contract in effect assigned to Scott Bader the whole responsibility for managing the construction in China of the necessary plant and bringing it on stream. The one-off payment only became due when those conditions had been satisfied.

As the cards fell, it was Don Wildman, whom we have already met in connection with the work of finding an adequately green resin for the *Perpetua,* who took over the on-the-spot responsibility in China for seeing this project through to a successful conclusion. He has kindly written me a complete account of what happened:

In 1965 Brian Parkyn was invited to China to negotiate a contract for a polyester resin manufacturing plant. The resulting contract required Scott Bader to supply all the components of the plant, resin formulations, raw materials and technicians to oversee the installation of the plant and supervise the resin manufacture to the agreed specifications.

The components of the plant and the raw materials required were listed in the contract, and these were ordered for delivery to Scott Bader prior to shipment to China. Due to delays in supply, wrong parts and errors, the shipment was late being despatched.

When it was established that the shipment had arrived, two Scott Bader technicians, Eric Golbourn, plant manager, and John Umfreville, resin chemist, were sent to China in 1966 to carry out the supervision of the installation.

Difficulties were experienced by the technicians due to (1) the effects of the Cultural Revolution, (2) parts missing from the shipment, and (3) failure of some equipment, in particular the oil heating unit.

Because of these factors, the Chinese were less than co-operative and the job was made difficult for the technicians. Replacement parts were not available in China (even spares such as fuses) and these had to be sent out from England. In addition to these problems the technicians became ill and finally were allowed to return to Hong Kong (suffering from scurvy). Upon recovery they declined to go back into China and returned to England.

This and other problems upset the Chinese and they demanded that Scott Bader complete the terms of the contract. Nothing continued at the plant, the Chinese technicians being sent out to work on the farms.

Meetings were held at the Chinese Embassy in London and finally, in late 1967, Scott Bader agreed to send one person to China to resolve the situation.

I agreed to go after being fully briefed on the difficulties involved. To help with language, Mr Chan of Jardine Matheson (our agent in Hong Kong) would accompany me to Beijing. The date was February 1968.

Upon arrival in Beijing – the journey was an adventure in itself – contact was made with the Chinese Ministry and a meeting was arranged. Slow and extended negotiations took place, often with reference back to Scott Bader by cable for agreement. The result after 10 days of talks was an agreement to complete the contract in a way acceptable to both parties.

I travelled alone to the plant at Changchow, as Mr Chan was not allowed to visit that part of China. The Chinese technicians had been reassembled at the plant and work started to put the reactor in order. Nothing had been touched since the Scott Bader technicians had left. When everything was operating correctly to the satisfaction of the Chinese inspectors, resin production was started. Two batches of each type of resin listed in the contract were required to be manufactured within agreed specifications – 24 batches in total. The Chinese chemists operating the plant carried out the manufacture with great dedication, in spite of restrictions imposed on them by the Cultural Revolution.

After eight weeks the task was completed to the satisfaction of the local Revolutionary Committee and was celebrated by a banquet and a ritual signing of the certificate of completion.

In consideration of the work, the Revolutionary Committee arranged for me to have a five days' tour of the successes of the Cultural Revolution, to schools, factories, projects and farms, before permitting me to return to Hong Kong.

Scott Bader presented the completion certificate to the Chinese Embassy in London and payment for the contract was obtained.

The Traxton/Reeves diary seems to have got the date wrong by one year. It records: '1967. Polyester resin plant commissioned in Changchow, China.'

There can be no real doubt that in the development by Scott Bader of its market for unsaturated polyester resins, the discovery of the special 'greener' resin needed for larger boat hulls like that of the *Perpetua* has been that much more consequential than bringing into production the new plant, built under licence in China. Nevertheless Don Wildman's contribution was clearly both important and exemplary. I like to think it might be possible for him to visit China again now in his retirement, and when the economy is apparently growing at a terrific pace. And I like to think of him being asked by a Chinese tourist guide about his memories of his 1968 visit. I imagine that he would express satisfaction at having overseen the completion of the Changchow resin plant. But what about his 'five days' tour of the successes of the Cultural Revolution', those schools. factories, projects and farms? Somehow I can't help feeling that they would have impressed Ernest Bader more than Don Wildman.

If we stand back for a moment from the details of Scott Bader's success in having created and then played a leading part in expanding and diversifying the domestic and overseas market for GRP, we may reflect that what was involved was as much 'pre-marketing' as a more conventional sales and marketing campaign. GRP may in some sense have been the new wonder material, but an essentially sceptical world had first to be convinced of that. I mentioned earlier two articles written by Brian Parkyn in the technical plastics press as long ago as 1950, one of which seems to have been decisive in securing that order in Blyth for the building of the first GRP hull for a 16ft sailing dinghy. The point to make here is that Brian Parkyn has been writing and lecturing about this same subject – and writing books as well as just articles – ever since. The Traxton/Reeves diary includes, among its 1953 items: 'The first edition of the Scott Bader Polyester Handbook published.' It has been more or less continuously updated ever since. Altogether, and now over half a century, Scott Bader has exposed the public to a continuous tutorial about the virtues of GRP. It has been a tremendous pre-marketing effort. It must be doubtful whether in its absence the market could have been developed as it was and thus whether the business could have survived.

As for the licensing of Scott Bader's polyester resins for manufacture by others abroad, I noted above that this appears to have declined between the end of the 1960s and 1980. Later, and especially in the 1990s, the company, as we shall see, substantially shifted its policy in this area towards setting up or acquiring overseas subsidiaries, and manufacturing abroad on its own account. Still it must be doubtful whether that would have been a realistic policy in the years down to 1972 which we have been considering. Furthermore, and though the data is sometimes missing and sometimes problematic, there seems little doubt that down at least to the mid-1970s net licence fee income made a substantial contribution to profits. Brian Parkyn believes that it frequently went as high as 30% or even more.

We will move on next to no more than the briefest summary account of those of Scott Bader's activities during the period down to 1972 which related not to unsaturated polyester resins but to its range of other products, notably its range of polymers. But before that we need just to flag up one more polyester item from the invaluable Traxton/Reeves diary. It comes from 1968 when Godric Bader still held both the top posts – those of chairman and managing director: '1968: New 22,000 tonne per annum polyester resin plant came on stream at Wollaston.'

POLYMERS, PAINT RESINS AND OTHER PRODUCTS
USED IN SURFACE COATINGS

In 1953 Scott Bader was organised into three business divisions. They were the polymer division, directed by Godric Bader, the paint resins division, directed by John Hand (who had by that time rejoined the company), and the polyester division, directed by Brian Parkyn. Already in that year, according to Parkyn's autobiography, the company was 'manufacturing and selling many tons of polyester resin all over the world' and was 'also making a substantial profit'. Eight years later, in 1961, we learn from the same source that the 'polyester division ... was making more profit than all the other activities of the company put together'. The profits of the division must have come to exceed 50% of the company's total profit some time during the second half of the 1950s.

But that is not the point which needs to be emphasised here. Instead we need to start by remembering the years before the polyester division started making any profit at all and what a close-run thing it was that it actually managed to survive to the point when those profits began to be made. Brian Parkyn had started to work at Wollaston in January 1947. His key meeting with Ernest Bader, when it was agreed to appoint John Edwards as an independent consultant on the polyester division's prospects was 'shortly after Easter' in 1950. At that stage the division was still making a loss and was widely seen as a 'major drain' on the firm. Only at some date between then and 1953 did it evidently start making a profit.

In effect for at least four and possibly five years from the beginning of 1947, the polyester division was being carried by Scott Bader's other activities. Moreover as late as 1955, in the second edition of *New Life in Industry: Handbook and Charter for the Staff of Scott Bader and Co* it is stated that 'most of the company's products are used in the paint, printing ink, linoleum, textiles, leather and paper trades'.

If there is any surviving written evidence about the relative profitability of the non-polyester divisions – the polymer division and the paint resins division – and of the various different products manufactured by them in 1953 and in the earlier post-war years, it has not proved to be at all readily accessible. However, the balance of the evidence from discussion seems to be that both the polymer division and those working with paint resins and driers contributed strongly to the commercial success of the business in those years. That seems plausible enough, given that three of the four licences brought back from America by John Hand after his two post-war visits were associated with polymers. Moreover, according to the Traxton/Reeves diary, one of those agreements, that with the American Polymer Corporation, was going well enough in 1953 for it to be extended 'to include polyvinyl acetate emulsions'.

The relative success of Scott Bader's polymer production in the late 1940s was all the more remarkable because three senior members of staff, the then technical director, the chief chemist, and the company secretary, all broke their contracts, without warning, and left the country for South Africa – to start a rival business on the basis of Scott Bader know-how – early in 1948. The sudden loss of the technical director, a man called James, was particularly damaging because he had had responsibility for overseeing the building of what was to be the company's new polymer plant, and had been designed to take maximum advantage of the new polymer licences from America.

However, the day was triumphantly saved by Godric Bader. In his autobiography Brian Parkyn fills in some of the details:

> Godric was appointed by Ernest to take over from James and sort out the chaos. In my opinion what Godric achieved in little more than six weeks was one of his greatest contributions to the company. He quickly made a number of changes and finally completed the building and installation of the plant so that it was up and running in time for the grand opening on 20 May.

It would be good news if reliable extra information was to become available which would make it possible to understand in more detail how it was that Scott Bader's non-polyester divisions managed to sustain a sufficient level of profitability from 1947 onwards to a) cover the 'major drain' of the polyester division's losses, and b) achieve at least a slim measure of overall profitability. It was, to repeat once again, a close-run thing. Staff numbers declined through natural wastage in both 1952 and 1953, and it was not until 1955 that the total numbers employed climbed back just over the number (161) on the books when the Commonwealth had been launched four years before.

What seems striking today is the considerable variety of non-polyester manufacturing in which Scott Bader was engaged at this time. Both Godric Bader and Brian Parkyn believe that those Nuodex paint driers, which began to be manufactured at Wollaston in 1946, after John Hand had brought back from America the licence to make them, may have been specially important as contributors to profit. That Scott Bader was on to something of a good thing in the case of this licence seems to be confirmed by a rather specific recollection that comes from Godric, that the licence was abruptly and unilaterally revoked by the licensor.

Others remember coatings for wallpapers as a market in which Scott Bader established an important position in the late 1940s and early 1950s. Taking advantage of the concentration of shoemaking and leather-dressing activity in its Northamptonshire neighbourhood, the company was evidently also something of a leader in developing special lacquers, including surface coatings for patent leather, for these nearby customers over those years. Without wishing to detract from the commercial and entrepreneurial merit involved in these and similar successes, those who were already working for the company in the years immediately following the war are inclined to make an important general point about those times: namely that such were the shortages that almost anything that could be manufactured could be sold.

But in the absence of reliable written records and of any systematic data, it probably makes most sense to stand back from the detail and do no more than remind ourselves about the main sources of Scott Bader's successful business record over the first 10 post-war years. There were two key decisions, first, to send John Hand to America with the mission of bringing back licences, and so to make possible the manufacture of American products at Wollaston; and secondly, to 'hang in' with the polyester resin project despite its losses, and allow it enough time to become profitable.

For the second of those decisions to have been successful it was necessary for the non-polyester parts of the business to make significantly greater efforts than would otherwise have been necessary. Arguably it was the people working in and leading those parts of the business who were the real business heroes of those early Commonwealth years.

But by 1955 the polyester division had started to make significant profits and numbers employed had just managed to exceed the 1951 total. Between that year and 1972 total employment more than doubled – to 385, over 50% above the limit laid down in the original set of principles. Furthermore, profits before tax in the same year amounted to £377,000 as against a previous highest ever of £299,000 in 1971. Ernest Bader's two great gambles – of introducing the Commonwealth and of backing the new material of GRP until well after that policy had started to hurt the business – must both have been widely judged to have paid off. What's more, eight years earlier, in 1963, the Bader family had given up its final 10% shareholding and thus relinquished control. It had also agreed to other constitutional changes. It is to those matters that we will move on in a moment.

GODRIC BADER TAKES OVER FROM HIS FATHER AT THE TOP

But first a few words about 'the succession', when Ernest Bader stood down from the post of managing director in 1957 and then from the post of chairman in 1966. As we have seen, his son Godric took over from him in both cases. These are matters about which board minutes are characteristically reticent. Nevertheless each of the two events is covered with some helpful comment by Susanna Hoe, and the first with additional detail by Brian Parkyn in his autobiography. The latter also refers to a 1960 initiative by Ernest Bader which might possibly have led to the replacement of Godric by himself in the position of managing director.

About the first of these changes Susanna Hoe (p 150) has an excellently persuasive account so far as it goes and I quote it in full:

> When the time came for Ernest to stand down in 1956–7 he was torn. There is some evidence to show that, although his son was his deputy, he considered the idea very seriously of asking his nephew Brian to take over as Managing Director.
>
> In many ways Brian was more like Ernest's business persona than was Godric but in the end it was the Commonwealth that was to triumph. Ernest knew that where the Commonwealth was concerned he and his son, though their methods would be different, were headed towards the same mystical goal. He could never be sure that the politician pragmatist in his nephew would not triumph over the idealism of the Commonwealth.

Brian Parkyn gets to the same outcome with a good deal of colourful detail and a fundamentally different explanation. He reports a conversation in which his uncle told him that he would 'like me to take over as managing director'. On the other hand he had also been told by his uncle that his aunt was 'implacably opposed to the appointment'. Evidently her view prevailed. And so it appears to have done later, in 1960, when Ernest apparently approached Brian and in effect invited him to '*seize the opportunity and take over from Godric* [emphasis original]'. His nephew replied that he 'would only take over from Godric if Godric fully agreed'. Parkyn concludes his account of this episode by reporting a visit to his office a few days later by Ernest, who told him, 'I'm sorry Brian, very, very sorry, but it's just not possible.'

There are no apparent conflicts of evidence when we come on to what happened when Ernest finally stepped down as chairman in 1966. I can do no better than quote Susanna Hoe's account (p 184): '[Ernest] was 76 years old. It was time he moved on from the chairmanship. But he was worried about this final succession.'

Godric describes how the end came about:

> Yes there was a tremendous hassle. In the Commonwealth centre there was a great question as to whether the new chairman should

come from the main Community Council; they had the right to confirm the appointment. He did and he didn't want to retire ... I remember the sweat literally pouring off him in the Commonwealth centre when the question of the appointment of the chairman was being debated by all members.

As soon as it was seen that he would appoint Godric and it would be accepted, Ernest could relax and give in to retirement.

1963: CONSTITUTIONAL CHANGES AND THE FINAL DIVESTMENT OF THE BADER SHAREHOLDING

Both Susanna Hoe and Brian Parkyn in his autobiography give prominence to the case of a secretary, Mrs Sayer, who was the subject of a more or less summary dismissal by Ernest Bader, then still managing director as well as chairman, in 1953. Her offence, according to Parkyn, was no more than 'some trivial mistake'. Her right of appeal lay with a wholly elected representative body which was officially called the general council at that time and was sometimes described as the 'standing committee' of the Commonwealth. Brian Parkyn had been elected to the council's chairmanship some months before. A senior member of the company's management team, Ron Smith, who held the post of chief buyer, but was also committed to quite radical versions of both socialism and pacifism, agreed to present her case to the council should Mrs Sayer wish to appeal against the dismissal. She did and following presentations by first Ron Smith and then Ernest Bader, the council decided unanimously in her favour. Ernest, albeit apparently with considerable reluctance, left the room during the discussion which led up to the decision.

Not altogether surprisingly, the managing director acquiesced. He told his nephew, who reported the decision to him, that he saw 'no alternative but to accept this verdict'; and he went on, 'If I don't it will be the end of the Commonwealth.'

The episode is worth reporting not so much as evidence that Ernest Bader was a 'compulsive sacker' – Susanna Hoe's phrase – though no doubt he was. What it shows is that when Scott Bader moved on from the earlier Fellowship to the Commonwealth it moved into a different world, a world governed by a framework of law rather than one which was the ex gratia creation of a capitalist business owner.

Ernest Bader's temperament may well have remained autocratic until his death. But once the Commonwealth had become 'by law established' he, like all other of its members, was governed by its laws.

That is worth emphasising because it marks a real – and not just a superficial – change towards more democratic accountability on the part of the Scott Bader management. Brian Parkyn seems at least partly to have missed or misunderstood this point in his views about the final 10% family shareholding – sometimes alternatively known as the Founders' shareholding – which we will cite from Susanna Hoe shortly.

The episode is important too because it shows that already in 1953 there were influential members of the company's management team – Ron Smith as well as Brian Parkyn – who were prepared to side openly with what one might call the 'democratic forces'. In fact we know from other sources that those two were not alone within management in being on that side.

In tracing the run-up to the 1963 divestment by the family of the remaining 10% of family – or Founders' – shares, Susanna Hoe quotes extensively from an unpublished dissertation, written by Dr Roger Hadley, and successfully presented by him for a PhD to London University. It is entitled 'Participation and Common Ownership: A Study in Employee Participation in a Common Ownership Firm'. Hadley dates the beginning of the story as early as 1957:

> In 1957 the Founder suggested that the time had come for the Founders' shares to be transferred to the Commonwealth to complete the transition to common ownership. Employees showed themselves eager to examine the proposal and discussion groups were arranged by the Community Council. ... Nearly 60% of the membership of the Commonwealth took part in the discussions which were held in the evenings in the employees' [owners'] homes.

It seems that out of this process two reports emerged. That of the majority indicated a readiness both to accept the Founders' shares and to pay for them at their nominal value from Commonwealth funds. The minority report disagreed, apparently arguing that, with the existing arrangements continuing to work well, there was no real need for a change.

Roger Hadley, as quoted by Susanna Hoe (p 174), goes on to outline the associated proposal in the majority report about the election of directors following the transfer of the family shares to the

Commonwealth. She also reports Ernest Bader's response to it. The majority report, according to Hadley,

> ... pointed out that the acquisition of the shares would logically imply that directors would then be elected at the AGM of the Commonwealth. The Founder baulked at the last proposal. He wanted new appointments to the board to be made by the directors themselves, although he was prepared to see the board as a whole subject to periodic votes of confidence by general membership. He was unwilling to go further with the transfer of the Founders' shares on the basis of the proposals ... and his offer was withdrawn.

There, in effect, the matter rested for some time. But there were at least two good reasons why the issue was unlikely to go away and stay quietly out of sight. One, probably the less important, was that employee expectations had been raised by the whole project of discussing the possible transfer to the Commonwealth of the Founder's shares. Moreover, these expectations were more kept alive than not by an experiment in employee participation which got underway about this time with at least the formal support of top management and the board of directors. The experiment was conducted by two academic sociologists. One was Roger Hadley, an Englishman, from whose dissertation on Scott Bader, following Susanna Hoe, I have just quoted. The other was Fred Blum, an American, who in 1968 was to write a book effectively on the same subject of employee ownership at Scott Bader. Fred Blum's book, published by Routledge & Kegan Paul, was entitled *Work and Community – The Scott Bader Commonwealth and the Quest for a New Social Order*.

The subject matter of both Roger Hadley's dissertation and Fred Blum's book, namely the reality of employee involvement and participation at Scott Bader, is both unusually important and unusually problematic. It would be impossible to do justice to it here. It would also be a mistake to try because it could not be fitted coherently into what is an essentially narrative chapter. Some of the key issues which it covers are looked at more closely in chapter 11.

About Blum and Hadley's experimental work at Scott Bader at this time, I do no more here than follow Susanna Hoe (p 175) in making a narrative point: 'The less tangible but perhaps more significant results of their work were probably an influence on the 1963 Constitution and in creating a certain awareness of Scott Bader.'

But it is time to go back to what I suggest is the second, and more important, of the two reasons why the issue of the Founders' shares was unlikely to stay away for long. There was first, to repeat, the heightened expectations of employees. But second there was the opinion of Ernest Bader himself. Susanna Hoe first tells her readers (p 177) that in relation to the handing over of the Founders' shares Ernest 'knew he must do so for propaganda reasons'. She then goes on, brilliantly in my view, to quote John Leyland's judgement about Ernest Bader's thinking on this matter, namely: 'It's quite obvious that the outside world knows that I control it and I mustn't be seen to control it.'

Here I must break my own rule briefly and interrupt the narrative with a word about John Leyland. He comes from an old Quaker family in North Yorkshire. Though in his mid-80s he is still very much alive and well in a small house which he shares with his second wife, the artist Janet Rawlins. It has been owned by his family since the 18th century in the main street of the Pennine village of Askrigg. After distinguished service in Burma and Western China with one of the Quaker Ambulance units during the war, John Leyland responded to an advertisement in *The Friend* in 1954 and almost immediately joined Scott Bader as company secretary and head of finance. He was later honoured by Ernest Bader with an invitation to become one of the Founder shareholders. After some 27 years of service, he chose to take early retirement in September 1981. According to Godric he never charged Scott Bader for a taxi during all those years. When Tracy Smeathers interviewed company pensioners in a Scott Bader oral history project early in 2000, she found that John Leyland was perhaps the most widely respected of the Commonwealth's top management team in its first half century.

Susanna Hoe (p 131) quotes from John Leyland a telling comment about Ernest Bader made soon after his arrival at Wollaston: 'That man thinks I am here just to be a yes-man. I'm not here just to further the ego of E.B. but to help run an organisation in the way I think it should be run.'

Evidently Scott Bader in the 1950s was very different from John Leyland's Friends Ambulance Unit in the 1940s. For one thing the latter did not include an Ernest Bader. I have sometimes found myself reflecting how different Scott Bader would have been if it had been wholly staffed by people with John Leyland's values. In that situation it would hardly have been necessary to embark on Fred Blum's 'Quest for a New Social Order' because one would already have arrived. But a moment's thought is enough to make clear that that prospect is utopian to the point of absurdity. It reminds me of another, in this case politically incorrect and utopian absurdity, which is also closer to street level: 'If the Windmill ran the railways we'd all have a wonderful time.'

John Leyland has left his mark on Scott Bader and will not be forgotten. He has also generously contributed some personal memories in a piece which is printed at the end of this book. But I cannot leave him now without passing on what was almost his final remark to me after he and his artist wife had entertained me to a delicious lunch in faraway Askrigg in the spring of 2000. 'Even if the results of the experiment have in some ways been disappointing,' he told me, 'I count it as a privilege to have been involved and I would not have missed it for anything.'

But to return, once again, to the issue of the Founders' shares and the associated constitutional changes over the election of directors, which public opinion seemed to demand but were unacceptable to Ernest Bader. As we shall see in a moment, a compromise was eventually reached. But before that I want to share with readers an account of what would today be called a memorable *spat* between Ernest Bader and his nephew Brian Parkyn. It is highly relevant to the issue of the Founders' shares and, more generally, to the evolution of Scott Bader's constitution in a democratic direction. Both Brian Parkyn and Susanna Hoe (p 177) give fairly full accounts of it.

There is no real dispute about the facts. The occasion of the spat was an article published in *Tribune*, the London left-wing political weekly, on 6 February 1961. The subject matter was Scott Bader and the piece was entitled 'An Experiment in Common Ownership'. It was written by the editor, David Boulton, who had apparently paid two visits to Wollaston for the collection of material and discussions with people. The question of the possible transfer of the Founders' shares and associated changes to the constitution was found by *Tribune*'s editor to be very much in the air. About the latter, and especially about the powers and composition of a democratised board of directors, Susanna Hoe records that both Godric and the then Commonwealth secretary, Ted Nichols, had spoken to Boulton about a possible compromise: assigning certain powers of veto to a new body of trustees.

Having referred to that possibility in her account of the episode, Susanna Hoe then goes on immediately to identify a 'paragraph' in the Boulton article 'that was to blow the issue wide open'. The paragraph read: 'However, another Director, Mr Brian Parkyn, forcefully argues for a whole-hog transference of power. 'The experiment really only begins when we get that far. Until we do we can reasonably be accused of humbug.'

In his autobiography Brian Parkyn quotes exactly the same paragraph from the Boulton piece which I have reproduced from Susanna Hoe above. But he also offers an account of his own thinking which lay behind that rather forcefully stated opinion. He begins by explaining that while 90% of the shares had been transferred [in 1951] as a free gift to the Commonwealth, '10% was retained ... as *Founder Shares*. In certain events, such as constitutional changes, or action to be taken should the company ever run at a loss, our *Founder shares* had their voting value increased tenfold so that we could take whatever action we considered appropriate.' And he goes on:

> I was somewhat unhappy about this aspect of the ... constitution. From 1951 to 1963 we had *Founder Members'* meetings which seemed to me exactly like shareholders' meetings. We still had virtually the same power, and we could *dismiss anybody* [emphasis added] or appoint anybody. As a fervent believer at that time in a simplistic Rousseau type of direct democracy, I wanted to see *all* the power of the former shareholders transferred to the democratically elected Commonwealth board.

I hope it is not a pedantic quibble to refer back to the case of Mrs Sayer and suggest that a power of dismissal associated with a right of appeal is 'not virtually the same' as the power of dismissal without that right. But, if not a quibble that is perhaps a detail. In any case we must move on to the end of the spat between Brian Parkyn and his uncle. The latter, according to Susanna Hoe, insisted on a public apology from his nephew over his use of the word 'humbug'. She also tells us that 'correspondence raged on between them for months'. Those who have known both men well enough to be entitled to a reliable opinion have assured me that both will, on balance, have greatly enjoyed the whole punch-up.

It remains to indicate briefly the main terms of the constitutional compromises which were reached when the ownership of the Founders' shares was eventually transferred to the Commonwealth in 1963. The treatment here is brief because I defer a full discussion until the chapter towards the end of the book which is devoted to the constitution in all its Byzantine glory and to how it has evolved over the 50 years since 1951. I shall confine myself here to just four points:

1 A new constitutional entity, a body of *trustees*, was added to the existing binary set-up of the Scott Bader Commonwealth and the Scott Bader company. The body is composed of a mixture of different elements. In the 1963 version both Ernest and Godric Bader are trustees for life; three trustees must come from outside and three are elected by the Commonwealth board. It has reserve powers similar to those described above by Brian Parkyn as has having been enjoyed by the 10% Founders' shares: that is relating to certain specified situations like proposals for constitutional change and if the company starts to make losses.

2 The board of the operating company is made subject to a vote of confidence at the annual general meeting of the membership. This confidence vote is precisely assigned to a 'jury' of 12 selected by lot from those attending the meeting. If the vote goes against the board, its effect is temporarily suspended, but an extended procedure of 'hearings' is set in motion which allows for the original vote of no confidence to be rescinded. This is perhaps both the most innovative and most complex of the new constitutional arrangements introduced in 1963. On at least two occasions during the 1960s a jury chosen by lot actually passed a vote of no confidence in the operating company's board, but in each case this was later rescinded in the procedure. However, this whole innovation was set aside in a further batch of later constitutional changes.

3 While retaining the preamble to the 1951 constitution, a second one was added, namely a preamble to the 1963 constitution.

4 Commonwealth members were required to commit themselves to a set of rules of conduct, containing 12 main points and three subsidiary ones. (These were softened with a revised description as a 'code of practice' in 1972.)

In effect Ernest Bader agreed early in 1963 that the ownership of the Founders' shares should be transferred to the Commonwealth. However, and if only as a point of detail, I need to explain further that (a) the Commonwealth *paid* £5,000 for them, namely their nominal value, but (b) the money went not to the Founder shareholders but to what we would now call a Third World charity which had recently been set up by Ernest Bader. It was the Society for Training Rural Industries and Village Enterprises and was generally known by its acronym as STRIVE. It was later amalgamated with the Intermediate Technology Development Group (ITDG) which was founded by E. F. Schumacher and has since become famous and survived to this day. However, as explained in the preface, we do not discuss either STRIVE or the ITDG group in this book.

CHANGE IN THE COMMONWEALTH'S OBJECTS CLAUSE

As a final postscript to this constitutional discussion, I must add a word of explanation about what may seem on the face of it to have been a rather surprising related development. It happened four years later, in 1967, and was just briefly mentioned earlier, namely an insistence by the Charity Commission that the objects clause in the Commonwealth's Memorandum of Association would have to be changed if it was not to be struck off the Charities' register. For convenience I will repeat the objects clause and then go on to quote from the objections to it put in writing by the Charity Commission in a letter dated 24 January 1967.

The relevant objects clause reads:

The objects for which the Commonwealth is established are the promotion of the Christian ethics and the encouragement of Christian principles in industry with a view to ensuring good relations between management and labour in industry and the discharge by persons engaged in industry and in particular in the paint and plastics trades of their social obligations to the community...

The letter from the Charity Commission reads in part:

The Commissioners are now of the provisional opinion that the objects are not charitable in law and that the company must be removed from the register...

The opening words of the objects clause refer to the 'promotion of Christian ethics and the encouragement of Christian principles in industry', and even if it is maintained that these are the main objects of the company I do not think that either of them can be related to the advancement of religion as such; but in any event these 'objects' are qualified by the words 'with a view to' immediately following and these words in my view lead to the main objects of the company: 'ensuring good relations between management and labour in industry and the discharge by people engaged in industry ... of their social obligations to the community... good relations and social obligations' must be regarded as the real objects of the company and the use of Christian principles is merely a means to an end. The Christian ethic here is merely the springboard or inspiration and so in a sense no more than the motive....

The company is obviously not concerned with the promotion of industry and commerce *per se* but (if we look at the statement by the subscribers printed ... immediately before the memorandum) ... with a variety of loosely declared purposes such as the establishment of common ownership in industry on principles based on Quaker and Christian/Pacifist movements, including the refusal to take an active part in rearmament; the idea being to 'present an alternative to a war based economy on the one hand and to communism on the other'. There are references to the power politics of governments, the profit-seeking of capitalists, the pressure for higher wages on the part of the employed, and the need to conduct individual and corporate life in accordance with the demands of peace against the current of a society war-based between capitalism and communism; the solution being the principle of common ownership as an essential step to a 'true Christian Industrial and Social Order'. *All of this is political and non-charitable* [emphasis added]; embracing propaganda, elimination of war and achievement of peace.

The 'discharge of ... social obligations to the community' is too wide and uncertain. I know of no authority to support a contention that this kind of thing can be charitable.

In short I think that the Scott Bader Commonwealth Limited's objects can fairly be stated as the establishment of a particular kind of politico-economic utopia; not necessarily for the benefit of the public, for it does not seem possible to accept that it is for the benefit of the public to, in the words of the subscribers to the memorandum, 'attempt to conduct business on lines not approved by Government nor the large majority of our fellow men [emphasis added]'.

By way of clarification it may be helpful to point out that where the Commission's letter uses the phrase – as it does more than once – 'in the words of the subscribers to the memorandum', it is referring quite specifically to the so-called 'preamble' to the constitution. And it seems reasonable to comment that the Commission's letter devotes much more space to the preamble than to the actual objects clause in the memorandum and bases its case for the ineligibility of the Commonwealth for charitable status much more on the former than the latter. On the other hand, it is also necessary to explain that in a paragraph of the letter which I have omitted the Commission justifies, with a cited precedent, the use of the preamble when trying to establish the 'dominant object' of a corporate body.

For what it is worth, that was a contention which was unsuccessfully challenged by Scott Bader's lawyers in their response to the Commission's letter. For the record, the company accepted a standard and more or less anodyne replacement of the object clause of the Commonwealth's memorandum. Having done so its charitable status was reinstated. Was it required, as a further condition of that reinstatement, to drop – or somehow otherwise extinguish – the offending preamble? I do not know. But it is still regularly reprinted as the 'preamble to the 1951 constitution'.

THE BRUCE REED REPORT: ITS ORIGIN AND MAIN OUTCOME

If only because of its date (1969) and what was probably its single most important short-term outcome, in 1970, I need to add a postscript here about a report prepared for the company's board of directors by the Revd Bruce Reed of London's Grubb Institute of Behavioural Studies, and entitled 'The Task and Role of the Board of Directors'.

The report was commissioned by Godric Bader while he still held each of the two top posts in the business, of chairman and managing director. It was apparently commissioned because of what were widely perceived inside Scott Bader as confusions, both about responsibilities, for example between the company and the Commonwealth, and about the relative priorities between the various different 'tasks' of the organisation. Its most important short-term result was the separation of the post managing director and non-executive chairman. That happened, as we already know, in 1970, when Godric resigned as managing director and Nick Broome was brought in from outside to take over.

At least in parts the report seems to me to be one of the most interesting discussions of Scott Bader that have emerged in the 50-year life of the Commonwealth. I shall refer to it again more than once. Here I shall do no more than highlight a few salient points:

a) It argues that the company board has wrongly lost powers to other bodies.

b) It criticises as unhelpful the standards of behaviour laid down in the 'rules of conduct'.

c) It identifies four distinct tasks with which the Scott Bader *organisation* – the term it uses to refer to the Company and the Commonwealth taken together – must be concerned:

    1 The economic task

    2 The technical task

    3 The social task

    4 The political task

Whatever else is true, this analysis into four separate tasks has been most influential – now for rather more than 30 years – as a framework for helping to define Scott Bader thinking.

Looking back now, and with the benefit of hindsight, the report can perhaps be seen, at least in part, as one of the earliest in a long series of steps, the effect of which has been to bring Scott Bader more into line with professional business practice without sacrificing the core values of trustee ownership and management accountability. Those steps have usually been thought of as having been started by Nick Broome and then greatly extended by Ralph Woolf. It is therefore interesting to find a forerunner when Godric still held the post of chief executive as well as of chairman, for a second forerunner of a similar kind was introduced when Godric was occupying both those positions.

As its final item for the year 1969, the Traxton/Reeves diary records the introduction of the 'method of job evaluation'. Many readers will know that that is one of a number of systems which claim to offer a 'scientific' basis for establishing relative rates of pay. We will look at it in some detail in chapter 11. Here it is enough to make just two points: first, while the Hay-MSL system is the subject of almost unceasing argument at Wollaston, it is still very much being used The second and final point to make in this context is that, whatever may have been made public at the time, Godric now makes no secret of the fact that he personally was against its introduction in 1969.

5
Continuity with Change at the Top: the Middle Years of the 1970s

From the early 1970s (and indeed from even earlier) down to the late 1990s – and also since then – there is a continuity both in the core products manufactured by Scott Bader on its parent site in Wollaston and in the tonnages shipped to its main customers. Year after year, and almost without exception, the statistics show that, whether measured by weight or by value in constant prices, the output and sale of polyesters was ahead of all others by a substantial margin.

Moreover, this pattern of polyester dominance seems to hold notwithstanding the huge recession in sales in 1980 and 1981 and during the years of only gradual recovery afterwards. Under the polyester heading I include gelcoats. As explained in the last chapter, these are polyesters with special qualities. Though not themselves reinforced with either glass fibre or any other stiffening material, they are almost exclusively sold to the buyers of those key unsaturated polyester resins which constitute the main component of reinforced plastics: what had been in the 1950s the new 'wonder material' and in the manufacture and sale of which Scott Bader, as we have seen, managed to grab onto a lead in its early years. As between the polyesters, on the one hand, and the gelcoats, on the other, the breakdown in an average year is that gelcoats account for roughly one third or a little more of the combined tonnages. The annual polyester tonnages between the start of the 1970s and the end of the 1990s have ranged from lows of just over 13,000 to highs up to 23,000.

The second enduring core product, in this case stretching all the way back to John Hand's two visits to America in 1945 and 1946 – and indeed on into the 21st century – is, of course, the company's range of polymers. Measured by weight, year by year, almost without exception, the polymers come second to polyesters in the output and sales score sheet. A surprising example to the contrary, so surprising indeed that it can almost be presented as strengthening the basic point, is the year

1974 when, at 7,555 tonnes, home sales of plasticisers were higher than those of polymers; and the same is also the case if we add the much smaller Wollaston export sales to those in the home market. It is true that there have been important changes over the years in the variety of the polymers manufactured and sold by the company – and in the markets to which they have been shipped, especially those within the paints, lacquers and other surface coating industries. But that should not obscure the extraordinary continuity of polymer production and technology at Wollaston over what is now more than half a century. It has been a continuity which extends to the actual plant and reactors in which these polymers have been manufactured. It was as late as the year 2000 that the company announced a start on the building of a new polymer plant and new reactors – to replace equipment, some of which has seen service since 1948. Readers will recall that it was Godric Bader who stepped in as a young man to bring the then new polymer plant into an operational state in May of that year. That had previously been the responsibility of a senior manager who had broken his contract and flown the coop under cover of darkness – only a month or so before the scheduled plant opening.

As for the annual output of polymers manufactured and sold from Wollaston, these have ranged, since 1970, from a low of just under 7,500 to a high of over 12,000 As indicated earlier, they typically command a lower margin than the unsaturated polyesters. Nevertheless, and since having been outstripped by the polyesters in the late 1950s, they have remained the second of the twin pillars on which the business has rested.

The logic of Scott Bader's main acquisitions in the UK over this period – and indeed before it – can best be understood in relation to these two core products and especially to the polyesters. In the last chapter we noted the acquisition in 1968, during Godric Bader's watch as managing director, of Artrite Resins Ltd, the polyester division of Turner and Newall. We will come on soon to other important examples of acquisitions in the 1970s and 1980s. These are similarly explained: namely by their position in the reinforced plastics market.

We should also note at this early stage that one or other, or both, of these core products have characterised the production and sales of Scott Bader's overseas subsidiaries as well as the parent business in Wollaston. For example, what became in 1974 its wholly owned French subsidiary, as Scott Bader SA, was engaged, to begin with, in the manufacture and sale of polymers only. Polyesters were added some

years later and after a special study. As for the much more recent overseas subsidiaries of the 1990s, in South Africa and the Arab Emirates,
each began with just polyesters. Additions, if any, came later. Finally
and most recently, the prospective wholly-owned subsidiary in Croatia
– in which in the year 2000 Scott Bader held loan stock convertible into
a majority equity holding – has had polyesters and alkyds, though not
emulsion polymers, as two of its core products since its first links with
Wollaston and indeed even before. But it is also exceptional in that it
manufactures and sells vinyl ester resins.

SECONDARY PRODUCTS

As a helpful starting point for a brief discussion of the secondary and
non-core products manufactured at Wollaston over this second phase
of the Commonwealth's first half century, Scott Bader's output and
sales numbers in the home market for 1975 are worth spelling out as
an illustration. After the polyesters – with a combined total of 17,288
tonnes, including the gelcoats – and the polymers, with 8,321 tonnes,
we have:

Plasticisers	6,482 tonnes
Other (mainly polyurethane)	517 tonnes

Both will need a word or two of explanation. But before that some
background.

To begin with, we need to emphasise two fundamental points and
what has been their main effect taken together. There is first the so-
called guarantee of permanent employment given to all those employees
who have been accepted as members of the Commonwealth. This is one
of the key provisions of its original 1951 constitution and was initially
embodied in a Certificate of Mutual Security. It was later replaced – as
we already know – by arrangements which allow for voluntary though
not compulsory redundancy on the part of members. However, it is not
that change, perhaps in any case more one of form than substance,
which concerns us here. Instead what needs to concern us is the
theoretical counterpart obligation which the guarantee lays upon
management: namely to have available jobs, or at least be well placed to
create jobs, in secondary activities which can take up slack when
markets for the company's existing main products dry up, or when
improvements in productivity run ahead of increases in market share.

The second fundamental point is that, on occasions, the company's markets have indeed dried up for one reason or another. And so, for that as well as other reasons, the management's obligation to have available – or be in a position to create – jobs associated with new activities ceases to be theoretical and becomes real, sometimes urgently so. Essentially it has been the interaction of these two fundamental points which mainly explains the secondary activities developed by Scott Bader at Wollaston since as long ago as the 1950s. Those secondary developments have also in part been driven by the hope, sadly not yet realised, that they would form the basis of a new core activity. We may note in parenthesis that where, as in the company's overseas subsidiaries, there was no substantial Commonwealth membership before the year 2000 – secondary activities have on the whole not been developed.

Having emphasised those two fundamental points in the background to the company's 'secondary' product lines, we must not overlook the more directly operational contribution to them of Scott Bader's research and development department. This is not the place for even a brief description – let alone any attempt at an evaluation – of R & D at Scott Bader. But it scarcely needs to be said that in-house R & D work has been critical to the company's success in bringing new secondary products to the market over the Commonwealth's 50 plus years. That very much applies to the two lines – plasticisers and polyurethane – we are now considering, but perhaps especially to the latter.

At least as it is remembered by Godric Bader, the genesis of plasticiser manufacture at Wollaston is a textbook example of the effects of the interaction of the two fundamental points that have just been identified. Readers will recall from the last chapter the sudden cancellation in 1953 by the American Nuodex company of the licence to manufacture its paint driers at Wollaston, one of those which John Hand had negotiated in the 1940s. It is easy to believe that this sudden cancellation left a number of employees at Wollaston – the actual number was apparently between 10 and 20 – with nothing to do which could make a positive contribution to the cash flow. A project of diversification was urgently needed. What Godric remembers, and he was after all in charge of the polymer division at the time, is that John Hand came up with an in-house Scott Bader plasticiser alternative to those Nuodex driers. Godric concedes that a changeover, which must have required some reactor modification as well as the retraining of some staff, was not achieved over a weekend. He remembers too that for an interim period of weeks – if not perhaps of months – some of those previously engaged in the manufacture of Nuodex driers were redeployed on the estate kitchen gardens and what was still then characterised as the company's farm. (Amazingly, there was a small herd of Jersey cows as well as some fowls to be looked after.) However, Godric is clear that, after a necessary interval of redeployment, the majority of those who had previously worked to manufacture the Nuodex driers were re-employed making John Hand's plasticisers. Brian Elgood doesn't seriously challenge Godric's story. But he adds a postscript to it. In developing his Scott Bader plasticisers, according to Brian, John Hand was materially assisted by the know-how embodied in another licence from an American company, namely Hercules Powder Inc.

We will come on to these plasticisers again shortly when we turn our attention to Nick Broome's years as chief executive between the end of 1970 and 1977. But first a summary account of the company's other secondary product of the 1970s, its polyurethane. Work on the development of Scott Bader's own in-house polyurethanes was in fact started somewhat earlier, in the second half of the 1960s, and had an interestingly hybrid origin. It resulted from an approach to Wollaston from the well-known, long-established and Quaker-owned English shoemaking business, C. & J. Clark of Street in Somerset. What follows is an edited version of an account kindly contributed by Tony Lovell, who led both the development project and the business which resulted from it. In effect he worked at Wollaston with Scott Bader for the whole of his professional life and held a series of research and management positions up to the time of his retirement in the 1990s.

Because of technical complexity and the constraints of space – but chiefly the latter – his contribution has had to be substantially cut. But before starting on the story I must guard against a misunderstanding. As some readers will know, the main use of polyurethane in today's world is for sponge-type packaging and cushion-filling. As we shall see, Scott Bader's own polyurethane had very different uses. Against that background here is Tony Lovell's story:

> During the latter part of the 1960s, the footwear manufacturers C. & J. Clark became very interested in a new invention which they saw as a potential market winner. Although what they saw at that stage was very basic, it was a polyurethane product based on a special saturated polyester resin and a high-quality di-isocyanate. This polyurethane produced high-quality properties, foremost of which were high abrasion resistance, good flexibility and light weight. These properties were recognised as being ideally suitable

as a shoe soling compound. Clarks – the trading name it favours, as buyers of its footwear will know – obtained the original formulation from an Austrian chemist, but they did not have the necessary chemical manufacturing expertise [for] the manufacture of the high quality polyurethane.

The person responsible for the polyurethane project at Clarks was Maurice Cuthbert, who as a boy at Wellingborough Grammar School had been a fellow pupil of Scott Bader's Robert Bridgeford, who had been appointed research and development director at Wollaston about this time. That previous relationship was unquestionably an important factor behind an approach by Clarks to Scott Bader for the latter to become its partner in the manufacture of the chemicals needed to produce the special kind of polyurethane. The proposal was accepted and a small but very dedicated team, consisting of Tony Lovell, Brian Taylor and Sue Deacon, was established at Wollaston, later to be joined by Trevor Osborne and a few assistants. Later again, Brian Hickman joined the team with responsibility for international sales.

A very high priority was given to the project and a close relationship developed between the two companies. For well over a year there were weekly progress meetings. Shoes were manufactured and given trials.

After lengthy evaluation of the shoes that had been given trials, Clarks were satisfied that the polyurethane system that had been developed in-house by the two companies was a marketable product worthy of their name, and bulk amounts were made by Scott Bader under the Clarks-devised name of Sorane.

As the system became well established, other Clarks factories throughout the world – and not just the parent factory at Street – became interested. Agreement was reached to the effect that Scott Bader would produce all the polyurethane needed in the UK, and its licensees would manufacture and sell the product overseas. In particular, licensees in Australia, New Zealand and South Africa took up the challenge.

Interest in the system rapidly increased throughout the Clarks organisation world wide to the point where it became uneconomic for the footwear manufacturer to buy the chemical components from Scott Bader. So facilities to manufacture these were made available by Scott Bader to Avalon Industries, a Clarks subsidiary in Shepton Mallet.

In return it was agreed that Scott Bader should be free to sell the product to any of the increasing number of footwear manufacturers interested in buying it and was free to do so under its own different brand name of Crestapol.

Simultaneously with the work done and experience gained on the development of polyurethane products for the footwear industry, several other speciality saturated polyesters had been developed for the polyurethane industry. ... A requirement by an engineering company to spray-coat large metal articles with a polyurethane system which exhibited very good abrasion resistance ... was worked on by Scott Bader in close co-operation with this company. ... This business flourished and was recognised as being very successful when personal contact was made with the company over 20 years later.

A further addition to the Scott Bader range of polyurethane products was a line of polyester-based fully reacted systems in solution. These were used for depositing very thin coatings of polyurethane onto various fabrics. The Scott Bader involvement in this market was considerable. Large quantities were produced for the fabric coating industry. The resulting products exhibited leather-like characteristics. The fabrics were ideally suited for use in the furniture industry for the production of easy chairs and settees. ... Leather-type cladded furniture was in vogue at the time. Applications were extended for the use of some coated fabrics in baggage ...

Having started the in-house development of saturated polyester-based polyurethane in the 1960s, by the middle of the 1970s Scott Bader had a considerable range of products available for the polyurethane industry. ... However the polyurethane business within Scott Bader had always been considered the poor relation of the organisation. The demise of the business section within the company finally came about in the late 1970s when it was sold with its technology to a competitor. Fundamentally the reason for the sale was the very low comparative return generated by the whole activity. In what had become a serious international business, Scott Bader's sales costs were very high, and so – upstream at the production end – were scrap rates.

However, in line with the Commonwealth philosophy, the staff involved in the polyurethane project were retained within the organisation and progressed in other capacities.

This long digression about the Wollaston polyurethane project is a fair illustration, both in its origin and at its end, of the workings of the company's employment guarantee. We can take it that even if the numbers were never very large, the prospect of new jobs in polyurethane manufacture was a significant consideration behind the company's positive response to the original Clarks proposal. And Tony Lovell has rightly chosen to emphasise that the staff were redeployed into other Wollaston activities when it came to an end.

Coming back from the particular to the more general, it makes sense, I think, to see Scott Bader's employment guarantee (or its 'no compulsory redundancy' rule) as imposing a special urgency on the duty of its research and development department to come up with those kinds of know-how which will either sustain existing jobs or create new ones. The real prize would of course be to develop a 'third pillar' on which, alongside its polymers and polyesters, the business might rest. That has so far turned out to be rather an elusive quest. On the other hand, as we shall see, the department has come up since the 1970s with more than one new set of secondary product lines in succession to the plasticisers and the polyurethane of earlier years.

Though it is by no means the whole story, the ups and downs of this long second period of the Commonwealth's first 50 years can probably be best understood as having been driven by the need to maintain the quality and range of jobs – and to a lesser extent the number of those jobs – in the parent business at Wollaston. That certainly explains the series of important acquisitions started by Godric Bader in the late 1960s and running right through to Ian Henderson's decade as chief executive in the 1990s. In that final decade of the 20th century it also explains the flurry of overseas activity: the creation of manufacturing subsidiaries in South Africa and the Arab Emirates and the progressive acquisition of the leading synthetic resin business in Croatia. But this admittedly complex thrust has been partly obscured, first by a recurrent obeisance to the ideology of 'small is beautiful', and second by recurrent 'de-manning adjustments' – through voluntary redundancy – at Wollaston. The latter have been made necessary by the need to remain competitive. A minority of the jobs at Wollaston have had to be sacrificed at different dates from the end of the 1970s onwards, in order that a larger number might be sustained.

In many ways this whole long period should be seen as one. But for convenience it is divided into three main parts in what follows. In the rest of this chapter we run through the years of Nick Broome's tenure of the post of chief executive. In the next two we move on to the late 1970s and the 1980s when Ralph Woolf occupied the chief executive's position. In the last narrative chapter we focus on Ian Henderson's years at the top in the 1990s. As a rather separate story on its own, we will also fit in a chapter on the record of Scott Bader SA in France before we start to look at the 1990s.

There is a second recurrent tendency, as well as the imperative of preserving the central core of jobs at Wollaston, which will help us to understand the evolution of the Commonwealth over the last 30 years or so: a tendency to adopt more professional business practices so long as these are compatible with retaining the fundamental principles on which the whole experiment was initially grounded. That tendency was particularly marked during Ralph Woolf's years. But in fact, as we have seen, there are cases of it even during Godric's time as chief executive, like the introduction in 1969 of the Hay-MSL system of job evaluation. Some of these examples are perhaps more sensitive than others, as when, starting as early as 1972 with the supply of the fire-resistant coating Crystic Fireguard to the Royal Navy, Scott Bader's pacifist principles began to be reinterpreted. More of that later.

NICK BROOME'S STEWARDSHIP AS CHIEF EXECUTIVE: LATE 1970 TO EARLY 1977

Readers will remember a notably specific recommendation which figured in the report presented to Scott Bader's company board by the Revd Bruce Reed at the end of 1969, that the two top positions – of chairman and managing director – should be split, in line with what by then had probably become best professional practice. Along with others, this recommendation went pretty quickly through a fairly well-established process of group discussion at Wollaston. Then, in 1970, following a formal decision by the company board to accept the proposal, Godric decided in the early summer – with the agreement of his company board colleagues – to hand over to an acting chief executive while a search for a more permanent successor was carried out. Cecil Philips, a man with a miner's family background, who had won scholarships to take him through university and on to a chemical engineering degree, was offered and accepted the position of acting chief executive. At Wollaston he had come to be respected as a strong manager and held the position of production director when he took over temporarily from Godric in 1970.

The search for a new chief executive was assigned to a firm of professional headhunters, as had by then become standard practice. But there was a prior question which needed to be addressed: should the search cover insiders as well as outsiders? For one rather specific reason this was far from being an academic issue. It was not just academic because Brian Parkyn, who had been MP for Bedford during the second Wilson government, starting in 1966, had just lost his seat in the general election of June 1970 when Wilson had been defeated by Ted Heath. Susanna Hoe, who discusses this episode of succession at some length (pp 193 and 194), tells us that Brian was 'determined to get back' into Parliament and that he 'did not press any claim he might have had too hard'. Against the success of a Brian Parkyn candidacy, there was also evidently some feeling at Wollaston that to retain the two top jobs within what amounted to the one Bader family could be a mistake: it might not send out the required professional and entrepreneurial business messages. Moreover, and essentially for reasons of personal chemistry and rivalry, such a double harness arrangement might not, some thought, work out all that smoothly. For these reasons it was decided, after considerable discussion, that the focus of the headhunters' search should be on outside candidates. After an extended pre-selection process, and from a final short list of two, the job was offered to Nick Broome. The voice of Godric was evidently decisive. What counted most in his view was Broome's high-level experience in the distribution and sales of products which overlapped with those of Scott Bader. In particular Nick Broome had spent a number of years as the general manager and a director of the Methylating Co Ltd, part of the chemicals and plastics division of the Distillers Company. It so happened that the executive head of Scott Bader's sales and marketing division had been lost to the company by an untimely death quite shortly before.

What a number of people now know about this first real 'leadership succession' test at Scott Bader – and an informed minority knew at the time – is that the choice of an outsider was made against what was an interim recommendation of the headhunters. Perhaps in part because they believed it would be both the easiest and the most acceptable solution, their recommendation, after interviewing a set of outsider candidates, was that Brian Parkyn should be offered the job. That was given the thumbs down. Some have argued otherwise, but it does not seem to me that either of the two chief players in this drama – the first cousins Brian Parkyn and Godric Bader – need feel in the least bit uneasy about what happened.

Nick Broome was appointed in September 1970. He resigned to take up another appointment in the middle of 1977. Thus at least in terms of output and sales his years are perhaps best seen as covering a phase of transition from the period of explosive growth, driven by the sales of the new 'wonder material' in the 1950s and 1960s, and into the company's first decade of levelling off, albeit doing so at what were for Scott Bader high rates of both output and profits. Some production tonnages have already been cited. Measured as a return on sales, profits between 1972 and 1976 average over 7% – higher than anything achieved since the golden years of the late 1950s and early 1960s, and higher than anything achieved over a comparable sequence of years thereafter.

Yet the Nick Broome years, between 1970 and 1977, were ones in which the political and socio-economic weather outside Scott Bader was probably as inclement and turbulent as any during the 50-year life of the Commonwealth. Essentially these were the years of Ted Heath's only government and Harold Wilson's last one. The episode of the now largely forgotten 'three-day week' in the autumn of 1972 was a potentially testing time, especially for a business, like Scott Bader, with high levels of energy consumption. More generally new labour laws enacted by Robert Carr, Ted Heath's Minister of Labour, and the new Industrial Relations Court established *inter alia* by them, provoked quite widespread explosions of official and unofficial union unrest. The newspapers at the time frequently carried headlines about the defiance by union activists and officials of orders issued by the new court, and subsequent stories about an almost medieval court officer called 'the tipstaff', mobilised from no one knew quite where, to enforce them. Then, in 1973, there was the first of the huge oil price increases concerted by the Organisation of Oil Producing and Exporting Countries (OPEC) under Arab leadership. The price of oil, the single most important constituent of Scott Bader's costs, increased three-fold overnight. The UK economy entered a period when prices rose more rapidly than at any time since the war and output more or less stood still. The combination became known as stagflation and only started to come to an end when Denis Healey began to get prices under control, with some help from the IMF, towards the end of 1976.

Given what was achieved in terms of maintained levels of output and profit margins, it is reasonable to claim that, with one qualification, Scott Bader under Nick Broome's leadership weathered these difficulties with considerable credit. Indeed in the particular case of the 'three-day week' it seems to have excelled itself. The key regulation

specified that businesses in the Scott Bader category of high energy con-
sumers could draw power from the grid for no more than three days
each week, meaning by that over not more than 72 (3 x 24) hours. The
headline point about this experience at Scott Bader is that, because of
a combination of much tightened scheduling and enhanced employee
commitment, the tonnages achieved exceeded the best since records
had started to be kept. Brian Elgood, who chaired an extended forum
when it was all over, believes that two important and positive developments can be attributed to it. The first was a significant improvement, at a time when the manufacturing process was still largely in a
pre-computerised stage, in the company's production scheduling skills.
The second was the acquisition of sufficient in-house energy-generating
capacity to offer a fair protection against the worst consequences of
future energy rationing by the grid. Perhaps predictably, a contemporary issue of the *Reactor* claimed to observe evidence of a 'Dunkirk
spirit' as having been evoked by the whole experience. It chose to make
no judgement about whether that spirit was maintained once conditions had returned to normal.

It was also during Ted Heath's government and again in the autumn
of 1972 that Wollaston experienced its only episode of industrial action
during the 50 years of the Commonwealth, and the first after the
famous strike in 1948 during the 'Fellowship' period. But the timing of
this action, which took the form of an overtime ban and was restricted
to no more than the 20 or so people employed in the so-called works
control laboratory, seems to have had little or nothing to do with the
industrial relations turbulence which characterised much of British
industry at that time. In a letter to the issue of the *Reactor* dated 10
October, Paddy Hall explained his own and his colleagues' case in
imposing the ban. So far as I know his facts have never been challenged.
They were that over the previous six years, since 1966, there had been a
progressive erosion in the premium rates paid to those working over
weekends in the works control laboratory, in effect the company's key
quality control mechanism at that time. In 1966, according to the Hall
letter, this overtime had been paid at 1.75 of the normal rate. That had
declined, by the time the ban was imposed, to 'between 1.3 and 1.4'.

The issue was eventually resolved following a switch over by Scott
Bader's manufacturing plants in November 1972 from three-shift (five-
day) to four-shift (seven-day) working. The staff of the company's
works control lab, though not of its R & D labs, made the switchover
at the same time. What is perhaps most striking in the whole affair is

the position adopted by the Community Council – in effect by that time Scott Bader's elected works council – and the part it played in the solution. After rejecting a proposal that a special 'emergency payment' out of the Bonus Fund should be made to the works control laboratory staff, the council passed by a majority vote a wonderfully even-handed, as well as businesslike, resolution in the following terms:

> The works laboratory staff may have a grievance, but they have attempted to resolve it in the wrong manner. The company and its management on the other hand rely on overtime to maintain production which in the view of the Council is wrong. They recommend to the board and the management concerned to produce a suitable four-shift system by Monday morning 2 October.

On the issue of any spin-off into Scott Bader of the industrial relations turbulence of Ted Heath's years as prime minister, Brian Elgood remembers that one of the leading technical and professional unions, then called the ASTMS, had some success at extending its membership among the company's staff at this time. Moreover there is a paragraph in Godric Bader's chairman's address to the company's AGM in October 1973 which suggests that industrial relations at Wollaston may have rather chilled over at that time:

> In case anyone ... should infer I am despairing or pessimistic about our company, let me say I consider the travail we are going through, while hurtful and hard and often downright destructive and harmful, is also exciting and real and essential for our growth.

It also seems at least possible that in the absence of the national socio-economic climate of the Heath and Wilson governments of the 1970s, management would have been tougher in resisting demands at Wollaston to take on additional labour during Nick Broome's time as chief executive between 1970 and 1977. As it was, total numbers employed increased by more than 25%, from 376 to 453 between those two dates.

But it is easy to be wise after the event. Management must surely have taken great comfort at the evidence of profit margins holding up despite the great oil price shock of 1973 and the roaring inflation rates of the middle 1970s under Harold Wilson. What's more, in 1974, about midway between the start and the finish of Nick Broome's years as chief executive, Scott Bader acquired the unsaturated polyester division of Bakelite Xylonite Ltd (BXL), in effect the latter's customer list and special know-how. Tonnages shipped to BXL's former customers were recorded separately in 1975 and 1976. In 1975 they totalled just under 1,500 tonnes and in 1976 just over 2,000 tonnes. It would not have been hard to argue that extra tonnages needed extra labour. There is also quite specific, even if later, evidence about the thrust of basic management thinking at this time. It comes from a note written by Ralph Woolf in September 1980 and headed 'Scott Bader's options in the present economic climate'. Though marked 'Confidential', it was evidently intended for widespread discussion and circulated accordingly. The passage is about fundamental board policy in relation to the business outlook: 'This policy, prior to 1979, assumed that the polyester industry would continue to provide growth and opportunities into the future.'

Well, as we know, Scott Bader was effectively forced to offer two packages of voluntary redundancy to its Wollaston employees in quick time at the end of the 1970s and the early 1980s. The de-manning itself happened in 1979 and 1981. The discussion and agreement of the relevant terms happened in each of the two preceding years. In other words, Scott Bader was facing its first redundancy in the year immediately following Nick Broome's departure. It is hard to resist the conclusion that he and his management team at Wollaston team had been caught napping by an undetected growth of overmanning during his years as chief executive.

Still it is pleasant to draw to the end of this review of Nick Broome's years with a number of more positive points. The first is that he must be given much of the credit for the company's decision to sustain Scott Bader SA in France when it was making serious losses, and after the parent company's remaining partner had pulled out at the end of 1973. As we shall see when we focus on the subsequent fortunes of this subsidiary in France, that decision looks as if it has unquestionably stood the test of time. Moreover, if we measure the success of decisions at Scott Bader by the number of man-years of good quality jobs resulting from them, then this decision to sustain Scott Bader SA was a quite outstanding success.

Secondly, it seems clear that under Nick Broome the Wollaston top management took a number of steps towards greater business professionalism. This was a process which was undoubtedly extended during the years of his successor Ralph Woolf and indeed, as we have seen, stretched back into Godric's time. One of the most specific achievements under Nick Broome may have been to set Wollaston firmly on the road to computer fluency. There is a reference to something of the kind in Godric's address to the AGM in November 1971, just 12 months after Broome had taken up his post.

My last general point about Nick Broome at Scott Bader is that he seems to have been better liked by non-management staff at Wollaston than either of his two successors. But that of course may be partly explained by the absence of any redundancy schemes during his years of office.

One quite specific point of detail, plus the opening of a story and a discussion about it which continue to the end of this book and indeed beyond, should be added to this account of the Nick Broome years at Scott Bader. The first is about John Hand's plasticisers. The Scott Bader know-how and customer list were sold to BP in the middle 1970s for the latter to use as an ingredient making for enhanced plasticity in its PVC products. However, the records show that Scott Bader tonnages of plasticisers continued after that sale for a number of years. That is explained by a deal negotiated with a plasticiser raw material manufacturer. Under it, Scott Bader undertook to manufacture plasticisers to the latter's specifications and on a so-called toll basis – an arrangement under which a business contracts to convert raw materials into finished goods for a fee. It is always to a customer's specifications and sometimes includes a free issue of raw materials. The deal was not of the stuff which makes for big headlines. But it managed to sustain a worthwhile number of Scott Bader jobs at Wollaston and to make a worthwhile contribution to its cash flow.

THE LONG-RUNNING AND UNFINISHED SAGA OF CLOSED MOULD FORMING

We will come later on to a decision, taken in 1998 during Ian Henderson's years as chief executive, to close down National Composites Inc in the United States. That same story, as we shall see when we come on to look at the record and achievements of Scott Bader in France, has continued into the 21st century and was still continuing when this was written early in 2001. And its long history can be tracked back at Wollaston as a project to Nick Broome's years as chief executive, and as a patent application to the 1950s. What was closed down in America in 1998 still continues in France, and this long Wollaston background is what I have called in the heading the 'closed mould forming' of glass-reinforced plastics (GRP).

There cannot be the least doubt as to the importance to Scott Bader of its long-running and continuing quest to come up with a viable system which would enable it to offer closed mould forming solutions to its single most important group of customers: those who buy its Crystic polyester resins to be used, together with glass fibre, to make glass-reinforced plastics (GRP) by the method of wet hand lay-up described in an earlier chapter. As that description implies, wet hand lay-up is hugely labour intensive and quite unsuitable when what is required is the controlled mass production of standard articles with minimum variation. But that is not its only drawback. Because it generates styrene emissions in considerable quantities, wet hand lay-up is systematically threatened by anti-pollution laws in developed countries, and is already close to being outlawed in those where public opinion on these issues is strong. It is very strong in the Nordic countries, and to a lesser extent, the US. Above all there is a growing belief in the reinforced plastics industry that the life expectation of wet hand lay-up in developed countries is not all that long, and certainly cannot be counted upon to extend into an indefinite future. Though, as we shall see, it was not the first Scott Bader project in this field, I will begin with Crystic Systems Ltd, which started life during Nick Broome's period as chief executive in the middle 1970s, and was closed during that of his successor in the early 1980s. Its position here is partly explained because it is a story with a definite beginning, middle and end. Its link with Nick Broome may be explained in part by the fact that he came to Scott Bader with considerable knowledge if the Scandinavian market for polyester resins.

CRYSTIC SYSTEMS LTD. THE JOINT VENTURE WITH THE LOTUS GROUP & THE VARI TECHNOLOGY: 1976–81

That a closed mould technology of one kind or another would eventually prevail in the manufacture of reinforced plastics seems in fact to have been foreseen very early at Wollaston: in 1950 or even before. In that year, according to John Raymond, one particular system of closed mould forming, the system of so-called vacuum-assisted resin injection (VARI), was the subject of a successful patent application by Scott Bader. As some readers may recall, that was the year when Scott Bader made its first sale of a GRP boat in the UK – to a boat-builder in Blythe. Given the cost and complexity of any alternative, there was no question at that time of using anything but wet hand lay-up in the process of building those first boats.

In chapter 8, which is devoted to Scott Bader SA in France, the difference will be briefly explained between two polyester resin and glass fibre compounds successively developed by Scott Bader for use in closed mould forming, namely Sheet Moulding Compound (SMC) and what at Wollaston has been given the brand name Impreg. There is no need to anticipate that discussion here. What we will focus on now is the experience of Crystic Systems, under John Raymond as director and general manager between 1976 and 1981, and on its Vaccuum Assisted Resin Injection (VARI) system of closed mould forming.

To begin with I should make clear that whatever the scope and validity of the patent taken out by Scott Bader in 1950, the development and application of the VARI technology was not the work of Scott Bader. That had been done by a business which was then known officially as the ACBC Group, after its founder and first chief executive, the late Mr A. Colin B. Chapman, and more colloquially after its most famous sports car product as the Lotus Group. In the years before 1976, when the Lotus group and Scott Bader together established Crystic Systems as a joint venture, the former had not only developed its own VARI system for the closed mould forming of reinforced plastics. It had also successfully applied it to make the body and other parts for its Lotus Elite car and the hull and some other parts for two of its lines of power-boats: the 46ft Marauder and the 42ft Mystère.

Scott Bader held 51% of the share capital of the new joint venture. Within the Lotus Group its 49% shareholding was owned by Technocraft Ltd, which specialised in VARI and particularly in the moulds and other tooling associated with it. It is understood that the proposal for the joint venture came from Scott Bader and was very possibly the actual brainchild of Nick Broome. To repeat, he had a special knowledge of Scandinavian polyester markets and thus of Nordic hostility to styrene emissions and so to systems of wet hand lay-up. As for John Raymond, before being appointed to take charge of the new joint venture, he had been head of the materials science laboratory at Wollaston.

I hope I have said enough about the logic of Scott Bader's need to find a successful closed mould GRP forming system for its interest in Crystic Systems to require no further explanation. About the Lotus Group interest, the obvious hypothesis is that such was the prestige at this time of the Scott Bader name in the field of reinforced plastics that there was an expectation that the joint venture would bring greatly increased sales of the Technocraft technology, and thus of an improved return on the £1m which the group had already invested in VARI.

Before going any further, it needs to be made clear that the main output of Crystic Systems was neither moulds nor compounds, nor indeed any of the material elements of the VARI system. It consisted fundamentally of know-how. It is true that some of its know-how was in fact embodied in moulds and other specialised components which Crystic Systems supplied to its clients. And while the latter were free in theory to purchase the necessary specialised polyester resins and other compound ingredients from any source, to choose to buy from a third party would have meant foregoing the Scott Bader guarantee of the quality of what was supplied from Wollaston.

In any event, given the character of its main output, the Crystic Systems workforce never climbed into double figures. Indeed, according to John Raymond, a maximum of himself and four others ever actually worked for it. He further explains that personnel from Technocraft came on secondment to work on special projects, but without becoming formally employed. It was located throughout its life on the Scott Bader Wollaston estate, sometimes in the big house, at others in a portacabin . He was himself the only ex-Scott Bader employee who became a Crystic Systems employee. On the other hand, one of the two assistants who helped him in the office went on to become a big name at Scott Bader after the joint venture had ceased to exist. She is Denise Sayer, and will be well known to all present and many former Scott Bader employees. She held the post of personal assistant to Ian Henderson during most of his years as chief executive. Then, in 1999, she was elected to succeed Mick Jones as Commonwealth secretary.

What of Crystic System's success as a business in selling the VARI closed mould know-how? Given that it made a standing start from scratch, albeit with the reputations of its two joint venture backers to support it, one of John Raymond's central claims – that it showed an audited profit in all but one of its completed years – seems at the very least to be modestly positive. John Raymond is also persuasively positive when he argues about the quality and number of the businesses from which enquiries about its know-how were received, and about the percentage of enquiries which led on to firm contracts. In an unsigned article in the magazine *Reinforced Plastics* of July 1979, the claim is made that the percentage of enquiries that have led on to actual contracts was over 6% and expected to rise.

On the other hand, the venture had to cope with a number of pieces of ill fortune in the later years of its short life. To begin with there was an understandable loss of confidence by John Raymond in his ability to go on working well within a joint venture with the Lotus Group. That difficulty was, it is true, quite speedily and satisfactorily resolved. The latter agreed that its shareholding should be bought out by Scott Bader for a nominal capital sum in an agreement which also permitted the Wollaston company continuing access at reasonable costs to the Lotus technology. On the other hand, with Lotus gone, John Raymond was left in effect to speak up for Crystic Systems very much on his own, and with no significant constituency of full-time Wollaston employees to back him.

If only from the date of its close-down, many readers will be able to guess the final piece of ill fortune which Crystic Systems had to confront: the calamitous downturn in the demand for polyester resins and GRP which set in early in 1980 and was the trigger for the second episode of voluntary redundancy at Scott Bader. For Crystic Systems the end came in May 1981, when the company board blew the whistle. For what it may be worth, the voluntary redundancy terms on offer to Scott Bader's employees were not extended to those who had worked with John Raymond in Crystic Systems. But that is another story.

PRODUCTION AND SALE OF SHEET MOULDING COMPOUND (SMC) IN MODEST QUANTITIES IN THE 1970S

Overlapping in time with Crystic Systems, but quite distinct from it, is an intriguing development first referred to in the Traxton/ Reeves diary for 1977: 'Major expansion of SMC activity commenced at Wollaston.'

There is a press release in the archives dated 31 March 1977 which is clearly the source of the diary item. The first two sentences are worth quoting:

> Scott Bader is expanding its SMC production capacity at Wollaston and announce appointments in this division of their activities.
>
> David Townsend becomes a product manager, sheet moulding compounds, and will seek to increase Scott Bader's share of the compounds market, co-ordinate the SMC activity in the company, and formulate long term marketing plans.

In the archives, even if not in the diary, there is evidence of where the major expansion of 1977 was coming from. A press release, dated June 1971, announces: 'Another new venture for Scott Bader'. In the main paragraph we read: 'As part of [SB's] expansion programme in the polyester field, a further manufacturing unit has been set up within the company to produce polyester sheet moulding compounds (SMC).'

The archives also contain the minutes of an important meeting which took place in February of that same year and which in effect defined the strategic policy which the company should adopt in relation to the development of in-house SMC capacity and for SMC sales under the brand name Crystic SMC Materials. The first minuted point spells out the chief strategic objective with admirable clarity: 'It is our intention to become significantly involved with the supply of Crystic resins for the preparation of compounds.'

However, that February meeting also noted a factor making for restraint in the development of full compound manufacturing capacity at Wollaston, namely the near-certain prediction that major users of SMC would want to develop their own in-house manufacturing capacity as soon as possible. Anticipating this response, or so it was argued at that February 1972 meeting, Scott Bader should offer a package deal 'providing technical know-how, plant and production technology in return for contractual arrangements to supply Crystic resin over a specified period'.

On the other hand, this seminal meeting also recognised that 'a need will continue to exist for SMC by the smaller and middle distance [*sic*] user in selected market areas and we will attempt to satisfy this need from our plant at Wollaston.'

We will return in later chapters to this extended and continuing quest by Scott Bader to find a commercially successful method of making GRP by closed mould forming. But, for the record, sales of SMC from the Wollaston plant started at 3 tonnes in 1971 and rose to 1,200 tonnes in 1978.

There was a gradual decline in the early 1980s and production was discontinued after 1982. Margins were rather low and costs, partly because of scrap rates, rather high. That explains why production was discontinued after just a dozen years.

6
Two Voluntary Redundancies and a Key Acquisition: 1978–81

WHAT HAPPENS WHEN A CO-OPERATIVE COMPANY
NEEDS TO SHED WORKERS?

This was the question posed by Godric in the first sentence of an article written by him as Scott Bader's chairman and published in the *Guardian* on 21 October 1981. We will come to his answer later. Here I will simply highlight the fact that in the collective memory of the Scott Bader community the 12-year stewardship of Ralph Woolf as chief executive will always be mainly remembered – doubtless in part unjustly – for the two massive downward adjustments in the Wollaston workforce that happened in quick succession during his first four years. The injustice of this memory bias, if it is unjust, is explained by the fact that his years as CEO also included events – like the acquisition of Strand Glassfibre shortly after he took over – which would now be almost universally regarded as positive. And yet, as we shall see in a moment, 'Ralph Woolf's redundancies' were in many ways just as positive as his acquisition of Strand Glassfibre. The implied criterion of what is positive in a Scott Bader decision at that time is, of course, the extent to which it serves to protect the long-term future of the business, even if at the cost of considerable de-manning.

Those two voluntary redundancies and the Strand Glassfibre acquisition apart, Ralph Woolf's dozen years as chief executive will also be remembered for the purchase of the Unilever subsidiary Synthetic Resins Ltd (SRL) outside Liverpool, and the subsequent three-year attempt to transplant the industrial relations culture of Wollaston into the rather different environment of a strongly unionised Merseyside. It was a bold attempt and the story of what happened is told by Brian Elgood, who was also at the centre of the experience for much of it. As many readers will know, the attempt failed in at least two senses, in that a) transplanting the culture proved impossible and b) the SRL business on Merseyside had eventually to be closed down with nearly 100 compulsory redundancies. For those outside the Scott Bader community, I should make clear that until his retirement in 1997 Brian had spent most of his professional life working for Scott Bader, latterly as a member of the top management team. For a senior manager he was also unusually active over many years in the life of the Commonwealth and was elected to the chairmanship of the Commonwealth board of management (CBoM) three times.

I suspect that, having read it, many readers will agree with John Leyland's assessment that it was worth making the attempt even if it failed. However that whole experience of Scott Bader on Merseyside is held over to the following chapter. An unusual number of what are called 'exceptionals' in the shorthand of company accounts happened during Ralph Woolf's long stewardship of more than a dozen years as chief executive. To make the narrative more digestible it is split into two chapters: the second begins in 1982 with the experience on Merseyside.

For the rest, and leaving the exceptionals on one side for the moment, we need to remember as we follow the narrative of events over Ralph Woolf's stewardship years, that Wollaston's core products – its polyesters and its polymers – remained unchanged and did so, except for the recession years of the early 1980s, with relatively stable tonnages of output. There were however important changes in each of its two main secondary product lines. The 'toll' (see above) production of plasticisers was discontinued and the polyurethane business was sold. They were both replaced, in the 1980s, by the manufacture of alkyds at Wollaston, supplied initially to former SRL customers; and by Texipols, perhaps the most important new range of products to be developed in the Wollaston laboratories since the pioneering days of the 1940s and 1950s. We shall come on later to the notable story of how these Texipols came to be developed.

Ralph Woolf came to Scott Bader from a top management post with Cossor Electronics, where he had special responsibility for the 'design, sale and manufacture of data terminals'. Before that he had spent four years as managing director of BARIC, a joint venture between Barclays Bank and ICL, one of the leaders of Britain's first generation of computer makers. BARIC had a workforce of about 1,000 at that time. Having previously worked for ICL itself, Ralph Woolf had been appointed BARIC's MD at the age of 37. He was, in short, a rising and still fairly young industrial manager who had acquired at least a fair understanding of computers at an early stage in their development.

His professional colleagues at BARIC had happened to include a

Quaker classicist turned systems analyst called Brian Bridge, who was also a friend of Godric. Bridge had evidently been impressed, among other things, by a special Woolf interest in group psychology, and suggested that he might find a visit to Scott Bader in Wollaston rather rewarding. The advice was accepted. The visit was made. Ralph Woolf was indeed interested by what he saw and apparently got on well with Godric. And so, when in the summer of 1977 headhunters were appointed to search for a successor to Nick Broome, it is not surprising that they were advised to consider Ralph Woolf, who by that time had moved on to Cossor Electronics. A shortlist of recommended candidates were called for interview at Wollaston, and there seems to have been agreement round the table that Woolf was the best one. That was in the late summer of 1977, but Cossor Electronics insisted that he work out his notice and not move to Scott Bader before January 1978. During the interregnum Norman Parkinson, the then director of marketing and sales, took over as acting MD. Godric remembers that it was only with some difficulty that he persuaded the Community Council that Nick Broome's long-term successor should be allowed a rather superior company car. What Ralph Woolf remembers is that in accepting the job he lost his annual bonus at BARIC, which cut his total earnings when he moved to Wollaston by more than 20%.

As a footnote to this thumbnail sketch of Ralph Woolf and how he came to get the top job at Scott Bader, it is worth saying a little more about his interest in group psychology and what followed it after his years at Scott Bader. One of his innovations at Wollaston which is widely remembered, even if it has not survived, was a scheme of regular 'group tutorials' for senior managers, aimed at enabling them to work better together through having an improved understanding of each other's personal strengths and goals. Typically these sessions were led by experienced professionals from outside.

Though transferred in part to individuals, Ralph Woolf's interest in psychology did not peter out with his departure from Wollaston. Indeed while still the company's managing director, he took the first steps, funded by Scott Bader and allowed as a legitimate corporate expense by the Inland Revenue, to study psychoanalysis and related disciplines. Later, after leaving Scott Bader, he became involved in professional psychoanalytic work.

The year 1978, Ralph Woolf's first as chief executive. must be counted as one of the most consequential in the 50-year life of the

Commonwealth. It was marked both by agreements reached in November which led on to the first actual voluntary redundancies in January of 1979, and by the acquisition, in the early autumn, of Strand Glass-fibre, including its French subsidiary, Strand Glass SA. Many of those well placed to have an informed opinion on these matters have judged the Strand acquisition to have been the most successful of Scott Bader's acquisitions during the Commonwealth's first 50 years.

What may be less clear now – with more than a further 20 years of survival and relative business success behind it – than it apparently was to a number of the key players at the time, is just how critical the financial condition of the Wollaston business then was, in the early stages of Ralph Woolf's period in the post of chief executive. In what is in some ways a surprising show of consensus between them, Ralph Woolf and Brian Parkyn have separately argued to me that in the absence of the voluntary redundancy and of the Strand Glassfibre acquisition, the Wollaston business might well have faced a refusal by the bank to make available survival loans and thus gone under. Brian Parkyn's influence at this time may well have been greater than his formal positions as a non-executive director and a trustee would suggest. That was partly because Godric was prevented by illness from chairing board meetings for much of this time. It was also because, as both a fellow trustee and his nephew, Brian played a significant part in limiting the damage caused by the hostility of the Commonwealth's founder Ernest Bader to both the voluntary redundancy and especially the Strand Acquisition. More later about the danger of a forced liquidation and about the role of Ernest Bader in those critical times.

Because they might otherwise be unacceptably overshadowed by the dramatic developments between 1978 and 1981, a word is needed about the more qualitative achievements of Ralph Woolf's dozen years as Scott Bader's chief executive, taken as a whole. John Leyland, who stayed on until taking early retirement in 1981, remembers that the process started by Nick Broome of imposing greater business and financial discipline was given substantially more thrust and priority. Financial planning became more widespread as a normal pre-condition before non-routine decisions were taken. The Traxton/Reeves diary records the installation of IBM's computer system 34 in September 1979, and its replacement by the same company's system 38 in 1983, both clearly reflections of the same trend.

Echoing John Leyland's memory, other senior managers who were at Wollaston at this time remember the introduction of planning – and not just financial planning – as a central management activity. Within the framework of a rolling five-year plan, the new chief executive introduced a routine of successive one-year plans and the associated activities of data collection and evaluation. A planning discipline, as one of those involved has lately put it, was introduced into Scott Bader's management culture, and some of that seems unquestionably to have survived. But the version of it in the post-Woolf years has evidently been less demanding and time-consuming. Planning still figures in the process of reaching important decisions, but it has become less dominant within that process.

In a separate reflection on the changes experienced at Wollaston during the 1980s, Brian Elgood mentions a big shift of focus towards the needs of customers. Managers tried to become more 'market pulled' and less 'technology driven'. In this case we are perhaps talking more about a move to a more commercial management emphasis than just another change towards greater professionalism. A similar shift in the mid-1990s at America's then substantially employee-owned Polaroid Corporation has been quite extensively documented (Partnership Research, 1993).

At my request Brian has also kindly contributed both a recollection of Ralph Woolf's general policy position during his years as chief executive as well as some details about his management innovations:

> Ralph Woolf clearly recognised that it was the role of the managing director to be the *steward of the company and to run the company within the values embodied in the Commonwealth*. The managing director was not accountable for the stewardship of the Commonwealth, but his stewardship of the company would clearly have effects on it. The account of the two voluntary redundancies which follows brings that interaction into sharp focus. Ralph Woolf's approach overall was to provide clear information and argument to enable Commonwealth members to accept the need for radical change. Later he would devote much time and energy as an educator of Commonwealth members. He met frequently and regularly with the Community Council to provide an opportunity for the council to inform itself about plans; he participated in the Trust Group [see later] and was an enthusiastic participant in the subsequent Commonwealth Workshops – persuading the company board to provide substantial funding for running these [see also later]. More

generally, he encouraged constitutional development in a direction intended to promote autonomy and reduce dependency.

Among Ralph Woolf's management innovations Brian Elgood especially recalls:

The management team in the years of Ralph Woolf's stewardship and under his leadership tried in his words to 'match the democratic process with a management style that encouraged autonomy, participation in decision making at all levels and a sense of independence. I tried to set the example by working with the executive employing the systems we had established. The hope was that people would feel ownership and be involved.'

Brian's note of recollection continues:

There are many examples of changes intended to exemplify this style: For example, role analyses were introduced for jobs throughout the company – in many cases written by the person doing the job – so that people could better understand the boundaries and accountabilities of their jobs. Role analyses determined the size of the job in the company job evaluation scheme. Appeals against 'wrong' job evaluations diminished.

Performance appraisals were (re-)introduced in a form based on performance against the role analysis and took the form of a dialogue between appraiser and appraised, so as to improve understanding of each other's perceptions of performance – and to improve performance.

Briefing groups were introduced, where small groups of workers were briefed monthly on company performance, including in particular the part of the company on which they had most influence. While there was also other content, monthly sales figures were provided (with explanations of how and why we were performing). The briefing groups were intended to be two-way. Opportunities were provided for feedback. Managers agreed to provide answers to questions. An example of typical feedback was how better communications between groups of workers would improve feedback.

During this period 'walkabouts' were both practised by the managing director himself and encouraged in his management team – to minimise distance and to encourage two-way communication.

Detailed consultations on major issues continued. ... For example, strategic plans were devised 'bottom up' and subsequently widely presented and debated.

For the first time the managing director met regularly and frequently with the Community Council, providing an opportunity for the council to inform itself about plans and management to hear the council's aspirations. One outcome of this was a strengthening of the powers of the council to provide social funding. That made possible the building of the swimming pool, for example, and the purchase of minibuses.

Dick Matthews adds weight to these notes about Ralph Woolf's participative management style – and his encouragement of learning – during Dick's time as the then Beacon Plant supervisor. He recalls how he was personally encouraged to learn and grow and how he confidently invited Ralph to his (Dick's) briefing sessions for Beacon Plant people.

Like other industrial managers of this and other times, Ralph Woolf's underlying objectives were to educate and to draw attention to the need for change. But there are also items in these notes about Ralph Woolf's stewardship which are specific to Scott Bader, like the new funding for Community Council projects. With a similar Scott Bader focus, Brian has also recalled, as notable *social* innovations, the long-service awards scheme and the pension improvement provisions, which were introduced on the recommendations of Ralph Woolf. We will look at the award scheme towards the end of this chapter but postpone the pension improvements to chapter 11, devoted to the whole array of labour and employment policies at Wollaston.

But for the rest we may reasonably see the industrial relations and communications changes introduced when Ralph Woolf was chief executive as bringing practice at Wollaston more into line with progressive policies recommended by 'human resources' professionals in the 1980s. They are thus another aspect, albeit one of special relevance to Scott Bader, of the gradual movement towards more professional management at Wollaston: a movement which started, as we have seen, well before Ralph Woolf's appointment as CEO, and which was, of course, to continue indefinitely after his departure.

Perhaps the paradigm example of this movement towards greater managerial professionalism at Scott Bader during this period was the second voluntary redundancy scheme agreed in the autumn of 1980. For it was at least in part the result of a planning process as well as a move, like its forerunner, to assert the primacy of professional business standards. There are, as we shall see, important differences of detail between the circumstances which explain each one. But evidence of overmanning was what drove both of them. To face up to that evidence and to agree an appropriate response to it called for a major exercise in social engineering. But it also brought Scott Bader more closely into line with professional business practice. And that brings us back to the question at the start of Godric's 1981 *Guardian* article: 'What happens when a co-operative company finds that it needs to shed workers?'

THE TWO VOLUNTARY REDUNDANCIES: 1979 AND 1981

At the risk of stating what is both obvious and elementary, it may be best to begin with a piece of market economy logic. Other than in those cases where market demand can be reliably expected to increase indefinitely – as possibly in the case of care services for old people in today's developed countries – there will always be demand downturns of greater or less duration and sometimes demand will dry up permanently. In the face of what are no more than temporary demand downturns, businesses, if they wish to survive, have a choice between the alternatives of cutting either a) pay or b) numbers employed – or they may go for a combination of the two.

As we know, Scott Bader's original ideals – and indeed what is written in the preamble to the Commonwealth's 1951 constitution – appear to rule out the response of cutting labour. It was originally laid down that in the event of a recession in trade the necessary adjustment would be made by reductions in pay – with the highest paid taking the largest cuts – rather than by de-manning. Moreover the pre-Commonwealth history of Scott Bader offers at least a partial precedent for adjusting to adverse economic conditions by cutting pay rather than numbers employed. In 1950, faced with sky-high raw material prices caused by the Korean war, the salaries of all employees then earning more than £1,000 a year were cut by 10%. That at least is how Godric remembers what happened. For what it's worth the pay cuts – which were uniform above £1,000 a year and not pro-rata with salary – lasted less than one year and were restored in a single step.

What, if anything, can we learn from what has happened elsewhere? In the first place, it seems probable that the businesses associated with the older and stricter of the Israeli *kibbutzim* do indeed adjust to adverse economic conditions in this way, by securing members' acceptance of personal belt-tightening rather than by showing the door to those who are in some sense surplus to requirements. And the same is presumably true of those Christian monasteries and Buddhist (and other) ashrams where the inmates derive at least part of their livelihood from market-related activities. Given, on the other hand, that unlike Scott Bader, the *kibbutzim*, the monasteries and the ashrams are as much religious as working communities, if indeed not more so, such adjustments, in their rather different circumstances, will presumably enjoy widespread, if not perhaps quite universal, acceptance.

But it is true that there are examples too of actual businesses, that is of bodies with exclusively or substantially business aims, which react to reductions in demand for their products by cutting pay rather than shedding people. Most of those which have made that choice have been either conglomerates or groups of linked businesses. So they have been able to adjust in part by switching labour from one activity or another. There are still apparently a few examples of Japanese conglomerates which behave in this way. Moreover, as late as the early 1990s the co-operatives centred on the town of Mondragon in the Basque Provinces of Spain followed policies of redeploying labour between different co-operatives as one of their principal weapons against unemployment. Some may want to argue that businesses which include even a partial duty to sustain employment among their objectives are not really businesses at all. However this is not the place to plunge into linguistic arguments. For what matters is not so much the question of whether Scott Bader violated its own employment principles in the two Ralph Woolf redundancies. The crucial issue seems to me to be rather different: how the decisions about those redundancies were reached – whether democratically or otherwise.

That is to anticipate. Here I must highlight, as perhaps the most striking evidence from elsewhere, a famous and quite recent example of the avoidance of redundancy, achieved through the acceptance of pay reductions in place of cuts in workforce numbers. The business in question is much larger than Scott Bader. It has total workforce numbers in the high tens of thousands, and by a range of measures is normally ranked either top or second top of the corporate airline league in America: United Airlines or UAL. In 1994, in a pioneering deal led by its pilots' union and supported by its unionised machinists, pay cuts of up to 15%, buttressed by a range of other measures to improve labour productivity, were agreed between management, the two unions, and investment bankers representing the interests of UAL's public share-holders. As well as the wage cuts of up to 15%, with a potential dura-tion of up to six years, the unions were persuaded at the bargaining table to accept various other productivity-enhancing proposals. Even-tually a deal was struck which gave the workforce total job security for the same duration of up to six years, plus 55% of the new share capital in what was effectively a financially restructured airline. There were other key provisions in the deal. For example, labour, in the shape of the pilots' and machinists' unions, had a veto lock on the appointment of the new UAL's two most senior executives, and the seats on the new company's board were distributed on a more or less co-determinational basis.

It would not make sense to explore the details of that famous deal any further. In any case they are available in an extended case study – *Employee Ownership at United Airlines: Big Wins for Both Employees and Investors* – published by Partnership Research Ltd (now Job Own-ership Research Ltd) in 1997. The important point to grasp is what this example really tells us. It tells that in a growth industry, like air travel, labour leaders may well see it as in the interest of their unions' mem-bers to negotiate pay cuts rather than workforce cuts as a way of enabling the business to move out of losses and into profit. They may be especially inclined to choose such a strategy when the annual growth rates of the industry in question are unusually high and, above all, if substantial tax breaks are available when broadly based employee share ownership can be introduced in this way.

In other words, although it is true that at Scott Bader in 1978, and then again in 1980, a decision was made to go for voluntary redun-dancy rather than pay cuts, the alternative was not as it were unthink-able or preposterous. If growth rates in the demand for polyester resins could have been confidently projected to become that much higher, and if significant supports had been available from the tax system, a deci-sion to favour pay cuts rather than job cuts might rationally have been taken. However that, as we know, was *not* what was decided.

The discussions at Wollaston in late 1978, and then those in late 1980, which preceded the implementation of agreed schemes of volun-tary redundancy in 1979 and 1981, exhibit many common features and had similar outcomes, but the underlying background logic of the two sequences of events was very different in one most important respect. The overmanning addressed by the first scheme may be characterised as 'systemic' in that it had evidently built up over a number of years, and even perhaps over a decade. Its reality and its extent were essentially established by comparing Scott Bader's key employment and production numbers with those of similar undertakings. Only on the margin, if at all, was the overmanning identified in 1978 linked to a recession of demand. By contrast the underlying logic of the second redundancy was a precipitous decline in demand which began to be felt in the summer of 1980. By the first of its two de-manning exercises Scott Bader brought its manpower more or less into line with the (fairly steady) levels of demand for its main products – and especially for its unsaturated polyesters – in the second half of the 1970s. The need for the second exercise arose, to repeat, from a precipitous decline in those earlier levels which began to become alarmingly apparent in the summer of 1980.

THE FIRST SCHEME OF VOLUNTARY REDUNDANCY: 1 NOVEMBER 1978 TO 1 FEBRUARY 1979

First, two partly divergent accounts of how it began. Godric has a vivid and evergreen memory about an exchange which he reckons took place at Scott Bader's regular quarterly meeting for all Commonwealth members on 1 November 1978. It went like this:

> Ralph Woolf: There are a hundred of you too many.
> Voice (unidentified) from the back of the hall. 'OK. What's it worth to leave?'

Godric is in no doubt that when Ralph Woolf gave his figure of 100, that was essentially an order of magnitude. It was certainly *not* the result of a detailed manpower study, even though it apparently rested on the fairly solid foundations of comparative manning data supplied by Hay-MSL. In this respect, as we shall see quite clearly in a moment, the second redundancy was rather different. But here we must return to the earlier one and a partly different account of how the voluntary scheme originated.

David Ralley, the then Commonwealth secretary, wrote an article about this whole voluntary redundancy experience which was published in the *Reactor* on 1 March 1979, little more than a month after those who were leaving had said their farewells. He confirms that at the 1 November quarterly meeting Ralph Woolf gave the answer in response to a question, that 'Scott Bader had about 100 people more than there should be for the level of production'. But he has a different account of how the proposal for a voluntary redundancy scheme originated. David Ralley's version is supported by Ralph Woolf: 'Shortly after that day (of the quarterly meeting) an individual contacted the managing director enquiring what policy existed regarding voluntary redundancy.'

It is entirely possible that both versions of the origin of this first and pathbreaking voluntary redundancy scheme contain a part of the truth: that there was an exchange at the quarterly meeting between Ralph Woolf and an unidentified voice on the lines remembered by Godric; and that this was followed a few days later by the submission of a more or less formal request to the managing director for policy clarification. Ralph Woolf recalls a detail of this request, apparently made by phone, which seems to strengthen the likelihood that his memory is accurate. He says it came from a Commonwealth member who announced himself as '*one of those without real work*'.

But however that may be, the steps which then followed are not in any serious doubt and are carefully chronicled in David Ralley's *Reactor* article of 1 March 1979.

What seems remarkable now is, first, the speed with which the details of a voluntary redundancy scheme were then worked out, and the almost complete absence of hassle in the process of reaching what was essentially a democratic endorsement of them. Second, and perhaps even more striking, is the fact that the voluntary redundancy package which was eventually agreed was significantly oversubscribed: 118 asked to go. Only 93 could be spared.

Because of both its intrinsic importance and of the precedent-setting character of what was decided, it makes sense to reproduce here the main points from David Ralley's article:

On 13 November, the Managing Director informed the Community Council of the enquiry [viz. which had requested clarification of company policy on voluntary redundancy] relating that the member for personnel had been requested to put forward a package ... as no policy existed. Two members of the council ... were nominated by the council to assist in the formulation of the proposals.

On 20 November the policy committee of the Community Council ... met with the managing director and the Member for Personnel [Scott Bader's equivalent of a Personnel Director] to discuss the draft proposals and felt they were not generous enough. It was subsequently agreed to uplift the terms of two weeks pay for each year served plus three months pay, to three weeks plus three months pay.

On 21 November the Community Council, as a corporate [*sic*] body, considered the proposals [and] after increasing them to include part years served, unanimously gave support.

A management briefing paper was distributed that day with the backing of the council, offering people the opportunity to apply ...

On 19 December the policy committee of the council met with the managing director and were informed that 118 had applied for voluntary redundancy, which would necessitate some selection ... It was agreed that the procedure under the [earlier] management briefing ... regarding selection would be applied.

The number to go eventually became 93 and of course there was considerable difficulty for those that had been turned down and, I might add, for those that had to tell them.

On Wednesday morning, 31 January, I guess the most traumatic time in the history of Scott Bader was experienced whereby goodbyes commenced among many colleagues that had worked, rowed, loved and laughed together. At dinner time tears and beer mingled. Some pretty hard characters were choking up.

On Thursday, 1 February Scott Bader felt empty, quiet, and very, very different.

David Ralley concludes his account with a number of questions and reflections from which a selection deserve to be highlighted:

Could it have been handled better? Probably. Could anyone have shown us how to do it from the outside world? No.

The security of the Commonwealth and the company must [now] be stronger and provides the opportunity for us to build working relationships and go further.

We can show the outside world that there is another way. For many years, critics of common ownership have asked what happens in a downturn situation assuming we would revert to convention. Perhaps we have answered them.

It will be time, after we have reviewed the second experience of voluntary redundancy two years later, to try and evaluate these events. We will need to ask ourselves whether, by choosing to go down this road, the company and the Commonwealth were doing violence to one of the core values of the whole undertaking, or, on the other hand, finding a practical way of modifying an essentially secondary principle.

Here a word or two about the economics – that is about the costs and subsequent savings – associated with this first voluntary redundancy. About the costs an apparently exact answer is available. It comes from a paper written by the company's executive in the run-up to the second voluntary redundancy. It is headed 'Further Questions Answered by the Executive on the Options in the Present Economic Climate' and dated 20 October 1980. Question 47 reads: 'What was the cost of the previous voluntary redundancies?'

The answer is exemplarily specific: £396,000 for 94 people. The Government rebate has been taken into account in this figure.

I know of no similarly authoritative estimate of associated savings. However, we can arrive at an approximate order of magnitude if we multiply the average pay of Scott Bader employees in 1979 by 94. Records show that pay (expressed in current 1979 prices) averaged £5,225 in that year. Multiplied by 94 gives us annual savings of not much less than £500,000. Add in saved national insurance and private pension scheme payments and the total may reach £600,000. In other words the company will have recovered its net redundancy expenditures in less than one year.

That that should have been so reflects a more general point about business economics. So long as a business is fundamentally profitable and production can be sustained at its pre-redundancy levels, redundancy costs will normally be recovered rather quickly and are quite often financed by bank borrowing. Despite the relative generosity of Scott Bader's 1979 redundancy package, that seems to be true in this case as well. What's more, many would argue that the final package was not just rather generous but unusually so. According to David Ralley its value was roughly four times the statutory minimum.

THE SECOND VOLUNTARY REDUNDANCY: END-SEPTEMBER 1980 TO EARLY JANUARY 1981

A good starting point is supplied by a comparison between Wollaston's quarterly output and home market sales figures for polyesters and polymers in 1979 and 1980:

	Polyesters (tonnes)		Polymers (tonnes)	
	1979	1980	1979	1980
1st Q	5,039	3,718	2,971	2,674
2nd Q	4,139	2,780	2,612	1,558
3rd Q	3,546	2,277	2,693	1,417
4th Q	3,550	2,586	2,555	1,483
Total	16,274	11,361	10,831	7,132

Alarm bells evidently started to ring with a strength which could not be ignored about the end of the summer holidays, and once the results for the second quarter became known. As the table shows, second quarter home sales of polyesters were down by roughly one-third against the corresponding 1979 numbers, and showed a significant further deterioration compared with the first quarter. For polymers the comparisons and the rate of deterioration since the first quarter were significantly worse. The worsening situation and management's reaction to it are reflected in a paper signed with Ralph Woolf's initials and dated 26 September. It is headed 'Scott Bader's Options in the Present Economic Climate'.

The first paragraph sets out the evolution of the company's tonnage estimates for the crucial UK polyester market and then comments:

> When the budget and plan were prepared in March/April they reflected the position at that time with our tonnages for the year to date running at less than 10% below the 1979/1980 budget. The UK market for polyester resins in that year was forecast to be 56,000 tonnes and we budgeted for a further 10% reduction to 51,000 tonnes. But the last quarter in 79/80, three months after the budget had been prepared, showed a shortfall of 33% against budget. This, together with our July and August figures, leads us to forecast that the polyester market will now be only 40,000 tonnes for 1980/1981.

John Goring came to work at Wollaston from BXL as a senior chemist in polyester research in 1975. As we already know, its polyester resin division had been taken over by Scott Bader in 1974. He has kindly contributed his own memory of those difficult times. It makes those dry numbers come more alive:

> In the autumn of 1980, trade suffered a huge downturn. You could drive on the M1 for miles without seeing a lorry. It lasted

several months. Here, all the resins that went into consumer items died the death. The only resins to be made were industrial resins for rock anchors, body fillers, and resins for defence industries and transport. I was caught up in efforts to maximise sales of these and to ensure timely development of new and better products because that was my speciality.

According to Godric's 1981 *Guardian* article, a total of 73 Scott Bader employees accepted the second redundancy package which eventually emerged as a result of a sequence of steps and processes set off by Ralph Woolf's paper of 26 September 1980. The majority of those who took the package seem to have left the company in the first week of January 1981. The full details of what happened in between need not concern us because the terms of the package, their genesis, and how they were finally approved, were kept very much in line with what had happened two years before. Essentially management proposed the terms which, after discussions with the company's two representative bodies – the Community Council and the Commonwealth Board of Management – and some consequent modification, received formal democratic approval. And there was at least one important result when the second redundancy package was offered which was the same as in the case of the first. Both were oversubscribed: more people wanted to go than could be spared.

On the other hand, unlike the first, the second redundancy exercise exhibited a second mismatch as well. It was not only that more people wanted to go than could be spared. There were also employees whose jobs came to be judged inessential, but who wanted, contrary to the implication of those judgements, to stay on. That happened because this second redundancy exercise dovetailed into and was to some extent justified retrospectively by a more or less scientific 'manpower survey'. The survey sought to establish which jobs were really necessary and which were 'surplus to requirements'.

We need to understand more precisely how the manpower survey came to be linked to this second redundancy exercise. Full documentary evidence is not now available. But what seems to have happened is that, quite early on in the set of steps and processes initiated by Ralph Woolf's paper of 26 September, a decision was reached to the effect that a manpower survey should be associated with any scheme of voluntary redundancy which might be agreed. For partly overlapping reasons both the management and the company's elected representatives must have seen the case for an exercise designed to put Scott Bader's manning levels – and thus the scale and composition of the proposed redundancy – on a more scientific footing. Readers will remember that no similar research had been undertaken at the time of the first redundancy. The case for making good that earlier omission must have seemed strong. Moreover the questions to be explored were made that much more complex because, within the whole process leading up to the redundancy package, it was decided to revert back to a three-shift system of working and to reduce the numbers directly employed in manufacturing accordingly. What seems perhaps surprising is that the results of the study work, embodied in a so-called 'manpower plan', were only finalised and published in January 1981, after the majority of those who had successfully opted for the voluntary package had already left. But maybe there were good public relations reasons for the timing.

As its first item in 1981, the Traxton/Reeves diary bluntly states: 'Manpower plan identified 20 people without a role out of 280.'

It is not altogether straightforward to reconcile the various numbers. But we have to assume that the diary's '20 people without a role' takes into account only those who were left in that anomalous position after the majority of the 73 people who took this second redundancy package had said their goodbyes. In other words they must have been people like Mick Jones whose jobs were judged not to be essential but who said that they nevertheless wished to stay on.

Within that category of what Russians would call 'refuseniks', Mick Jones, one of three supervisors in the then works control laboratory, has already been mentioned. The year 1980 was the 20th of his service with Scott Bader and he was one of the more prominent of those 'without a role' who wished to stay. He had already held high elected office as one of the directors on the company board chosen by the Community Council and as an elected member of the Commonwealth Board of Management. Whether typically or otherwise, he was someone who took seriously Scott Bader's democratic institutions and the constitutional principle that management was ultimately subordinate to them. He may have been one of the '20 people without a role out of 280', but he knew his rights and was determined to hold on to them. His story in the situation in which he then found himself had a happy ending. More precisely he moved on into a quite different job and a long and successful 'second innings' with Scott Bader in Wollaston.

One of those who chose to go for this second voluntary redundancy package had been David Ralley, the chronicler of its predecessor, and the then holder of the key full-time post of Commonwealth secretary. Some time around mid-summer in 1981, as Mick remembers what happened, that post was the subject of an internal advertisement. There were apparently two applicants for it and Mick was not the unlucky one. It is an indirectly elected position. The final choice rests with members of the Commonwealth Board of Management (CBoM). In this case Mick believes that an influential voice in the process which ended when he was offered and accepted the post was that of the Revd Canon Frank Scuffham, at that time the appointed representative of the local rather than the working community on the CBoM. More about him in a moment. Here it is clearly right to suggest that the post and Mick Jones seem to have suited each other or, at minimum, that he satisfied the wishes of the CBoM which chose him in the first place, and then went on choosing him again and again and year by year. In fact he remained Commonwealth secretary from 1981 until he reached his 60th birthday. By then, in 1998, he had reached Scott Bader's official retiring age.

That is to anticipate. Here we must turn our attention to an important paper in the archives headed: 'Discussion Document from Community Council: Procedures following Voluntary Redundancy.'

It is unsigned. And so, as its heading implies, we must assume that it was a collective Community Council document. It is also undated, but from the internal evidence it must almost certainly have been written and circulated in December 1980. New Year's Day in 1981 fell on a Thursday and the following Monday was thus 5 January. The paper is divided into two, namely: (1) 'Immediate Arrangements from 5 January'; (2) 'Preparation, Publication and Implementation of Manpower Plan'.

The actual date of the voluntary redundancy is nowhere specified, and in this case we do not have anything similar to David Ralley's earlier chronicle to guide us. But there is a clear implication throughout that those who had already accepted the second voluntary redundancy package will have left by 5 January.

The paper's first part amounts to no more than a single paragraph, and essentially provides that those who have not accepted the package and are staying on will be subject to a temporary regime of 'flexibility – Individuals may be asked to work outside their previous tasks.'

Then, in the second and much longer part of the paper, it is explained that:

Executive members [that is members of the top management team] and the managing director will talk through the implications of the structure with the groups concerned in the development of the manpower plan. Someone who knows the company but is outside the executive structure will assist the process of these meetings. It is recommended that this person will be Frank Scuffham.

And then:

Following these meetings the manpower plan will be published together with any appropriate grade changes. If there are too many individuals in any particular role, the executive will decide who will be released for redeployment elsewhere. Individual counselling will be available to individuals affected to assist them to come to a decision. ...

Where individuals are offered alternative work, they may decide to accept it or not. If the work is a reasonable alternative, then the individual will have to choose whether to accept or leave the company. *There is no compensatory payment in this situation* [emphasis added].

If the work is not a reasonable alternative then the individual can apply to leave the company under the voluntary redundancy terms or to give the alternative work a trial for a period of a month without losing the right to apply for the redundancy terms.

And finally:

The tests for reasonableness will be those established by the practice in industrial relations law. These tests consider the matter from the individual's point of view, and take into account hours, pay and job content.

What we have then, in the second part of this important Community Council document, is a set of choices offered to the 20 people who were judged in the manpower plan to be without a role. The sting, for those readers who will see it as such, is what I have highlighted above: namely that no compensation will be offered to those who choose *not* to accept an alternative job which would qualify as a reasonable alternative under industrial relations law. And yet even in that situation a let-out is on offer: an apparently unattractive alternative may be given a one-month trial without the right to the compensation package being lost.

Further details are covered in the document, like how a downward pay adjustment will be phased in when the alternative job that has been offered and accepted is on a lower pay level. But to explore those further would take us beyond what we need to know. For the main point is, surely, that with such an array of choices, someone judged to be 'without a role' would have to have been almost unthinkably proud – or stubborn – to have left Scott Bader without compensation following the findings of the manpower plan. Of course the compensation terms themselves might have been challenged. Given, on the other hand, that they enjoyed the approval of the Community Council, such a challenge would have been unlikely to succeed.

I have not been able to establish what can be shown by contemporary records. But my guess is that not one of the '20 without a role' left Scott Bader without taking the voluntary redundancy package with them at this time. The particular experience of Mick Jones makes that all the more likely. He remembers a time lag of around six months between the publication of the manpower plan and his getting the job of Commonwealth secretary. During that 'temporary' period, he simply continued to do his old job as supervisor in the works control laboratory. He admits that he felt rather uncomfortable – doing a job for which there was no official role. On the other hand, to repeat, there was for him a satisfactory and indeed most satisfying outcome in the end.

To complete this account of Scott Bader's second voluntary redundancy scheme in the early years after Ralph Woolf took over as chief executive in 1978, two further points need to be flagged. First, compared with the scheme of two years before there were two quite specific and linked differences. According to Mick Jones there was a higher proportion of older and long-service employees who chose to go this second time round. Partly as a cause and partly as a consequence there was an important set of extra provisions. Those over 55 were allowed to take early retirement and enjoy their company pensions at once, as if they had already reached their 65th birthdays. The judgement was made that because unemployment levels were significantly higher than they had been two years earlier, those who left would have greater difficulty finding new jobs or starting themselves in self-employment.

Second, readers need to know a little more about Canon Frank Scuffham. I introduce him here because of his having been named in the Community Council's paper in connection with the manpower plan, and because of Mick Jones's acknowledgement of his important support. In fact his connection with Scott Bader went back long before the second redundancy scheme and continued long after. Its origins apparently went well back – to an approach made by Godric to the team of industrial chaplains in the diocese of Peterborough in the mid-1960s, led by Frank Scuffham. The Revd Mike Atkinson was initially assigned by the group to Scott Bader, to serve as a part-time industrial chaplain. Frank Scuffham replaced him two years later. Later again he was invited to become a member of the Commonwealth and chosen to represent the local community on Scott Bader's CBoM.

Frank Scuffham came to win the respect and trust of both management and non-management staff alike. Both are confirmed by his appearance in the Community Council's paper on the second redundancy. He was asked to perform many roles for the community (including being asked to chair the Commonwealth Board of Management – which he declined, believing it should be an employee). He was asked by successive Community Councils to lead their training and review sessions. We will meet him again in 1983 as part of Scott Bader's effort to change the culture of the former Unilever subsidiary, SRL, on Merseyside. Later in the decade we will find him accepting the challenge of leading what would now be called a cascade of company-wide workshops on the 'Scott Bader Values'. There was indeed a period during the 1980s when the amount of his work for Scott Bader was such that he was asked to become a consultant to the firm. Here however what deserve to be highlighted are a) his contribution to the second redundancy scheme and manpower plan – in helping to win their acceptance – and b) his support for Mick Jones in helping him to secure a new job in which he prospered.

THE SCOTT BADER REDUNDANCIES AND THE NEED FOR BALANCES TO BE FAIR

Taking the two redundancy schemes together, a total of 167 employees (94 plus 73) left the employment of Scott Bader at Wollaston. Most of them, though the actual number has not been recorded, were Commonwealth members and had therefore believed, according to Godric, that they would keep their jobs until retirement. The jobs which they had held amounted to more than half of the 280 which were judged to be permanently secure according to the company's 1981 manpower plan. In other words Scott Bader at Wollaston shed rather more than one-third of its workforce as a result of the two schemes. Behind the departure of the larger number in the first scheme was overmanning, which had evidently grown up over a longish period of years and was not connected with any immediate market downturn, Behind the second was a sharp and savage downturn in the demand for Wollaston's main products.

In an interview given to Tracy Smeathers as part of the Commonwealth's Golden Jubilee oral history programme, David Ralley looked back, early in the year 2000, on the first redundancy scheme – in which as Commonwealth secretary he had played a notable part more than 20 years before, and of which he was also the chronicler. He is answering a question about his 'best memory' of Scott Bader:

> The best memory of how we did something was in fact the first lot of redundancies, because that was an unheard-of solution at Scott Bader. We had to find a solution which as a community we did together. People in that first round of redundancies left because they wanted to leave and they left with dignity.

The phrase 'leaving with dignity' may stimulate thoughts of hospice advertisements. But to the extent that periodic redundancies are almost inescapable in competitive business environments, we need not be totally dismissive of the parallels. Let us accept that redundancies like deaths are inescapable. Then the important first distinctions are between those which are well and those which are less well managed, and between those which are managed with more and less dignity. By these tests, or so it seems to me, the first Scott Bader redundancy could hardly have scored more highly. Quite apart from anything else, as David Ralley rightly emphasises, 'people left because they wanted to leave'.

It is true that that second claim cannot be advanced in the case of all those who left as a result of a combination of the second redundancy scheme and the manpower plan. Not all those 20 whom I have labelled the 'refuseniks' will have been as lucky as Mick Jones and have swapped their previous job for a better one. Some, perhaps even a majority, may well have been persuaded into accepting an alternative job for which they had little enthusiasm.

In relation to those 'refuseniks' and more generally, reasonable people must I think subject these two redundancies to a pair of key tests. The first is about how the decisions were reached: whether democratically or otherwise. The second is what balance was struck between the interests of those who left, those who stayed on, and those who were yet to come in – as future employees of Scott Bader and members of the Commonwealth. A business which proclaims its commitment to 'trusteeship' must perhaps be specially mindful of the interest of future employees. Readers must decide for themselves how well these Scott Bader redundancies should be judged against those two criteria.

Godric, in his 1981 *Guardian* article with which I opened this discussion of the two 'pioneering' voluntary redundancies at Scott Bader, offers a verdict which also seems to reflect at least in part the need to have in mind the needs of the future:

> It would be quite wrong to suggest that [these schemes of voluntary redundancies] occurred without pain. The pain was particularly deep in that we should have to carry through this exercise on two separate occasions. But the leaner membership is feeling a lot healthier. Even with redundancy costs, the company was in profit in the year to last June of around £102,000. It has also maintained excellent liquidity.

Readers, again, must decide for themselves how nearly in these two redundancies Scott Bader came to striking the right balance between easing the pain for those who left and ensuring the better health of those who stayed on. They must also judge whether in accepting the necessity of these redundancies, the Commonwealth was being false to its core values. My own answer would be 'no'. And it would be 'no' for one overwhelming reason, namely that it would have been madness to retain as a core value a principle that was bound to prove unsustainable in the long run.

I would like to end this discussion with a rather different point. What I myself find most surprising is that each of the two redundancy packages was oversubscribed. Perhaps we underestimate people's readiness to take risks. Simone Weil says somewhere that people need risk as well as security in their lives. Perhaps at least for an important minority of its employees life at Scott Bader offered something less than an ideal mixture of risk and security in the 1960s and 1970s.

THE ACQUISITION OF STRAND GLASSFIBRE AND STRAND GLASS SA: 1978

The first half of Ralph Woolf's dozen years as chief executive were dominated, as must already have become clear, by what are referred to in company accounts as 'exceptional items'. By the test of their contribution to the sustainability of the Wollaston business, the two redundancies were doubtless the most consequential of these. But the acquisition of Strand Glassfibre and of Strand SA, its subsidiary in France, cannot come far behind. As for the third of these 'exceptionals', the acquisition and subsequent close-down of Synthetic Resins Ltd (SRL) on Merseyside, its long-term contribution to sustainability may quite well, contrary to first appearances, have been positive, even if there are big costs, financial and other, to set on the other side. But that is to anticipate. We will come to look at Scott Bader's foray into the Merseyside area only in the next chapter after we have fully taken in the Strand Glassfibre acquisition and its implications.

When Scott Bader took over Strand Glassfibre and its French subsidiary, it paid £1.2m in cash and in return became the owner of the share capital of those two businesses. In effect, and as had not happened in the case of the earlier acquisitions under first Godric and then Nick Broome, the business was taken over as a going concern and, while Ralph Woolf became chairman of the board, everything else was initially left as it had been. According to a statement by its pre-takeover directors, which has been preserved in the Wollaston archives, the deal became effective on Monday 25 September 1978. A member of Scott Bader's senior management, Martin Maule, was given the task of explaining the Scott Bader set-up to the staff at Strand, a first step on a road which led eventually to the complete integration – social and political as well as commercial – of the two businesses.

Here we must focus on the commercial and economic, as opposed to the social and political aspects of the acquisition. Essentially Strand Glassfibre (Strand) contributed to the sustainability of the Wollaston operation, and more specifically of its polyester business, in two distinguishable but linked ways. There was first a quantitative contribution. At the time of the acquisition Strand, according to a valuable note written by Martin Maule in October 1978, was initially selling unsaturated polyester resins and gelcoats at an annual rates of 4,500 tonnes and 800 tonnes respectively – or roughly 25% of the then Wollaston numbers in the latter's best years. But what was acquired was much more than just these tonnages. With help from a prodigiously efficient manager, Jill Jones, and from his own brother, an accountant, the business had been built up by a young entrepreneur called Rodney Paris over rather more than 15 years, to become Britain's leading distributor and retailer of GRP, with the astonishing number of 2,000 account customers. As well as distributing and selling the polyester resins and the gelcoats themselves, the operation also covered the associated fibreglass together with various ancillary items, like brushes, rollers and catalysts. Scott Bader had from time to time been one of Strand's suppliers of polyesters and gelcoats but for the most part these had apparently been bought from other sources, especially ICI. So the polyesters and gelcoats which, following the acquisition, could be sold to Strand's customers constituted an unqualified gain – in effect an add-on to its previous market share – for Scott Bader. As we shall see in a moment, this notable gain in market share was associated with other significant financial benefits as well.

Strand's head office was at Brentford on the then Great West Road out of London. Roughly half of its 130-odd employees were based there. The balance were spread around a network of branches which totalled 15 in the UK at the time of the acquisition, plus one just outside Paris and one in Dublin. With the exception of Southampton, where there was simply a retail business, all these branches served as both distribution depots and retail shops. This extensive network had enabled Strand, and thus Scott Bader after the acquisition, to get much closer to small and do-it-yourself customers than would ever have been remotely possible from a single selling and distribution point in Northamptonshire. Typical of the small customers supplied by Strand were those who used GRP for small patching jobs, whether on cars and trucks, or for roofing and other building repairs.

Not counting Brentford, Strand's 15 UK branches acquired by Scott Bader in 1978 were at: Ashford (Kent), Birmingham, Bristol, Cardiff, Derby, Glasgow, Ilford, Leeds, Liverpool, Norwich, Portsmouth, Plymouth, Southampton, Stockport, Stockton. Out of these were eventually to come five of the seven regional distribution and retail centres which Scott Bader operates today. Glasgow, Leeds, Stockport, Portsmouth and Plymouth have survived, the last two reflecting the company's continuing dominance in the marine market for GRP. The remaining two centres at the start of the 21st century are at Cambridge and in the West Midlands.

The process of shrinking the old Strand network was more or less continuous following the 1978 takeover. Put differently, efforts have continually been made to create a more strategic regional network and one which, from the early 1980s onwards, came to serve the needs of Scott Bader's own polyester and gelcoat customers as well as those of the typically much smaller clients which Strand had brought with it. There was a gradual merging of the distribution, sales and marketing activities of the two companies highlighted by the closure in 1983 of Strand's former head office in Brentford and its transfer to Williams Way in Wollaston, within easy walking distance of Wollaston Hall. An item in the Traxton/Reeves diary for 1985 records 'Full integration of Strand and SB completed.'

In the summer of 1984 Jill Jones, Strand's managing director, gave an interview to the then flourishing GRP glossy magazine called the *International Reinforced Plastics Industry (IRPI)*. The headline message of the article was that Strand, or more exactly Strand and Scott Bader taken together, were working to 'get closer to our customers'. And yet, as she explained in the article, this was being achieved by a) a shrinking of the distribution and sales network and b) the bringing of certain functions into the centre. Some readers may be inclined to see a contradiction here between the objective (of getting closer to customers) and the means chosen to promote it (reducing branch numbers and centralising some functions). However it seems sensible to suppose that there was no real contradiction. The hypothesis must be that gains in efficiency resulting from the new set-up were sufficient to make possible a closer attention to customer needs. And that perhaps is the enduring business contribution which Strand under Jill Jones brought to Scott Bader. For it may be seen as having paved the way for the opening at Wollaston, by the Duke of Kent in 1992, of Scott Bader's £1.4m Customer Service Centre, the physical embodiment of its latterly dominant commitment to customer service. More of that later.

Even in the dark recession days of the autumn and winter of 1980/81, which forced the second Wollaston scheme of voluntary redundancy, the separate accounts of Strand Fibreglass show that it was operating profitably. Moreover, those results ignore the enormous contribution made by its sales of unsaturated polyester resins and gelcoats to Scott Bader's overall position in the markets for those products. Objective truth is notoriously hard to arrive at so long – 20 years – after the event. But if independent accountants were commissioned to examine retrospectively what Strand, following its acquisition, contributed to Scott Bader's finances, it would be most surprising if they failed to confirm the impressionistic judgement that in financial and economic terms this has proved to be easily the most successful of Scott Bader's acquisitions. It must have repaid its initial purchase price of £1.2m many times over.

There is a long-standing and romantic tradition at Scott Bader about how that price was arrived at. It is that, like one of the classic types of entrepreneur in the textbooks, Rodney Paris's ambition from the start had been to build up a business, sell it for a millionaire's million, and then get out. So when Ralph Woolf offered him £1.2m, the deal was done with a minimum of fussing. Sadly the then chief executive has a quite different and more prosaic version of what happened. According to what he remembers, the price offered by Scott Bader was based on a standard discounted cash flow formula which the company applied to acquisitions. But he does add a detail about Rodney Paris which is romantic in a rather different way. Apparently once the business had been put on the market, its founder went off to serve out in Papua New Guinea an assignment with Voluntary Service Overseas (VSO), leaving his accountant brother to select, from among the would-be purchasers, to which the business should be sold. Scott Bader's bid was successful, according to Ralph Woolf, because of a feeling at Strand that 'we would care for both the business and the people'.

In any event, and despite hiccups on the way, the employees of Strand came before too long to be fully integrated into the Scott Bader system. They came to enjoy precisely the same rights to apply for Commonwealth membership and to elect their representatives to the Community Council as the company's Wollaston Hall employees. In the process of ensuring that these rights were extended to Strand's employees in the UK, it seems that the voice of the community rather than of management was decisive. John Goring, who was chairman of the Commonwealth Board of Management in the early 1980s, remembers that management initially opposed extending the possibility of Commonwealth membership to all Strand employees. In the management view, according to Goring, the likelihood of early closures at some of the Strand branches made it imprudent to offer Commonwealth membership unconditionally. Mick Jones, who became involved when he took over as Commonwealth secretary in the summer of 1981, has the same memory of the Scott Bader management's initial position on this issue. However in this case, as fundamentally in that of the two voluntary redundancies, the voice of the community, or more formally of the CBoM and the Community Council, prevailed.

THE VOLUNTARY REDUNDANCIES AND THE STRAND ACQUISITION TAKEN TOGETHER

I noted earlier, for fuller discussion at a more appropriate place, a remarkable shared judgement – remarkable because shared between Brian Parkyn and Ralph Woolf – on the one hand and the extreme opposite judgement on the other. The judgement in question is about voluntary redundancies and the Strand Acquisition taken together. The person who ferociously opposed the Parkyn/Woolf judgement was, of course, the Founder of both Scott Bader the company and Scott Bader the Commonwealth, namely Ernest Bader. Now that we are reasonably clear about what actually happened, it makes sense to introduce that discussion.

To begin with Brian Parkyn and Ralph Woolf, the essential point of the judgement which they share is that Scott Bader needed *both* the two redundancies *and* the Strand acquisition for it to have survived the years between 1978 and 1981, and that conversely, without them, that is all three of them, the business would have gone under. Ralph Woolf has framed his judgement partly in quantitative terms. As he sees it, the company's financial position was potentially so dire that 'it needed a very successful acquisition and for about 160 people to leave before reasonable profitability could be achieved'.

He goes on to point out that when he took over as chief executive in January 1978 'Redundancy ... was against a core value of S.B. and Strand was not for sale.'

Ralph Woolf has in fact gone so far as to estimate what would have been the company's financial results – more precisely its losses – in 1979/1980 and 1980/81 – if Strand had not been acquired and if the voluntary redundancies had not taken place. He concludes in the light of them that 'By early 1980 they [the bank] would have, I imagine, called in their loans. We would probably have had to declare ourselves bankrupt.'

So much for Ralph Woolf's judgement, which seems to have had one quite specific and longer-term consequence: what he reckoned had been a looming danger of bankruptcy was a powerful factor behind his subsequent insistence on building liquidity.

As for Brian Parkyn, I must first recall that because of Godric's frequent absence from Wollaston over this period owing to illness, Brian's influence was unquestionably greater than his two formal positions in the company, as a non-executive director and a trustee, would normally have led one to expect. In a letter to me, written in November 2000, Brian was at pains to emphasise that 'over the Strand deal and the redundancies ... I supported [Ralph Woolf] totally as did John Leyland. I knew how serious the position really was and in his position I would have made the same unpopular choice.'

Especially perhaps in relation to the Strand deal, which began to be discussed as a possibility in the early summer of 1978 – nearly six months before the overmanning issue was first raised at the general meeting in November – Brian Parkyn is in no doubt that its approval by the company's two representative bodies was far from being an advance certainty. Ernest Bader's opposition simply could not have been more ferocious, sustained and potentially dangerous. Brian writes bluntly: 'My support for Ralph over that period was known throughout the company and made it impossible for Ernest and his supporters (although they tried hard) to wreck the firm.'

About Ernest's opposition to the Strand deal there is voluminous evidence in the archives. They also contain evidence of opposition from Roger Sawtell, who is described by Brian Parkyn as a 'semi-outsider'. We shall meet Roger again later in chapter 12, as the first chief executive of Trylon, a free-standing business in Wollaston with a 'trustee' or an 'in common' form of ownership. He also contributes his own evaluation of Scott Bader's achievement at the end.

For our purposes here it is enough to say that Ernest's and Roger's opposition to the Strand deal – and the former's opposition to both that and the voluntary redundancies – were entirely ideological in character. They regarded what they saw as an essentially capitalist takeover of Strand as a going concern as a violation of both Scott Bader's ownership arrangements and its ideals. They were either unaware of or unwilling to address the gravity of the financial situation towards which the business was then heading at an accelerating pace.

Something of the emotional passion which Ernest put into his hostility to the Strand takeover should perhaps be included in this record. Here are the concluding words of a letter he wrote to all office holders at Scott Bader. It is dated 30 September 1978:

> … Although it may be too late to stop the takeover, I hope you will accept what I say as a serious warning, so that none of you share the fate of being thrown on the rubbish heap as I have been myself. Together with my wife our only comfort is now the saying 'better to have loved and lost than never to have loved at all'.

It was Brian Parkyn who first drew my attention to the extent of his uncle's hostility to those decisions, taken between 1978 and 1980, about the Strand acquisition and the voluntary redundancies. He now rates what he contributed to securing their democratic approval as on a par in its importance with his contribution to the development of the company's lead in the manufacture of GRP in the 1950s and 1960s. He evidently sees it as a close-run thing that the necessary democratic approval for those decisions was achieved.

7

A Mixed Outcome on Merseyside, but Strengthened Liquidity and 'Values Workshops': 1981–90

By 1982, when it acquired Synthetic Resins Ltd (SRL) from Unilever on Merseyside, Scott Bader already had behind it at least three polyester resin takeovers which were both substantial and successful. On the other hand, in the case of the first two, namely Artrite Resins in 1968 and BXL in 1974, what had been acquired were not going concern businesses but simply combinations of customer lists and knowhow. Only in the case of Strand Glassfibre, which has just been reviewed, did the Wollaston-based company become responsible for actually managing a business with its own life and people. No doubt there were hiccups in the process by which Scott Bader and Strand came to be integrated. Some may argue that more attention should have been paid to them. But it would be hard now to argue convincingly that the takeover of Strand by Scott Bader has not been beneficial to both businesses, to each of the two workforces, and to their two sets of customers and suppliers.

Because it ended in close-down and what was up to then the only scheme of compulsory redundancy in Scott Bader's history, the case of SRL was much more problematic. And so it makes sense, I believe, for the story of what happened to be written by someone who was both an eyewitness of and major actor in those events on Merseyside. It is thus singularly fortunate that Brian Elgood has agreed to put his version of the events on record.

The story is worth telling in some detail for reasons which include, but go well beyond, its importance in Scott Bader's company record. For the student of British industrial relations in the prime ministerships of Harold Wilson and Edward Heath in the 1970s, it offers an almost laboratory demonstration of the gulf between the relationships in a conventionally unionised business on Merseyside on the one hand, and those which had evolved within the essentially co-determinational framework of the Scott Bader Commonwealth on the other. As for Scott Bader itself, there were substantial business benefits in the medium and long term which stemmed from this whole venture in Liverpool, especially the acquisition of SRL's technologies and customer lists, and in particular those for its unsaturated polyesters and alkyds. And there was even a benefit to Scott Bader SA in France: an old but serviceable polyester reactor used by SRL to process its unsaturated resins was shipped across the channel to Picardy in the later 1970s where it made possible a big increase in the Amiens capacity to supply resin to the continental GRP market. But that is to anticipate. Here is Brian's account of what happened:

Scott Bader acquired Synthetic Resins Ltd (SRL) from Unilever in July 1982, for a purchase price of £1.08m plus stock and debtors. The decision to purchase was made by the board of the Scott Bader Company Ltd, and ratified by members of the Scott Bader Commonwealth in general meeting.

SRL's product range consisted of unsaturated polyester resins, surface coating resins (principally alkyds and modified alkyds but also some urethane-based products) and phenolic resins. Phenolics, of course, are the oldest known type of thermosetting resin, familiar under the famous brand name Bakelite. They find use in, for example, electrical and thermal insulation applications, in fire retardant uses, and in foundry sand binders. There was also a speciality range – branded as Kollercast. Kollercast applications were as diverse as pub signs and industrial flooring.

The central driver for the acquisition was the wish to preserve jobs on Merseyside. As will be seen later, Scott Bader was to spend considerable sums to try to turn the business around. That needs to be highlighted because the extent of the *social motivation* for the acquisition has sometimes been forgotten. But there was also the opportunity to increase Scott Bader's share of the polyester market and there was the expectation of synergy between SRL's surface coating resins business and Scott Bader's existing polymer emulsion business.

An exciting opportunity would also be provided for the extension of the Scott Bader Commonwealth values into an area where a different model of industrial relations was the norm. The management team responsible for the acquisition recognised at the outset that the change might be slow; for example they agreed at the outset that there would be trade union recognition at SRL's Speke (Merseyside) site 'for as long as employees wish'. It was hoped that the Commonwealth would learn in turn about the transferability of the Commonwealth's values.

Polyester production was transferred to Scott Bader's Wollaston plant before the formal acquisition date of 1 July 1982 and production of the remaining products continued at the SRL Speke site thereafter. To repeat, Scott Bader intended that the Speke site should be run as a going concern. 128 people were employed by SRL at the acquisition date.

The polyester business was absorbed into the Scott Bader business from even before the outset; indications (from the third quarter 1982 figures) are that *at the beginning* it made up 11% of polyester resin sales and 35% of polyester compound (including gelcoat) sales. This would represent an approximate increase in annual margin to Scott Bader of £620,000.

Meanwhile at SRL, the surface coating and phenolic businesses continued with no significant change in sales volumes following the transfer of ownership.

Denis Gregory, a consultant from Ruskin College, was asked to advise about participation (meaning participation in management, of which he took a broad view) at Speke. His report was called 'Restructuring Participation at SRL: Draft Proposal, based on ideas and opinions expressed at a series of meetings with the workforce between September 1982 and February1983 ... in itself an example of participation'. Gregory made proposals in four areas. He proposed monthly briefing groups, with some two-way communication as a means of workgroup-based participation. He proposed a quarterly review body elected on a workgroup basis (and notes that 'shop stewards had no objection to this') with elements thus of Scott Bader's Community Council and quarterly meeting. He proposed links with Wollaston by the formation of a Scott Bader group council with representation from workforces at all Scott Bader plants. And for what he described as the 'first tier of participation' he recommended 'leaving the existing trade union structures and procedures as they are'. He noted, however, that 'some participants ...recognised that pay negotiations at Speke could not long be carried out independent of the process at Wollaston'.

Briefing groups did happen subsequently and (with help from

Frank Scuffham and members of Scott Bader's board, Commonwealth board and Community Council, and from the Wollaston
branch of the TGWU) a management and trade union forum was
formed. Some of the meetings have been described by Dave
McMonnies of the Department of Political Theory and Institutions, University of Liverpool who, in his published paper the
'Scott Bader – Synthetic Resins Saga', also discusses the '1983 pay
issue' [see later].

Bob Bridgeford from Scott Bader took on general responsibility
for the management of the site in December 1982. Losses for the
second half of 1982 (i.e. the first period in Scott Bader's ownership) totalled £202,000 after interest payments.

In 1983 SRL sold 15,160 tonnes, the highest rate in Scott
Bader's ownership. Despite strenuous efforts by joint Scott
Bader/SRL marketing teams, margins however did not reach the
levels enjoyed before the ownership transfer. The business was at
that stage of the cycle when raw material costs are rising and there
is substantial difficulty in recovering these in selling prices.

Some industrial action (in June-August) followed Scott Bader's
initial unwillingness to grant an across-the-board pay increase
(which the board did not believe it appropriate to grant – at a time
of financial stringency – to workers at Strand or Scott Bader
either). McMonnies contrasts the stance of USDAW (the production workers' trade union), which he describes as 'traditional
confrontation' with that of ASTMS (representing white collar and
scientific staff). For ASTMS a district official visited Scott Bader
and 'met with several members of the various bodies and tried to
explain and understand the confusion'.

Whether or not this visit was influential, following it Scott
Bader agreed to a 3% increase, and sanctions ceased. The trade
unions (USDAW, ASTMS and the craft unions) agreed to work
with the Scott Bader Community Council 'to determine procedures by April 1984 for pay negotiations, to prevent a repetition
of this year's events'. The Community Council was intended to be,
and remains at the present time, the Scott Bader institution providing a co-operative alternative to pay bargaining. A Community
Council at Speke might, eventually, have provided a similar alternative.

'The 1983 pay issue' was to have more repercussions. At an
extraordinary general meeting of the Scott Bader Commonwealth

on 31 October 1983, the manner of allocating the bonus payments was discussed. The main issue was whether or not the bonus payments should be made to SRL personnel. ('Bonus' here means that part of profit allocated to members and non-members at Scott Bader. The manner of allocating it follows a recommendation of the Community Council; they usually recommend that it be shared equally. There is an exactly matching payment to charity.)

Following a vigorous debate – and with Scott Bader managers concerned with SRL speaking in favour of paying it to SRL personnel – the matter was decided by postal ballot. A majority of Commonwealth members voted not to pay the bonus to SRL personnel – possibly reflecting displeasure at their un-Commonwealth methods of negotiation, and the fact that they were already earning more than people were at Scott Bader and Strand. Some Commonwealth members took up a collection and sent it to SRL so it could be used for local charities.

During 1983 Brian Elgood from Scott Bader was appointed general manager in succession to Bob Bridgeford. Losses for the year totalled £745,000.

In both 1983 and 1984, cost reduction programmes were implemented at SRL. Costs of energy were reduced; stocks were reduced. While savings were made they were not at a level to stem the continuing losses. Total employment came down from 128 to 121. Margins however still, intractably, failed to reach pre-takeover levels.

The updated 5-year strategic plan, produced by Scott Bader and SRL managers in February 1984, showed a very low probability of bringing the business into profit while manufacturing continued on the Speke site. Having agreed to spend £1 million to turn the business round, and with losses already totalling £947,000, the board was minded to shut down manufacturing at SRL, to avoid damaging the whole Scott Bader enterprise.

Some £10,000 was made available to enable alternative plans to be drawn up which might possibly permit production at Speke to continue, and joint management/trade union teams worked on them with help from students at Manchester Business School. The alternative plans envisaged further cost-cutting on the Speke site, more aggressive growth in the export sales of surface coating resins, particularly in the Far East, and the production of non-resin material.

These alternative plans were presented to the board of Scott Bader by the joint team. Subsequently they were rejected by the board. It argued that the substantial capital investment required would put the whole group at risk and that there was a low probability of the plans being successful. It was decided to close the Speke site on 28 June 1985.

The decision was put to members of the Scott Bader Commonwealth in a general meeting and was ratified, with 155 members voting for and 50 members voting against. Thirteen observers from SRL attended the meeting but, of course, as non-members of the Commonwealth, had no vote.

In August a plan was accepted by the board for the production of alkyds and similar materials at Wollaston in what had previously been the plasticiser plant. On the other hand, those working in the plant argued strongly that the transfer of SRL's urethane range of resins was undesirable because of the toxicity of the raw material and the proximity of the village. That range was not transferred to Wollaston. Of the remaining SRL products, it was decided that the phenolics business would be sold if possible and that the Kollercast materials would be manufactured on a toll basis if there was an adequate demand.

Discussions with the trade unions in the third and fourth quarter of 1984 led to an agreement for the orderly closure of the site and for substantial redundancy payments in what was Scott Bader's only compulsory redundancy in Britain. The negotiated terms were broadly equivalent to those of the earlier voluntary redundancies at Wollaston. The assurances given earlier, that should Speke employees be made redundant within five years the terms would be at least as good as they would have been if Unilever had remained the employer, were honoured. Opportunities for transfer to Wollaston were also offered and eventually taken up by 12 people.

In 1984 SRL sold 15,090 tonnes of which 20% were exported. The export agent was changed from a branch of Unilever to an independent company in a successful move to grow export sales more rapidly. But margins remained low and losses in 1984 totalled £846,000.

By the end of the first quarter of 1985, the production of alkyds was running in parallel at Wollaston and in the SRL Speke plant. Numbers of people at Speke were now down to 105, after 'early leavers' had gone. Both money and resources were made available to help people explore alternative means of earning a living. Job-seeking consultancy was offered to everyone leaving. The Speke plant was formally closed on 30 June 1985, and everyone working there either left under the redundancy terms or transferred to work for Scott Bader elsewhere. Total redundancy costs were £750,000. In fact, a small team continued at Speke for the rest of the year to effect an orderly close-down of the site. In the first half of 1985 SRL sold 6,940 tonnes, of which 19% were exported. SRL losses for this period totalled £602,000.

What were the outcomes – positive and negative – of Scott Bader's experience with SRL?

Three years was evidently insufficient time for the values and institutions of the Commonwealth to be implanted – and doubt-less modified – on Merseyside. The Scott Bader of 2001 has been able to draw on this learning about the significant impact of local cultural factors when trying to extend Commonwealth member-ship to its more recently acquired subsidiaries.

Economic rather than industrial relations arguments led to the closure of the Speke site: after three years of losses, closure was judged to be the only way in which the putting at risk of the whole Scott Bader operation could be avoided.

At Speke during those years over 100 people were probably employed for longer than they would have been if SRL had been taken over by a conventional capitalist business. When redun-dancy became inevitable, one group of workers had the painful experience of voting for the job losses of another, elsewhere. The redundancy was carried out with 'good' terms and more opportu-nities for transfer to Scott Bader were offered than were taken up.

The unsaturated polyester business acquired from SRL has continued to be important in the product range of Scott Bader's composite business. In the three years of its operation of SRL's Speke site, that polyester business added about £1.85m in margin and has continued to be a positive contributor. The phenolic business was not, in fact, sold. Production on a toll basis continued for a year or two, but Scott Bader does not market phenolic resins today. It would be hard to argue that substantial synergies were experienced between SRL's surface coatings business and Scott Bader's emulsion polymer business, though today a number of cus-tomers buy both these product ranges. SRL's experience in selling powder-coating resins for surface coatings made possible Scott Bader's entry into this market when the technology for making these resins had been developed in the Wollaston labs. Parts of the Kollercast business have been sold and others have formed one of the bases of Scott Bader's current 'solid surfaces' activity. Finally, SRL's alkyd business has continued to yield significant margins of up to £1m a year within Scott Bader's speciality polymer business.

Overall a *business* verdict on the SRL acquisition must be positive. A net contribution to profits started to be made after about five years and has continued ever since.

1978–89: LEGACIES OF IMPROVED PERFORMANCE AND STRONGER LIQUIDITY

I quoted earlier from a question-and-answer document written and circulated by Scott Bader's top management in the run-up to the second voluntary redundancy in the winter of 1980. The same source is worth quoting from here because it underlines the huge difference in assumptions about the future of the polyester market in the period before Ralph Woolf took over as chief executive in 1978 and what the management at Wollaston came to believe soon afterwards:

> Our... strategies prior to 1978 seem to have been based on the assumption that the company could survive as predominantly a polyester company and at the same time could afford considerable overstaffing. Profit levels were too low during the period to permit a significant diversification activity.

John Goring claims to remember that when Ralph Woolf first took over as chief executive he was impressed by the good health of the business and by the opportunities for higher profits. But what the latter remembers is rather different:

> I recognised from the accounting information I had seen before joining that the company's financial and trading positions were not strong. [But] I [also] misread the accounts and believed that [the company] had some cash and was not using its overdraft. When I arrived I found that the cash was not there: the asset was, I believe, something to do with tax and could not be turned into cash.

More in line with those negative views of the new chief executive about the company's financial and trading position, John Goring also remembers that very soon after his arrival – in his first months – Ralph Woolf had come to see Scott Bader's operation at Wollaston as 'grossly overmanned'. He had evidently studied comparative data supplied by the consultants Hay-MSL. In any event it was then only a matter of a few more months before he made his famous pronouncement at that historic company meeting on 1 November 1978: 'There are a hundred of you too many.'

We can make a judgement, at least in broad-brush terms, about the difference in the state of business health at Scott Bader as between the beginning and the end of Ralph Woolf's 12-year period as chief executive. One way of doing that involves two simple steps: first, to compare the average output and sales of the company's core products – its polyesters and its polymers – for his first two and his last two years: that is 1978/79 and 1988/89; second, to set against those 'before and after' tonnages the numbers employed by the company in the same two pairs of years.

Whether we are talking about the polyester tonnages taken alone or about the polyesters and polymers taken together, the numbers show similar quite modest increases for the averages of 1978/79 and those for 1988/89.

Output and Sales: Average in tonnes	1978/79	1988/89
Polyesters	19,549	20,528
Polyesters & Polymers	31,088	32,722

It is by the measure of numbers employed, rather than of its core product output and sales, that we see a quite substantial difference between the averages for the first and the last two years of Ralph Woolf's term as chief executive. The numbers employed average out at 527 for 1978/79 and 445 for 1988/89.

So, by the rough and ready measure of manpower/tonnage productivity for its two core products we can say that there was an improvement from about 58 to 78 – or of roughly one-third – between the start and the end of Ralph Woolf's years. Of course productivity changes measured in tonnes are not necessarily in line with those measured in money. Of course, too, productivity changes in core products may not be at all similar to those in secondary ones.

However in this case we can, I think, be quite confident that the physical productivity improvement of about one-third which we have just identified understates the financial improvement achieved between the last two years of the 1970s and those of the 1980s. That is because of the improvement in profits, measured as a percent of sales between the two pairs of dates. By this measure profits almost doubled between the start and the finish of Ralph Woolf's years: from 3.5% to 6.8%.

How can we explain this much greater improvement in profit margins? Ignoring price movements, about which it seems difficult to obtain reliable data and over which in any case the company has little control, I believe that there are three main reasons. The first is the acquisition of Strand. I suspect that, especially after the integration of its activities with those of Scott Bader following the move of its head office to Wollaston, the group achieved a better return for its distribution and sales activities. Secondly, and though the numbers are incomplete, I suspect that there was at least a small improvement – that is a decline – in the ratio of pay to value added between the beginning and end of the period when Ralph Woolf was chief executive. In 1980 the percentage was 57%. For the average of 1988 and 1989, it was 55%. Ever since 1982, when he took over from responsibility for Scott Bader's finances, Andrew Gunn has never tired of repeating the message that if the business is to be sustainable then employment costs must be prevented from increasing their share of value added: or to put the same point more simply – if less precisely – that wages must not be allowed to rise faster than profits.

I originally thought that the third most important reason for the increase in Scott Bader's profit margins between the start and finish of the 1980s was the development of its Texipols, which were first sold in the middle of the decade. That story is important and I will come on to it in a moment. But I now accept that in the early years after their introduction Texipols, to quote Ralph Woolf, 'had a large gross margin but their net contribution was very small or even negative'. I also accept from the same source that profit margins were improved during this period by 'the decision to deliberately concentrate the polyester business in markets that yielded higher margins and to extract full value for our gelcoats'.

One last set of financial statistics is worth highlighting in this effort to characterise and evaluate Scott Bader's business record over Ralph Woolf's long reign as chief executive: the evolution of its borrowing over the 1980s. By way of background, readers should know that over the Commonwealth's first 21 years – that is down to 1971 – the company had no borrowings at all. Even the acquisition of Artrite

Resins, the polyester division of Turner and Newall in 1968, when Godric still held each of the top two posts, was financed without any bank borrowing at all. But a combination of later acquisitions and the first redundancy changed all that. Expressed as a percentage of equity, borrowings jumped from just 3.6% to 35.9% between 1972 and 1973 (because of the BXL acquisition) and reached a peak of 59.6% in 1979, which presumably reflected both the acquisition of Strand and the first voluntary redundancy. That was Ralph Woolf's second year. By 1990, the year of his departure, that figure had fallen to 0.6%.

Yet that pair of statistics do not remotely do justice to Ralph Woolf's 'stewardship of cash' between the beginning and the end his years as chief executive. That is because they fail to take account of the significant cash mountain that had been accumulated in the balance sheet by 1990. Readers will remember that following what he came to see as a fairly imminent bankruptcy before the Strand acquisition and the voluntary redundancies, Ralph Woolf continuously insisted on the need to build up liquidity. Well, by the time he left there was £6m of cash in the balance sheet.

There are, of course, two main and essentially opposite ways of evaluating a business policy of building up liquidity, not taking on new borrowings and reducing debt, as was broadly the case under Ralph Woolf in his years as chief executive after 1979. It can be judged positively as exhibiting a salutary reluctance to become overstretched, and as creating a cushion of security against a future rainy day. Or it can be judged negatively as evidence of some failure to make adequate investment for the future. Perhaps a balanced judgement in this case is that Ralph Woolf's build-up of liquidity enabled Ian Henderson subsequently to modernise the whole manufacturing process at Wollaston.

That is to anticipate. About Ralph Woolf's years of stewardship from 1978 to 1990 fair-minded readers will, I think, be bound to give a predominantly positive verdict so far as the state of the business is concerned. That does not necessarily mean a total acceptance of Ralph Woolf's own later judgement that Scott Bader was 'close to extinction' when he arrived. But we do have to accept that by 1978 the business had become horribly overmanned, and that by the autumn of 1980, because of a catastrophic downturn in the demand for its main products, it had become seriously overmanned a second time. It is to Ralph Woolf's enduring credit that he alerted the working Scott Bader community to these crises relatively early, when there was still time to make big changes without seriously undermining the long-term sustainability of the business. He must get the credit in other words for having forcefully sounded the alarm in these two cases.

For the fact that – with some qualification about the 'refuseniks' of the second de-manning exercise – the necessary adjustments enjoyed democratic consent, I share the view expressed by Godric in his *Guardian* article, that Scott Bader's democratic institutions deserve great credit. For the achievement of that democratic consent, I would also want to highlight contributions by Brian Parkyn, John Leyland and David Ralley – and doubtless other trusted members of the Commonwealth who advised their fellow members to approve what had been provisionally agreed. And I would want to make the same points in relation to the Strand acquisition. The credit for identifying the possibility and for proposing an acceptable deal must go to Ralph Woolf; that for securing the Commonwealth's democratic consent to it should be shared with others. The acquisition and subsequent close-down of SRL will be fairly seen in a slightly different light. It is true that in this case too all the big decisions were democratically approved. But in the case of SRL the degree of management responsibility was that much greater. For what happened on Merseyside, the main credit, if credit it is, must go to Ralph Woolf as MD. I suspect that after reading Brian Elgood's account most readers will say that the whole exercise resulted in some real net gain for the Scott Bader business in the long term. For those on Merseyside the best available verdict is that what happened was for them almost certainly the least bad possibility for two reasons. In the first place the operation was almost certainly kept open longer by Scott Bader than it would have been by a more conventional business competitor. In the second place what Scott Bader offered as compensation to those whose employment ended with compulsory redundancy was almost certainly more generous than could have been realistically expected from a more normal business.

THE TEXIPOL STORY

Most of those at Scott Bader in a position to make an informed judgement will tell you that the development of these Texipols or 'inverse emulsions' was – after the much earlier development of unsaturated polyester resins for GRP – the most important new product contribution of the company's laboratory staff to its business success over the first 50 years of the Commonwealth's life. For those like the present writer who won't know without being told what a Texipol is, let me explain that it is a special kind of liquid thickening agent with important applications in textile printing or the colour coatings of textiles. From 1985 until 1989, Texipol output and sales figures were included in the polymer totals. By 1989, not less than 20% of the total Scott Bader output and sale of polymers consisted of these Texipols.

The word itself is, of course, the name of a Scott Bader brand or rather family of brands – as, for example, is gelcoat. You won't find either of them in any normal dictionary. The generally accepted chemical description of Texipols is that they are inverse emulsions. For the non-chemist that requires some explanation. The best starting point is the word emulsion. My *Concise Oxford* offers the definition: 'Emulsion (noun) fine dispersion of one liquid in another, especially as paint etc.'

The typical emulsion polymers manufactured by Scott Bader at Wollaston since John Hand's post-war visits to America have been dispersions of oil droplets in a medium of water. In an inverse polymer those two liquids swap roles. They thus consist of droplets of water in an oil medium. One of their most widespread uses, as indicated earlier, is as thickening agents, especially for applications in textile printing.

After this brief introduction for the benefit of readers who are not chemists, Barry Sauntson kindly takes over. For members and ex-members of the Scott Bader community, Barry will need no introduction. For others it is enough to say that he has worked for the company since the 1960s. Currently he is head of research and development, as indeed he already was at the time of the events he describes:

During the 1970s the company's emulsion polymer business was yet again under a cloud. A proposal was made to strengthen it by entering water treatment chemicals and particularly the flocculants market, which was seen as a growth area with attractive margins. A large project team was put together to develop the case involving all aspects of technology, product development, manufacturing and marketing. Several manufacturing processes for those very high molecular weight polyacrylamide copolymers were considered and the emerging *inverse emulsion* [emphasis added] polymerisation technology was selected as the most appropriate. In this case the water soluble polymers were produced in a water and toluene [an organic solvent] mixture followed by precipitation in methanol and drying to produce the product in powder form.

Eventually in the late 1970s a case was put together for very significant expenditure on new plants and technical and business structures to enter these products and markets. The timing was not good. A new MD had recently started, the recession of that time was hurting, and the board rightly decided not to proceed due to the high level of risk, i.e. large expenditures, new product technology, and a new market. The project was officially stopped.

Unofficially however that was the start. We felt there was something in this technology we could exploit and the technical work was continued (smuggled) via the original R&D team. The inverse emulsion was improved to make it stable, have a more acceptable solvent part, and make it self-inverting in water. In principle these products could be made on existing plant and used without the need to precipitate and dry. The inclusion of a crosslinking agent in these high molecular weight products produced a powerful thickening agent whereby a few drops added to a water-based mix produced a very high viscosity immediately.

All that was needed now was a suitable application and a receptive customer! Many uses were developed, ranging from paint thickeners and drilling mud additives in oil recovery to replacements for our existing Texigels. The use and application of the technology was patented and still we appeared to escape formal notice and justification of the work. Or did we? Certainly the acquisition of Strand and SRL provided somewhat of a diversion.

Breaking into the market, however, and actually selling some was proving difficult. Some luck was needed and it arrived in the form of a major worldwide company particularly active in textiles. They visited us to see if we could toll manufacture a thickener for them which consisted of dispersing a solid polymer in a mixture of water and hydrocarbon to form an inverse emulsion We said there was no need for that since we already had this type of product polymerised directly.

Co-operation was started, the product tuned to their application, and after some ups and downs they started to purchase and Wollaston production was established.

We learned from this. Firstly, textiles were an attractive area, and secondly we needed to work with key customers and distributors to fine-tune the technology to their individual needs.

The business started to grow further when a determined product champion, Dr Arshad Chaudhry, joined the small team, first in the technical area and later in the business. His contribution gave us more drive and impetus.

At one stage in the mid-80s we reconsidered entering the water treatment flocculant market (where we started from) but put this to one side when we became toll manufacturers for Calgon, who were very active in this area. The arrangement with Calgon did not last long, but somehow it was used by those involved to justify the purchase of a new reactor set which soon became full of Texipol.

Sales to textiles continued to grow and were supplemented by other uses including wallpaper adhesives and other thickener applications. Far East exports commenced and through the 1980s sales almost doubled year on year.

This, however, was not without pain. Part of the success in textile applications was due to the superior quality of Texipols over competitive products, particularly in the absence of 'bits' – swollen particles that blocked printing screens. This high quality stemmed from extremely tight product release specifications which ensured any lower grade material was kept in-house. Unfortunately there were many periods when the product produced failed to meet these specifications. Often the reasons were not identified; sometimes it was raw material quality, for example, and sometimes processing variations. There were many arguments around relaxing the specifications, not robust enough formulations and technology, around whose fault it was and whether to stop the business.

During the early and middle 1990s, with the support of the new MD and Dr Chaudhry, improvements were gradually made and the problem was reduced to manageable proportions by sheer hard work from everyone.

Sales growth continued in established markets, new speciality applications were found, and additional capacity installed. Sometimes the new areas themselves presented their own problems in making and supplying top grade product, sometimes we had to legally defend the patented, in-house technology – but it's all established now.

Today Texipols are exported around the world and constitute the largest single component of the company's UK polymer emulsion business.

Market pull is fine, but sometimes a good technical push is beneficial too!
Where is the next one? [emphasis added]

A possible answer to that final question might concern itself with the
company's long struggle to develop 'closed form moulding'. We will
have to explore that story later.

Teamwork is always or nearly always a necessary condition of
success in R&D work. It is however most notable that Barry Sauntson,
his first boss at Wollaston, assigns much of the credit for developing
Texipols and bringing them to market to Dr Chaudhry. By the measure
of the jobs and incomes which they have created and sustained,
Texipols, to repeat, must rank second only to Brian Parkyn's unsaturated polyester resins as a home-grown Wollaston development.

But we should also, finally, give some credit to the Scott Bader system
for having allowed this development to happen. That is partly because
in the company's laboratories the system clearly remained *bricolage*-
friendly in the 1970s and 1980s in the way pioneered by Brian Parkyn
in the 1940s and 1950s. But it is also surely because, at least in the
laboratories, the Scott Bader system is not dedicated to the dogmas of
control freaks. The company board, as Barry Sauntson tells us in no
uncertain terms, had ordered that the then current project of developing a range of water treatment products should be stopped in its tracks.
And he also tells us that it *was* stopped. Nevertheless the management
seems to have chosen not to prevent the pursuit, at a tangent arising out
of the water treatment work, of a home-grown Scott Bader inverse
polymer. Its tolerance of some rejection of top control may not always
have served the company well. But in this case it made possible the
development of a winner.

1978–90: CONSTITUTIONAL AND OTHER CHANGES OF A NOT DIRECTLY BUSINESS CHARACTER

For 1978, Ralph Woolf's first year as MD and, of course, the year when
the first voluntary redundancy scheme was agreed and Strand Fibreglass was acquired, the Traxton/Reeves diary has an item which, in the
absence of further information, might be taken to record no more than
a change of window dressing. It reads: '27-Year Award established,
being 27 years since the formation of the Commonwealth.'

In fact this 'award' for 27 years' length of service at Scott Bader is not, as may seem probable at first sight, the company's equivalent of the 'long service and good conduct medal' in the British Army. It is essentially a foreign travel sabbatical, intended for education in its widest sense, paid for by the company. The 27-year service qualification was fixed initially – as the Traxton/Reeves diary tells us – to reflect the length of time which separated the year of the Commonwealth's formation (1951) from that of the award's introduction. Later the qualifying length of service was reduced to 25 years.

The amount of money paid to those qualifying for the award is the same for everyone and does not reflect differences in rates of pay. Initially it was fixed at six months of the average pay earned by the company's employees, with Scott Bader covering the associated tax liabilities. In the tougher financial environment of the 1990s the money payment was adjusted to a fixed sum of £8,000, but with the company continuing to cover the tax liability. There is only one condition: the money must be spent on foreign travel or study. The records show just three cases where that condition could not be met – because of bereavement or other similarly personal and compassionate reasons. In at least one case the prospective recipient insisted that the money be diverted to charity. Whether he or either of the other two had the option of deflecting the money to meet other personal needs or wants is not entirely clear. But I rather think that was not permitted on the grounds that an unfortunate precedent might otherwise have been set of being able to use the award for purposes other than foreign travel. Libertarians will rightly object to the restriction. On the other hand there is quite explicit evidence from Brian Elgood about how the award is valued by those who have enjoyed it:

> I do know that those of us who have received a 25/27 year award see them as very significant. Spouses and partners of Scott Bader people think so too – Margaret Elgood describes the award as a life-changing opportunity. What's more it provided the occasion for one of the most astonishing coincidences of my own and Margaret's life. We bumped into Alan Green and his wife on the Great Barrier Reef. We were travelling in opposite directions around the world, the Greens eastward.

As all Scott Bader readers will know, until his retirement in 2000 Alan Green spent almost all of his working life with Scott Bader, most of it as an industrial chemist. We will meet him again later on but as a specialist in the development of Scott Bader's constitution and not as a chemist.

But to return to the foreign travel sabbaticals. When awarded these allow absence for six months. But especially since the money sum was fixed at £8,000, it seems that many are in fact away from work for less time and there is a tendency to choose a number of shorter foreign expeditions rather than one long one.

My guess is that for those who work on the shop floor at Wollaston, these '27-year awards' may be ranked about fifth among the conditions they most value: after relatively good pay rates and holidays, after employment security and after pension benefits. But we will return to that point when we review the whole range of Scott Bader's labour and employment policies in chapter 9.

It is worth remembering that though these awards are in some sense Commonwealth and Community Council matters, because of their financial implications they could only have been introduced by the company board. It was Ralph Woolf who proposed them to the board. Brian Elgood points out that they were introduced at a time when pay policy was moving towards greater emphasis on performance and less on length of service. The awards may therefore also be seen in part as a way of mitigating that movement, and recognising the contribution of long-serving members.

In the same year of 1978, Ralph Woolf put forward proposals to change the composition of the company board. After they had won the support of both the Community Council and the Commonwealth Board of Management, these were embodied in a revision of the company's articles of association in the following year.

The most eye-catching of these changes can be presented – and was so presented by its supporters at the time – as a move from direct to representative democracy. In any event, once they had been approved and constitutionally enacted, the managing director became the one and only member of the top management team to sit on the company board. Where before he had been joined by three top management colleagues – normally the heads of the production, sales and marketing, and finance – he now sat alone.

Brian Elgood has kindly contributed additional background to the thinking behind these changes:

The Bruce Reed report, which had recommended the split in the roles of chairman and managing director, had also commented on the difficulties of executive directors' participation in board meetings. It is possible to see these changes as part of a continuum of changes emanating from that report. The report also argued that it was desirably the job of the board to deliberate about all four tasks of the organisation, and that this would be more possible if there were no executive directors having to fight their corners.

On that new company board, following the change of the articles, the managing director was joined, on the one hand, by four elected directors, two from the Community Council (CC) and two 'community directors' elected by Commonwealth members in an election organised by the Commonwealth Board of Management (CBoM); and, on the other hand, by the chairman – still then, of course, Godric – and three chairman's nominees from outside. In other words, the arithmetic was such that if the chairman and his nominees were to support the managing director, their votes would prevail over those of the elected directors. However, as a final democratic grace note to these new arrangements, it was provided that the new board would be inquorate without one if the Commonwealth directors present.

The change could be presented as a move from direct to representative democracy because, concurrently with these changes in the company board, important rights previously enjoyed by Commonwealth members in general meeting were stripped away: for example the right to approve (or otherwise) all proposed capital expenditures above a quite modest limit, and the right to elect a panel of representatives able to pass provisional votes of no confidence in the company board. It is not clear to me that the extinction of those previously enjoyed 'direct democracy' rights was greatly regretted by anyone or any major interest group. Apart from anything else, their previous exercise had apparently been more formal than real. Moreover when, in the future, really mega-sized issues came up for decision, the approval of the Commonwealth's members in general meeting remained a political even if not a legal requirement. That happened, for example, with the decisions about the two schemes of voluntary redundancy, about the acquisitions of Strand and SRL, and about both the possible extension of profit-sharing and the final close-down of the business in the case of the latter. In other words the old direct democracy was not mourned in part because it had been largely a matter of form and not of substance, and in part because, where it really did matter, it survived.

But the reality of the new representative democracy was also in some ways problematic. John Goring was chairman of the CBoM at the time when these changes were still at the proposal stage. He remembers putting great efforts into an attempt to persuade his colleagues to seek a total of six CC and CBoM directors on the company board, thus assigning the ultimate power of decision to those representative bodies. There are clearly a number of possible reasons which might explain why he failed. My own guess is that given what had gone before – and the tricky state that the business was in at the end of the 1970s – the representative institutions were not then ready to take on that ultimate responsibility.

That hypothesis is no more than probably correct. On the other hand, and whatever its intention, the effect of leaving the chief executive as the only member of the top management team on the company board was almost bound to shift the main forum for the discussion of business issues to the meetings of the top management team by themselves, held in their capacity as the 'executive'. If that is true, then its result will surely have been to strengthen certain quite specific views and feelings among rank-and-file Commonwealth members which on other evidence had already been formed. Above all it must surely have increased the belief of rank-and-file members that on certain issues top management might well have its own special interests and agendas which were not always, after the changes, subjected to properly transparent debate. If that analysis is more right than wrong, it could well turn out to be of unusual importance. If those feelings were indeed thereby strengthened, that could help to explain what seems to be a quite deeply embedded suspicion among rank-and-file Commonwealth members at Wollaston: that whatever the appearances and indeed the constitutional provisions to the contrary, top management might well on any particular issue be furthering its own interests rather than those of the working community as a whole. Of course the existence of such a suspicion does not at all mean that it is justified.

At this stage I will add no more than that the existence of this rank-and-file suspicion seems to be supported by two published sources: by Professor Jack Quarter in his book *Beyond the Bottom Line* published in Canada in 2000; and by Professors Roger Hadley and Maurice Goldsmith in a famous learned article in 1995. The latter was published in *Economic and Industrial Democracy*, vol 16 (1995) and had a rather long title: 'Development or Convergence? Change and Stability in a Common Ownership Enterprise over Three Decades: 1960–89.'

Earlier I suggested, if with qualifications, that a predominantly favourable verdict on Ralph Woolf's stewardship at Wollaston was in order so far as the business was concerned. About the 'constitutional changes' which took place during his stewardship I would offer the judgement that it is still too early to say how beneficial or otherwise they have been to the organisation as a whole: that is, to the company and the community taken together. It is a subject on which there are still, after 20 years, a number of rather widely different opinions.

THE COMMONWEALTH VALUES WORKSHOPS 1983–8

The years are 1983 and 1984. Once again the invaluable Traxton/Reeves diary supplies a starting point:

> 1983 Commonwealth workshops introduced to consist of two and a half days off-site participation.
> 1984 Commonwealth workshops Phase I started at Wadenhoe House.

There was in fact a series of workshops which took place between 1984 and 1988. Brian Elgood has kindly explained that the formal initiative which led on to them stemmed from a resolution passed by the CBoM, in the exercise of a duty laid upon it in its constitution, namely to 'organise small groups in which all questions related to the development of the Commonwealth … can be adequately discussed'.

Brian has also tried to look behind the formal initiative. He writes:

> What neither of these sources make clear, however, is the earlier genesis of the workshops. They sprang from an attempt to help the continuing problem of lack of trust within Scott Bader. From an offer made by Frank Scuffham to facilitate matters if members wanted to come together to explore issues of trust, a group was formed from across the community. The group, which contained people who were members of most of the bodies of company and Commonwealth, including Ralph Woolf, met on nine occasions. The idea emerged to explore trust *within* this group. The group then felt that it would be good if the rest of the community had this experience too. Frank Scuffham was asked to put forward proposals as to how this might be done.

Whether they were known from the start as 'values' workshops, I am not sure. What is certain is that one of the principal outcomes of the series was a list of values which became known as 'the Scott Bader values' and which will be enumerated shortly. What is certain too is that all the workshops in the series shared one key feature. They were headed by Frank Scuffham, who managed to combine the roles of director, facilitator and champion. He has already been introduced. In a communication with Brian Elgood, Frank Scuffham has himself explained what happened next:

I consulted widely within the community and outside. As a member of the CBoM, I was very aware of the issues of membership of the Commonwealth; what did it mean? How were members to be selected? What training or initiation did they need? Each applicant had to be employed by the company for 18 months before they were able to apply. An assessment was made by members of the CBoM in an interview with both the applicant and their work group to determine whether they 'would make a good Commonwealth member'. They were asked to read the constitution and indicate whether they were willing to accept it as the basis for membership. Applicants would answer 'yes', but later express concern about what that constitution really meant.

So I made an analysis of the constitution to draw out and to make clear the fundamental basis on which it was built. Whilst it is a specifically Christian document expressed in Christian language, it was important, since within the community there were Christians, Jews, Muslims, Sikhs, agnostics and atheists, that the basic values should be expressed in non-religious/secular language. These were discussed and accepted as helpful by the workshops' steering group [which consisted of management and non-management members of Scott Bader's institutions].

Brian Elgood goes on:

Before each of the phases of workshops, case studies were prepared, volunteer facilitators were organised and a video was commissioned. The investment in time was considerable and there was a substantial financial cost.

While generically Commonwealth workshops, they eventually became known as values workshops. As such they set out to explore 'values in and through business'. The participants were enabled to tease out the values found in the constitution – helped by Frank Scuffham's analysis referred to earlier – and do case studies from which they could recommend actions arising from specific values. They were thus offered some experience in using the values in possible work situations. All the workshops were principally facilitated by Frank Scuffham with the help of a team of facilitators.

Notwithstanding Frank Scuffham's conclusively remembered origin of these workshops in his so-called 'trust' group of 1982, it is also possible that, in their later stages, they came to be effected by what were clearly two of the most traumatic voting issues which had ever come before Scott Bader in a general meeting of Commonwealth members. As an indication of the strength and the pain of the feelings generated at Wollaston by the whole SRL affair, I will quote here something said to Professor Jack Quarter, not indeed about the decision to exclude ex-SRL employees from profit shares in 1983, but about the second – and in many ways more traumatic – decision to close the whole Merseyside business down, which came a year later. The speaker is Dick Matthews, who spent more than 30 years with Scott Bader at Wollaston. Having started in the company's unskilled blue-collar ranks in the 1960s, he had climbed up to be a senior line manager well before his retirement in the year 2000. At various times he has served on both the company board and the CBoM. Here is what he told Jack Quarter about the decision to close down SRL:

> There I was, a working lad, making a decision to close them down. I never thought I had to go on that board and make that decision. In a conventional company you can blame the so-called bosses; but we only have ourselves to blame.

To repeat, a direct link between these value workshops and the difficulties experienced by Scott Bader on Merseyside is pure speculation on my part. Yet it seems intuitively possible that what happened on Merseyside was at least a psychological factor in the balance of forces which coloured the later stages of the values workshops.

In any event, following the CBoM's resolution of 1983 and the approval by the company board of the expenditures to be incurred, a first round of workshops was held in 1984. These were three-day events held off-site at company expense and centred round a weekend. Attendance was voluntary, but substantial efforts were made to encourage Commonwealth members to sign up. Mick Jones, by then Commonwealth secretary, wrote a flyer: 'Everyone can experience the pleasure of going on these workshops which are free and open to all.'

In all there were 11 of these weekend events during 1984, and about

150 people – or more than half of the then Commonwealth members – went along. Two objectives were defined:

1 To create greater understanding of what the Commonwealth should or could mean in order to create a deeper commitment to it.
2 To develop a greater understanding of each other as human beings and to value our distinctive contributions and roles.

Between this first set in 1984 and the last set in 1988, there was a great deal of what one might call processing and participatory staff work. Feedback from the 1984 set was collected and analysed. There were extensive small group discussions on-site. All this constituted Phase 2. Out of that, in turn, emerged the beginnings of an agenda for the third and final phase of these values workshops. Brian Elgood remembers that it was at this point that a consensus began to develop to the effect that the company's traditional language of 'common ownership' should be abandoned and replaced with the language of 'trusteeship', a change which has stuck – at least in part – and which is perhaps the single most important and specific outcome of the workshop series as a whole. Commonwealth members were thus encouraged to think of themselves as trustees of the Scott Bader endowment rather than as owners of it. As trustees or stewards they had an obvious duty to pass it on in a state at least as good as it had been when they took it over.

During 1987 a small team, including the holders of the two top positions – Godric Bader and Ralph Woolf – together with Frank Scuffham and Peter Mattli, combined to take the material forward in a way which could lead on to a final workshop series in 1988. Peter Mattli was in the 1980s, as indeed he had been for many years since joining the company in the early 1950s, the company's top works chemist. However, and equally important in this context, he had come over the years to be much respected, along with Godric, as the voice and conscience of the 'original Scott Bader values'.

To introduce the final 1988 phase of these workshops, a letter was written to all Commonwealth members and signed jointly by Christine Riddle and Godric, as holding the chairs of the CBoM and the company respectively. The letter included an injunction to the effect that all members of the Commonwealth would be expected to attend a workshop. It also defined the main purpose first of Scott Bader and second of the final set of values workshops: SB's main purpose was to 'practise and propagate the Commonwealth's beliefs and values'. That of the workshops was to 'enable us to live out our lives in and through business'.

This final series of workshops lasted for two and a half days and were apparently very well attended. Their most specific output was a defining list of 'Scott Bader values', drawn from the Constitution, of which there are seven, namely:

> Overall Love
> Love of Neighbour
> Peace
> Integrity
> Self-Giving
> Stewardship
> Equality

It may help to remind ourselves of Frank Scuffham's comment about his aim of expressing the Scott Bader values in non-religious or secular language. He has explained that 'overall love' was used to stand for God or whatever else participants felt to be the 'ground of our being', and added that the same participants hardly ever claimed to find difficulty with the words used to define what the values meant to them.

But it also makes sense, I think, to remind readers of the warning expressed in his report on Scott Bader by the Revd Bruce Reed in 1979, namely that there can be negative consequences if people are required to commit themselves to a set of ideals which they may reasonably feel are beyond their reach.

But, in any case, I suspect that it is not mainly by specific declaratory outcomes that the worth of a series of events like these Scott Bader values workshops should be judged. They have a more immediate function: to make the rank and file, that is the non-management people, feel at home, feel confident enough to speak their minds, and more generally to enjoy themselves and let off steam. If at the same time those rank-and-file participants – and indeed at least as importantly the managers – could be reminded that despite any appearances to the contrary Scott Bader differed from conventional capitalist businesses in some important ways, even if not in others – that is probably the best that the promoters of these events could reasonably have hoped for. Alas, there were no equivalents of exit polls which can guide our judgements whether those goals were achieved.

What there is, on the other hand, is some important evidence from

Mick Jones in his contribution to Scott Bader's millennium oral history project. In his words, the workshops sought to 'bring out in laymen's terms what the constitution and the philosophy of common ownership actually meant'. But perhaps more importantly, and looking back on what actually happened, he expresses the view that 'by and large ... the workshops were very successful, people that did attend were pleased and I think that the majority attended.' He argues further that the workshops helped the participants 'to understand what other people's problems were and that we were all interdependent on one another'. And he goes on: 'So that was the upside, the fact that people met other people and widened their scope of contacts within the organisation.'

The credibility of Mick Jones's account is reinforced, I think, by the criticisms which he also reports: 'One of the criticisms was that they were too spiritually inclined and this was probably due to the fact that they were run mostly by industrial chaplains who obviously had a very large spiritual input.' The team designing the workshops might respond that, while they were concerned with things of the spirit, the workshops were designed to be couched in non-religious terms.

And then a more general and inescapably persuasive criticism:

> The downside was that when people came back to Wollaston having attended a three-day workshop and having been wined and dined in good company, and came back on a high, then they didn't see anything different happening within the organisation after the workshops and that I think was a bit of a let-down.

Many of us will be tempted to respond with the question: Realistically, could that let-down have been avoided? Frank Scuffham argues that it might have been, by proceeding with a next phase where there would be workshop-type events held for groups of people within the same department. This phase was not proceeded with at the time, though something like it would appear in the late 1990s.

ATTEMPTS AT INSTITUTIONAL REFORM

At the request of Frank Scuffham, Brian Elgood has contributed the following paragraphs to provide an accessible record of these attempts in the late 1980s. Brian writes:

As was already indicated in chapter 2, the binary nature of Scott

Bader's constitution has not always been as helpful to the growth of the organisation or of individual members as had been hoped. Attempts have been made to *understand* this (as in the values workshops just discussed) and to reform the organisation's institutions. One of these attempts took place in the late 1980s.

The work went on from 1987 to 1989. A joint meeting of the company and Commonwealth boards early in 1988 noted *inter alia* that the separation of the two boards 'provides competition, conflict and distrust within the organisation. The two-board structure encourages the view (which is held by the majority) of separation into:

Values and philosophy – the Commonwealth board

Business and the material world – company board.'

The same meeting concluded that the separation 'impedes the progress of the organisation' and decided that 'a working party from the two boards [will be formed] to develop the means for an integration of the functions of the two boards'.

It is clear that from the outset this process had the support of both chairs and of the managing director, Ralph Woolf. Working parties were set up to explore both future structure and the setting up of a learning centre to provide understanding. The boards held joint meetings over much of the 1988/89 period to experience working together on 'value-based issues'.

The Joint Boards Structures Group developed a model which would better enable the carrying out of all tasks within one organisation. The group consisted of elected members of both company and Commonwealth boards facilitated by Frank Scuffham. After much work, they developed a model which envisaged a Policy Board and an Executive Board. Both would deal with all of the four tasks distinguished by the Bruce Reed report. Both would have elected directors, and there would be equal numbers of elected directors to appointed ones on the executive board. They also recommended a Community Council with extended powers. When this proposal was discussed by a joint meeting of the two boards in September 1989, and after the appointment of a new chairman, it was agreed to go on meeting jointly, but to put the 'work on new structures' in abeyance for six months.

The proposal was not subsequently put to members in this form, but further work on the structures went on into the 1990s.

It may be appropriate to see these attempts at institutional reform as forming a continuum with the change in the composition of the company board implemented in 1979. All were intended to improve the performance of Scott Bader institutions *and* to improve the progress of the whole Scott Bader organisation.

TAILPIECE

As a tailpiece to this long discussion of the Scott Bader values workshops and of the efforts at institutional reform in the late 1980s, I want to quote, without any comment, from a letter written to the *Reactor* by Ralph Woolf in the closing days of his stewardship as managing director, when his retirement had already been announced and after he had *not* been invited to succeed Godric as company chairman. The date of publication in the *Reactor* is April 1990. The extract from the letter can in fact serve as a tailpiece not only to those values workshops but also to Ralph Woolf's long 12-year stewardship of the business:

> My position is that through personal growth will come organisational growth. Individual growth comes through love. I had better say what I mean by love, which is, the will to extend oneself for the purpose of nurturing one's own or another's spiritual growth.

Earlier in the same letter the retiring chief steward had written:

> When I was rejected as chairman, Godric told me that it was because, among other things, I had failed to create an appropriate management style, and that the Community Council would not accept me as chairman.

Towards the end of the letter comes a sentence with rather different but also vitally important subject matter: 'Never again do I want Scott Bader to be as near extinction as it was when I became MD.'

As we have seen, by building up a strong liquidity in Scott Bader's balance sheet, the retiring chief steward had indeed created a most valuable cushion against that happening.

8

Scott Bader France

Of the four Scott Bader overseas manufacturing subsidiaries which were operational in the year 2000, that in France was easily the oldest, by a margin of some 25 years, and the most substantial. Measured by employment numbers its total workforce, of approximately 110, was a little less than one-third of that of the parent business in the UK. Measured in tonnes of output and sales, the French subsidiary was comfortably more than half the size of its parent.

But as compared with the three other overseas manufacturing subsidiaries – in the Middle East, in South Africa, and (in fact if not by formal legal status) in Croatia – the Scott Bader business in France differs perhaps most importantly in the logic of its origin. The other three all result from a policy decision taken in the early 1990s aimed at strengthening the sustainability of the Wollaston parent, to be achieved by the setting up – or acquisition – of overseas subsidiaries which would then make significant contributions from their profits, and in other ways, to the parent's overheads in general, and to its research and development costs in particular. We shall see in the next chapter how far that policy has succeeded. By contrast, and despite what can now be seen as two false starts, the Scott Bader subsidiary in France was set up from the outset to be much more of a business in its own right. It had perhaps also a second start-up purpose: to serve as something of a Scott Bader bridgehead in what was then normally called the European Economic Community (EEC). Moreover, down to the end of the year 2000 it had never contributed any of its profits – or paid any dividends – to Wollaston.

Jean-Marc Bain joined the French subsidiary in 1996, and took over as chief executive in early 1999. He writes persuasively that what he 'discovered' when he joined was a 'rather radical company' and then gives two quite separate reasons for that judgement. The first was its small size, at least relative to the giants which dominate the world of industrial chemicals. Second, he discovered a company which was 'not driven exclusively by shareholder value'. It was for these reasons, he writes, that the company appealed to him.

They are also two of the reasons which make its record and survival, over what had reached a total of 35 years by the year 2000, of interest and importance to people outside the circle of the Scott Bader community alone. It is true that its Wollaston parent has shown over a significantly longer period that business survival in the world of international chemicals, together with at least a tolerable level of economic prosperity, are compatible with small size and with a set of drivers more subtle and complex than shareholder value by itself. All the same, it is good news that the Scott Bader business in France has shown that the same achievements are possible on a notably even smaller scale and with no more than a watered-down version of the huge advantage enjoyed by Wollaston from the early 1950s onwards, by virtue of its world lead in the manufacture of the new material of glass fibre reinforced plastics (GRP). What's more, the French business has achieved what it has achieved as a *subsidiary* of its Wollaston parent and as a subsidiary which, at least since 1974, has had to rely entirely, or almost entirely, on its own financial resources. I should add that it is not only its own survival and reasonable prosperity which it has managed to finance. Especially since the late 1980s it has itself financed significant growth, including the acquisition of a business in south-western France engaged in the so-called closed mould forming of GRP, and called simply Scott Bader Composites. More of that later.

As for the relationship between the French subsidiary and its Wollaston parent, that has in fact evolved in a rather unusual way and reached a rather unusual equilibrium. In law the subsidiary has always been constitutionally subordinate to its parent. But in practice, since the mid-1970s it has been substantially free to make its own decisions and manage its own affairs. Since about the same time too, there has been an elegant equilibrium in the financial relationship between the two businesses. Scott Bader in France, to repeat, has had to rely almost entirely on its own financial resources. But conversely it has never been required to pay a dividend on its share capital which remains 100% owned by its parent. Though for accounting purposes its financial results are consolidated with those of its parent, it is free in practice to spend its own profits as it chooses. But it must make good its own losses. In many ways this is a relationship between subsidiary and parent which looks like an almost exemplary model of 'subsidiarity': that is of a relationship in which the maximum possible responsibility and autonomy is assigned to the subordinate entity. Though he makes no explicit mention of this feature in his account of why Scott Bader in France appealed to him, it is hard not to believe that Jean-Marc Bain rated it rather highly.

But of course in business, perhaps even more than in other spheres of human activity, not much is for ever. As readers will see in the Postscript to chapter 9 of this book, Scott Bader's strategy for the first decade of the 21st century is based on treating all its operations in Europe, including its Wollaston operations, as a single whole. The exemplary subsidiarity in the relationship between Wollaston and Scott Bader France was thus already, when the Postscript and this paragraph were written, substantially in the past.

The 35-year history of the business is divided by Stuart Fearon, who was chief executive from 1974 until his retirement in early 1999, into four successive periods with the following dates and characterisations:

> 1966–1972: Chaos
> 1972–1980: Struggle to survive
> 1980–1986: Consolidation
> 1986–2000: Growth and expansion

I shall adopt broadly the same breakdown into sequential time periods in what follows.

TWO FALSE STARTS AND TWO JOINT VENTURES IN AMIENS: 1966–72

The first item which relates to France in the Traxton/Reeves diary is dated not in 1966 but three years earlier: '1963: Production of Scott Bader Emulsion Polymers commenced in France.'

What the diary does not tell us is that this involved not a Scott Bader manufacturing operation but no more than a licensing agreement. That had been negotiated with a French private company called Promaco, located in the industrial town of Mulhouse in eastern France near the borders with Germany and Switzerland. The licensing agreement was unusual in Scott Bader's history in that it covered not polyester resins but a number of specified emulsion polymers. Between 1963 and 1974 the diary goes on to identify a number of new developments and changes relating to Scott Bader in France:

1966: Creation of tripartite venture in France by Promaco, SA

Sturge and Scott Bader to manufacture and sell polymer emulsions. New production plant at Amiens in France.
1967: Withdrawal of Promaco, France, from joint venture. Company becomes Scott Bader Sturge, a 50:50 joint venture.
1974: SA Sturge withdraws from French joint venture. Company becomes Scott Bader SA (Société Anonyme).

At around the time when the tripartite venture was giving place to the 50:50 arrangement with SA Sturge, we find a positive if also circumspect set of comments on developments in France included in Godric Bader's chairman's report to the Wollaston annual general meeting on 26 November 1967. Godric seems to be unsure whether Promaco is still involved or not. For while he names the company 'SBPS' – the initials of Scott Bader, Promaco and Sturge – in the same sentence he also refers to Scott Bader's 'half-share' with Sturge. However that may be explained, what is more important for our purposes here is what Godric had to say about the actual state of the business. It had evidently *not* got off to a flying start:

> Whilst the formation [of the company in France] has proceeded according to plan and according to the formation costs budgeted, the development of sales has not done so. In this case the estimates were not prepared by our own people alone but in collaboration with our French colleagues who had some claim to know their markets.

Nevertheless Godric went on to affirm his belief in the basic good sense of the project:

> This is not to question at all our move to participate in a company in the EEC, as this is a good move, but to say that the likelihood of quick growth and any great royalty return to us here is further ahead in time than originally envisaged.

Godric in that report offered no estimate of just when a 'any great royalty return' might be expected. As it turned out the first actual royalty payment made to Wollaston by the SBSA in France was not transmitted until 1998. But that is to anticipate. Here a few words are needed about SA Sturge, which was to soldier on as Scott Bader's 50:50 partner until 1974, and about Amiens itself.

SA Sturge was also the subsidiary of a UK parent, being wholly owned by the private company John & E. Sturge based in Birmingham.

Its chief activity was the manufacture of calcium carbonate, which gave it valuable links with the French wallpaper industry, an important market for the joint venture's emulsion polymers.

But much more than for its links with the wallpaper industry, SA Sturge needs to be celebrated in this history for having been responsible for bringing Scott Bader to Amiens. Sturge itself had evidently been operating there since the 1930s. There may be disadvantages – at least as compared with the Wollaston Hall estate – about the actual site in Amiens: about three and a half acres in extent on the west side of the town. And it need hardly be said that its unpretentious and functional buildings cannot compete with those of Wollaston Hall even if the reactors on both sites have to be housed, because of their height, in fairly similar structures rising three storeys above ground. Still SBSA was happy enough to remain a tenant of Sturge for many years and eventually, in 1991, to make an offer for the freehold which was accepted. In fact, though very different in size and in other ways, the sites in both Wollaston and Amiens share an important common feature: both are more or less surrounded by high-density housing, so both have to face similarly tough anti-pollution rules and have strictly limited scope for expansion. If either ever becomes willing and able to compete in size with the giants of the industry it will have to move elsewhere to do so.

But of course it is the town itself, the capital of France's pre-1789 province of Picardy, rather than the industrial site they have occupied since 1966, which deserves to be celebrated by Scott Bader personnel. As many readers will know, Amiens boasts one of the finest and oldest of the great medieval Gothic cathedrals in France, having been built to virtual completion as early as the 13th century. It was greatly admired by one of Britain's most famous Victorians, John Ruskin, whose collected works include a volume with the striking title of *The Bible of Amiens*. Ruskin perhaps somewhat hyperbolically describes the cathedral as 'the Parthenon of Gothic architecture', while Amiens itself is called 'the Venice of France'. *The Bible of Amiens* is mainly devoted to a series of descriptions of statues of the Apostles in the central porch of the cathedral's west front, 'each statue with its representative virtue and opposite vice'.

But his links with Amiens apart, the main point about Ruskin in the Scott Bader context is that he is at least as well known as a friend of working people and as an advocate of trade union rights as he is as an art critic: the trade union college as well as the fine art and drawing school in Oxford are named after him. In his time he was as passionate a critic of conventional capitalism as Ernest Bader was later to become. I feel sure that the founder of the Commonwealth would have substantially endorsed Ruskin's famous aphorism 'There is no wealth but life'. Equally, I feel entitled to be sure that Ruskin would have had nothing but praise for Scott Bader's replacement of conventional capitalist ownership by trusteeship arrangements.

Finally I should make clear that though I missed it inexcusably in earlier readings, Ruskin in fact appears on the last page but one (p 228) of Susanna Hoe's book, at the end of her Appendix 7. It was contributed by the founder of the Commonwealth himself and explicitly addresses the question 'Why I started the Scott Bader Commonwealth'. This is not the place to attempt a summary. But towards the end Ernest names three sages and claims that the Commonwealth should be understood as belonging to their 'tradition'. As already flagged in chapter 2, they are Rousseau, Ruskin and Robert Owen.

American researchers who, in the 1980s and 1990s, explored the factors behind the choices in the US of locations in which new businesses were set up, found that proximity to a top-quality golf course was one of the single most important variables. I simply don't know whether similar studies have been undertaken in Britain or in mainland Europe. Nor would I confidently predict that, if they have been, then 'falling within the shadow of a great medieval cathedral' would have emerged as a key variable. On the other hand what must surely be beyond dispute is that visitors from Scott Bader in Wollaston to Scott Bader in France enjoy almost unanimously positive feelings about Sturge's choice of Amiens to become SBSA's location. And for those who are not specially interested in medieval cathedrals? Well, I would myself be inclined to mention the Amiens cuisine, especially its magnificent seafood dishes and those with freshwater fish as one of their main ingredients.

So much for Sturge's cultural legacy to Scott Bader in the shape of Amiens. What about the business in which Sturge and Scott Bader were joint 50:50 partners from 1967 to early 1974 when Sturge withdrew? According to Stuart Fearon, its results showed losses in every single year down to and including 1973. In a historical review and record which he wrote for Ralph Woolf in 1982, he cites some actual numbers for the financial year 1969: on a turnover of FF 2.3m, the joint venture, which then had share capital of FF 250,000, made operating losses of some FF 112,000. Its physical output at that time consisted only of the original emulsion polymers, and its annual production was in the range 800 to 1,000 tonnes.

But that is not by any means the whole story of the joint venture with Sturge in Amiens in the years following 1967. As Stuart Fearon also noted in his 1982 review, the production of polyesters was first added to that of the emulsion polymers as early as 1970. It is worth quoting the two relevant paragraphs from that same Stuart Fearon review:

> At the end of 1969, the writer was seconded to SBS [i.e. Scott Bader Sturge] as a technical representative to assist in the evaluation of the polyester market in France with a view to manufacturing these products at Amiens if the potential justified such a decision.
>
> By the end of 1970 sales of polyester products had progressed to the extent that a small reactor (of 1,000 tonnes per annum capacity) was transferred from Wollaston and installed at Amiens. Sales continued to develop and were accelerated by the termination of the agreement with the Dutch licensee of Scott Bader, Sythese BV, an Akzo subsidiary. This gave access to the Benelux market and effectively doubled sales over a period of three months. Capacity was insufficient and a new reactor was commissioned and brought on stream in 1972, bringing polyester capacity up to the present [1982] level of 3,500 tonnes.

But though the output and sales of polyesters continued to increase from then on, those of the emulsion polymers apparently managed to do little better than stagnate, and losses increased to over FF 500,000 in 1971. In the following year the two UK parents of the 50:50 joint venture judged that the Amiens operation was in crisis, and in September Mike Truman and Stuart Fearon from Wollaston were appointed chief executive and commercial manager respectively. Fairly soon afterwards, the UK parent of SA Sturge made clear its wish to pull out. Agreement was reached to the effect that it would only continue to cover 50% of the Amiens losses up to the end of 1973, and that it would legally withdraw from the joint venture as early as possible in 1974.

According to Stuart Fearon, Sturge's own operations on the Amiens site as well as the joint venture were in bad shape when he and Mike Truman took over their new responsibilities in late 1972. All the same, what stands out from this account of the last days of the Amiens joint venture is the readiness of Scott Bader at Wollaston to take a quite exceptionally long view. I suggested earlier that this was perhaps one of the most important decisions taken during the years when Nick Broome was chief executive of the parent business. From the viewpoint of the local economy in Amiens, and from the perspective of future employment in that cathedral town, it was clearly of outstanding importance. Here perhaps is a clear example of a decision in which trustee ownership was important and other criteria beyond shareholder value were taken into account. I like to think that Ruskin would have approved.

THE WATERSHED OF 1973 AND THE LONG STRUGGLE TO
SURVIVE AND REPAY DEBTS, DOWN TO ABOUT 1980

Mike Truman stepped down as chief executive of what had by then become Scott Bader SA, a wholly owned subsidiary of Scott Bader, in February 1974. Starting in September 1972, in the days when the 50:50 joint venture with Sturge still survived, he had held the top Scott Bader post in Amiens for just less than 18 months. But he seems to have accomplished much. The Paris office had been closed down and its work shifted to Amiens. More important in the judgement of Stuart Fearon, who succeeded him in the top post, was a change of morale. In his view it had come about because 'quality and logistics had improved to the point where a young and dynamic sales force had sufficient confidence to go out and sell'.

Rates of pay for the blue-collar workforce at Amiens were also increased during Mike Truman's time, with what was presumably a positive effect on morale. Moreover during 1973 Scott Bader made the last in a series of increases in the share capital of the business, though that stemmed from the provisions of French company law rather any particular persuasiveness on Mike Truman's part.

Yet his achievements were not without cost. The business made a loss of FF 650,000 in 1972. The reported figure was the same in 1973. But that result seems to have involved some creative accounting. For, according to Stuart Fearon, the real loss was probably closer to FF1 million. The upshot, he told Ralph Woolf in his 1982 report, was that the business when he took over was 'technically and almost in reality insolvent'. And he went on in the same report: 'The primary objective of Scott Bader SA was survival, the method chosen being expansion of sales.'

Especially if measured by the volumes of polyester sales, the chosen method was implemented with a considerable degree of success during Stuart Fearon's first seven years as chief executive, from 1974 to 1980.

Polyester Sales from Amiens in tonnes: 1974–80

	1974	1975	1976	1977	1978	1979	1980
Exports	830	800	769	782	1,319	912	611
In France	782	850	1,248	1,554	1,441	1,900	2,131
Total	1,612	1,650	2,017	2,336	2,760	2,812	2,742

Moreover, in the years running down to 1980 Amiens' sales of emulsion polymers also showed rapid improvement, increasing by more than 50% to some 4,200 tonnes over just four years. Looked at in this way, through the prism of rapidly increasing sales numbers, these years begin to seem less like a hard slog and a struggle to survive and more like easy riding. Having eventually installed adequate polyester capacity, so the explanation would run, SBSA was at last in a position to achieve its destiny by making and selling those polyester resins in relation to which its Wollaston parent enjoyed its greatest comparative advantage.

There is clearly something in that line of thought. What it ignores is the tough realities, particularly the industrial relations realities, which were having to be faced on he ground. We get a glimpse of these in a report sent by Stuart Fearon to Wollaston and dated 27 October 1977, i.e. during the interregnum between the resignation of Nick Broome and the arrival of Ralph Woolf. The report is headed 'Social conflict at Scott Bader France'. Its main focus is on a strike threat made by the Amiens blue-collar workforce earlier in the month, and it goes on to explain how an actual strike was averted by meeting the demands of the strikers halfway. It seeks to cover both what actually happened and the relevant background. But before moving on to quote from the report itself, a word about trade union membership among Amiens blue-collar workers may be helpful.

Among those working in the actual manufacturing plant in Amiens, union membership seems to have been considerable. There was nothing which remotely resembled a closed shop and actual membership may even have been below 50% of those eligible to take it up. Nevertheless confrontational attitudes towards management were widespread if not universal and it was quite common, as we shall see, for known union members to hold elected office, for example as elected and statutorily recognised delegates or deputy delegates, positions similar to but by no means exactly the same as those of shop stewards and their deputies in the UK. Nevertheless, it was not until the late 1998 that a whole union-backed list of candidates was voted into office as delegates or deputy delegates.

But to return to Stuart Fearon's 1977 report, this begins by tracing the story all the way back to what had been found at Amiens by the Wollaston team when it took over in September 1972: 'On his arrival at Amiens [Mike Truman] found an unskilled, unstable, and disgruntled workforce, and one immediate priority was to increase salaries in the factory area.'

Less than 18 months later, in January 1974:

The factory personnel requested further increases and the initial offer was rejected. A strike of short duration (2 days) took place. A compromise solution was reached …

No further general increase in real salaries was made in the period up to October 1975, though individual merit increases were given. By this time the salary structure in the factory was far from coherent and following a refusal by the company to accept a demand for a 10% increase a second strike took place which lasted for four of five days. Following this [new] salaries were established …

At the beginning of 1977 a new salary structure broadly based on the Wollaston system for defined jobs was proposed and accepted [Wollaston rates were and are derived from Hay-MSL job evaluations].

Following elections at the beginning of October Mr Wlusek was elected as delegate and Mr Bertin as deputy. One obligation of management is to receive delegates once per month and to give written replies to questions within 6 days. The first meeting with new delegates was held on Monday 17 October and amongst other requests were:

1) General immediate increase in salaries of 200 F per month [about 9% for those on lowest rates] in the factory area.

2) a fifth week's paid holiday.

3) Bonus to be paid for working in conditions acknowledged to be dirty (*prime de salissure*).

To these requests the management offered written responses the details of which need not concern us. They were in any case not acceptable. The report goes on:

On Thursday 20 October, Mr Wlusek informed me ... that unless an acceptable agreement was reached work would stop on Monday 24 October at 6.00 hours. ... A further meeting was arranged on Friday, 21 October at which the following [terms] were agreed.

In other words, a compromise was reached. The management went some way towards meeting the workers' latest demands and its new proposals were accepted. Once again the details need not concern us. But this whole industrial relations episode at Amiens in October 1977, including its background and outcome, needs to be fully taken in by readers who wish to have a proper understanding of SBSA – or of Scott Bader France (SBF) as it is also often called in the records – and of how it differs from its parent in Wollaston. Stuart Fearon's report indicates that there were two actual strikes in just four years, together with two separate strike threats which were met with management compromise offers that were accepted. In other words, whatever the formal trade union position, union attitudes and a propensity to take union-type actions were widespread, at least among the blue-collar workforce. The contrast with the position at Wollaston hardly needs to be laboured.

It is also true and important that Stuart Fearon in this report expresses some sympathy with the position of the leaders of the Amiens blue-collar workforce, or at minimum a good understanding of it. He does so partly in a section of the report which is revealingly headed 'Us/Them Situation'. Addressing management colleagues in Wollaston, he writes:

Whatever we may like to think, this situation [viz. of us/them] still exists and is extremely difficult to break down. This is not peculiar to SBF and is extremely prevalent and deeply entrenched in French attitudes. Social intercourse between office and factory personnel is virtually non-existent and neither group seeks to improve the situation. Company meetings which initially were reasonably successful have fallen by the wayside mainly because of the physical impossibility of 20–25 people meeting together in one place due to lack of space. Thus there is still an element of mistrust about company motives and [a widespread belief] that the company will not give anything until forced to do so. Perhaps there is some justification in this attitude given the situation in which the company operates. It is also true that the workforce sees little alternative to threatened strike action (as distinct from an actual strike) once a demand has been refused ...

This general discussion of the industrial relations background at SBF would presumably have applied to any dispute which arose – or might have arisen – between management and the union at Amiens at that time. But Stuart Fearon's October 1977 report to Wollaston also includes valuable points about what was at issue on this particular occasion:

> The basic justification of the increase [demanded] by the workforce was the significantly increased volume of production coupled with poor working conditions.

And the report offers valuable data on both points: 'Sales volume increased by 17.3% in the first six months of the year and value by 19.1%.'
As for the working conditions:

> Whilst improvements have been made in many areas, there is still a lot of frustration in the production area. Some equipment is old and dates from the initial start up at Amiens. The conditions under which the maintenance men work are lamentable although this should now be resolved at the beginning of November.
>
> Processing of capital expenditure requests is unbelievably slow, the prime example being the high pressure cleaning gun where our formal request has been pending for six months, despite the social and practical desirability of this item. The factory is dirty mainly because of continuing high volume throughput ... The whole is symptomatic of lack of commitment to developing SBF and the day-to-day nature of the actual operation at Amiens.

By way of additional background to the claim for higher wages, Stuart Fearon's report of October 1977 also includes a comparative table with rates at Wollaston set against those at Amiens. On the basis of these numbers he offers the calculation that 'Wollaston salaries for factory personnel are 23% higher than those at Amiens'. We shall return shortly to the question of relative rates of pay as between the UK parent and its French subsidiary, and how these have evolved since 1977, and to the related issue of comparative labour productivity.
I cannot leave this report without quoting a number of points made towards the end and from the final conclusion:

Although it may sound cynical and perhaps an oversimplification, I am confident that if salaries in the factory area at Amiens were similar in proportion to those at Wollaston this sort of problem would not arise .

However, whilst the company continues to operate in what is essentially a day-to-day survival situation it is difficult to adopt any but the conventional employer's role to keep costs within reasonable limits related to the company's actual performance.

Salaries at SBF are thus governed by the going rate in the labour market rather than the result of a defined policy.

Both in operating and social spheres there is very little integration with the parent company to the point that if this situation does not change the basic question is raised as to whether or not SBF should exist at all.

And then in conclusion:

Suffice it to say that lessons must be learned from the recent experience, and either it is accepted that such situations will arise from time to time or the necessary effort and resource is applied to SBF so that personnel at all levels consider themselves justly rewarded for their contribution and can take some pride in belonging to and hopefully one day co-owning SBF, providing the Scott Bader Commonwealth defines its position concerning its French subsidiary in the near future.

This remarkable report by Stuart Fearon of October 1977 will surely be sufficient to dispel any readers' presumptions – based on the steadily improving output and sales figures of these years – that this was a period of 'easy riding' for the management of SBF in Amiens. But something also needs to be said about how Wollaston responded, especially to the assertion in the report's conclusion about the need for 'the necessary effort and resource' to be applied to SBF. Though unstated, the implication of that assertion can only be that any new 'effort and resource' would have to come from the parent company. The short answer must be that this was not forthcoming. As we know, SBF has had to rely entirely on its own financial resources ever since the final infusion of additional share capital from Wollaston in 1973. As for the Commonwealth, the first Frenchman was admitted to membership only in the year 2000.

Those facts need to be emphasised even if it is also true and important, as Stuart Fearon has been good enough to emphasise for me in a recent note, that a) SBSA has always enjoyed the strongest moral support from its parent and b) that he himself greatly benefited from the support and advice of whoever was in the top position at Wollaston and especially, since his overlap with them was that much longer, with Ralph Woolf and Ian Henderson. He has further pointed out that this support included letters from Wollaston to SBF's bankers in France when additional credits were needed by the Amiens business. And he has of course acknowledged Wollaston's notable financial forbearance, which had extended over more than a quarter of a century by the year 2000, in not requiring any dividend payments out of profits made by its Amiens subsidiary.

Given the absence of any additional finance from Wollaston, it was the singular achievement of Stuart Fearon and those who worked with him in Amiens to have secured by themselves one of the most specific objectives implied in his October 1977 report, namely the upward movement of Amiens rates of pay until they equalled those at Wollaston. In fact Amiens rates had already probably drawn level with those at Wollaston by the end of the 1980s. Ignoring the loss by the Euro – and thus by the French Franc – of almost 25% of its exchange value between January 1999 and December 2000, my guess is that the Amiens rates have almost certainly moved well ahead of those at Wollaston since then. But I have to concede at once that I know of no systematic empirical study of this pay relationship over time. My own guess relies heavily on the much higher levels of productivity currently achieved at Amiens. More of that in a moment.

I need next to introduce a set of related points of fundamental contrast between the Amiens business and its own mainly French market on the one hand, and that of its Wollaston parent and its mainly UK market on the other. The first contrast is about their respective market positions and margins. For reasons which are not altogether clear, anyway not to the writer of this book, margins, especially for the polyester resins, have apparently always been wider in Britain. However it also seems probable that in some subsectors of this resin market, the Scott Bader parent is still to some extent a market leader and price setter. The contrast with the position of Amiens in its markets could hardly be sharper: margins are very substantially narrower and Amiens, as a late arrival in the business, has always inescapably been a price taker.

On the other hand, when we turn from the respective market positions of the two businesses to their respective levels of productivity the contrast is in the reverse direction and could scarcely be more marked. It seems that at least since the later 1970s the physical productivity of the Amiens blue-collar workforce, its tonnage of output per person and per unit of time, has been ahead of the corresponding Wollaston numbers. Measured in this way the comparison eliminates any distortions due to currency exchange rates. Moreover it seems that this gap between the Amiens and Wollaston levels of blue-collar productivity has been increasing as time has gone on. For what it is worth and on a spot check basis, the physical productivity of the Amiens workforce was well over 50% ahead of its Wollaston counterpart in the year 2000.

Much of the credit due to Amiens in this respect is convincingly assigned to a Frenchman, Michel Maille, who has held the key post of production manager of the business since 1975. His skills in the complex set of tasks associated with the production and scheduling of polyester resins and emulsion polymers are said to be of an unusually high order. And that no doubt partly explains not only Amiens' early lead over Wollaston by this measure but also the subsequent widening of this productivity gap.

To be fair to Wollaston, part of the difference may be explained by objective factors, namely the much wider production range of the parent as against that of its subsidiary. But I have also to report a view, essentially about the slower rate of improvement in this productivity measure at Wollaston, which seems to be quite widely held among managers in the parent business. It is simply to the effect that resistance to changes in working practices is notably greater among Wollaston's blue-collar employee owners than among their wage-earning counterparts in Amiens. Many readers will see that fact, if fact it is, as counterintuitive. It needs to be qualified in two ways.

The first qualification is an important repetition: I know of no systematic empirical study of these apparent productivity differences and thus of no attempt to track the changes and to analyse their causes over time. Second, I would suggest what amounts to a linguistic or perhaps better a conceptual adjustment. I suggest that it may be more fruitful if we think not so much about resistance to change on the part of the blue-collar workforce at Wollaston as about a joint management/workforce failure to find an acceptable set of processes leading to productivity improvements. In cases of such joint failures, some readers are likely to assign the chief responsibility to management.

Stuart Fearon never clearly states what marked the end of his period of a survival struggle by SBSA and the start of the consolidation phase which followed it. However in his 1982 report to Ralph Woolf from which I quoted earlier, he wrote that 'the elimination of accumulated losses has taken six years, or eight years for fiscal purposes'. If we take that as marking the transition to the consolidation phase, it implies a year between 1979 and 1981 as the relevant date. However, in the same 1982 report to Ralph Woolf he was at pains to stress that 'profits have remained modest'.

CONSOLIDATION AND THE STEP CHANGE OF 1986:
EARLY 1980S TO MID-1980S

In fact, according to some notes which he made much later, in the year 2000, Stuart Fearon came to think that closure was still on the cards when Ralph Woolf took over in Wollaston in 1978. But however that may be, he is quite unambiguous in identifying a step change for the better which took place in 1986 and in putting his finger on what made it possible. He writes:

> However, this situation [viz. when the closure of SBF was still on the cards] was to change in the mid eighties when the misfortunes of one group company, Synthetic Resins Ltd (at Speke), was to benefit another, SBF. In 1985 it was announced that SRL would close in the following year. A considerable quantity of hardware (reactors, blenders, storage vessels etc) became available at knockdown prices. SBF, never slow to take an opportunity, acquired a number of vessels very cheaply, some of which were banked for later use, and one of which, a polyester reactor, was installed in the Amiens factory in record time. The low hardware cost enabled the capital project to meet stringent financial criteria set by the Wollaston parent. The installation effectively doubled polyester capacity overnight. The project which from memory cost FF 500,000 was financed totally by SBF and completed in 1986 ...
>
> The project was arguably the single most important event in SBF's development since it removed the capacity bind and opened up a growth mentality amongst French personnel. Timing was fortuitous but impeccable. Inflation in the mid eighties was reducing rapidly, economic growth had returned and business confidence

was high. An increasingly confident young company was now poised to take advantage of these favourable circumstances and in fact did so.

GROWTH ACQUISITIONS AND A BUSINESS CYCLE
DOWNTURN: MID-1980S TO 2000

With two rather different qualifications, the years following the step change of 1986 were ones of steady and cumulative success for Scott Bader France. One of the qualifications will be dealt with separately at the end. That is partly because it concerns neither of its two core businesses at Amiens, its polyester resins and its emulsion polymers, but the much newer technology of *composites* or compound manufacture: essentially the pre-mixing of resin and glass fibre for so-called closed mould forming into GRP. Separate treatment also makes sense in this case because the story of composites manufacture is one which has impinged on Scott Bader elsewhere – for example in both the UK and US – and not only on SBF. The second qualification about this otherwise steadily improving period relates to a long downturn in the business cycle, which began in 1995 and which, of course, had significant negative consequences both for SBF's well-established manufacturing activities at Amiens and, for good measure, on its fledgling project in the new field of composites.

Apart from the proper celebration of SBF's 25th anniversary or silver jubilee in 1991, a number of highlights are worth picking out from this long 15-year period down to the end of the century. Two are acquisitions. In this respect Scott Bader SA in the 1990s was following a path pioneered by Godric Bader at Wollaston in the late 1960s, and by his two successors, Nick Broome and Ralph Woolf, in the 1970s and 1980s. The first of these took place in 1994 and was of a French manufacturer of polyester resins called Convert. The bid from Scott Bader SA succeeded against stiff competition from two of its much larger international competitors, Cray Valley and Dutch State Mines (DSM). As with a number of Wollaston's acquisitions, what was purchased was not the business as a going concern but simply its technology and customer list. Then in 1997 Scott Bader SA acquired an American-owned resin company in France called Arizona, located at Niort, south-west of Tours, towards the Atlantic coast. Arizona's products are officially chemical emulsions, but that is apparently no more than a different description of emulsion polymers. As with

Convert, what was purchased was the know-how and the customer list. So far as I know it is unique in Scott Bader's history as being the acquisition of a non-polyester business. But then, among Wollaston's overseas subsidiaries, SBF is also unique as having started by making polymers and having only added polyesters four years later. By the time of this second acquisition Jean-Marc Bain had joined Scott Bader SA as business director under Stuart Fearon.

But it would be a mistake to put too much emphasis on these acquisitions. There was also organic expansion during this 15-year period. Excluding the composites venture, SBF employment, which had been scarcely more than 40 in the early 1980s, had reached well over 90 by the end of the century. Moreover, because of the company's success in improving its productivity, those employment numbers understate the increase in the output and sales of its polyesters and emulsion polymers. New capacity in each of the two main product lines was commissioned on the Amiens site during this period. So indeed was new capacity for gelcoats, if they are to be classified separately from the other polyester resins.

A highlight of a rather different kind is identified by the Traxton/ Reeves diary entry for 1992, the year following the purchase by Scott Bader SA of the freehold of the Amiens site which it had rented from Sturge since the joint venture was wound up in 1974. Included in this diary entry is: 'Conversion of old 1930s Sturge premises into offices, *gelcoat and polyester technical laboratories* [emphasis added] [and a] gelcoat production and spray application centre.'

I have given special emphasis to the new technical laboratories on the Amiens site for a quite specific reason. Within what by then had become the Scott Bader *Group* this is the only example of any laboratory building outside the home base at Wollaston. In a note by Jean-Marc Bain, which I quote in a moment, he refers to new polyester resins developed by SBSA, presumably in these new laboratories on the Amiens site. They offer an excellent additional example of the considerable autonomy which SBSA has come to enjoy.

But to give readers more of feel for what these years were like, I must quote from notes which have kindly been supplied by Stuart Fearon and Jean-Marc Bain. Here first are some extracts from Stuart Fearon's notes:

The period from the mid eighties to the economic downturn which began in 1994/95 was one of high growth for SBF.

Increased profits meant additional resources for investment and further capacity increases were made initially in emulsion polymers and subsequently in polyesters and gelcoats. By any standards, SBF was highly successful with profits, whether expressed as return on sales or capital, at record levels, and had become an important instead of a marginal contributor to what was from the 1990s group profit.

No history of SBF would be complete without a mention of the 25th anniversary of the company celebrated in 1991. There were two main events: the first – for company personnel and partners – was an evening dinner and dance boat trip along the Somme River... The second evening of celebration was for customers and suppliers and was centred round a dinner cruise on the Seine on a delightful summer evening in June. Some 130 guests attended this memorable occasion and a particular pleasure was to unite for one evening our three former presidents (Charlie Stumm, Mike Truman and Ralph Woolf) and the then current incumbent, Ian Henderson.

By 1992 a significant cash balance had been accumulated despite financing capital investment and the not inconsiderable growth in the working capital requirement. It gave considerable pleasure to SBF management to have interest received as a contributor to profit rather than the reverse. Other more personal landmarks of this time included signing our first corporation tax cheque once previous losses had been all used, and also identifying the specific invoice in the year concerned which took turnover through the FF 100 million sales barrier.

As is still the case, the economic cycle on the Continent was not in phase with that in the UK and for a period in the early nineties the French business was still growing strongly as the UK entered recession. This resulted in the French profit on a month by month basis being comparable with or even exceeding that of the Wollaston-based business. This gave an additional element of spice to performance in a period of continuing high autonomy ...

An economic growth blip in early 1995 resulted in massive price increases for key raw materials and plummeting margins. Profits in the base business slumped despite the positive impact of the Convert acquisition. However, recovery got underway and profitability ... so that by 1998 profits on the base business were at the lower end of the group target range, with 1999 a bumper year, as growing demand was combined with attractive input costs and as a consequence good margins.

Jean-Marc Bain in his separate notes has additional details about the position and prospects of SBSA at the turn of the century which should be on the record:

> From 14,500 tonnes in 1996, the output of the Amiens site in the year 2000 will be around 22,000 tonnes and the expectation is that it will produce over 25,000 tonnes in the coming years. This is a 'must' if we are to compete in Continental Europe with our big competitors. The increase in sales has been developed in France and the export countries with which we deal, especially in Germany, where we have developed a good presence starting from scratch in my time with SBSA. This is also the case with our more traditional export markets such as the Netherlands and Italy where we already had a real presence long before 1996. These increases have been achieved not only as a result of our well-established points of excellence, that is, our customer orientation, our technical and commercial services, and our adaptability to customer demands. It is also explained by the fact that we have at Amiens developed some good new polyester resins. As for our emulsion polymers, there has been no significant increase in the tonnage of our business but we have changed our mix to concentrate more on adhesive products and those for the surface coating of textiles.
>
> ...The independence of Scott Bader is a very well-received advantage and makes us able to work in good harmony even with some tough competitors.

THE COMPOSITES PROJECT: SMC AND IMPREG

We move on now to what Stuart and Jean-Marc have written for me in their notes about the composites project in south-western France. To understand what has been happening we need at least a minimal knowledge of the process involved.

For readers of this book who, like the writer, went through their education without ever entering a chemistry laboratory or opening a chemistry textbook, I make no apology for going back to the beginning. The process of manufacturing and finishing in its final form the new post-war material of GRP (plastics reinforced by glass or other stiffening material) can follow at least two main different paths. The first is described in chapter 2 and essentially involves bringing together the 'plastic' (viz. the polyester resin) and the stiffening material, not in the manufacturing process itself, but when the resin is applied together with the stiffening material by the method of wet hand lay-up – where it is used, for example, to form the hulls of smaller or larger boats or even of small ships. A homely and easy to imagine parallel would be if a familiar kitchen jelly mould came into existence as a result of a process – *in situ* in the kitchen – in which extra ingredients were 'paint rollered' on to a layer of liquid plastic to make something firm which could hold the shape to which it had been moulded.

In sharp contrast to the above is the path of the 'closed mould forming' of the same GRP. The essential difference is that the stiffening material and the polyester resin are brought together in the manufacturing process itself. So, that has as its output what may reasonably be described as a polyester moulding compound. Stuart Fearon has kindly explained to me that there are a number of these and that they consist of 'resin, glass, fillers and various additives'. Here, because our focus is on Scott Bader SA, we discuss only two, namely sheet moulding compound (SMC) and what, by its Scott Bader registered trade name, is known as 'Impreg'. As we shall see elsewhere, whatever the compound which may be used, closed form moulding may itself involve different processes as well as different compounds. Readers may remember that Scott Bader was involved in a joint venture from 1976 to 1981 with Lotus – the maker of small sports cars – which explored and marketed a closed mould system called vacuum assisted resin injection (VARI). This was dealt with in chapter 5 and there is no need to repeat the discussion here.

About SMC, Stuart Fearon explains that this is a material which is ready to use when delivered to customers 'either in rolled or lapped sheet form'. He goes on to make clear that it needs several days to 'mature', during which the 'initially sticky resin system thickens up … to give a non-tacky product and one easy to handle'. At this stage it is despatched to the customer who cuts it to size and moulds it under 'heat and under pressure' in a 'closed mould'. Within the closed mould, he goes on to explain, 'curing time is very short', no more than a 'matter of minutes'. As a result, he points out, the process is highly productive compared with conventional processes of wet hand lay-up. On the other hand, it is a capital-intensive method and so depends on customers who want to buy long runs. Moreover, apart from 'the initial maturation period pre-delivery, another drawback is that the SMC has a limited shelf or storage life once made and thus has to be used within a "moulding window" which is usually a maximum of one or two months.'

Finally, about the Scott Bader patented Impreg technology, its essential logic is to overcome the drawbacks from which SMC suffers. First by the use of what amounts to a thickening agent it seeks to minimise the pre-delivery 'maturation' phase of the manufacturing process. Second, after delivery to the customer, the Impreg compound enjoys a 'moulding window' of almost unlimited duration. What's more, and always as compared with SMC, it can be moulded under very low pressures. Stuart Fearon concedes that the overcoming of the drawbacks of SMC has meant modestly higher manufacturing costs. But he argues that the advantages are such that great excitement was generated when Impreg emerged successfully from the Wollaston laboratories after a series of tough and extended trials.

Not surprisingly in all the circumstances, new compound or composite manufacture came to be seen by many at Scott Bader in the late 1980s as not so much a new 'wonder material' as a means of making possible a new 'wonder process' which would enable GRP to sweep into new markets and to replace sheet metal across a wide range of products, including for example car bodies and other car parts.

Stuart Fearon takes that story forward:

> By 1992 the emerging Impreg technology was showing the potential to be a major profit earner in the field of polyester moulding compounds by the end of the decade. The potential markets were essentially in Continental Europe and North America, and having taken the strategic decision to enter compound manufacture in Europe, rather than offer resin systems to compounders, it was decided to achieve this by the acquisition of a compounding company if possible.
>
> In early 1993 a suitable candidate was identified and purchase of its assets together with those of an associated moulding company was completed by the end of that year. Thus Scott Bader Composites in Auch, and Stradour Industries near Tarbes, both in SW France, joined the SB group on 1 January 1994.

But the results turned out to be disappointing:

> In fact it was clear by 1998 that we as a group were unable to

convert the undoubtedly attractive technological concept [viz. of Impreg] into viable industrial products within an acceptable time scale and, by the time of my departure, there was serious doubt about whether an acceptable return on total investment would ever be achieved.

By the time Stuart wrote those notes for me in the summer of the year 2000, the moulding company had in fact already been disposed of through the mechanism of a management buy-out.

On the other hand, and despite the disposal of Stradour, Jean-Marc Bain managed to be rather more optimistic about the future of Impreg and SMC in France, based on SB Composites, in the notes he wrote for me at the same time:

> The past years have been used to strengthen our product range on Impreg low-pressure compounds as well our SMC products. We aim to produce 'robust' products able to satisfy very demanding customers who see Scott Bader as a small player.
>
> We have demonstrated our know-how through various automotive projects in competition with the best competitors in the European market. Even if commercially we have not been successful, we are now considered as a high-quality supplier and get many requests from possible partners.

We will need to go back to compounds and composites, Impreg and SMC in the next final narrative chapter, on Scott Bader in the 1990s. As we shall see, the results elsewhere, and especially in the US, have been disappointing. But let us leave the continuing project of SB Composites at Auch in south-western France with the more optimistic and even romantic exit line from Jean-Marc's notes: '... *many requests from possible partners*'.

Here, to conclude this record of SBSA as a business, an overdue brief word about Strand Glass SA (SGSA). As many readers will know, this was originally the French operation of Strand Glassfibre Ltd. It was engaged , like its UK parent, in the distribution and sale of the materials needed for GRP, including the glass fibre, rather than in manufacture.

STRAND GLASS SA

When Strand Glassfibre was acquired in 1978, under Ralph Woolf's leadership, responsibility for SGSA was effectively assigned by Wollaston to Amiens where it has remained. Stuart Fearon has kindly supplied me with a thumbnail sketch of what the French business amounted to at that time:

> It had been created in 1975 and was still in the embryo stage at the time of acquisition, with annual sales of around FF 5 million and three employees. It was operating at a loss from a single branch in the greater Paris area. Glass sales were disproportionately higher than resin sales and in fact at my departure this imbalance was still not redressed ...
>
> We developed the business from its small foundations to a national composites distribution business with sales rising from 20 tonnes a month of resin to 1,400 tonnes in the peak year of 1992, with glass sales about double. Three additional branches were opened and in the record year sales totalled FF 60 million with pre-tax profits around four to five million. The company then employed 23 people ... But subsequently the business declined. Sales reduced to just over FF 50 million and profits to zero or a small loss.

It seems that the overhead costs of the distribution and sales network were too much for the volume of traffic. But Stuart Fearon reports that a programme of closures was already underway before his own departure in 1999.

The nearly-always-positive Jean-Marc Bain takes the story down to the second half of the year 2000:

> The distribution business has been reorganised and strengthened by the closure of depots and by having the depot staff more involved, and trained to be sales assistants and small accounts managers. The improvement of sales and the decrease of costs made the Strand activity a very profitable one after a difficult period of time in 1996/97.
>
> We plan to pursue this effort to better manage our [distribution and sales] costs with the opening in 2001 of a logistic platform in Amiens to deal with the storage of all packaged products. The *leitmotiv* is competitiveness and reactivity, but we now invest in image and more and more in working conditions to offer our staff the best environment to work to the best practice.

INVOLVEMENT BY NON-MANAGEMENT STAFF AT SBSA

As noted earlier, it was only in the year 2000 that French applications to become members of the Scott Bader Commonwealth, considered in that context as a group rather than as a narrowly Wollaston entity, were first approved. A total of seven SBSA employees applied for Commonwealth membership, and all were accepted following well-established procedures. Over earlier years there had been quite widespread questioning about this, especially from rank-and-file Commonwealth members at Wollaston. The thrust of the questions was to ask why opportunities for Commonwealth membership had not already been opened up to the group's French employees.

A similar question has also been raised over a number of years about why a Community Council, on Wollaston lines, has not been developed at Amiens.

At least in relation to the second of these questions it seems to me that the Wollaston management has a persuasive answer. It is that under French industrial relations law, works councils have been a statutory requirement for all businesses above a minimum size for many years. The pioneering legislation on this issue was first introduced into what was then West Germany in the late 1940s and 1950s. It passed from there into French law through the influence of what was then the EEC and has, of course, more recently become a key feature of the Social Chapter of the European Union to which Britain signed up only after Mr Tony Blair's government succeeded Mr John Major's in 1997. In both France and Germany, and indeed elsewhere in the EU, these works council institutions sit reasonably comfortably alongside traditional relations between businesses and the unions which they recognise. To the question, 'Why not a Community Council at SBSA?', there is a reasonable answer: namely that there is already a statutory *comité d'entreprise* (essentially the French equivalent of a British works council) in Amiens. It is true that as compared with those of the Community Council in Wollaston the powers of Amiens *comité d'entreprise* are much less strong. However, and I am indebted for this point to Stuart Fearon, there would surely be nothing to prevent the granting, above what is prescribed in law, of equivalent extra powers to the latter if that was felt to be desirable.

A similar response is available should a question be asked about why Wollaston's profit-sharing arrangements are not extended to SBSA's employees in Amiens. It is that there has been statutory financial participation by French employees in the companies for which they work since the presidential terms of General de Gaulle in the 1960s, and tax assistance for voluntary schemes since the prime ministership of Antoine Pinay some years before, and an array of new voluntary measures dating from 1986. This is not the place to go into details. It is enough to say, first, that as well as its statutory scheme, a voluntary scheme is in place at Amiens. Second, and in case there are readers with a special interest in employee financial participation, it is worth acknowledging that this is an area of tax law in which the French can justly claim to lead the European Union.

Before closing, we come back to the point of departure of this discussion: what about the Scott Bader Commonwealth, the Wollaston institution which has nothing to do either with employee financial participation or with industrial relations but which was established by Ernest Bader with a number of objectives:

1 To hold the share capital of the Scott Bader business.
2 By opening its membership to all employees to ensure that management became constitutionally subordinate to the 'community' of all employees.
3 To receive any dividends distributed by the business and to assign the resulting money between reinvestment in the business, the employees as individuals, and charitable donations.

If we leave out the charitable donations as a matter slightly on one side, it seems reasonable to argue that what is missing at SBSA is a constitutional accountability by the French management to the French working community. In discussion with the writer and with Brian Elgood in the early autumn of 2000, Jean-Marc Bain appeared to have some sympathy with this judgement but also expressed the view that the concept of a Commonwealth had little resonance in France. It rang no bells either about proposals for co-operative businesses put forward by English and Dutch radicals in the 1640s and 1650s or about the post-Second World War transition into the British Commonwealth of the British Empire. On the other hand, or so Jean-Marc seemed to be persuasively arguing, if the second of the above objectives could be achieved by converting SBSA into a French production co-operative, the new language could have significant resonance with its French workforce. Because of the provisions of French co-operative law, such a conversion would satisfy the second of the two Scott Bader Commonwealth objectives. It remains to add only two final points. The first is that such a conversion could result in significant corporate tax advantages. Secondly it would serve to underline that as between Wollaston and Amiens, the constitutional relationship was one of a truly exemplary subsidiarity,

Such a constitutional relationship would not, I think, need to be at variance with the new Europeanwide management focus of the Scott Bader group agreed after Allan Bell replaced Ian Henderson as group managing director in 2000, and presented to customers and other trade partners early in 2001. But of course with the new focus the old exemplary subsidiarity will cease to apply in the management sphere. The new focus itself is covered, if with inescapable brevity, in the Postscript at the end of the next chapter.

9

New Responses to Tough Old Problems in the 1990s

INTRODUCTION

It should come as no surprise that over the decade of the 1990s Scott Bader faced more difficult market conditions than those of the 1980s, just as those of the 1980s had been tougher than those of the 1970s. Its core products, most of its emulsion polymers and above all its polyester resins – the key ingredient for what was now the middle-aged and almost standard material of GRP – were now between 30 and 40 years old. Competition, especially in the UK market, was becoming more intense as every year passed. There was no return to the high demand growth rates of the 1960s and 1970s. Furthermore, as the decade moved into its second half, the strength of sterling made it increasingly difficult to sell Wollaston products abroad. As evidence that 1994 was perhaps the most difficult in the company's history, the Traxton/Reeves diary notes that the results showed an accounting – though not an operating – loss for the first time ever. In line with the constitution that resulted in a temporary, even if very largely formal, intervention by the Scott Bader trustees in the following year.

In the 1980s, as readers will remember, the company's main responses to the tougher market environment had been a combination of a) acquisitions, especially of Strand Glassfibre, and b) controlled de-manning, using the mechanism of voluntary redundancy schemes. So it also mainly was in the 1990s. But in place of two de-manning episodes in the 1980s, there was only one in the 1990s, and the total numbers who left were far fewer: about 30 compared with over 160. As for acquisitions, their most striking feature in the 1990s – and what was new about them – was their international character.

The big change came in the mid-1990s. At the start of the decade what was soon to become the Scott Bader Group, but was still then just Scott Bader UK together with its wholly owned subsidiary, SBSA, in France, were employing about 470 people, with rather less than 100 of them in France. In one jump between 1992 and 1993, the total employed by the group increased by about 80 to just over 550. In the following year, between 1993 and 1994, total employment made a slightly bigger jump, increasing to approximately 640. Moreover this was the period when, following the latest voluntary redundancy scheme, employment in the UK – and mainly Wollaston – was cut by about 30. In other words, net of that reduction, the group's total work-force increased by some 200 during the middle years of the 1990s. By the end of the decade in 1999, it had grown further to a total of 670. Including what was by then over 100 in France, total employment in the group at the end of the century was split into two nearly equal halves, with just over 50% in the UK and just under 50% overseas. Excluding single digit numbers employed in three overseas distribution and sales offices, the great majority of extra people were employed in three new international manufacturing operations outside the UK: in South Africa, the Middle East, and Croatia.

For a year or two in the middle of the decade the total numbers employed included up to 20 people working in an American subsidiary, National Composites Inc, but that was closed in 1998.

On the other hand, the total workforce at the end of the decade also included single digit numbers employed by Scott Bader in three over-seas distribution and sales offices: in the US, Sweden, and in the Czech Republic.

The old, more or less self-contained, universe of the parent company at Wollaston with its French subsidiary in Amiens had effectively come to an end. The challenge was to integrate the new overseas businesses into a coherent whole. Some progress towards that admittedly difficult objective began to be made towards the end of the decade, and more so at the start of the new century. See the Postscript to this chapter for the latter.

In the world of global business nothing, of course, is certain. But for each of its three new overseas manufacturing businesses of the 1990s, medium-term market prospects, when reviewed in the year 2000, looked fairly good. That at least *seemed* more true than untrue, despite particular difficulties which had come up in South Africa and Croatia, in part because of high raw material prices. Those difficulties seem to have been rather successfully negotiated by the new Middle East sub-sidiary. Moreover, the three new sales and distribution offices, two in mainland Europe and the third in the US, were judged to be doing well.

Among the overseas acquisitions of the 1990s, however, one major disappointment must also be acknowledged here, even if it is mainly part of a different and longer story, with roots going back to Scott Bader's 1970s, and with an important surviving project, in the shape of a subsidiary of Scott Bader France, gallantly soldiering on into the next decade. What turned into a big disappointment was the acquisition of National Composites Inc, an innovative new company in America's plastic composite – or plastic compound – industry, located at South Bend in the Midwestern state of Indiana. After taking a minority stake in the early 1990s, the share capital of the business was fully acquired by Scott Bader in 1996. But not long afterwards, in 1998, what must have been a most difficult decision was taken by the company board at Wollaston: to close the business down. Later on in this chapter we will treat the whole episode as a continuing part of the much longer story of compounds and closed mould forming, to which readers have already been introduced.

Because it substantially changed the character of Scott Bader into a 'mini-multinational business', the development of overseas manufacturing subsidiaries was the company's most important new response to the ever tougher market conditions which it had to face in the 1990s. But it was not the only one.

IAN HENDERSON'S NEW INVESTMENTS

During the years when Ralph Woolf was chief steward, substantial cash reserves were built up, as we have seen. Ian Henderson, who took over in 1990, was an industrial chemist by profession and came from a senior management position at BP Chemicals. It was no doubt predictable that with such a background he should have at once concerned himself with the state of the manufacturing plant and equipment at Wollaston. In fact the focus of the new investment he initiated was significantly wider. For example, it extended to include anti-pollution and other environmental protection systems and more advanced safety equipment. Equally important were new investments, initiated by Ian Henderson early on in the 1990s, in the area of customer service. They found their most emphatic expression in a new (£1.4m) 'customer service centre' built on the Wollaston Hall estate and opened by the Duke of Kent in 1992. A new and consolidated site warehouse, to and from which all incoming and outgoing materials are directed, was built alongside the new centre as both part of it and as a distinct entity. As important, if less visible, was the initiative, early in Ian Henderson's stewardship, to invest in the software and hardware for a new 'commercial system' for the whole of Scott Bader's business processes.

About the new modernising investment in the plant and machinery at Wollaston, which took place during the early years of Ian Henderson's term as chief executive, Chris Webb has kindly contributed the following summary account. He was at the time – and indeed still continued to be when this was written in the early months of 2001 – the head of the engineering department in the parent business. Plant by plant he has identified the following main investments during the 1990s and supplied approximate estimates of the expenditures involved:

Polyester plant: Reactor automation; improved storage, handling and metering of raw materials, and including new bulk tanks; improved distillation systems; improved finished product handling, with a new packaging plant building, product storage tanks and filing system. All for approx. £1.7m.

Gelcoat plant: Installation of three large and four small gelcoat mixers and one paste mixer to improve productivity, with associated equipment for raw material handling and finished product packing. All for approx. £1.4m.

Alkyd plant: Installation of a further reactor for solid (powder coating) resin production and a belt cooler for this resin; additional reactor and blender systems for alkyd production and improved raw material handling systems. All for approx. £1.7m.

Polymer plant: Improved storage and handling of raw materials for Texipols (including bulk storage); improved Texipol productivity by installation of a preparation vessel and full automation of two reactors; environmental improvements – a fume-abatement system and a system for the recovery and re-use of wash water; capacity increased by partial automation of two further reactors and provision of additional finished product storage tanks. All for approx. £1.3m.

Site Infrastructure: The new technical centre building; new liquid nitrogen storage and distribution; new air compressors and a new process steam boiler. All for approx. £2.2m.

Looking back on his decade at Wollaston in the summer of the year 2000, Ian Henderson was inclined to put at least as much emphasis on the 'people-focused' investments and changes of his early years as on those which were concerned with plant and machinery. For example, in a special signed article written for the *Reactor* in its issue of May 2000, he highlights the decision in 1990 to go for the so-called ISO 9001 standard and its successful achievement in the following year. For non-specialist readers I should explain that to satisfy the conditions for achieving this standard, a manufacturing business must write down, for the standard-awarding authority, in complete and exhaustive detail, and in images and graphics as well as in words, an account of its entire set of manufacturing processes including full specifications of all the materials used. For the outside world in general and for customers in particular, the award of ISO 9001 and its subsequent retention acts as a kind of independent voucher of material and manufacturing process quality. Inside the business it provides an invaluably tight description of what is supposed to be happening. In any particular business it may also necessitate the introduction of new systems to ensure that what is supposed to happen does happen. According to Ian Henderson, ISO 9001 was specially valuable at Wollaston because it required the introduction of precisely those kinds of new systems. It thus made possible a major improvement in quality control and so a reduction of cost.

Other 'people focused' improvements which Ian Henderson clearly made were in the building of effective working teams as, for example, in the business unit management structure mentioned next. For example, he devoted much time and energy into revitalising the system of briefing meetings.

Seen by Ian Henderson in broadly the same light was a switch to a so-called 'business unit management structure' in 1994. I take the phrase from a familiar source – the Traxton/Reeves diary for that year. For non-specialist readers I should explain that this involves the division of the overall business into semi-autonomous business units: at Wollaston in 1994 into just two units, the (polyester) composites business and the speciality polymers business. Functions like sales and marketing, and production planning, which had previously been exercised on the level of the Wollaston enterprise as a whole, were decentralised down to the two new business units. These changes were in line with developments in UK industrial management thinking which came to be quite widely adopted in the 1980s and 1990s. Their essential logic is to bring responsibility for decisions to those most directly involved in their implementation, and thus to increase the speed of response to internal and external changes and to improve the motivation of those who do the responding. By all accounts they are changes that have worked reasonably well at Wollaston even if their contribution to improved performance has not been easy to quantify.

Somewhat less successful, or so it seems, was another policy initiative introduced during Ian Henderson's earlier years. It is recorded briefly and simply as an item in the Traxton/ Reeves diary for 1992: 'Continuous improvement process endorsed by the board.'

As most readers will know, the main hypothesis behind the introduction of continuous improvement processes in business undertakings – or indeed almost any other kind of organisation – is clear enough: that there is always scope for improving quality and reducing waste. But there are also a number of subsidiary hypotheses. One is that much of the knowledge about how to achieve improvement is likely to be found in the heads of shop-floor workers rather than in those of management. And another is that a most valuable technique for identifying what needs to be improved is the measurement of statistical variation, as pioneered in Japan by the great American industrial engineer W. Edwards Deming, and later brought back to the West. Needless to say, whole books have been written about continuous improvement and how best it may be achieved. But for our purposes it is enough to assert that continuous improvement schemes have by now been widely adopted by business in the West and have generally resulted in significant success. That has perhaps been especially true in companies which are employee-owned in one way or another, and thus where it may be easier to motivate shop-floor employees behind projects for searching out and then implementing improvements. For non-specialist readers it makes sense to underline the rather specific approach which is commonly used in the search for improvements and is at the heart of Edwards Deming's teaching. The approach is made through an analysis of statistical variation – for example of product quality or changeover times. Typically, that provides an excellent starting point from which prospective improvements can be identified.

Continuous improvement is mentioned in the Traxton/Reeves diary only just the once – in 1992 as quoted above. What's more, it was not stressed by Ian Henderson to me when he was about to retire, as one of the successful initiatives launched in his time as chief executive. It is probably safe to suppose that though endorsed by the board it was an initiative which was tried, found unusually difficult, and then dropped. There is no real doubt that it was seriously attempted. Why it was found so difficult can probably be best explained by a widespread reluctance to change, coupled with that absence of trust between shop floor and management at Wollaston which has already surfaced more than once. For a limited period of time, as we shall shortly see, a once-off cost-saving project in the mid-1990s offered some kind of substitute. By definition, on the other hand, it was no substitute for a commitment to continuous improvement over an indefinite period of time.

THE PRODUCT STORY OF THE 1990S: SURVIVORS FROM THE PAST GO ON DOMINATING OUTPUT AND SALES

Including gelcoats in that overall category, polyester resins, sold mainly to manufacturers of GRP in selected market sectors, took first place among Wollaston's output and sales in the 1990s as they had done in the three previous decades. There was a similar continuity in second place, which was once again filled by emulsion polymers. In this latter case, on the other hand, Texipols, because of their higher values and increasing tonnages, came to be distinguished as a separate category of output and sales from 1994. They reached a peak total of over 6,000 tonnes in 1996. Readers will remember that Texipols had been developed in the Wollaston laboratories – in some sense by accident – during the 1980s, and that they operate as thickeners when added to surface coatings of one kind and another. Their main buyers, for use as liquid pigment thickeners, are the manufacturers of surface coatings in the textile printing industry. In the 1990s they also found uses in adhesives on both sides of the Atlantic.

Historians of business are probably more like than unlike their fellow historians in having an inescapable interest in change. As a result they often give insufficient credit to those whose task it is to sustain in the present successful activities inherited from the past. A case in point is the Wollaston staff, non-management and management alike, who have been responsible for sustaining the polyester business, including gelcoats. Among its top managers in the 1980s and 1990s were Ron Peacock and Dave Townsend. Both were retired by the time this was written. It is right that their contribution should be highlighted here.

Following on behind the core products, throughout the 1990s and into the next century, came the Wollaston alkyds. They had been reintroduced from SRL into the product mix of the parent company, despite some opposition from Scott Bader's environmental protection lobby, during Ralph Woolf's time in the 1980s. The rationale for the reintroduction of these low-margin and essentially 'commodity' products may perhaps be seen as having as much to do with sustaining employment in rural Northamptonshire as with their contribution to profits. Nevertheless from the first that contribution was positive, and so it continued. Sold mainly to buyers among the manufacturers of special paints, Wollaston's reintroduced alkyds quickly established a reputation for consistently high product quality. This was sustained throughout the 1990s. In one important case the company has even managed to go on selling its alkyds to a manufacturer which favours those from Scott Bader over similar products of its own.

For the rest, Scott Bader developed a quite new set of secondary products in the 1990s. These are indeed polyester resins, though in solid granular form rather than as the company's more familiar liquid resins. Their main buyers are the manufacturers of spray paints. Their output and sales fell back somewhat after peaking in the middle of the decade, but had started to increase again by the end of it. The Traxton/Reeves diary records the construction of a special plant at Wollaston for powder coatings manufacture in 1993.

But the big new line of secondary products promoted by the Scott Bader group, though not directly by the Wollaston parent in the 1990s, was not the powder coatings but the ready-mixed composites or compounds. As we have seen, these began to be manufactured in both the US and by Scott Bader France during Ian Henderson's years as chief executive. On the other hand, as we shall learn in more detail shortly, their manufacture at Wollaston had been discontinued in the 1980s. Reminding ourselves that this manufacture was still very much in progress in France early in the year 2001, when this was written, we will defer getting into the details of the story until later in this chapter.

BIG MARKET FLUCTUATIONS IN THE EARLY
AND MIDDLE 1990S

Between the year of Ian Henderson's arrival, 1990, and 1991, the output and sales of polyester resins In the UK by Scott Bader at Wollaston, measured in tonnes, fell by over 30%. It was the biggest ever reduction over a twelve-month period and seems to have been mainly caused by the collapse of business confidence which resulted from the Gulf War. Parts of the demand for GRP, for example that from the leisure boats industry, simply disappeared, as previously flourishing boat-builders shut up shop for the duration. It was a mark both of Scott Bader's commitment to its labour-friendly philosophy and policies, and its relative strength in the market, that the crisis was survived without a single redundancy at Wollaston. For the most part the company was able to hold on to its margins in a collapsing market. On the other hand, its UK sales never climbed back to their 1990 levels – or even came close to them – during what was left of the century.

Then in the middle of the decade, halfway through Ian Henderson's years as chief executive, the Wollaston business was dealt a second devastating blow of a rather different kind: not a collapse of demand but a sudden and rocketing increase in the prices of its mainly oil-based raw materials. The chief cause was said to have been a blockage in the growth of oil refinery capacity and output. But whatever the cause, this was an especially serious crisis because the company was simply unable to protect its margins by raising its own prices.

Given that an overall wage reduction was no more acceptable in the 1990s under Ian Henderson than it had been under Ralph Woolf at the end of the 1970s and in the early 1980s, a voluntary redundancy scheme was the predictable response. The terms offered to those who left were similar to what they had been in the two earlier schemes. They were agreed by Wollaston's two representative social organs, the Commonwealth board of management and the Community Council, with the minimum of delay. Subsequently they were approved by a vote of Commonwealth members in a general meeting.

The company's two representative institutions once again demonstrated their huge virtue in enabling a crisis to be acceptably negotiated. Moreover, in a remarkable re-run of what had happened before, there were more redundancy volunteers than the company could spare. The actual numbers were 59 and 30. Thoughtful observers could only ask themselves again whether labour-friendly companies like Scott Bader should put greater emphasis in their self-publicity on having available a really generous set of voluntary redundancy provisions as part of their standard employment package.

As in the case of the two earlier voluntary redundancies during Ralph Woolf's term as chief executive, the compensation payments, however generous compared with what the state required, were quite quickly recovered through savings in wage and salary costs. Redundancy expenditures were estimated to have been £1.3m, and the subsequent payroll savings at an annual £450,000. So the former had been fully recovered after three years.

But the company's response to this crisis in the 1990s contained a quite new component as well as a by now well-tried project of voluntary redundancy. This was an organised and highly participative drive to reduce the costs of purchases and find other savings to add to those resulting from the voluntary redundancy of people. The approach seems to have been of a 'scatter-gun' character with suggestions for cost savings being invited from the entire workforce. Records show that as many as 285 suggestions were elicited. These were then subjected to scrutiny and evaluation by an ad hoc working party, bringing together people both from Scott Bader's two representative institutions and from management, all under Ian Henderson's chairmanship as chief executive.

The reported numbers suggest that this cost-reducing drive was rather a success and resulted in initial savings of over £1m at an annual rate. That figure has to be qualified as applying only to the initial results, because there was some later slipping back. For example, the former privilege of free tea and coffee, which was extinguished in this mid-1990s savings drive, was later reinstated. But an important and apparently enduring cost saving was achieved by raising the qualifications which newcomers would have to satisfy to be assigned a company car. The largest single saving was rather different in kind because it resulted not from a purchasing but a people change: an agreement to increase the working week by one hour without any increase in pay.

It is worth repeating that while this mid-1990s savings drive produced desirable results in the form of cost savings similar to what might be expected from successful programmes of continuous improvement, it cannot be classified as a genuine example of one of those. To begin with, it was explicitly a once-off rather than an ongoing project. Equally important its approach was, as I have described it, of a 'scatter-gun' character using an appeal for suggestions addressed to the entire workforce. It was not an approach, following the teaching of Deming, which would have started from an analysis of statistical variation. Each of these two approaches can, without question, generate valuable results. But evidence from both the US and Japan suggests that the gains likely to result from the Deming approach are likely to be that much more substantial.

A NEW STRATEGIC THRUST IN THE 1990S: OVERSEAS EXPANSION

Down to the end of the 1980s, and with the single exception of what became in 1974 its wholly-owned French subsidiary, Scott Bader SA, the Wollaston parent business chose to use a combination of direct exports and licensing agreements with overseas partners as the best way of maximising benefits accruing from its leading technology in the field of those unsaturated polyester resins used to make GRP. Brian Parkyn had been from the outset a most forceful and influential advocate of the search for licensee partners, and over the years more than 40 agreements had been signed around the world and delivered significant gross income at a quite modest level of on-going costs. Of course the licensees had to be kept happy and their know-how updated in line with new developments in the Wollaston laboratories. Once every two years their representatives were invited to Wollaston for a programme of teach-ins and the exchange of technical information. For the purpose of these gatherings, a special lecture theatre was included in the design of Wollaston's new 1960s Bryson building. However, despite the cost of these gatherings and other expenses, the total expenses only rarely exceeded 50% of total fee income, at least down to the start of the 1980s: a most satisfactory comparative margin, as Brian Parkyn and other supporters of the policy were not slow to point out.

However, for reasons which are not altogether clear but which may well have included inadequate protection against price inflation and the costs and difficulties of effective policing, licence fees measured as a percentage of profits fell dramatically between 1985 and 1991, from close on 20% to under 8%. They also fell by about 50% in inflation-adjusted cash terms. In any event, quite soon after taking over in 1990, Ian Henderson persuaded the company board that licensing agreements were not in all cases continuing to offer an adequate return on the technologies which had been developed and were continuously being improved at Wollaston. And he argued successfully for two new and linked policy departures. The first was for the development – whether by acquisition or otherwise – of Scott Bader overseas manufacturing subsidiaries in places where that could be justified by regional levels of demand. The second policy departure was for a parallel development, by acquisition or otherwise, of the company's own distribution and sales businesses overseas, so as to bring the business that much closer to offshore customers. The model was one which had already proved itself in the UK with the acquisition of Strand Glassfibre and its sales and distribution network in 1978.

This pair of new policies was successfully implemented during the 1990s in two separate and discrete phases: in its traditional market areas in the early years of the decade, and in two former ex-communist countries of Eastern Europe, starting from 1997.

OVERSEAS EXPANSION PHASE I: SCANDINAVIA, THE US,
SOUTH AFRICA, AND THE MIDDLE EAST

The new policy began to be implemented in the early 1990s. In 1991, the Traxton/Reeves diary tells us, a new start-up sales and distribution business was established in North America: '1991: Office in Hudson, Ohio, opened under Bill Fitzgibbons to develop the sale of emulsion polymers in North America.'

In the following year Scott Bader took over the business of its sales and distribution agent in Sweden, Niedert Trading.

Then in 1993 came the start of the two new manufacturing subsidiaries overseas, duly noted by Traxton/Reeves as they occurred:

> 1993: Inauguration of Scott Bader Proprietary (in South Africa).
> Scott Bader Middle East started trading.

To understand what happened in South Africa, some background is required. To begin with, as Brian Parkyn remembers, there was considerable opposition in Wollaston when the proposal of a South African licensee had first come forward in the early 1960s. Such a move was seen by many Commonwealth members as tantamount to supporting the country's then apartheid regime. However, the opposition, as we shall see, was later overcome by an imaginative, even if not altogether commercial, modification of the company's standard licensing arrangements. It was decided that royalty payments associated with this licence should stay in South Africa and be transferred to a trust to alleviate hardship among African farmers. There will be more about that decision in a later chapter. In the meantime, Andrew Gunn has kindly supplied the necessary commercial and related specifics which preceded the start-up of Scott Bader Proprietary in 1993:

> Scott Bader had been represented in South Africa since the 1960s via its licensee, NCS Plastics Proprietary Ltd. Over the years, while NCS Plastics remained in the ownership of the Hepburn business family, Scott Bader developed a close relationship with it. But in the late 1980s, as unrest and protest against the apartheid policies of the South African government became widespread, and the reaction to the protest became ever more violent, the Hepburn family, like many others, decided to move their capital abroad. They therefore sold their interest in NCS Plastics to the South African chemical giant, Sentrachem. From that time on the culture

of the company apparently changed. In any case Sentrachem was found in 1990 to be in breach of its licence agreement. Both in Australia and in the Middle East it had advertised goods for sale based on Scott Bader's technology.

Scott Bader informed NCS Plastics of the evidence that it was in breach of the licensing agreement. Extensive discussions and negotiations followed, during which it was agreed that a new licence between the two companies would be drawn up. Under it NCS Plastics would enjoy *non-exclusive* rights to manufacture and sell Scott Bader's products in South Africa. NCS was in fact the market leader in the manufacture and sale of polyesters in South Africa. Moreover Scott Bader's Crystic brand name had a dominant position in the market.

At about the same time, long-standing and senior former members of the NCS Plastics staff, who had left the business shortly after its acquisition by Sentrachem, approached Scott Bader with a proposal that they should themselves import the company's products and sell them into the South African market.

NCS had been informed that despite its new non-exclusive licence, Scott Bader itself planned to sell its own products in the South African market. On this basis discussions with the former senior staff members of NCS were continued. During these discussions an opportunity arose to bring in a small chemical manufacturing company, in which another former NCS senior staff member was involved. As a result, and in due course, a three-way joint venture was formed: with SMG Proprietary Ltd providing the marketing and distribution expertise, Charter Chemicals Proprietary Ltd providing the manufacturing facilities, and Scott Bader providing the technology and financial resources. During its first trading year, the new joint venture showed sales of 2 million South African rands. During the following year it broke even, and in 1996, by which time it was operating at its capacity limits, it showed a profit of 2.6 million rands and had recovered the losses accumulated since its start-up.

But that is by no means the end of the Scott Bader story in the new post-apartheid South Africa, where the market for GRP and thus for polyester resins appears to be growing briskly. As the century came to an end, the annual rate of polyester sales by Scott Bader Proprietary were in excess of 4,000 tonnes and the business was contributing to its

Wollaston parent royalties linked to the value of its sales. By then, Scott Bader, having bought out the other two original partners, was the sole owner of the business. Numbers employed continued to rise and had reached 74 by the year 2000. In that same year staff at Scott Bader Pty were for the first time admitted into membership of the Commonwealth. It is true that mainly because of higher raw material costs the results in the year 2000 showed a modest loss. However, this does not seem to have constituted an enduring setback and in the first quarter of 2001 the results were back in profit.

If only as a footnote we should not forget NCS Plastics and its non-exclusive licence. Wollaston records show that in 1997 it contributed more than half of the total Scott Bader licence fee income from third parties. It may be claimed with some justice that after the detection of the NCS contract breach in 1990, Scott Bader played its cards successfully in South Africa with a mixture of reactions and initiatives. Little more than seven years on from 1993, the company is entitled to be at least modestly satisfied with the results.

The same is true, and financially even more so, if we turn from South Africa to Scott Bader's second new manufacturing subsidiary of the 1990s in the Middle East, or more precisely in the free trade zone of the Arab Emirate of Dubai. Once again Andrew Gunn has kindly supplied me with background details:

> Since the 1960s the Middle East has been an important export market for Scott Bader, and by the early 1990s the company was exporting approximately 4,000 tonnes of unsaturated polyester resins, compounds and gelcoats each year into the region. However, the market was fiercely price competitive with imports coming not only from Continental Europe but also from the Far East. Scott Bader's ability to be price competitive depended not only upon the reputation of its products, but also upon the relative value of Sterling against the Deutschmark and the US Dollar.
>
> In pursuit of the new strategy of international expansion, David Lovell and Les Pitcher, both of whom had long experience with Scott Bader as export managers supplying goods to the Middle East, made an assessment of the potential in the region, and of possible sites at which a plant might be located. They became aware of the recent construction of a polyester manufacturing plant in the Jebel Ali free trade zone in the Emirate of Dubai. After

a visit, they recommended that Scott Bader should seek to enter into a joint venture agreement with the company which owned the plant. It had been formed by Pakistani businessmen who had long experience of the oil industry in the Middle East.

However, it soon became apparent that Scott Bader was not the only European polyester manufacturing company interested in a new plant in Jebel Ali. Accordingly, Ian Henderson made an urgent visit to meet the owners of the Pakistani-led business in late 1992, and proposed a joint venture to them. This was agreed and the new joint venture company was formed in May 1993. It started off well and was quickly using most of its capacity. Plans were made to add a second reactor to the single one already installed and in use.

However these plans were dealt a severe blow when, on 12 June 1994, the whole of the plant went up in a catastrophic fire. It took more than two years before, following site clearance, the drawing-up and approval of new plans, and the construction of new buildings and plant, the new unit was ready to be commissioned and start operating. It was opened by the then British secretary of state for trade and industry, Ian Lang, in the presence of HE Sultan Ahmed bin Sulayem, chairman of the Jebel Ali free trade zone authority, and HE Abdul Rahman Al Mutawee, the director general of the Dubai chamber of commerce and industry. The company had to struggle to regain its market over the next two years, in part because during the reconstruction of the joint venture plant a second polyester plant had been opened in the Jebel Ali free trade zone by a European competitor.

But as time went on relationships between the two venture capital partners became rather difficult, and both concluded that the business would be better run by a sole owner than as a joint venture. Accordingly each made bids to buy the other's shares. The matter was resolved in Scott Bader's favour in October 1998 when the local 49% interest was bought out and Joe McKeever was appointed general manager. Since then the business has made remarkable progress, recording a profit of $1.2m on a turnover of $13.3m in 1999. Already in the previous year it had made a first royalty payment, linked to its sales, to the parent business in Wollaston. Moreover, sales of its polyester resins were confidently expected to reach 10,000 tonnes in the year 2000 with productivity levels, measured in tonnes per person employed, coming close to the best levels in the group, those achieved by Scott Bader SA in France.

Some will detect in that achievement the influence of Michele Maille, the long-serving production manager of SBSA in Amiens and, since 1998, a director of the group's Middle East manufacturing business in Dubai.

Given the rebuilding of the business and subsequent recovery after the catastrophic fire in 1994, it is not too much to claim that Scott Bader in the Middle East had become the group's top economic and financial success story by the end of the 1990s. On the basis of this evidence, coupled with that of the new manufacturing subsidiary in South Africa, it also seems reasonable to claim that new international expansion strategy of the 1990s had been reasonably well vindicated by the end of the decade. Apart from Ian Henderson himself, Arne Strand, the head of overseas sales for the first half of the 1990s, should probably be given the main credit for having pushed it, and Ian Henderson would wish to give credit to the executive team, and particularly the overseas managers, for the later stages of the push. We will defer until later in the chapter a discussion of the second phase of the strategy, focused on ex-communist countries: the manufacturing venture in Zagreb, capital of Croatia, and the new sales and distribution office in Prague, capital of the Czech Republic.

CLOSED MOULD FORMING: NEW DEVELOPMENTS IN THE 1980S AND 1990S

As he did in the case of the evolution of Texipols in an earlier chapter, Barry Sauntson, the company's director of research and development, here takes up the story in more recent years of Scott Bader's quest for a viable system of making reinforced plastics by closed mould forming. The earlier stages of the story, those associated with Crystic Systems and Sheet Moulding Compound (SMC) were covered in chapter 5. There is an overlap reference to the latter in Barry's first sentence.

> During the early 80s the company had a small business at Wollaston making Sheet Moulding Compound (SMC). ... The UK 'free' market however was limited since many SMC producers were integrated into moulding and vice versa. As well as the difficult market problems ... there were many in-house problems stemming from variable consistency and quality of production.

Most of these problems came from the thickening process used to convert the liquid resin/filler combination into a thick paste. ...

At the same time, another separate business was being developed, called Crystic Impel, which was also part of the closed mould offering. This technology basically consisted of resin/filler/glass blends made on an extruder in dry pellet form, for injection moulding small parts in electrical and domestic appliance applications. The key behind this patented technology was the use of solid crystalline resins (melting points around 80C) as the main resin ingredient.

If these solid resins were heated and melted and then added to liquid resin, on cooling, we wondered, would they physically thicken the mixture to a potential SMC paste viscosity? In principle they did and the heavily patented Crystic Impreg technology was born. It was however too late to save the existing SMC business.

Much R & D work was started to optimise the crystalline thickening system ... Many patents were obtained in several countries. ...

While the work was proceeding strategy reviews again highlighted the importance of closed mould processing. Not only did it bring productivity and environmental improvements but it was the key to entry into the volume automotive business – a market with huge potential for composites. ...

Closed mould became a major strategy. Automotive became a key target market for us and Impreg became the key product/technology thrust within these (although not the only one). The plan was to sell Impreg resin as a moulding compound component to the major European compound producers and the automotive companies and grant them a licence to use the patented technology. The system, while slightly more expensive than traditional SMC, brought major advances in 'instant thickening', stock holding, consistency and quality, very long shelf life, ability to use any resin, and the ability to mould under low pressure (to become known as LPMC), giving potential savings in press and tooling costs.

Over the next two years or so only minor resin sales were developed and we were unable to make the breakthrough with the majors.

In the USA, a long-standing acquaintance of Scott Bader, who was a technical entrepreneur, was forming a company with some colleagues by borrowing heavily from private investors. Originally known as Total Composites (TC) this company later became National Composites Inc (NCI). They invested in a 'state of the art' compounding plant and moulding facilities. They became a customer and licensee for Impreg and the technology was the basis of their business.

There were ups and downs particularly in quality, consistency and scrap levels – many of the problems stemming from equipment and poor quality control – but the business grew. Volumes reached some thousands of tonnes and represented good sales of Impreg resin which was now being made in a special plant in France.

Sometimes there were resin problems resulting from contamination which affected the final product ... The main problems, however, were related to pricing, a volatile customer base and competitive reaction.

NCI had started to heavily promote and advertise their Impreg LPMC. The big US competitors became aware and concerned. While they couldn't copy the patented system, they did develop their own versions, and while these were often inferior, they seemed determined to 'keep NC out'... Customers did not want to pay for the benefits and whenever a new account was obtained, it seemed as though it was lost relatively quickly, mostly for price reasons. Even those customers that did stay never seemed to reach their projected offtake. ... As a result, the business moved from one project to another without establishing baseline sales, stability or profitability. ...

More money was put in. Eventually SB became the major shareholder and started to manage directly. An experienced technical person was seconded ... and he quickly installed a lower-cost, more flexible production unit, sorted out the quality control, and soon proved that the overall technology worked. Pricing and margin continued to be the problem.

About this time Scott Bader in France, SBSA, acquired a small SMC producing business called Auch in the south of the country, and along with it a sister moulding company called Stradour. This was to pursue the cold mould strategy in Europe.

Back at NCI, managers came and went but the business pattern continued. The moulding operation was shut and reductions to the cost base were made. Still more money was needed and despite continued optimistic forecasts losses continued.

Eventually in late 1998 the decision was made to shut the operation. Sometime after, the Stradour moulding operation in France was disposed of through the mechanism of a management buyout.

Hindsight suggests that there are many lessons to be learned – too many 'news' at the same time, (that is new technology, new market, new region). Then there was the competitive reaction. Did we move in too late to save the business? How far did we underestimate the real up front costs that that would have required? We all have our views but it would make a good business school case study of *'what would you have done'*?

Above all, perhaps, we must learn that development (whether business or technical) carries risk and uncertainty and that not all projects will be successful...

Finally, closed mould remains a key part of the strategy. Scott Bader Composites continues in France, more and more closed mould business has been gained with other products, complementary lines to Impreg are being produced and further new technologies for closed mould are being pursued.

'The Search' continues.

Perhaps we should stand back for a moment in drawing to an end this discussion about Scott Bader's quest for a viable closed mould system. According to John Raymond's evidence about the patent taken out in 1950, it had lasted, by the time this was written in early 2001, for more than 50 years – without so far reaching solid business success. But against that there was the optimistic exit line of Jean-Marc Bain about Scott Bader Composites in France: '...many requests from possible partners'. I should also perhaps quote more explicitly the view held widely in the reinforced plastics industry – and publicly endorsed among others by Brian Parkyn – that, at least in developed countries, the future lies with closed mould forming of one kind or another and not with wet hand lay-up.

INTERNATIONAL EXPANSION PHASE 2: THE CZECH REPUBLIC AND CROATIA

It was towards the end of the 1990s, precisely in 1998, that Scott Bader took the first of two steps in extending its new international expansion policy to the countries of Eastern Europe. It established a distribution and sales office in Prague, the capital from 1919 of Czechoslovakia and from the early 1990s of the Czech Republic. A look at the map will confirm Prague's advantages for distribution, placed as it is west of Vienna and almost due south of Berlin, but also with good access to the five most economically developed of its neighbouring ex-communist countries: Poland, Hungary and Slovakia (from which the Czech Republic had negotiated a friendly divorce in the early 1990s), and among the successor states of the former Yugoslavia, Slovenia and Croatia.

Then, in 1999, Scott Bader took a much more substantial step in the development of its activities in the region. It responded positively to an approach from a recently privatised resin manufacturing business in Croatia. Andrew Gunn has again supplied the background details:

> Around that time [viz. in 1998 and 1999] Chromos Tvornica Smola dd, a business with which there had been some contact over time, approached Scott Bader as a potential partner. It was a time of special difficulty for the Croatian business because of a recent devaluation of the local currency. Of particular interest to Scott Bader was the fact that Chromos had a reputation for the manufacture and sale of vinyl ester resins, which were not produced elsewhere in the group. It was also a manufacturer of alkyd resins, which were complementary to similar activities in the UK. Furthermore, the installed capacity at Chromos, added to that available in Amiens and Wollaston, would provide an opportunity for the achievement by the group of a 10% share in the Continental European market for polyesters.
>
> Accordingly in late 1999 Scott Bader purchased convertible unsecured loan stock in Chromos, which it intended would be converted in time into the equity of the company. In effect it took control of Chromos as of a subsidiary.

For the benefit of non-specialist readers, the main special quality of vinyl esters is that they are very much more resistant than ordinary polyesters to aggressive chemicals such as acids or bleaches. They are also more resistant to high temperatures. Given these qualities they are particularly used to make ducting for flues, for example flues coming from furnaces, for they have the power to contain hot and aggressive gases such as sulphur dioxide.

The control by Scott Bader at Wollaston of Chromos in Zagreb was still less than two years old when this was written early in 2001. The top management of the group does not wish to conceal the fact that considerable teething problems have been encountered. Many of these are probably common to a majority of formerly state-owned Croatian businesses privatised in the 1990s. However the same top management is also confident that, notwithstanding an accounting loss in the year 2000, the remaining difficulties will be overcome before too long and that the now well-established strengths of a) polyester resins made to Scott Bader's specifications and b) the quality of its customer service will enable Chromos to achieve its market goals – with the bonus of its own vinyl esters thrown in.

About both Chromos in Zagreb and the new sales and distribution centre in Prague, I should mention that their future is briefly revisited in the this chapter.

THE RELATIVE BUSINESS STRENGTH OF SCOTT BADER AT THE BEGINNING AND END OF THE 1990S

By the test of balance sheet strength, measured by cash in the bank, what by the end of the 1990s had become the Scott Bader Group was less strong than it had been at the start of the decade. Readers will remember that Ian Henderson's predecessor as chief executive had left a business with around £6m of cash in the bank and negligible borrowings. By the end of Ian Henderson's decade, in 1999, there was no net cash in the balance sheet. As for borrowings, these were still quite modest by industry standards but they were not negligible.

But, of course, as was discussed briefly earlier in this chapter, its balance sheet cash position is not the only test of business strength. As we have seen, there was much investment in plant and machinery at Wollaston during Ian Henderson's early years. There was also much investment in improved facilities, for example the new customer service centre and the new centralised warehouse built next to it. Above all there were the three new overseas manufacturing subsidiaries and the three, first ever, overseas distribution and sales centres which are legacies of Ian Henderson's decade as chief executive.

In the case of Ralph Woolf's tenure, it was possible to make a meaningful comparison between labour productivity, measured by tonnes of output per employee, as between when he arrived and when he left. That is not possible in the same way if we try to compare the data at the start and the end of the 1990s. The reason is that we are not comparing like with like, for by the end of the decade the numbers reflect the activities of a multinational group with very different component entities. For what it's worth, management data on the value of sales per person shows a decline of some 10% between 1990 and 1999. But quite apart from all the uncertainties of using money values in measurements of this kind, the character of the business reflected by the 1999 statistics was totally different at the end of the decade from what it was at the beginning. It seems to be true that, measured in tonnes output per employee, productivity was relatively rather low when the results from the new overseas subsidiaries started to become consolidated in those of the group. But that had evidently been foreseen and the reaction to it in Wollaston was not therefore one of alarm.

Perhaps the main achievement of Scott Bader in Ian Henderson's stewardship during the 1990s was to strengthen its potential for survival in the future. It did this in the first place by the international expansion which we have already looked at. What perhaps has not yet been sufficiently emphasised is that the three new markets to which during the decade it gained much closer and lower cost access – in the Middle East and South Asia, in South Africa and elsewhere on the African continent, and in Eastern Europe and Russia – are likely to show more rapid growth in the demand for traditional reinforced plastics associated with wet hand lay-up than are the domestic UK or other Western markets. That is because of the belief referred to earlier, and apparently growing more widespread all the time, that reinforced plastics associated with traditional wet hand lay-up will gradually come to be replaced in developed countries by reinforced plastics manufactured by closed mould forming of one kind an another.

Secondly, or so I believe, Scott Bader in the 1990s strengthened its potential for survival into the future by a further enhancement of the already high emphasis which it had placed for many years on customer service and customer care. It is not too much to claim that the reality of this new emphasis goes far beyond the new customer service centre which has already been mentioned. A systematic effort is being made to develop so-called 'partnership relationships' with Scott Bader's more important and regular customers. The model for these relationships originally comes, like so much else, from Japan. The logic behind the idea is that both parties to the relationship can come to have a serious economic interest in sustaining it over the long term. Visits to and discussions with senior people at two of Scott Bader's most important customers in the marine sector of the GRP market – Fairline Boats and Vosper Thorneycroft – suggest that such relationships can come to be seen as offering real benefits for buyers as well as sellers. Vosper Thorneycroft, which has bought material from Scott Bader to build minehunter ships for the Royal Navy since the beginning of the 1990s and even before, has recently bought out Halmatic. Readers will remember that Scott Bader had what was essentially its breakthrough success when it built the hull of Halmatic's ocean-going boat *Perpetua* in Crystic Resin 189 in 1954. They will also remember that Brian Parkyn was a non-executive director of the business in the 1970s and 1980s.

There is no space to offer further examples of how Scott Bader has evolved, and is determined to go on evolving, partnership relationships with its key trading partners, including its suppliers only slightly less importantly than its customers (slightly *less* because what it buys are substantially commodities). The main commercial point can probably best be put by saying that when what is being traded is essentially not a commodity, but something special for the trading partner, then long-term and high trust partnership relationships can work extremely well. What's more, because it is both independent and substantially immune from takeover offers, such relationships with Scott Bader have that much extra credibility.

Looking at in this way we can see some continuity in the fundamental driver of the business as between the 1980s and 1990s: the strengthening of Scott Bader's capacity to sustain itself in the future. At the end of the 1980s the result of that driver was the strength of the cash position in the balance sheet. At the end of the 1990s the result was perhaps two things: a) those three overseas manufacturing subsidiaries were well placed because of where they are to take advantage of more rapid demand, and b) a larger number of partnership relationships with trading partners.

These then are two main reasons why, or so it seems to me, a mainly positive verdict can be pronounced on Scott Bader, considered as a *business* during the decade of the 1990s. It was stronger in 2000 than in 1990 essentially because:

a) It had established good and relatively low-cost access to markets where demand for traditional wet hand lay-up GRP, and not GRP formed in closed moulds, was likely to grow more rapidly. In consequence, total sales of polyester resins of what had become the Scott Bader group had been significantly increased.

b) By putting even greater emphasis than before on customer service and care, it gave itself the best chance of keeping its existing customers over the long term and of establishing potentially long-term relationships with new ones.

Nevertheless, real and important as these successes were, they must not be allowed to obscure the fact with which we began this chapter: for a manufacturer with as its main product those polyester resins used to make GRP, competitive conditions had been becoming progressively tougher since the end of the 1970s. Moreover, at least as measured by the profit margin on sales, that process continued through the 1990s. If we compare the average value of that margin over the first five years of the decade with the same average over the last five, we find a reduction of nearly 20%.

THE EVOLUTION OF THE SCOTT BADER COMMUNITY OVER THE 1990S

Any account of how the community evolved during the 1990s cannot be made even minimally coherent unless we recognise at once that the evidence pulls in two quite contradictory directions. On the one hand there are a number of positive specifics, among which the opening of the Learning Centre, after long years of discussion, may serve as an example. On the other hand there is a pervasive and sustained accumulation of negative evidence, a continuing flow of negative muttering, punctuated by pained expressions of disappointment from friendly outsiders. The *Reactor* printed letters of discontent which are too many to be counted, and a special and anonymous 'agony uncle' column had to be instituted to cope with them. Successive chairmen of the Scott Bader trustees wrote articles which expressed their disappointment. Numerous professionally conducted 'opinion surveys' exhibited minor differences of detail but consistently reported levels of dissatisfaction in line with what would be expected in a conventional capitalist company – and in some cases rather worse. Assume for the moment – for discussion later – that such evidence has some objective content. The obvious question seems to be that if dissatisfaction is no lower here than elsewhere, is there much positive reality in the Scott Bader Commonwealth and about its thinking of itself as a working community at all?

But, to be fair to the 1990s, it seems that 'negative muttering' and 'negative feelings towards the high-ups' has a long history at Wollaston and can be traced back to the 1960s. There may indeed be more evidence for it in the 1990s. But that may well be explained by the openness of the *Reactor*'s 'agony uncle' column and the objectively tougher conditions within which the company had to operate. In these circumstances it seems best to defer the discussion of negative feelings in the community until we move on, in the next chapter, to consider the broader issues of the Commonwealth and the gradual extension of democratic authority. In this way we shall perhaps avoid attributing solely to Ian Henderson's years of chief stewardship discontent with management which was already deep-seated when he arrived.

However, it nevertheless makes sense to itemise here some specific and positive developments in the Scott Bader community during the 1990s. What are perhaps the three most important can, it seems, be attributed at least in part to the work and advocacy of Jim O'Brien. Having previously held top management position in British Rail, Jim emerged from a selection process to accept the position of Scott Bader's chairman designate. He took up the actual chairmanship shortly afterwards, and was the main voice behind the appointment of Ian Henderson as chief executive in 1990. He resigned from the post in 1994. And, before moving on, it is important to note that during Jim O'Brien's chairmanship there was also positive recognition by the wider community of the work of two members of the Scott Bader community. Keith Edwards received an MBE for his work on environmental stewardship and Pat Blackwell also received an MBE in recognition of her long and successful secretaryship of the Community Council.

THE LEARNING CENTRE AND TWO OTHER POSITIVE DEVELOPMENTS

When the Learning Centre opened its doors in October 1996, the *Reactor* devoted its cover story to the event. In the story's second paragraph, Les Pitcher, the senior manager who wrote it, spelled out its essential logic:

> The Learning Centre is all about individuals improving their skills, but the subjects can be of their own choice and do not have to be work-related. Encouraging a return to a learning mode is one of the main purposes of the Centre. The company must continually raise skill levels in its members if it is to survive in the 20th century.

Later in the same article the author returns to the idea that *individual* learning is what the centre aims to supply:

The distinction between learning and training within Scott Bader is that learning is an individual experience and can cover any chosen subject that interests the individual, whilst training is a more formal team-based event and the subject is work related.

What the *Reactor* article chooses not to discuss was the enormously long gestation period which preceded the decision to establish such a centre at all, and the evolution of the concept at the heart of it. The original concept can perhaps be traced back to Fred Blum, the religiously minded sociologist – he eventually took holy orders – who had worked at Scott Bader with Roger Hadley in the early 1960s and published *Work and Community: The Scott Bader Commonwealth and the Quest for a New Social Order* in 1968. Later, from the 1970s onwards, Godric became a tireless advocate. And its importance for him is highlighted in an open letter which he sent to all members of the Commonwealth towards the end of 1992, and in which calls on its readers 'to proceed now with launching and manning the "learning centre" concept and link the centre with progressive organisations and people, and even fund it at the expense of less profit distribution'.

It seems clear both from the advocacy of links with 'other organisations and people' and above all from Godric's use of the adjective 'progressive', that what he had in mind in this open letter was something rather different from the institution which is 'all about individuals improving their skills'. There may be some argument about what language would best describe what Godric then, and others before him, had in mind. But there can be no real doubt that what he essentially hoped for was some kind of ideological centre with as its main task the continuous reinforcement and development of Scott Bader *values* both inside and outside the business.

What is much less clear now is how – by what set of processes and steps – the concept advocated by Godric in his 1992 open letter became the actual Learning Centre celebrated upon its opening by the *Reactor* in November 1996. But it is perhaps sufficient to make just four points. The first is that the establishment of such centres became quite widely fashionable in UK business in the 1990s. The Ford Motor Company at Dagenham and the then employee-owned Baxi Partnership outside Preston are both, albeit in their different ways, good examples. Second there is widespread testimony at Wollaston to the effect that Jim O'Brien, though he had resigned some time before it opened, put his substantial authority as chairman behind the 'learning centre for individual improvement' concept. Third, it is surely a fair bet that inside the actual working community at Wollaston, the learning centre concept which actually prevailed was hugely more popular than its more ideological predecessor favoured by Godric. Finally, I need to highlight the fact that among the 'learning modules' made available in the centre opened by Les Pitcher are a number which make possible a better understanding of the Commonwealth.

The other two examples of what I have rather loosely characterised as positive developments within the Scott Bader community during the 1990s can be dealt with more rapidly. The first was a scheme for training employees elected to be members of the company board in the functions and duties of company directors. I have quoted John Goring in these pages before. He does not seem to be someone who scatters compliments with a gossamer light hand. He served on the company board both before and after the introduction of these specially designed training schemes. He is in no doubt about their value both to the individuals involved and to the quality of company board decisions. Jim O'Brien was evidently the prime mover behind them.

A third positive development in the life of the community was rather different again but should be featured here. It had to do with the Commonwealth's charitable giving. The old arrangement was that the distribution of all available charitable money should be by either direct or indirect collective decisions, that is either by the general meeting of the Commonwealth or by its elected board of management. Under the new arrangement, up to 50% of all the money to be distributed is assigned by individual Commonwealth members to charities of their own individual choice. The initiative behind this change came from the CBoM, led by Alan Green. Its aim, as he has explained, was to enable Commonwealth members to take a stronger personal interest in corporate charitable giving.

REVISITING SCOTT BADER VALUES AND INSTITUTIONAL REFORM IN THE 1990S

Readers will remember an extended series of 'values workshops' in the 1980s, formally initiated by the Commonwealth through the CBoM – in line with the latter's formal responsibility for the 'philosophical oversight' of the business – and led by Canon Frank Scuffham. Brian Elgood has kindly explained what happened next:

In the 1990–3 period, more work on the Scott Bader values was done at a 'Values Steering Group'. But before that, 'core values' had been proposed by the board of the Scott Bader company, to be added to the original list of seven, seen as part of the constitution. The additions were:

> Equality of humanness
> Equality of race, religion and sex
> Freedom and participative management
> Security
> Full growth and development of human beings

In December 1993, Ian Alexander (then chair of the CBoM) was writing on behalf of the Steering Group that 'over the years misunderstanding and lack of clarity have inhibited the growth of the Commonwealth as an entity and the realisation of the potential of its members'. The group was formed to 'agree the means to link Scott Bader beliefs and values to Scott Bader practice', and they saw it as their task to 'look at our principal values and offer definitions which might find greater acceptance'.

By the summer of 1994, a consensus had emerged with support in each of the four Wollaston power centres: the company board, the Community Council, the Commonwealth board of management (CBoM), and the trustees. Accordingly a booking was made at an 'events centre', converted out of a former United Reformed church, in the nearby village of Hastings Yardley. Representatives from each of the four bodies gathered there for an all-day meeting in December. Jennifer Wates, then the trustees' chairman, and Ian Henderson, the managing director, were leading participants. The outcome was a pair of agreed sets of seven vision statements and ten 'behaviour statements'. Both were approved by a general meeting of Commonwealth members in February 1995. They have since been framed and hung in the reception area at Wollaston Hall until the spring of 2001. It may be helpful to have an accessible record of them here.

A VISION STATEMENTS:
We strive to build and sustain an enterprise which is successful because:

1 We provide education and training and show willingness to learn, grow and accept responsibility.
2 Managers lead by example, involving their teams, and enabling each person to maximise their contribution.

3 We are committed to meeting our customers' needs by constantly improving our products and services.

4 We have the courage to face and resolve conflicts openly and honestly.

5 Our work is founded on collective responsibility and mutual trust and we commit ourselves to decisions once taken.

6 We make our decisions on an ethical basis, caring for each other, the wider world and the environment.

7 As joint stewards of all our economic resources, we use them effectively, not just for our own livelihood, but for coming generations.

B BEHAVIOUR STATEMENTS
In enhancing the vision we must:

1 Be committed to the care and welfare of the working community and those within it.

2 Meet the needs of customers by the dedication of our own skills within the framework of the vision statement.

3 Seek to use the resources as effectively as possible by flexible, waste-conscious, creative working practices.

4 Recognise our own failures and weaknesses and strive to improve ourselves.

5 Participate fully in the consultative and democratic processes of the community and support the decisions of community bodies.

6 Talk openly, directly, and honestly about others and not about them in their absence.

7 Act in a way which is worthy of the trust of others.

8 Carry out our own duties conscientiously, striving to meet work objectives and constantly improve the quality of what we do.

9 Support the good, positive and creative in others and avoid being negative.

10 Enjoy working co-operatively and enthusiastically with fellow workers.

It need hardly be said that there is some little distance between the 'overall love' and other 'arch values' which emerged from the workshops of the 1980s and the 'striving to meet work objectives' and other behaviour and vision statements of the 1990s. But maybe it would not have been easy to arrive at the second without having started from the first. More generally, these statements can perhaps best be seen as in part a creed of ethical business practice and in part as a guide to what Americans have lately started to call 'emotional intelligence'.

So much for the evolution of the Scott Bader values.

About later efforts to pick up the process of institutional reform Brian Elgood has also contributed the following paragraphs:

> From a meeting, proposed by Jim O'Brien, of all the constitutional bodies on 2 September 1992 a process was started designed '*either* to propose alterations to the existing structure of the company and Commonwealth *or* to agree to recognise and set down what we do at present'. The process was initially led by a team consisting of Peter Mattli, Frank Scuffham and Brian Elgood, in his then role of chair of the CBoM. The process was highly participative with presentations and discussions taking place with small groups of members and non-members throughout Britain and Ireland. Groups of members and non-members were then invited to continue to meet to develop proposals for an improved structure. These groups thus consisted of those who wanted to work on the process.
>
> A 'three-body' structure emerged (with a supervisory board, an executive board, and a Community Council with strengthened powers) i.e. with substantial similarities to that proposed as the end of the eighties. (It should be noted that there was some dissent that such a structure *did* emerge, the external trustees dissenting.)
>
> By the end of 1993 a majority of the 43 people who had continued to work on the process were in favour of 'maintaining the present structure of company and Commonwealth'.
>
> Later from 1995, further work took place in the ad hoc 'governance group' which was started as an early initiative of Derek Muir, the incoming Chairman of Scott Bader Company Limited. Derek had had a career in international business with Vickers; he had also been a non-executive director of the majority-employee-owned Tullis Russell. The governance group, over a long period, had members – usually the Chairs – drawn from the Company Board, Commonwealth Board of Management, the Community Council and international representation from the executive team. The group set out to 'update our corporate governance'. Early on, the group was 'indicating a need for a single worldwide

Commonwealth with membership open to all'. And it also sought to provide an appropriate institutional structure to serve the increasingly international Scott Bader. Consultation took the form, initially, of presentations to members and non-members followed by questionnaires. Subsequently small groups discussed the proposals. The governance group was initially helped by a consultant, Michael Nisbett; the later stages were led by Alan Green, in his role as chair of the CBoM, helped by Ian Henderson and Brian Elgood in a steering group.

Its final proposal, supported by a majority of four at a general meeting in March 2000, as described in chapter 10, left most of the bodies unchanged – notably the trustees, the CBoM, and the Community Council. It proposed overseas Community Councils and a local executive board for Scott Bader in the UK. It also proposed a new board as a 'co-ordinating body for all operations of Scott Bader throughout the world 'accountable to members in general meeting and have[ing] elected members'.

At the time of writing (mid-2001), and following a CBoM initiative providing extensive Commonwealth training, membership of the Commonwealth is spreading rapidly throughout the overseas parts of Scott Bader and a 'trial' local executive board for Scott Bader in the UK has begun meeting.

POSTSCRIPT: NEW DIRECTIONS BUILT ON
OLD FOUNDATIONS

Our move to participate in a company in the EEC ... is a good move.
Godric Bader, Annual Report to Scott Bader AGM, November 1967.

Readers with very good memories for detail may perhaps recall this notably affirmative pronouncement about what was to become Scott Bader France – but was still then a joint venture with SA Sturge in Amiens – at the company's AGM in Wollaston in 1967. I had almost totally forgotten it. It only resurfaced in my brain when I started to think about the new focus on 'one market Europe' which the company presented to its customers, other trading partners and friends, as the first major new development of the year 2000. But then I suspect that ever since the move to Wollaston in 1940 and the takeover by the company of the Wollaston Estate and Wollaston Hall, Scott Bader has been inescapably and perhaps in some measure subconsciously 'Wollaston-centric'. Perhaps inescapably too – at least up to now – any one writing about the business has operated with a similarly 'Wollastoncentric' vision.

Allan Bell, as we know, took over from Ian Henderson as managing director in the autumn of 1999. He was the first person to be appointed to that position from inside and had previously been in charge of Scott Bader's operations in the UK. Whether surprisingly or otherwise, given that background, his first major new policy initiative has been to persuade top management – including colleagues in mainland Europe, and especially, because of its age and weight, in Scott Bader France – to accept a new main focus on Europe.

Bold and radical as it is, the economic and commercial logic behind this huge shift of focus which is already underway seems solid enough. Scott Bader has still to transplant into mainland Europe the full competitive advantages of its polyester resin products and its special know-how and reputation in the field of GRP applications in the marine markets of boat-builders and shipbuilders.

Moreover, as a result of developments in the 1990s, Scott Bader at the start of the new century controls, including Wollaston itself, three production units in Europe – Chromos in the Croatian capital of Zagreb having been added to the facilities of Scott Bader France. There are also the two new distribution centres in mainland Europe in Sweden and the Czech Republic – aside from those of Chromos itself and Scott Bader France. It is easy for even laymen to see that there are great new advantages to be had, if the response to customers of this 'Scott Bader network' in Europe can efficiently co-ordinated and managed as if they were a single unit.

It is true that Scott Bader France will lose some of its autonomy and of its exemplary business 'subsidiarity' as a result of this new focus. But Jean-Marc Bain, the chief executive of Scott Bader France, seems to have readily added new Europe-wide responsibilities to those he will continue to exercise in France.

Together with this new focus on Europe as one market, Allan Bell is determined to press ahead with an initiative in the present decade started by his predecessor in the previous one: to encourage non-Wollaston employees of the group to become members of the Commonwealth. He sees that as Wollaston's duty to the democratic values with which the business has been endowed. But he also sees it as likely to confer commercial advantages through enhancing employee commitment to customer service and ethical business practices.

10

The Commonwealth and the Gradual Extension of Democratic Authority

Taking the long view, the original purpose of forming the Commonwealth was to raise employees to the status of responsible owners; or
in other words to liberate them from the wage nexus ... *Ernest Bader*
From an article published in the [American Free Church] 'Journal
of Current Social Issue', Winter 1971–2

INTRODUCTION

When Godric retired from the chairmanship of the company in 1990
and accepted the post of life president, some 70 years of Bader family
power in the business – if not indeed family influence – finally came to
an end. As we know, the family had relinquished its shareholding much
earlier, in two successive acts of benefaction: the first in 1951 when 90%
of the equity was passed to the Commonwealth, and the second in
1963, when the remaining 10% was handed over. We need just to note
here, for later discussion, that in the case of the final 10%, while the
actual shares, as in the original gift, went to the Commonwealth, the
right to exercise them was passed to a newly created body of trustees.

Dr Fritz Schumacher, the former National Coal Board economist and
author of the celebrated *Small Is Beautiful: A Study of Economics as if
People Mattered* (Blond and Briggs, 1973), became in later life a great
admirer of Scott Bader and was indeed successively an external non-
executive director and a trustee of the business. Of its ownership, once
that had been transferred from the family to the Commonwealth he
wrote that that changed 'the existential character of "ownership" in so
fundamental a way that it would be better to think of such a transfer as
effecting the *extinction* [emphasis original] of private ownership rather
than as the establishment of collective ownership' (*op. cit.* p 260). That
is the line that we will follow here. In its financial sense the Commonwealth's *ownership* of Scott Bader's share capital will be ignored in what
follows – except on the margin when we deal briefly with the distribution to charity of the dividend income from those shares.

Rather than on ownership we focus our first attention in this chapter on the question of constitutional power or, as some will prefer to describe it, constitutional authority. In effect we ask what happened to the power or authority which the Bader family gave up in line, though not always in step, with the relinquishing of its shares. Part of the answer, as we shall see, is that certain reserve powers, associated with its 10% shareholding, went to the new body of the trustees. But that is not the most interesting piece of the answer. Aside from anything else those powers have so far been used only in a limited and advisory way. Moreover there might be serious company law difficulties if they were to be used more actively. They are probably best understood as in part a transitional device and in part as a means of sounding a wake-up call.

But what then about the destination of the main powers which the Bader family began to give up in 1951, as the first step in a long process which ended when Godric retired from the chairmanship in 1990? The short answer is that they have gradually passed to not one but two representative and democratic bodies to which the Commonwealth itself has given birth: namely, what have been called since 1971 the Commonwealth board of management (CBoM) and the Community Council. But before going any further I should emphasise that once it reached those two destinations that power – some may feel more comfortable with the word authority – became legitimised by democratic consent or at the least by democratic acquiescence.

On the other hand this transfer of power to the new democratic organs is not by any means complete. With the essential consent of those organs themselves, considerable powers, including as has often happened in similar cases, the 'power to manage the business', have remained with its professional managers. Partly because the phrase is deliberately rather vague, power in today's Scott Bader can, I think, best be understood as resting in a 'power-sharing mix', a mix which is unquestionably most unusual and very likely unique. The identities of the two main parties to this power-sharing are clear enough. They are the democracy of the Commonwealth's two representative bodies on the one hand and the top executive management of the business on the other. What is less clear is the precise balance of power between the two. After we have been through the details, itself a not altogether straightforward task, some readers may come to believe that each of the two main parties may actually favour the present uncertainty. Some senior managers are happy to refer to it as a source of 'creative friction'. But not all. Others see it by contrast as a source of dysfunctional conflict.

For the moment we will leave that question on one side. What seems by contrast almost certain is that if now, 50 years after the Commonwealth was born, you were to ask any old Scott Bader hand what he or she sees as the 'gold' which has most notably survived in the hills of this whole pathbreaking project, the odds are that the answer will include a reference to the position of labour. The language used may well differ depending on the place within the business, management or professional or otherwise, occupied by the person answering the question. Or the choice of words may simply depend on what they are deemed to connote or leave out. For example, Godric Bader expresses a marked hostility to the use of 'labour' in this context, presumably because it doesn't reflect the special position of 'trustees in common'. But whatever words are chosen the following points are likely to figure in the response.

> That labour is treated 'decently' both in terms of its pay and conditions and of its rights in relation to executive management; its position does not depend on the grace and favour of the board of directors or of executive management but is embodied in legally binding rules which can not be changed without its consent. (Its resulting *power* has sometimes been a source of irritation or worse to some managers, but that is another story.)

The discussion which now follows has two main and distinct areas of focus. The first is essentially about the constitutional rights and duties of members of the Commonwealth, as these were originally established in 1951, and as they have evolved since then. The second is about the material conditions, essentially the pay and other benefits, which that same labour force, those same Commonwealth members, now enjoy. The second of these two topics is held over to the next chapter.

However, some points of clarification need to be made before the discussion starts. The first is a fairly minor detail but could become a source of confusion unless flagged at this stage. Though I have used the terms 'labour' and 'Commonwealth member' above as if they are synonymous, that is strictly speaking not the case. For one thing Commonwealth membership has always been voluntary, and a minority – varying up to about 25% but down to not much more than 10% at the turn of the century when this was written – of those who work or have worked at Wollaston have so far always chosen *not* to become members. Second, subject always to an appeal to all members in a general meeting, the Commonwealth's elected officers are empowered to withdraw – or withhold – membership in cases of serious misconduct. Both have happened only rarely but cases of both kinds are known. Third, the rules have always provided that a period of employment – changing in length between six months and two years – and a minimum age, 18 since 1971 – are necessary preconditions for membership. Fourth, the lack of enthusiasm to become Commonwealth members shown by a significant minority can be explained at least in part by the fact that non-members as well as members enjoy most of the non-wage benefits of the Wollaston workforce. For example, they participate in the pension scheme, the profit distributions, and are eligible for long service awards.

My second point of preliminary clarification is about how I use the word 'labour' in this discussion. The short answer is that I use it in two different ways. Sometimes, as in the last paragraph, I use it to embrace all grades of staff at Wollaston: top management, research scientists, people in selling and administrative positions, the blue-collar workers in the factory and warehouse, the cleaners and those who work in the canteen: the lot. At other times I use it in the same way as the phrase 'rank-and-file partners' is used in the John Lewis Partnership: to cover only those employees (partners) who enjoy no managerial or professional authority at all. Which of the two uses applies should be clear from the context in any particular case.

THE EVOLUTION OF THE RIGHTS AND DUTIES OF SCOTT BADER LABOUR

To begin with we need to remember that it was not the unencumbered Scott Bader business which Ernest and other members of the Bader family passed to the Commonwealth, in two successive acts of benefaction in 1951 and 1963. Rather as when the ownership of an estate is passed on to the heir in the next generation of a family, the gift came with a number of what may be called restrictive covenants. More precisely, in a series of constitutional and related documents, an array of duties and rules were imposed on both the Commonwealth and the business. What are in many ways the most important of these, what one may call the rules of corporate government, relate to the actual running of the business and the powers of various bodies either within it, like the company's board of directors; or linked closely to it, like the Commonwealth itself, from 1951 onwards, and then subsequently, from 1963, the trustees as well.

But there also were and still are rules and/or restrictive covenants of a more general character – *not* relating to the exercise of corporate power – with which the Commonwealth and its members were required to comply. Inevitably these, as well as those relating to corporate government, have been modified over the years. What is probably the majority view – though it is far from being unchallenged – is that, despite the modifications, most of the rules have managed to remain at least broadly faithful to the original intentions of Ernest Bader and his family. Their range was from the start and still remained after 50 years rather wide: for example they originally included rules about the maximum numbers of people who might be employed in the business. It seems that from the beginning there was also a rule about the maximum permitted difference between the highest and lowest rates of pay. From the beginning too these rules have also included a duty to share profits with charity. Similarly they also included from the start – and still include – an injunction against the manufacture of weapons of war and a duty, in the event of a business recession, to accept an overall cut in pay rather than to impose any compulsory redundancies. The latter, as we already know, was in fact modified at the end of the 1970s to allow for schemes of voluntary redundancy. However, as we also already know, neither the original rules nor its modified successor was applied to employees of subsidiaries, like those at SRL on Merseyside in the 1980s and at NCI in the US in the 1990s. Readers with a specialist interest in the whole subject of what is loosely called 'employee ownership' may be interested to know that at the German optical and glass works of Carl Zeiss a similar distinction is drawn between an inner circle of employees who enjoy special conditions, and an outer circle who enjoy those conditions only in somewhat diluted form.

In what was a rather radical step at the beginning, and way ahead of what was normal business practice when the Commonwealth was founded, these rules even include a duty to reduce 'any harmful effect of our work on the natural environment'. We will look later in a special discussion at how that particular duty has been honoured.

Essentially, both the original rules and covenants and their later modifications have sought to show that the business has, in the first place, duties of good neighbourly and co-operative behaviour between those who work in it, and secondly, duties of good corporate citizenship towards the outside world and the local neighbourhood – all that plus a duty to restrict its manufacturing activities within a framework acceptable to Christian Pacifist principles. And as if these duties were not enough, in July 1972 members of the Commonwealth imposed on themselves a code of practice which, following the language of the report written by the Revd Bruce Reed in 1969, included a duty to take on a 'political task'. The task was to promote and help to midwife businesses with structures and objectives similar to those of Scott Bader.

What is more, as the business expanded overseas, especially in the 1990s, there were further new challenges: essentially about how to extend the Scott Bader structures, institutions and *values* to embrace those working outside the UK. Some of those most recent new challenges had been only partially met when this was written early in 2001. But see also the Postscript at the end of chapter 9.

I have italicised the word 'values' in the last paragraph for a quite specific reason. Neither the founder nor his son Godric have made any real secret about what they see as the single most important long-term objective of the post-Commonwealth Scott Bader: to enable different behaviour patterns among those who work in the business. Like his father before him, Godric still believes today that when the business was given to the Commonwealth, the gift entailed a duty laid upon all those who worked in it: to strive for personal and collective transformation. A reader coming to Scott Bader for the first time might well ask at this point: transformation into what? As a first answer to that, let us follow Ernest Bader in the epigraph to this chapter and take the goal of the desired transformation as being to become 'responsible owners'. However, in discussion with Godric during the writing of this book it has often seemed to me that the transformation which he – like his father before him – has been hoping for would go a good deal further than what most people mean by the phrase 'responsible owner'. It is also true that the word 'owner' itself has been partly jettisoned as inappropriate since the values workshops of the 1980s.

THE CHANGES IN CORPORATE GOVERNMENT AND THE ACQUISITION OF POWER BY 'DEMOCRATIC BODIES'

Almost all readers who have any links with the Scott Bader community will know Alan Green. In fact he was introduced in chapter 7 when he and his wife bumped into Brian Elgood and his wife on Australia's Great Barrier Reef. It was already foreseen, when he was then introduced, that we would meet him again in a rather different setting.

Alan's final assignment was as a special assistant to the chief executive with a double brief. Its first part was to advise about how best to extend Commonwealth membership to employees in overseas subsidiaries. Its second part was to discuss with the management and employees of those subsidiaries whether, and if so how best, they should adopt Scott Bader's values and ways of working, albeit as appropriately adapted to their own local conditions. He was well qualified for that task for he had twice been the CBoM's elected chairman. And he was several times an elected member of the company board as well as of the CBoM. Before his retirement Alan kindly wrote what for me has been a most helpful document entitled 'The Organs of Scott Bader and Their Functions, 1951–1971'.

Under this heading the document is divided into three columns: 1951, 1963 and 1971, the years of each of the three successive constitutions by which Scott Bader has so far been governed. Some would argue that changes in the composition of the company board (as opposed to the CBoM or the Community Council), introduced on the recommendation of Ralph Woolf in 1978, were sufficiently consequential to count as a change of constitution in their own right. More of them later.

In a general way, and most importantly for today's and tomorrow's Scott Bader, the changes as between Alan Green's three constitutions trace movement of power away from both the Bader family, and from the executive board of a conventional private company, and in the direction of what, following current Wollaston usage, Alan calls in a footnote 'the democratic bodies'. But here I must warn readers that the shift of power which needs to be described is neither altogether straightforward nor altogether unambiguous.

THE TRUSTEE BODY

The movement of power away from the Bader family was complex enough, even if, as we already know, it took place in line with the progressive relinquishment by the family of its original 100% shareholding. But the relinquishment of family *power* lagged well behind that of the family's shares and extended over a much longer period. Between 1951 and 1963 the lag in the movement of power happened because of the special and overriding voting rights enjoyed by the family's remaining 10% shareholding. After 1963 it happened partly because the special powers of that 10% shareholding were transferred not in the direction of 'the democratic bodies' but to the new institution which I have already referred to more than once: the trustees. Of the first trustee body, the two Baders, father and son, were members, as was Ernest's nephew, Brian Parkyn. So, if we take the trustee body into account, family power extended well beyond the giving up by the Baders of their final 10% shareholding.

Even so, and whatever the present powers of the trustees by virtue of their 10% shareholding, I think it is best to see this particular constitutional entity as having fulfilled an essentially historical and transitional function, to ease what must surely have been Ernest Bader's real pain in giving up the shares still held by the family in 1963. By contrast and in today's world I think the trustees are perhaps best understood as performing functions similar to those enjoyed by constitutional monarchs. In other words they can 'advise, encourage and warn'. What's more, especially in the 1990s, that is very much what some of them, with complete propriety, but perhaps more doubtful outcomes, have chosen to do.

It is true that one of the two special powers of the trustees permits, though it does not require, them to move in and act as arbiters in serious disputes between Scott Bader's company board and what has been since 1971 its new community council, of which more later. It is I suppose just possible that in a supreme crisis the trustees could successfully act as arbiters in such a dispute. However, the fact is that they have so far never done so. I shall assume from now on that that is not going to happen and I shall therefore ignore the trustees in my attempt to explain what has happened to the more ordinary powers given up by the family and by the executive directors of the original private company.

But we still need to mention the second of the two powers enjoyed by the trustees. They may, though again they need not, intervene and make what may be called (so as to avoid any conflict with company law) 'advisory pronouncements' should the accounts ever move from a profit into loss. Furthermore, after the accounts had shown just that in 1994, the trustees did make a move in 1995. However the consensus, rightly in my view, is that their move at that time was more formal than substantial. The trustees behaved, to repeat my earlier analogy, like constitutional monarchs. Indeed their then chairman, Roger Hadley, spoke most eloquently in a speech to a general meeting of Commonwealth members from which I will later quote. But in no sense at all did the trustees then take power.

I should only add that at the time of writing there are seven trustees, as there have indeed been since 1971 – four elected from inside by the democratic bodies and three chosen from outside. In the latter case the company board and the CBoM put forward a joint list of candidates and the final decisions are made by a general meeting of the Commonwealth. By convention, though not by any legally binding rule, the chairman of the trustee body has always been – up to the time of writing in early 2001 – one of the outsiders.

GODRIC BECOMES LIFE PRESIDENT

But I still have to complete the story of the movement of power away from the Bader family, or more precisely from Godric. In the 1971 constitution, having resigned as managing director the year before, he was named as life chairman of the company. He held on to that position until 1990 when he stepped down and became life president. In the latter post he remains enormously influential. He retains membership of the Commonwealth and attends meetings of trustees. But the life president has no formal powers. As chairman he had enjoyed the right to nominate three outside directors to the company board: making, together with himself and the chief executive, a total of five. At least in theory those five could always outvote the four that came to be elected by Alan Green's 'democratic bodies'. So the final power which the family gave up when Godric stepped down from the chairmanship in 1990 was not negligible.

Thus those who wish to may argue that whereas the family had completely relinquished its shares by 1963, just 12 years after the establishment of the Commonwealth, it was not until 1990 that it finally let go of power – when Godric ceased to be chairman.

A DIFFUSION OF EXECUTIVE POWERS

There is a key footnote at the bottom of the third (1971 constitution) column of Alan Green's paper to which I have already referred:

> The board of Scott Bader Company Ltd became non-executive in nature in 1978. First one, then two additional directors were elected from amongst Commonwealth members who had previously served on one of the democratic bodies. These directors are called community directors. A managing director's group manages the business of the Scott Bader company.

In other words at least some of the powers exercised by the board of the company before it 'became non-executive in nature', essentially those of 'managing the business', were passed in 1978 to a managing director's group. In Wollaston today, as in the past, that group is known as 'the Executive'. But at least since 1978 it appears to exercise its powers by convention and not by formal constitutional rule.

Some readers may however remember the case of Mrs Sayer, in the very first years after the formation of the Commonwealth, and the unsuccessful attempt by Ernest Bader to give her the sack. They will remember that Ernest climbed down in the face of a challenge by one of the Commonwealth's two elected representative bodies, then the General Council. In other words, a power which under traditional UK company law normally rests with the executive had already in the early 1950s been transferred by convention to a 'democratic body'.

In the case of those readers whose memories extend back no further than the late 1970s they will remember an even more fundamental example of the transfer of a traditionally executive power to a 'democratic body': the approval by the Commonwealth members in a general meeting in December 1978 of what had earlier been no more than a provisional proposal to implement a scheme of voluntary redundancy and the approval of its terms. It may be argued that in neither case, neither that of Mrs Sayer and the thwarting of Ernest Bader's attempt to sack her, nor in the later case of the approval of the proposed voluntary redundancy scheme and its terms, was the democratic body exercising a right which it enjoyed under a constitutional rule. But I would be inclined to suggest that flexibility is one of the strengths and not a weakness of the mixed co-determinational system which has evolved at Scott Bader. In any case, as we shall see in a moment, under the 1971 constitution a democratic body became formally responsible for discipline by a legally binding rule. As for the issue of voluntary redundancy, we must assume that once the final decision was assigned in 1978 to the general meeting of Commonwealth members, that became a precedent which from then on has not been set aside and is unlikely to be so, except perhaps in the most extraordinary circumstances.

Indeed the need for key decisions to be approved by Commonwealth members in a general meeting has since been extended beyond the most sensitive issue of voluntary redundancy in the parent business at Wollaston. One example of special importance during the 1980s was the provisional decision, sent to a general meeting of the Commonwealth for final confirmation or otherwise, to close down SRL on Merseyside. Most recently, the Commonwealth in March 2000 voted to approve a complex set of proposals for changes in corporate structures, to better reflect the new multinational character of the business. The details need not concern us here. The key point is that because the margin of approval was almost minimally slim – some four votes in over 200 – the proposal was in effect 'remitted' for further discussion.

It is true that some, notably Godric Bader, argue that 'key decisions have always had to be approved by [Commonwealth] members'. Unless the decisions to which he refers as 'key' are very narrowly restricted, or unless he accepts that decisions which 'had to be' were not in fact so approved, the record tells me that Godric's pronouncement is less true than untrue.

As against the progressive relinquishment of the Bader family's power and its final disappearance in 1990, we can thus, I think, characterise what has happened to the executive power of the formerly conventional private company as its *diffusion*: in part to professional managers and in part to democratic bodies, in other words, as suggested earlier, to an arrangement of mixed co-determinational power-sharing.

DIRECT AND REPRESENTATIVE DEMOCRACY, AND THE 1971 CONSTITUTION

But the process of power diffusion and the resulting mix of power-sharing has been partly masked by what was described, when it happened in 1971, as a move from direct to representative democracy. Under the constitutional arrangements established in 1963, a form of supposedly direct democracy was put in place. As spelt out by Alan Green, this had two elements. The more eye-catching took the form of a panel of representatives chosen at random from the attendees at the annual general meeting each year. He goes on to specify the panel's chief and apparently its only task:

> To give a vote of confidence or no confidence in the board of Scott Bader Company Ltd.
>
> Should they give a vote of no confidence, then the AGM would be adjourned for no more than three months when a second panel would be formed to repeat the vote. If the second panel gave a vote of no confidence, the trustees would be asked to determine what changes if any in the said board of directors are desirable.

For the record, the archives show that an initial vote of no confidence was passed at two AGMs between 1963 and 1970. On the other hand it seems that the company board always managed to survive the second of the two 'direct democracy' tests prescribed in the 1963 constitution. So the trustees were never asked to intervene.

The second element in the direct democracy of the 1963 constitution was rather more straightforward: a right and a duty imposed on all members attending the Commonwealth AGM to approve – or otherwise – all items of capital expenditure above a specified threshold, originally £5,000, later £10,000. On the other hand, I can find no record in the archives or elsewhere of any such item from which the approval of the 'direct democracy' was withheld. The operational reality of that earlier 'direct democracy' may thus be open to sceptical question.

However that may be, in a paper delivered by Godric to the Business History Unit at the London School of Economics in May 1983, he ascribes the move away from so called direct democracy to the growing numbers employed at Wollaston. He told his audience:

> Direct democracy with numbers approaching 400 was proving difficult and so the Community Council, a standing committee of members and staff in general meeting, was formed. This was given deeper involvement in policy-making powers, the responsibility for the confirmation of appointments and remuneration of directors, and explicit rights to stand them down.

To avoid any misunderstanding I should make clear that this Community Council was not simply created out of thin air. It was the successor to a body which went back to 1951. It had had the General Council as its original name and later the Council of Reference. From the beginning it was a mainly elected and thus mainly democratic body, and its more important functions were exercised within the company, as opposed to the Commonwealth. It enjoyed the prestige of having successfully challenged Ernest Bader when he had wanted to sack Mrs Sayer. In effect in 1971 its powers were greatly enlarged and it underwent its third name change. To have decided to call it the Community Council was a source of perhaps needless confusion. For that, since 1951, had been the name of the more important of Scott Bader's two democratic bodies. When its earlier name became no longer available in 1971, the other and essentially Commonwealth-related body also changed *its* name and became, as it has mercifully since remained, the Commonwealth Board of Management (CBoM).

This last point is made in parenthesis to avoid confusion. What can be in no doubt is that the new 1971 Community Council quickly became, to repeat, the more powerful of the two democratic bodies at

Scott Bader. As well as its powers in relation to the company's board of directors, specified above by Godric, Alan Green, after describing its composition, enumerates its further tasks and powers:

> Membership: Up to 24 members elected from constituencies agreed by the council and approved by members.
>
> Tasks and Powers: To appoint two of their number as directors.
>
> To discuss any matter referred to it and make recommendations to the board.
>
> To consider any matter of dispute affecting disciplinary action and come to a decision on it. Such decisions can not be set aside by any individual organ of the company.
>
> To recommend to members the distribution of any declared bonus.

It makes sense, I think, to have on the record at least briefly here, as it is at some length in Susanna Hoe's book (pp 196–201), the intense and, in one memorable episode, theatrical opposition of Ernest Bader to the democratic advances embodied in the 1971 constitution. Both David Ralley and Brian Parkyn are quoted persuasively in *The Man Who Gave His Company Away* about the source of the founder's opposition. As David Ralley saw it (p 196):

> The change in the constitution was basically taking some of the power away from the company board and giving it to the community. The establishment was having to give up some of the power. Ernest clearly saw this as his power which technically he didn't have. He wouldn't be able to manipulate his son. Here was his son giving up the power. It was quite unacceptable.

Further down the same page comes Bryan Parkyn's assessment of Ernest Bader's opposition:

> He felt that the new constitution was putting real power into the hands of the workers. Ernest has always been in support of an *elite*. He would not like to use these words but he's always believed that some are born to train and govern and be leaders and others to be led.

On the same page again Susanna Hoe cites David Ralley's opinion on a separate matter – Godric's view of the proposed constitutional changes: 'I think Godric saw it as a move forward in the organic growth of the community – and I'm sure he is right – and developing people.'

At this point we come on to the famous theatrical expression of Ernest Bader's opposition to the 1971 constitution. The scene is an informal meeting of Commonwealth members in March 1971, called to discuss the proposed changes. To understand what then happened I should make clear that not long before, to mark his 80th birthday in November 1970, Ernest had been presented with a fine portrait bust of himself, cast in polyester resin. Here is how Susanna Hoe (p 199) tells us what next happened at the meeting:

> Suddenly Ernest appeared. He was dressed in sackcloth and ashes. The sack was tied toga-style on one shoulder. He had bare feet with a big label tied round his front with string which read 'I am a fool of Christ'. In his hand was a polythene bag full of something that looked like peat or burnt glass fibre. He threw it on the table in front of Godric and cried, 'Here you are! Here are my ashes – the ashes of your bust – because I am so disgusted with what you've done. This is what I think of *your* rotten new constitution.' With that broken little speech, emphasising the word *your,* he left.

About Ernest's self-description as a 'fool of Christ', Susanna Hoe helpfully points her readers to St Paul's First Epistle to the Corinthians, chapter 4, verse 10 (though, less helpfully, she cites it as the Second Epistle), which includes the phrase 'we are fools for Christ's sake'. But however that may be interpreted, what now seems most extraordinary is how modest was the fire behind the smoke of the bust-burning. Susanna Hoe tells us on her very next page (200):

> Ernest obviously picked himself up and dusted himself down. John Leyland, trying to account for the calm afterwards and for the storm itself, says, 'It's difficult to identify what he didn't like because just a short time afterwards he wrote this article for *The Journal.* It spelt out just what the Scott Bader Commonwealth was. ... He went through the constitution and spelt out how it worked after the changes – after the bust-burning. And he was quite rational – he said why it was sensible compared with its pre-decessor.

As many older readers among the Scott Bader community will surely know, *The Journal* to which John Leyland is referring is an American Free Church review. The article which Ernest wrote for it in 1971 is the one from which the epigraph to this chapter has been taken.

Both Alan Green in his 'Organs of Scott Bader and Their Functions,

1951–71', and Godric in his address to the Business History Unit in 1983, are quite clear about the key importance, in the 1971 constitution, of its new democratically elected Community Council, with its wide range of powers including for the first time the formal recognition of a democratic control over matters of discipline. Godric adds a last special piece to this jigsaw of diffused power, or mixed power-sharing, which resulted from the 1971 constitution: 'The Community Council ... whilst not constitutionally mandatory on pay scales ... [its] support and agreement is obtained by management before implementation.' In other words the Community Council has a key influence on rates of pay and associated conditions of employment.

Here then is an example if not quite of a power, at least of a most influential say which the Community Council came to enjoy from 1971 onwards. But I need to emphasise that this was not a matter of constitutional right, but the result of a convention. In some ways it seems to resemble the power enjoyed, according to Alan Green's key footnote, by the 'managing director's group' – or the 'executive' as it is almost always referred to in Wollaston – to 'manage the company'. Both are clearly of first class importance but they are powers enjoyed, to repeat, not by constitutional rules but by convention. Together they may account for much of the ambiguity which seems to be widely felt – and even voiced – at Wollaston about where the final responsibility for key business decisions actually lies. I hasten to add that this ambiguity is openly acknowledged by Scott Bader's top managers. It has indeed, to repeat, been described as a source of 'creative friction'. Maybe that is one good way to look at it. But it also seems to reflect a reluctance by the Commonwealth's democracy to accept final and formal responsibility outside the circumscribed area of disciplinary questions.

And that, a reluctance by the Commonwealth democracy to accept an *overall* responsibility, seems to me to explain, or at least partly explain, what happened when in 1978, on the recommendation of Ralph Woolf, the composition of the company board was changed. We have already described that change in chapter 7. It was, I need hardly say, the change described in Alan Green's footnote as the company board having become 'non-executive' in nature.

It will be helpful to recall what was involved. Once the change had been implemented, the managing director became the only executive on the company board. His former executive colleagues – the heads of production, marketing and finance – lost their seats. Of the new board of nine members, four were appointed by the democratic institutions of the Commonwealth. Of the remaining four, one was the non-executive chairman – Godric in both 1971 and 1978 – and three were the chairman's non-executive nominees, chosen from outside. But the main point I want to emphasise here is rather different. It is not about what happened in 1978 but about what *might* have happened. I refer to the efforts of John Goring, the chairman at that time of what by then had become the CBoM, to seek to insist on an increase to six from four in the number of democratic representatives on the new company board. Had he succeeded, those representatives would have formed a majority on the new board and would thus have had to assume overall responsibility for final decisions.

The apparent reluctance of the Commonwealth's democratic bodies to accept overall and final responsibility for the company is undeniably puzzling. And so too is the corresponding unwillingness by top management to press them to do so.

What we need next is a brief introduction to the Commonwealth Board of Management (CBoM) from the chairmanship of which John Goring called on his colleagues to join him in trying to take their destiny more firmly into their own hands. It is of course the second of two democratic institutions which have evolved at Scott Bader. As we have seen, it took its present name in 1972. Alan Green tells us about its membership: six are elected by the Commonwealth in a secret ballot. They are joined by the chairman of the company plus one outsider. He or she is appointed by the 'insider' seven to represent the interests of the local (Northamptonshire) – as opposed to the working (Scott Bader) – community. As for its history, it is as old as the Commonwealth itself, dating from 1951. It is a source of the rather tiresome confusion noted earlier that its own original name was the Community Council. Ernest Bader was its first chairman.

To make the situation less confusing, I should remind readers that in essence the two democratic bodies of today's Scott Bader – the Community Council and the CBoM – each go back to 1951, and that each underwent a name change in 1971. With closer links to the company, the present Community Council and the bodies which came before its name change act as something like a works council at Wollaston and perform a range of economic and industrial relations, disciplinary and other functions. It also appoints two members to the company board. Reflecting Scott Bader's normal concern with clarity they are called *Commonwealth* board members.

By contrast the CBoM does not itself appoint any members to the company board. Instead the Commonwealth office organises an election for the two remaining internal and non-executive posts on the company board. All Commonwealth members have a vote in that election. Readers will not be surprised that those elected are called *Community* board members.

As for the CBoM itself, its functions cover: responsibility for charitable giving; responsibility for Commonwealth membership; a general responsibility for 'philosophical oversight' or values. That then is the most unusual mix of power-sharing, essentially between labour and top management, which has evolved at Wollaston over 50 years. The first steps in the process, the two-stage relinquishment of its shareholding by the Bader family, can now best be seen as a prelude to the transfer of power. Some will challenge my language and prefer to talk about the 'democratic bodies' rather than 'labour' as the partner with which top management has come to share power. Others again may prefer to use the phrase 'the community'. So be it. The case for using the word 'labour' is the pervasive evidence of a continuing psychological division between the management and other employees, and especially between the management and blue-collar employees at Wollaston.

Many will argue that what is most unusual about this Wollaston mix is that it is neither one thing nor the other. Final responsibility for what happens to the business does not lie clearly with management, as it does for example in the John Lewis Partnership and in the Scottish paper manufacturer, Tullis Russell, probably the two leading employee-owned businesses in today's UK. But nor does it clearly lie with a non-executive board, as is the case with the manufacturing and other businesses within the Mondragon group of co-operatives in the Basque provinces of Spain, and with Italy's two most famous and successful manufacturing co-ops, SACMI and La Ceramica, both of which have their parent business in the small town of Imola outside Bologna. At Wollaston final responsibility does not rest with a non-executive board because in a sense there is not one but two of these: the company board *and* the CBoM. But equally, at least under its 1971 constitution as modified by the 1978 changes, it doesn't rest with an executive board. And it cannot presumably rest with what Alan Green calls 'a managing director's group' and what at Wollaston is normally called the 'executive'. That at least *seems* impossible given that this top management group has no status in law or in the company constitution.

On the other hand I should not conceal that some, including Godric Bader, have argued forcefully that this co-determinational-type arrangement is deliberate: to avoid vesting final authority in a single power centre. But whatever the historical validity of that argument, it does not of course settle the question of how well this power-sharing has worked.

In practice, even if with one exception, it has become true that when the decision to be taken is really big – about voluntary redundancy for example – ultimate responsibility remains where perhaps in theory it has always been: with a general meeting of Commonwealth members; and that has so far worked well at least four times. The general meeting on those occasions has become in effect a non-executive final decision-making body. Brian Elgood has indeed suggested that to the question of where final responsibility fundamentally rests at Scott Bader, the least bad answer may be: with the Commonwealth members in their general meetings.

As I have already reported, there is no firm consensus among top managers at Wollaston about the consequences of these arrangements for company performance. To repeat once again, some see them as a source of 'creative friction', and others of 'dysfunctional conflict'. It remains to be seen whether over the longer run their contribution to sustainability will be more positive or more negative.

However, before closing this discussion I need to flag up, if only for the record, the exception just noted to the paramountcy of Commonwealth members: a major vote by the members of the Commonwealth in a general meeting which was later overruled. The date was 1986. The subject was what should happen to profits accruing to Scott Bader under the licence granted by the company to NCS Plastics in South Africa and going back to the early 1960s. Up to that time, as with profits arising out of Scott Bader's other overseas licensing agreements, the net licence fees coming in from South Africa were simply included in the total profits of the Wollaston business. But by 1986 international and British public hostility to the apartheid government of P. W. Botha in Pretoria had climbed to such exceptionally high levels that even President Reagan in Washington could no longer afford to ignore it. Against that background a proposal, originated by management, was put before Commonwealth members in a general meeting. It called for the establishment of a special charitable fund to be set up in South Africa, for future licence fees from NCS Plastics to be transferred to it, and for that money then to be spent on projects in the field of black

African education and improvement inside the country. By a significant – but neither very large nor very small – majority the Commonwealth members voted the proposal down. However that vote was later set aside by the CBoM.

So far as I know, that had never happened before and has not happened again, anyway up to the time that this was written. Thus what happened in 1986 appears not to have become a precedent. Beyond making the familiar linguistic point that an exception tests a rule – and citing the difference between parliamentary and public opinion in this country on the issue of capital punishment as a partial parallel – there is nothing useful that can be said.

THE COMMONWEALTH'S DUTY OF CORPORATE CHARITABLE GIVING

Given the charitable status of the Commonwealth, it is right to begin with the duty of a distribution to charity of a percentage of any profits made by the Scott Bader business. Readers may recall that since the original 1951 constitution not less than 60% of any profits must be ploughed back, and that only the remainder could be distributed, to a combination of an employee bonus fund and to charity. According to the original rule, the amount to go to charity was linked to the amount of the bonus by a sliding scale which climbed to a maximum of 10% when the bonus took 30%. But the charity maximum was actually increased in 1953, two years after the Commonwealth came into being, and increased, not by the command of Ernest Bader but by a popular vote in the then Community Council. Susanna Hoe tells the story (p 201) of how it happened, and does so in the words of Ted Nichols, the first in a long line of Commonwealth secretaries:

> We had been working at it about two years when one of the Community Council chaps – Sid Andrews working in the resin plant – had said quietly at one meeting, 'Don't you think, Mr Bader, that if we really believe in what we are doing that we should give an equal amount to charities as we take in bonus?' [i.e. a maximum of 20%]. We did and it's been that ever since.

Susanna Hoe goes on to tell her readers, though not as if it was a surprise, that 'Ernest was delighted with this reaction'.

No one can claim that in this respect the Commonwealth and its members have shown anything less than 100% fidelity to the wishes of its founder. Measured as a percent of profits, the records show that what was given to charity reached a peak of 16% in 1973. As we already know, the company has found it much harder to make profits in the last 20 years of the Commonwealth's half century than in the first 30. The eight years from 1979, which included two voluntary redundancies, were particularly tough for making profits and, with Ralph Woolf determined to build up cash in the balance sheet, they were even tougher for staff bonuses and charitable giving. Not a penny was paid out under either heading over this period. All the same, by a process of adding and averaging it can shown that over the Commonwealth's first half century the average annual Scott Bader payment to charity, measured as a percent of profits, was 5%. It must be doubtful whether any other UK private company can match that percentage over so long a period.

Moreover, data collected by the Percent Club, which is a part of Business in the Community and tries to keep track of British corporate charitable giving, puts Scott Bader at number four in its league table for 1999. What the table ostensibly records is the percentage of pre-tax profits given by companies to charity. Because businesses are permitted to include in that figure the costs of staff and management time made available to charity, and the value of gifts in kind, as well as actual money payments, the numbers are in fact a little more complex than that. However, for the record, the first five businesses listed in the Percent Club's table for 1999, with the percentage of 'pre-tax profits' given by them to charity, were:

COMPANY	PERCENT
Bernstein Group	15.00
Buy As You View	10.15
Anglia TV	8.76
Scott Bader	7.78
Marshall Group	6.98

For what it's worth, and for the year 2000, the Percent Club data indicates that companies in contact with it recorded total charitable giving of just over £370m, a year when the gross operating surplus of corporations came to just over £200,000m. That suggests that corporate charitable contributions reported to the club are now running at about 0.2% of pre-tax corporate profits. On the basis of its 1999 contribution Scott Bader seems to have deflected to charity between 30 and 40 times that percentage number. But then the Commonwealth, the body which made the contribution, is itself a charity and may therefore be thought to have a rather special obligation in this respect.

Next in this discussion of the Commonwealth's charitable giving, two general and two special points need to be made. The two general points are essentially clarifications. First, whereas the present rules provide that the total of any profits distributed to employees should not *exceed* what the Commonwealth gives to charity, the act of charitable giving in no way requires either a similar distribution to employees – or any distribution to employees at all. The second general point is one of anticipation. As we shall see shortly, over a number of years, starting from 1973, it was decided that a part of the money which would otherwise be distributed to charity should be assigned to a new entity: the Commonwealth Development Fund (CDF).

Of my two special points one has in fact just been mentioned: the unprecedented setting aside in 1986 by the CBoM of an earlier vote by Commonwealth members at a general meeting *not* to set up a special charitable fund in South Africa. There is no need to go over that again here.

The second special point was about the initiative pressed on the Commonwealth by the CBoM and especially by Alan Green in the early 1990s. It was already mentioned briefly in chapter 9. The aim was to make it possible that the choice of charities to which donations should be made each year should be taken not by the CBoM alone but should be shared with individual Commonwealth members. Initially the individual members were permitted to decide on an allocation of up to £150, a sum which was later increased to £200. By its take-up – over 85 of all Commonwealth members by 1999 – and the satisfaction reported in feedback, this modest but imaginative scheme seems to have been a triumph.

Changed arrangements can be the source of similar satisfactions. In her Scott Bader half-century oral history project, Tracy Smeathers has found that there are a surprising number of retired old-timers who single out for special mention the warm memories they have of distributing firewood and food parcels to elderly Wollaston folk in need. In its selection of events in 1979, the Traxton/Reeves diary includes without comment: 'Old people's parcels scheme replaced by voucher scheme.'

Evidently the distribution of firewood had been discontinued some time before, perhaps following the first batch of clean air laws in the 1960s. The Traxton/Reeves diary is silent. Nor does it record the later wind-up of the voucher scheme.

But despite the warm memories of those Scott Bader old-timers, we should certainly not conclude that everything to do with the original firewood and food parcels scheme of the Commonwealth's early years was sweetness and light. As part of her course work as student at the Bells Park Training College in Hertford, Diana Green wrote an essay in 1964 entitled 'The Effects of Industry on Wollaston'. It includes an unforgettable thumbnail sketch of the slightly separate firewood and parcels schemes:

> During the winter months the members of the Commonwealth distribute gifts of firewood to the deserving old people in the village. Already they meet an obstacle: Who are to decide which are the deserving old people? Names are handed in to the firm of people known to employees, and thus some really deserving people can be left out. This is the same with the weekly parcels of groceries which are distributed to about a 100 old people. Quickly the cry goes up 'Why didn't the old lady in our street get a parcel, she's much more deserving than Mrs XXX?' ... The petty bickering and unpleasantness amongst the villagers tend to spoil attempts at kindness. The annual dinner which the firm gave for the old people was stopped for a while because the invitations could never be distributed to the satisfaction of the villagers.

So far as I know, that annual dinner has not survived. What there is, on the other hand, is a pre-Christmas coach outing to which all Wollaston's pensioners, and not only Scott Bader's, are invited.

CHRISTIAN PACIFISM AND WORK FOR DEFENCE INDUSTRIES

The preamble to the original 1951 constitution of the Commonwealth which later, as we have seen, caused so much consternation at the Charity Commission that, along with the 'objects clause' in the Commonwealth's Memorandum, it had to be revised, contains a commitment in the last sentence of clause 5 to 'a refusal take an active part in rearmament'.

At least from his 30s onwards Ernest Bader is sometimes presented as a fundamentalist in the causes to which he became committed, to Christian pacifism, for example, to vegetarianism, and to a life of total abstinence from alcohol. It is not a portrait which should be accepted without qualification. Brian Parkyn has an unforgettable picture of his uncle enjoying a large glass of German beer on a visit to the Leipzig trade fair in the 1950s. In his forthcoming autobiography he also presents his uncle as having a fairly pragmatic view of what was required by his commitment to pacifism. The date is the early 1950s and the occasion is a visit to Wollaston 'by a very senior civil servant from the Ministry of Supply called Hardy'. The topic for discussion was the nature and limits of any defence contracts which Scott Bader might be prepared to undertake for the ministry:

> Ernest *at that time* [emphasis original] was happy for us to continue to supply resins for making radomes, aircraft panels, ducting and so forth, but not for specific weapons of war such as bombs, rockets and torpedoes, or for the manufacture of explosives.

From Brian Parkyn's account it appears that Ernest's line later became a good deal tougher, and it is known that in the 1960s the company imposed on itself a severe self-denying ordinance when it came to bidding for work put out to tender by the Navy. And yet, as was briefly noted in an earlier chapter, we find apparently uncontested sales in the early 1970s to the Royal Navy of a thick, fire-resistant, surface coating material called Crystic Fireguard.

Les Norwood, who spent more than 30 years in senior professional and management positions at Wollaston from the middle 1960s onwards, has contributed the following account of how Scott Bader came to make sales of altogether more substantial material for naval shipbuilding, to build the hulls not indeed of battleships, as Brian Parkyn has always dreamed, but of minesweepers of far from negligible size:

> When the proposal came along in the mid-1960s to build Mine Counter Measure Vessels (MCMVs) in GRP, the potential business and the prestige of such applications were very attractive to any resin supplier, and especially to Scott Bader who were dominant in the UK marine market. Debates in Scott Bader about the nature of these vessels as offensive or defensive weapons went on and so did a very large development programme which resulted in SB's *The Large Ships Report* in 1969. The outcome of this work was a resin to meet the Ministry of Defence D.G. Ships 1180 requirements, and SB Crystic 625 TV was listed in Annex F as one of the materials currently approved. For *commercial* reasons [emphasis added] we never supplied Crystic 625TV for MCMV production and the major supplier became BP Chemicals with a

Cellobond resin. However we continued to forge links with the manufacturers, Vosper Thorneycroft (UK) Ltd. Then during the late 1970s SB were approached by a research group ... who were working for the MOD and Vosper Thornycroft for a tough gap-fill resin; Crestomer was supplied and the results were so good that eventually Crestomer was used on MCMVs to improve the shock resistance of the structure during mine blast. Gradually the requirement for improvements in the laminating resin were felt to be necessary and Crystic 489 PA became approved to NES 167 and MCMV hulls began to be constructed from Crystic products in the mid-1980s.

Les Norwood has also contributed the following comment:

I believe that the general attitude within SB to selling for defensive purposes is positive and MCMVs are used to clear up the mess after conflicts and are not used offensively. We have to accept that we live in a state which behaves defensively rather than aggressively to other nations and that there will be an armaments policy. If we can provide the appropriate materials to assist such a policy, then we should do so: to support our rights to independence and freedom.

Some who read Les Norwood's comments in draft have challenged his assertion that 'we live in a state which behaves defensively rather than aggressively to other nations' and have recalled what the Iraqis and the Serbs have suffered from British weaponry in recent years. I hope it is not mere casuistry to argue that aggression against the attackers of peoples unable adequately to defend themselves – the Kuwaitis and the Kosovars – can fall within what a state which 'behaves defensively' may be permitted to do.

EMPLOYMENT NUMBERS AND INCOME DIFFERENTIALS

A limit on the maximum number of members of the Commonwealth, and thus indirectly on the numbers who may be employed, goes back to its original articles of association in 1951. The number was fixed at 250. It appears that Ernest Bader, perhaps because of his Swiss origins, was a believer in the doctrine of 'small is beautiful' well before Dr Schumacher first published his famous book with that title in 1973, and indeed well before the first meeting between the two men.

Records show that actual numbers employed at Wollaston first reached 250 in 1961. Presumably to allow for some additional leeway, the maximum was lifted to 350 in the Commonwealth's revised articles of association in 1963. In the year 2000 the now multinational Scott Bader group employed approximately 650 people worldwide. So far as I can establish, the 1963 limit has never been formally set aside. What has happened can perhaps best be seen as an expression of a continuing belief in the human value of small scale, but one which has been allowed to accommodate itself to business imperatives. The unstated guideline now is that the group should operate at the smallest size that is compatible with reasonably vigorous sustainability.

A similar evolution may be observed in relation to maximum permitted differentials of pay. According to both Godric Bader and Brian Parkyn, this was the subject of a Scott Bader rule from the very start of the Commonwealth in 1951, when the limiting ratio between top and bottom was five to one, increased a few years later to six to one. I have no doubt at all that what they remember about this matter is correct, though I have found nothing on paper to support it. But what is certain is that under a new article introduced in January 1966, it was laid down that the maximum difference between highest and lowest pre-tax salaries must not exceed 7:1. Then in January 1990 the reference to any specific ratio was removed. It was replaced by an injunction to the effect that this differential should not be excessive. At least on paper the distance between top and bottom in the year 2000 was about 13 to 1. In practice it appears to have been rather less. Different readers will doubtless make different judgements about whether this evolution falls within what is acceptable according to Scott Bader values. It is perhaps worth noting for comparison that there has been a similar widening over 50-odd years of their existence in the maximum differentials that are paid within the Mondragon co-operatives in the Basque Provinces of Spain.

A DUTY TO RESPECT THE PHYSICAL ENVIRONMENT

The code of practice adopted by and for Commonwealth members in 1972 provides that 'Our social responsibility extends to reducing any harmful effect of our work on the natural environment by rigorously avoiding the negligent discharge of pollutants, [and] questioning whether any of our activities are unnecessarily wasteful of the earth's natural resources.'

Rather as the so-called ISO 9001 sets an international standard of good manufacturing practice and invites businesses to undertake extended and closely monitored programmes of compliance if they wish to obtain a certificate under it, so it is, more or less, with the lately established international standard for what we may call 'good environmental housekeeping', embodied in ISO 14001. As noted in our narrative chapter on the 1990s, early in that decade Scott Bader went through the extended series of steps necessary to achieve its ISO 9001 certificate. Later in the same decade it embarked on the long process of achieving the environmental housekeeping counterpart. During the year 2000 that process was completed and the company obtained its ISO 14001 certificate.

In effect, the corporate holders of that certificate commit themselves to go well beyond what is required by national laws in respect of good environmental housekeeping and to make regular checks on their own performance.

With the benefit of some hindsight, the achievement of that 14001 certificate in the year 2000 can be seen as a stage in a more active Scott Bader policy of environmental concern which had begun in the mid-1990s. As the quotation from the code of practice tells us, Commonwealth members had indeed been specifically enjoined to be so concerned since at least 1972. But the acceptance of an obligation does not always, as we know, result in early action. In any event, during 1994 the company for the first time appointed an experienced professional, Hugh Fenton, to take charge full time of policy in this whole area and for its implementation. The various tasks, starting from the oversight of Scott Bader's compliance with the relevant government regulations and covering, for example, responsibility for health and safety on the Wollaston site, had previously been divided between different people who also had other jobs.

Then in 1998 it was decided to collect and circulate information about what Scott Bader was actually doing in its policies and behaviour towards the natural environment and in various related aspects of its policy and behaviour, for example in its employment policies and in its compliance with ethical business standards. The result was a document, called *Scott Bader 1998 Social Account,* divided into five sections. The two most relevant for our purposes here are headed in the document 'To make better use of the earth's resources' and 'To be a good neighbour'.

There is not the space for a long or detailed discussion. I will simply highlight two points. My own view, for what it's worth, is that the relevant parts of this *Social Account* show that Scott Bader is taking seriously its obligations under those two headings. But for clarification I should note that more of the company's policies and initiatives under the 'good neighbour' heading are dealt with in the chapter devoted to Wollaston later in the book.

1 Energy consumption: A chart shows that over the six years ending 1997, Scott Bader managed to cut its consumption of energy per tonne of output by some 20%. No comparative data is cited but that seems like a useful saving of the earth's non-renewable resources. The *Social Account* notes that the Wollaston site 'presently uses no renewable energy sources apart from those used to generate the energy bought'. But it also reports the commissioning of external consultants to advise us on the best long-term means of generating the energy needs on the Wollaston site.

2 Complaints:

> We have a procedure that requires urgent response to a complaint about our environmental performance. ... We report numbers weekly and monthly and look at trends every six months. ... Whilst any increase in the number of complaints is contrary to our intent, we recognise that our neighbours are now less tolerant of any intrusion in their privacy, whether it be by smell, noise or traffic movement. ... For smell complaints, we determine whether or not we can find cause on our site. In 1997, we found no cause in 31 smell complaints, 60% of the total.

THE SO-CALLED POLITICAL TASK AND THE PROMOTION OF BUSINESSES ON THE SCOTT BADER MODEL

Readers will remember the report written by the Revd Bruce Reed of London's Grubb Institute in 1969. It had as probably its main result a separation of the two top positions, of chairman and managing director which were at the time both held by Godric. But it was also important in having proposed that the company and the Commonwealth should think of themselves as having four more or less separate tasks: economic, technical, social and *political*. The founding documents in 1951 were of course overflowing with political implications. But it was not, I think, before the Reed report that an attempt was made to define in words a specific political task as such. Here is how the subject was introduced in the Reed report:

It was assumed by Ernest Bader that some of the political and social unrest of present-day society would be ameliorated if other industrial companies would follow the example of Scott Bader. ... The inputs are requests for literature and speakers, visitors, enquiries from the external environment about the operation of the Scott Bader organisation; the conversion process is the answering of these queries by means of articles speakers, conducted tours, books etc ; the *outputs are men and women in society with an increased sense of social responsibility in their own sphere of influence.* [emphasis added]. The hope is that some other companies would wish to follow the Scott Bader example.

Against this background the report goes on to define Scott Bader's political task as 'to encourage other men and women to change society by offering them an example by being economically healthy and socially responsible.'

As noted earlier, Commonwealth members shortly afterwards made an explicit political commitment. Already in its second provision a code of practice adopted in July 1972 echoed the language of the Reed report and referred to four tasks in which members were involved: economic, technical, social and political.

Many readers will be as familiar as the writer with the hard truth that propositions on paper of this kind, whether codes of practice, principles, mission statements or whatever else, can not themselves be 'performative'. They can neither directly make to happen nor actually constitute their own desired results. Their logic and the criteria by which they are judged are rather different, namely whether they succeed in motivating human agents into taking actions which they would not otherwise have taken, and doing so in the real world rather than in that of multiplying statements on paper.

By that test, perhaps the supreme example of success in the last 200 years of British history were the famous Principles of Co-operation, promulgated by the Rochdale Pioneers when they founded their first retail co-operative store in Rochdale's Toad Lane in the 1840s. The measure of the success of those principles was that in less than 50 years literally hundreds of similar retail shops had been founded and were up and running all over the country on the basis of just those principles. On the other hand, most historians would surely now agree that it was not mainly the principles by themselves but their relevance and impact in conjunction with the prevailing conditions of the time which succeeded in 'motivating human agents into taking actions which they would not otherwise have taken'.

It need hardly be said, indeed it seems almost bad manners to say it, that by the yardstick of what can be attributed to the Rochdale Principles, the outcomes which can be traced back to the first explicit statement of Scott Bader's political task in the report of the Revd Bruce Reed in 1969, and to its subsequent legitimation in the Commonwealth code of practice in 1972, are rather modest. But they are not by any means negligible. Out of the latter, even if on a much smaller scale than the former, came a new piece of law. Also out of the latter, even if in far smaller numbers than out the former, came a combination of small numbers of 'common ownership' enterprises started from scratch, and of existing businesses restructured on more of less Scott Bader's 'common ownership' lines. I put the phrase common ownership within inverted commas because, as we know, the favoured Wollaston language partially threw out the word 'ownership' in the 1980s and replaced it with the word 'trusteeship'.

THE INDUSTRIAL COMMON OWNERSHIP MOVEMENT (ICOM) AND INDUSTRIAL COMMON OWNERSHIP FINANCE (ICOF)

Next, and at least in part as a result of help stemming from Scott Bader's commitment to the 'political task' enshrined in the in 1972 code of practice of the Commonwealth, are two institutions dating from the 1970s which were still very much alive and well when this was written in 2001: the Industrial Common Ownership Movement, and Industrial Common Ownership Finance. I take ICOM first because it started earlier and in fact can trace a history going back before the Bruce Reed report.

The original body which became ICOM in or about 1971 – and had started to receive some support from Scott Bader in 1972 – had been known by the acronym DEMINTRY and is said by Susanna Hoe (pp 107–8) to have been 'co-founded' by Ernest Bader 'in the late 'fifties'. The acronym apparently reflected the idea of *Democratic Integration in Industry*, by which was meant some kind of coming together of management and shop floor within individual businesses. Susanna Hoe tells us that Ernest fell out with his co-founders of DEMINTRY and later with ICOM, which he seems to have joined briefly, after the name change, as an individual member.

In the genesis of ICOF, the link with Scott Bader and its 'political task' is that much closer, and the financial debt that much greater. For reasons of space I hope it is enough to state just three key steps in its genesis:

1 Towards the end of 1971, following the necessary changes in the relevant corporate articles, Scott Bader set up a new institution: The Commonwealth Development Fund (CDF). It was financed by grants from the post-tax profits of the Scott Bader company and managed by the CBoM. Its task was to offer financial assistance to businesses structured on Scott Bader lines, whether 'new start' undertakings or conversions.

2 In 1973, on the initiative of ICOM and Scott Bader together, ICOF was set up.

3 In 1974 Scott Bader passed to ICOF, in return for appropriate fees, the management of the CDF and the financial resources to enable its work to continue.

Following the start made by the CDF, and working separately or sometimes together, ICOM and ICOF have helped to midwife perhaps as many as 2,000 new co-operative type businesses since 1974, of which perhaps as many as 1,000 still survive today. More about them in a moment. However I must acknowledge at once that among those which did not survive was Sunderlandia Ltd, a building co-operative in Sunderland with which the writer of this book was most closely associated, and which had received valuable financial support from the CDF, and went into voluntary liquidation towards the end of the 1970s.

But here, in the context of what can be at least partly traced back to Scott Bader's 'political task', it would be unreasonable not to mention the national Co-operative Development Agency (CDA) established by James Callaghan's government in 1979. The importance of Scott Bader in the thinking which had preceded it was strikingly recognised when Ralph Woolf was appointed in the mid-1980s to succeed its first chairman, Lord Oram. Later Ralph Woolf was awarded the CBE for this work.

Though the national CDA did not itself survive beyond the end of Mrs Thatcher's second government, it became the model for large numbers of local CDAs set up in the1980s by mainly Labour party dominated local authorities. Some have done good work. Among these an important minority have survived.

The national and local CDAs are an interesting story in their own right. However, and if only for reasons of space, I must limit myself to the more direct outcomes of Commonwealth's new commitment, starting from the early 1970s, to its political task. In that connection I will return to ICOF and ICOM shortly.

THE INDUSTRIAL COMMON OWNERSHIP ACT 1976

About both the new law and also the co-operatives and other businesses which reflected the thinking behind it, either directly or indirectly, I rely mainly, aside from a description of the law itself, on Roger Sawtell. He has already made a first appearance in these pages as a friend of Ernest Bader, and one who spoke out – as we also know the founder did – against the acquisition of Strand Glassfibre in 1978. And he will reappear again, first, in chapter 12 as the founder of Trylon, and second, as the contributor of a 'critical celebration' of the Commonwealth's first 50 years, near the end. I hope it is reasonable to characterise Roger's values as coming from both the Quaker and the humanist traditions, though he has chosen to remain outside the Society of Friends. For me he is also something of a 'small is beautiful' fundamentalist. His 'critical celebration' right at the end of this book is my main evidence for that judgement.

Rather unusually for a new law of any kind, but especially so for one dealing with the subject matter of industrial ownership, the Act which became law on 22 November 1976 started its life as a private member's bill. David Watkins, the then Labour MP for the then steel town of Consett in County Durham, was the private member who sponsored it. He had a close relationship with what was then the Amalgamated Union of Engineering Workers (AUEW) and was for some years secretary of its parliamentary group.

David Watkins was himself the author of a Fabian Tract (number 455) published in April 1978 with the simple (or otherwise) title of 'Industrial Common Ownership'. Already on the tract's second page he gives a clear summary of its content:

> The Act has two main provisions. First, it enables the secretary of state for industry to provide loans for the development of common ownership and co-operative enterprises as well as to make grants to bodies whose purpose is to encourage such enterprises. The amount of the grants and loans is extremely modest but the principle has far-reaching implications. It lays a

foundation stone upon which could be built the *Co-operative Development Agency* [emphasis added] promised in both Labour's 1974 manifestos.

Second, the Act provides for the first time a proper legal definition of what constitutes enterprises of a common owner-ship and industrial co-operative nature. This ends the legal limbo in which common ownership companies and workers' co-operatives have found themselves whereby they were neither provided for in company law nor in industrial and provident societies legislation.

About the ICO Act itself and what has followed after it, Roger Sawtell wrote me a helpful letter in May 2000. After observing that it was 'drafted by me and mauled by parliamentary draughtsman', he went on:

> It has had v. little effect and few registrations, to the best of my knowledge. Far more effective have been the various ICOM model rules (first edition written by me in 1976 and 1977 as the 'ICOM Green Guide') – probably over 2,000 registrations by now but, of course many fall out. ... I think my figure of 1,000 ... is safe ... for the year 2000.

Some final points of clarification are in order. The first and most important is about the ICOM model rules to which Roger refers. It was perhaps his greatest contribution in this whole field to have achieved what I see as a double-barrelled success with the Registrar of Compa-nies: first, the acceptance by the latter of the idea of a pre-drafted set of model rules – simplified language to describe the Memorandum and Articles of Companies Act – and secondly its acceptance of the actual rules drafted by him. I should perhaps add that, for our purposes here, just two of those rules need to be emphasised:

1 A democratic rule, such that only those working in the business can have a voice in its decisions, and that that voice must reflect the prin-ciple, one worker one vote.
2 What Dr Schumacher called the 'extinction of capital'. These are Companies by Guarantee without a share capital.

For the rest I should make clear that almost all of the 1,000 of these businesses which Roger reckons were in existence in the year 2000 – and most of which presumably still are – have workforces which are small or very small in number, perhaps an average of five or even less.

That is one of the reasons why I see their impact and importance as much less, by a whole order of magnitude, than that of the retail co-ops formed in the second half of the 19th century in line with the Rochdale Principles.

As for registrations under the ICO Act, Godric is keen to remind anyone who will listen that certificate number one was issued to Scott Bader under it. The fact that no one seems to know of any others must tells us that not many have been applied for, and perhaps not even one by a business of Scott Bader's size.

On the other hand, Roger Sawtell has confirmed for me that Michael Jones, the well-known Northampton jeweller formed as a family business in 1919, followed something like the Scott Bader route into common ownership in 1970 and is today in a very flourishing state. Roger makes no claim about the degree of Scott Bader's influence on Michael Jones's ownership change. But given the town's proximity to Wollaston and the fact that Ernest Bader scarcely kept his ownership views secret, it will hardly have been non-existent.

It remains to say a final word about ICOM and ICOF. I should make clear first that both benefited for short periods from what David Watkins had described as the 'extremely modest' sums of money made available under the ICO Act. But both have now been entirely independent of government financial support for many years.

In the case of ICOM, its main tasks are to provide a range of services to the large number of admittedly on average rather small businesses which have used Roger Sawtell's ICOM model rules under which to get themselves registered, and to help those who continue to seek such registration. It invites these businesses to become members of ICOM and charges a membership fee to those which take that up. Its services are the familiar range supplied by such organisations: registration services apart, it supplies training, runs seminars and conferences, conducts research, offers consultancy, and acts as the advocate and representative of the ICOM movement with government and other agencies.

As for ICOF, its historical links with Scott Bader were for many years embodied in the person of David Ralley, its first executive director and someone whom we have already met many times in these pages. Among his many achievements with ICOF David Ralley was responsible for its pioneering and successful first share issue in 1987. His latest successor, Andrew Hibbert, was one of the main speakers at an event on 28 April 2001 to mark the actual 50th birthday of the Scott Bader

Commonwealth. He presides over total ICOF financial resources of over £6m, and his annual disbursements of equity and loan funds are running at around £750,000. In the 12 months ending with the Commonwealth's birthday, ICOF was able to respond to around 40 approaches for financial help with an average amount of some £18,000.

11

Labour and the (Working) Community in the Parent Company

Our community will not see the Scott Bader enterprise fail with the loss of all our livelihoods as well as our (and the founder's) aspirations to show an alternative way of doing business.   *Roger Scott, Community Council chairman. Letter to the author, 16 May 2000.*

INTRODUCTION

As long ago as 1968, but already 17 years after the establishment of the Scott Bader Commonwealth, Fred Blum published the first in what later became almost a library of major studies about it. Blum, an academic sociologist who became an Anglican priest later in life, gave his book a double title – *Work and Community*: *The Scott Bader Community and the Quest for a New Social Order* (London, RKP). Among other things, it presented the findings of a piece of research about the extent to which the company's employees were taking advantage of the Commonwealth's new democratic institutions. The research had been conducted jointly with Roger Hadley, whom we have already met several times in these pages and will do so again. However for my purpose here I want to emphasise just two points about Fred Blum's book. The first is that the research results were disappointing. What Blum and Hadley found was that only a rather small percentage of Commonwealth members chose to play an active part in its democratic institutions. Secondly, Blum expressed the view that these results were not really surprising. The typical Scott Bader employees were not, after all, a self-selected band of brothers – like the people one might find, for example, in an Israeli kibbutz. They came from ordinary backgrounds and had in effect been so conditioned before joining Scott Bader that the impact of the Commonwealth's democratic institutions and its other much publicised features – like, for example, its ownership arrangements – had been inescapably limited.

Susanna Hoe heads her chapter on the Commonwealth's first

quinquennium (1951–6) 'Bliss was it in that Dawn'. Well so perhaps it was then for a few, and perhaps even for a small or medium-sized minority. But to understand Scott Bader as it is today and as it surely has been since Fred Blum's and Roger Hadley's researches in the 1960s – and indeed mainly was before – it is necessary to start from a quite opposite position. Scott Bader's workforce today, its managers, its rank-and-file employees, and those in the middle, are essentially ordinary. Put in a slightly different way, they are more like than unlike their counterparts in businesses engaged in similar activities in today's UK. Whatever the founder, and still today his son Godric, may have predicted and hoped, the great majority of Scott Bader's employees do not seem to be more than minimally driven by unusual enthusiasms, not anyway at work.

It is true that, in discussing today's Scott Bader workforce and Commonwealth members, it is far from easy to strike an appropriate balance. There are some marvellous anecdotes: one of those who joined the Wollaston blue-collar workforce after a spell at a conventional company was said to have muttered that he seemed to have 'dropped into heaven'. Moreover, the workforce may indeed exhibit some fairly distinctive features. For example, its age and length of service profiles may, I think, be somewhat exceptional. That might be because, for those recruits who settle down, there are attractions about staying on. More important and no doubt more directly attributable to Commonwealth values, Scott Bader's pay differentials may be somewhat narrower than normal and somewhat biased in favour of the lower paid. As we saw in the last chapter, Commonwealth members have also, as a corporate body, an outstanding record of charitable giving.

I am also inclined to think, though this is hard to measure, that they mostly behave with notable good manners and unaggressively towards each other, and follow ethical business practices in their relationships with trading partners. In a real crisis, as Roger Scott's epigraph suggests, they just might be prepared to make personal sacrifices to keep the business alive which would go beyond what might be expected in the mainstream and conventional undertakings of private capitalism. But readers must not expect a management or a workforce which has been dramatically transformed by the experience of working in the Commonwealth, with its democratic institutions and what now seems to be called either its common ownership or its common trusteeship. For that is not what is to be found within the parent company at

Left Breitling Orbiter. Scott Bader played a key role in the production of the Gondola for the world record-breaking Breitling Orbiter 3 Round the World Balloon, manufactured by W. & J. od. *Right* Burj-al Arab Hotel, Dubai. Standing 321 metres high on its own man-made island in the Arabian Gulf, many of the internal features of the Burj-al Arab are made of Crystic resins.

eft Aston Martin V12, Aston Martin's most technologically advanced vehicle to date. It utilises Crystic resins. *Right* Minehunter from Vosper Thorneycroft. The first commercial application for Crystic Crestomer structural adhesives was in the manufacture of minehunters where they were used to prevent explosion induced forces from delaminating a ship's structure.

Left The Princess 65. Built using Crystic resins by Marine Projects, the largest production boatbuilder in Britain and the leading powerboat builder in Europe. *Right* TGV. Crystic resins are used in the production of France's TGV high-speed trains.

Left Flexible Packaging. A key application for Scott Bader emulsion polymers is high gloss and functional coatings to enhance paper, board and film substrates used for packaged goods. Many examples can be seen in our supermarkets.

Right Industrial Coatings. Scott Bader's powder-coating resins are used in high performance, solvent-free coatings that have high gloss

Ernest Bader, Founder   Godric Bader, Life President

Left Allan Bell, Group Managing Director. *Right* Andrew Gunn, currently Head of Finance, will become the Company's first internally appointed Chairman, outside of the family, in 2002.

Left Wollaston Hall. Scott Bader's headquarters is set in 44 acres of Northamptonshire parkland. *Right* The Customer Services Centre. Opened in 1992 as part of the Company's drive towards total quality management.

Ernest Bader Technical Centre, opened in 1990. This 1,160m² building houses the largest full scale closed mould demonstration facility in Europe.

Wollaston after the Commonwealth's first half century. The typical rank-and-file employees do not behave like Stakhanovites in the early years of the Soviet Union. Equally, the typical managers have no special capacities to inspire with special enthusiasms and no special gifts of business prescience. No doubt one fundamental question is whether the differences between the company and its conventional counterparts, and especially those which can be attributed to the Commonwealth, are as strong as might reasonably have been expected. And a similar question may be asked about business performance. But we do not address either of them here.

Instead, the focus of what follows now is labour and management, or the 'working community' at Wollaston at the end of the Commonwealth's first 50 years. I emphasise at once that it is the *Wollaston* labour force in the parent business, together with those working in its UK offshoots in the company's sales and distribution network, with which we are going to be concerned. For that is where, if anywhere, within what became in the 1990s the mini-multinational Scott Bader group, that we should look for any changes to which 50 years of the Commonwealth experience have given rise.

Whatever the precise extent to which they managed to transform themselves into a true working community and/or – to borrow the founder's phrase – into 'responsible owners', we need first to have a sharper understanding of who these people now are, classified by traditional categories of occupation and by age, gender and length of service. Next we will need at least an indication of rates of pay and other employment conditions and a closer understanding than was appropriate in the last chapter about how final decisions on these matters are reached.

Thirdly we shall need to look closely at the prevalent attitudes within this working community such as they emerge – or appear to emerge – from professionally conducted attitude surveys and other evidence. The latter will include assessments by supposedly sympathetic outsiders, for example by a succession of external trustees.

THE COMPOSITION OF THE WORKING COMMUNITY AND RATES OF PAY

Helen Dollimore, head of the human resources department, has kindly supplied me with data for the position as it was in July of 2000. In round figures we are talking about a total employee population of some

360, of whom about two-thirds, approximately 240, are classified as not falling into any one of six higher-paid occupational categories: categories devised by the London-based management consultants, Hay (formerly and in earlier chapters Hay-MSL). We will come back to the actual categories later.

In commonly used language, those in this majority group of 240 are not managers; but equally, they are not professionals and they are not 'on the road' as mainly autonomous senior members of the company's travelling sales force. In the John Lewis Partnership the corresponding majority group would be referred to as 'rank-and-file partners'. At Scott Bader, with the possible and rather appealing exception of 'non-suits', there is no generally accepted – or politically correct – way of referring to them as a whole. It is true that they are sometimes called the non-management employees and sometimes the 'blue-collar staff'. Neither description is accurate at Scott Bader in Wollaston. As we will see in a moment, there are plenty of Scott Bader's non-managers – the professionals, the technicians and a large percentage of those engaged in selling – who do not fall into the majority group of 240. Conversely there are plenty of non-blue-collar employees within that majority group.

In line with what apparently remains typical in the industrials chemicals sector of the UK economy, the gender balance at Scott Bader is still heavily male-dominated. Less than one in four of the workforce were female in July of 2000. After a small but necessary adjustment to make the total come to 360, Helen Dollimore's figures are 281 male and 79 female. So far as I know, no women have yet been recruited to work in the actual resin manufacturing plants. I suspect that the existing blue-collar workforce would not be specially enthusiastic in the welcome they would offer to new female recruits. Who knows? Some negative feelings might well be mutual between the two sexes on this issue. No doubt change will come but it may come rather slowly.

What may, on the other hand, be rather unusual in the industrial chemicals businesses of today's UK are the profiles of Scott Bader's workforce by age and length of service. Rather over 200 employees, between 55 and 60% of the total, had more than 10 years' service when Helen Dollimore made her calculations for me in the summer of 2000, and approximately the same number – or just a few more – were 41 years old or older.

Thus if we look at Scott Bader's UK workforce in mid-2000, and in broad-brush terms, there seem to be three dominant features. Two are likely to be typical at least of most of the country's industrial chemicals businesses at start of the new century: 1) A ratio of roughly two to one between 'non-suit' and 'higher' employee grades; 2) A ratio of nearly four to one of males to females.

It seems intuitively probable – though I have no direct data to confirm it – that the third of these dominant characteristics is untypical and fairly special to Scott Bader: the fact that over 55% of the workforce in the year 2000 were either over 41 years of age or had more than 10 years' service or both. That may well be both part cause and part effect of the rather unusually generous pension arrangements which have been a notable feature of Scott Bader's employee compensation package since the 1970s.

But first we need to get a more detailed understanding of the Hay system of classifying occupations for the purposes of rates of pay, and to know something about rates which were actually operational in the summer of the year 2000. At Scott Bader the system is referred to as one of *job grades*. Including the managing director, who is in the top grade on his own, there have for some years been 11 of these. They run up the scale from 21 at the bottom to 31 (the MD's grade) at the top.

Here is how Helen Dollimore describes the different clusters of grades between 21 and 30:

> Those in 21 and 22 are either cleaners, receptionists or catering staff. As far as grades 23, 24 and 25 are concerned, these grades mostly cover process operators, laboratory assistants, clerical and administration staff, team leaders, engineers, chemical assistants, trainers and marketing assistants. Those in grades 26 to 30 are either managers or professionals. The sales people do not earn a commission but are positioned in grade 26.

As no doubt happens in other businesses which apply either the Hay or a similar job grade system, the rates of pay in each grade may vary between a bottom and a top percentage level. At Scott Bader in Wollaston, in the summer of 2000, the top rate in each grade was set at 120% and the bottom at 80%. For example, the actual rates that then applied to grade 25 fell between £17,320 at the 80% bottom and £25,980 at the 120% top. To understand the system more clearly, readers should also know that the grades are stepped in such a way that 80% of each grade is always significantly above 100% of the grade below.

It should also be specified that as between the pay for those in grade 21 at the bottom and the MD's grade 31 at the top, the ratio was approximately 13 to 1. The 100% figures in each of these two job grades were £11,441 and £152,949 respectively. Both rates are pre-tax and so therefore is the ratio number. The post-tax distance between top and bottom is, of course, less. I have not got the data which would make possible an objective judgement about how far Scott Bader's rates for its job grades in the summer of the year 2000 were in line with the then going rates for industrial chemicals businesses of an employment and turnover size similar to its own. But, as I understand it, the company believes that with one qualification there is a rough correspondence between its own rates and those paid by its peers. The qualification is that there is something of an upward bias in the Scott Bader rates for the lower job grades. So the pay structure is more egalitarian than is normal in the industry.

PENSIONS, REDUNDANCY COMPENSATION, AND THE 25-YEAR TRAVEL AWARD

But it is when we move on from rates of pay to pensions that the Scott Bader employment benefit package seems to be rather exceptional, and is known to be valued most highly by the company's employees. The pension's policy statement at Wollaston is notably forthright and not a little ambitious: 'Our company's policy is to provide a pension based on final salary and years of service *which is better than the UK industrial average* [emphasis added].'

To a non-pension specialist, three specifics tell us most of what we want to know:

1 In return for an employee contribution of just 3.5% of pre-tax salary, pensioners receive 1/55th of final salary for each completed year of service between the ages of 20 and 60, the prescribed age of retirement. In other words, those who have contributed for the maximum of 40 years of service will enjoy a pension up to the limit allowed by the Inland Revenue, namely two-thirds of final salary.

2 In principle employees may choose to take early retirement from their 55th birthday onwards and then take their pensions, as the technical language has it, *without actuarial loss*. That means that while their final salary will normally be lower than it would have been had they soldiered on until their 60th birthday, the formula

which determines their actual pension will not be adjusted downwards to take account of the fact that they may expect to receive that pension for longer.

3 Given that the Inland Revenue's limit on tax relief for employee contributions to private pension funds is 15% of pay, against the 3.5% laid down for Scott Bader employees, there is plenty of room for making additional voluntary contributions (AVCs). It will come as no surprise that since the relief is at the highest rate at which the AVC maker pays tax, a relatively greater percentage of higher-paid employees take advantage of these possibilities.

We may recall from the earlier narrative history that the opportunity to 'retire at 55 without actuarial loss' was first introduced in 1978, on the recommendation of the then chief executive, Ralph Woolf. It coincided with a concurrent lowering of the normal retiring age from 65 to 60. Both may be seen as partly a reflection of the unusual overmanning difficulties with which Scott Bader was contending at that time. Early retirement could be presented as a reasonable alternative to voluntary redundancy as long as the terms on offer were fair.

The arithmetic of the comparison is not altogether straightforward and I will not attempt to present it here. All the same, given a) the importance of its voluntary redundancy schemes in the company's history since the end of the 1970s; b) the fact that they have been oversubscribed on three different occasions; and c) that they are now almost permanently available as a standing offer, it would be a mistake not to have the now well-established formula on which they are based on the record. The formula gives us the lump sum redundancy payment expressed in terms of numbers of weeks of salary. This formula is twelve weeks' pay, plus two weeks for each year of age over 20, plus one week for every year of service. It thus takes account of the employee's age and length of service as well as of his or her rate of pay.

Helen Dollimore has calculated how the formula would work out for someone with 20 years' service and earning an annual salary of £20,000: 12 + 40 weeks (equals 52) + 20 weeks (equals 72) x £20,000 divided by 52. Thus the redundancy payment due to an employee with those qualifications of age, length of service and salary level would be rather more than one year and four months – exactly one year plus 5/13 – of his or her annual salary on becoming voluntarily redundant. Such a payment level is understood to be well over three times what the law would require.

The special 'travelling sabbatical award', for which employees now become eligible after 25 years' service has already been described. There is no need to repeat that here. On the other hand it makes sense to suggest that it shares a common logic with the two items in the Wollaston employment conditions that we have just reviewed: the deliberately rather generous terms of the private pension scheme and of the compensation for voluntary redundancy. However, there is a double educational rationale behind it which is quite separate and distinct: first, the travel itself is seen as having educational content, and secondly the award may be used to finance a period of study rather than travel, though there are few if any examples of the educational alternative having been actually chosen.

Though there is nothing – so far as I know – on paper to this effect, all three are persuasively presented at Wollaston, by those who have thought carefully about these questions, as offering something of an alternative to the benefits which Commonwealth members might enjoy if they held some actual shares in the Scott Bader business. The logic of this partial equivalence is perhaps most obvious in the case of the private pension scheme and, perhaps in particular, of its provisions for special early retirement at 55 without actuarial loss. By accepting pension costs which are higher than normal, the business is somehow acknowledging that Commonwealth members, and especially members with extended lengths of service, have certain special claims on any resources which are surplus to other requirements. The formal argument can only be pressed up to a point, because the same pension scheme provisions are open to employees who are not Commonwealth members. Still it seems rather persuasive and should certainly count for something.

A quite separate argument for encouraging early retirement is that the recurrent costs of the business are likely to fall when younger employees replace older ones.

It is also perhaps worth mentioning in this context that unusually generous pension scheme arrangements have also, at least in good times, been an important feature of the Carl Zeiss optical business in Germany. As noted earlier, Zeiss has been almost literally 'trustee owned' – by a German charitable foundation or *Stiftung* – since the 1890s. Alternatively, in Dr Schumacher's language, its ownership is 'extinguished', and has been for more than twice as long as that of Scott Bader. It is true that in the much tougher economic climate of the middle and later 1990s, the business was forced to revise the terms of its pension scheme in order to reduce costs. But my point is rather different: that we should expect the employees in businesses owned in these ways to press successfully for 'above average' pension arrangements. It was indeed true of Zeiss before its 1990s pension cutbacks, as it still sometimes is at Scott Bader, that when the state pension is added to what the company provides, there are some among the lower paid who have more money coming in after their retirement than before.

And the same is surely true about compensation terms in cases of redundancy. We should *expect* that, so long as they can be afforded, they will be that much higher in businesses like Scott Bader where employee influence is strong. Maybe those 'travel sabbaticals' awarded to those who complete 25 years of service are something of a special case. But it is easy to see that a similar logic can be applied in their case too. In any event John Lewis has for many years offered sabbaticals to long service employees, though without the obligation to undertake either foreign travel or private study.

There then is what had by the 1990s become the most distinctive feature of the employment conditions package at Scott Bader in the UK: its pension scheme arrangements, its more or less 'standing' redundancy compensation terms, and its 25-year award, all three linked by the logic of their special appeal to older and more long-serving employees. Evidence is not lacking about the effectiveness of this appeal:

a) The results of a survey in 2000 showed beyond any doubt that a majority of Scott Bader's UK employees assign the highest value to their pension rights.

b) That on the three occasions – twice when Ralph Woolf was chief executive and once after Ian Henderson had taken over in the 1990s – more people wanted to take their voluntary redundancy payments and leave than the company was able to release.

c) Only three times has the 25-year award been declined by an employee who had qualified for it, and all three have been in quite exceptional circumstances.

It seems plausible to suppose therefore that these employment benefits are of special interest to the older people employed by Scott Bader in the UK and may explain at least in part the rather high percentages in the total workforce who have either 10 years' length of service or have passed their 41st birthday, or both. For a man or woman in, say, the middle 30s with a fair number of years already in Scott

Bader employment, the strength of the case for staying on must surely be enhanced by the prospect of fairly generous early retirement benefits at 55, and ones which are almost correspondingly attractive should the employee decide to leave earlier under what are almost standing voluntary redundancy arrangements.

Moreover, it is also almost certainly fair to claim that both the early retirement provisions of the pension scheme and the redundancy payments, despite their up-front costs, will normally result quite quickly in improvements in the company's business performance. They will have tended to improve labour productivity and to reduce the proportion of the company's value added which is directly related to the pay and conditions of employees.

OTHER FEATURES OF THE EMPLOYMENT CONDITIONS AT SCOTT BADER UK

Labour turnover and rates of unscheduled absence – whether due to sickness or otherwise – are widely taken as evidence of workforce satisfaction, with higher numbers taken as indicating lower levels of morale and vice versa. By these measures the record of Scott Bader in the UK seems to have been very reasonable or rather better over the seven years to mid-2000 for which data is easily accessible. Excluding all retirements, the early ones as well as those associated with the retiring age of 60, annual labour turnover for those seven years averaged 7.6% of the total. On the other hand, 1994 and 1995 were years in which a formal voluntary redundancy scheme was in operation. If those are excluded the annual average comes down by just over a full percentage point to 6.5.

For businesses which continue to pay people who are sick over the really long term – that is over a number of years – the sickness percentage is inescapably made up of two quite distinct components: a long-term and a short-term sick component. Scott Bader in the UK is one of those companies. About its record in this respect over the 12 months to 30 April 2000 Helen Dollimore writes:

> The total number of days lost was 3,165.
>
> There are two people classed as long-term sick which accounts for 520 days.
>
> Assuming an average of 369 employees working 260 days per year, giving 95,940 possible days, the following calculations apply:

a) Including long term sick: 3,165 / 95,940 = 3.29%
b) Excluding long term sick: 2,645 / 9,940 = 2.76%

Those numbers look to me to be quite competitive. I remember hearing an interesting view expressed by a senior person in the Mondragon group of co-ops who was concerned with these matters. It was his judgement that if you could get the short-term sick numbers down to wholly genuine and unavoidable cases, you might expect an annual average of 1.5%. But he did not claim that the co-ops had actually succeeded in reaching it. As for conventionally-owned manufacturing businesses, the range of annual sickness percentages is quite wide, but Scott Bader's numbers are significantly better than average.

Finally about holiday pay, the present position is that all full-time staff who have completed 12 months' service are entitled to 25 days plus 8 statutory holidays. That seems to be rather above the industrial average. Moreover, for those working for Scott Bader in the UK up to four extra days are associated with longer service.

HOW CHANGES IN PAY AND CONDITIONS ARE DECIDED

There are two starting points for this discussion. The first is that from the very beginnings of the Commonwealth, and indeed from the days when Scott Bader was still a more or less conventional family business, there has been no recognition of unions for wage and related bargaining purposes. Moreover, as readers will remember, the Chemical Workers' Union, the main one in the industry during Scott Bader's early days, gave its formal consent to that as part of the deal which brought the 1948 strike to an end, and which included a company commitment to move to a co-operative type legal framework and, at least by implication, to pay labour at above union rates. For what it's worth, Ernest Bader and the union's then general secretary, Bob Edwards, who reached that deal between them, later became good friends. Later again, in 1963, by which time he had been elected a Labour MP, Bob Edwards accepted an invitation to become one of the Commonwealth's first set of external trustees.

Not to recognise a union or unions for wage bargaining purposes is, of course, not at all the same thing as a blanket non-recognition of union membership. The latter has never applied at Scott Bader, and a minority of the workforce – sometimes up to 25% – have always chosen to pay their union dues. However, given that the company does not bargain with a union or unions over wages, there needs to be some other mechanism for reaching decisions about them. Until the introduction of the new constitution in 1971, that mechanism was simplicity itself: wages and other conditions of employment were matters for unilateral management decision, albeit sometimes only after extensive discussion within the framework of the Commonwealth.

On the other hand, as we already know, the 1971 constitution changed all that – which brings us to our second starting point. I quoted in the last chapter what Godric told the Business History Unit at the London School of Economics in his 1983 paper about the role of the new Community Council in decision making about wages after 1971. It makes sense to repeat that here: 'Whilst not constitutionally mandatory on pay scales … its [i.e. the Community Council's] agreement is obtained by management before implementation.'

I myself originally took this less than transparent formula to mean that, in the event of a disagreement over these matters between the council and management, the voice of the former would prevail. But that is not what happens nor was it apparently intended. In effect the formula imposes on both parties a duty to reach their decisions by consensus. But what if a consensus cannot be reached? The first response to that question is that so far it has not happened. And if it was to? Under the constitution, the answer seems to be that one of the two powers of the trustees would be invoked: the power to arbitrate between the two parties.

However it is scarcely surprising that the process of reaching agreement about Godric's 'pay scales' can take time, especially when the economic climate is tough, as it undoubtedly was for Scott Bader during most of the 1990s and into the 21st century. A good illustration is provided by the extended process which was needed during the year 2000 and into 2001 to reach a new agreement about both wages and the main other components of the compensation package for Scott Bader employees in the UK. A special and widely representative working party was formed under the chairmanship of Andrew Gunn. It took just over 12 months for the necessary consensus to be reached. Rather in parenthesis, it may be helpful for readers to know that a survey set up by this working party provided the information about the key employee preference which has already been highlighted, namely that it was their pensions to which a majority of employees attached the greatest value.

What was probably most important in the outcome of the many sessions of this working party was an agreement for some change of emphasis in how annual wage adjustments are to be agreed. At least on the margin the effect of the newly agreed emphasis should be twofold:

1 To reduce the pressure to set across-the-board annual wage increases either to keep pace with inflation or to leapfrog ahead of it.
2 Conversely to link wage increases more closely with individual performance.

To understand what these changes mean it is necessary to understand what has happened in the recent past. Under the former regime, the pay of Scott Bader employees was divided into two quite distinct components: first, basic pay linked to the employee's job grade on the Hay scale; second, 'progression' pay, an extra above the basic component, varying upwards from zero, and dependent on an individual performance assessment made by the responsible manager.

Under the old regime, the basic component in the pay packets of *all* employees has been adjusted each year by the same amount – to reflect the movement of prices. By definition, on the other hand, the annual adjustments of employees' progression pay has varied quite widely: from nil to significant percentage increases.

Under the new regime agreed by Andrew Gunn's working party the distinction between these two components in the annual adjustment of individual employees' pay will be blurred if not eliminated. Of the total extra money allocated to the company's annual pay adjustment, a much higher proportion will be linked to the assessed performance of individual employees. In extreme cases under the new regime, where an individual's performance is assessed as having been well below average, that individual might find that his or her annual adjustment was zero, and in such cases he or she would not be compensated for any loss of purchasing power brought about by price inflation.

To repeat, the logic of these changes is clear enough: to reduce or eliminate the link between annual wage adjustments and inflation and instead to link them as closely as possible with improvements in individual employee performance.

One of the key criteria by which the 'responsibility' of owners is normally judged is about the degree to which the future as well as the present is taken into account. By that test the changes agreed by Andrew Gunn's working party at the turn of the century look as if they are rather in line with Ernest Bader's objectives in establishing the Commonwealth in the first place – to transform the company's employees into 'responsible owners'. It is true that much earlier, in the 1980s, they demonstrated a notable advantage in this respect compared with the unionised labour force of SRL on Merseyside. The decisions of Andrew Gunn's working party can be seen as having significantly strengthened that comparative advantage.

SELECTED EVIDENCE ABOUT EMPLOYEE ATTITUDES

As has already been suggested, those who try to understand Scott Bader – and especially perhaps those who do so from a standpoint of admiring and caring about its social democratic and social Christian ideals and objectives – have somehow to deal with an unusually stubborn difficulty: the evidence for the quite widespread 'comparative dissatisfaction' of its workforce. There is a great deal of 'attitude survey evidence', going back at least to the 1970s, on which to base that judgement. So much so that it has made this writer's head swim even to look through the files. By 'comparative dissatisfaction' I mean reported satisfaction levels which are not significantly higher than those reported in conventional capitalist companies, and sharply lower than in some other 'co-operative' or 'co-operative type' companies.

For me, the most persuasive summary of this evidence comes in a learned article written by Roger Hadley and Maurice Goldsmith and published in the international journal *Economic and Industrial Democracy* (volume 16, number 2) in May 1995. Both authors, Maurice Goldsmith as well as Roger Hadley, must be counted as friends of Scott Bader. At different times in the 1980s the former was a member of the company board and chairman of the trustees. In his professional life he was the author of many books on science and technology and their social impact. In the mid-1990s, when the article was published, he was the director of the London-based International Science Policy Foundation. Roger Hadley needs no introduction.

The passage from the article I want to highlight is about job satisfaction at Scott Bader in 1989 (pp 183 and 184). The evidence comes from self-assessment by a sample of employees:

> Scott Bader workers' self assessment ... suggested that just over a third enjoyed their jobs very much, a little over one-half said they enjoyed their jobs 'somewhat', one in 14 'little' and one worker

'not at all'. *This suggested level of satisfaction is very close to the findings of a contemporary national survey for all kinds of jobs in Britain in which a similar, although not identical, question was asked* [emphasis added]. In the national study, 34% said they were very satisfied with their jobs, 48% said they were fairly satisfied, 8% were fairly dissatisfied and 2% very dissatisfied. In contrast, a study of three American co-operative enterprises … *suggested much higher satisfaction levels with 84% either rating their jobs as the most satisfying they have ever done or as 'very satisfying'* [emphasis added].

The article also reports (p 182) responses from the same sample of Scott Bader's Wollaston workforce to questions about whether Scott Bader was a democracy or not. It seems that 'one half … felt the need to enter caveats … about the extent to which the organisation could be considered democratic'.

And the article goes on:

Three main types of reservation were expressed. The first of these was the abuse or potential abuse of power by management. As one factory worker put it, after saying that in theory the Commonwealth was a democracy, 'it's gone away from the founder's ideals. There is more direction from above and less say by the workforce.' A second type of reservation identified members' failure to use their powers as the problem. … Finally a third type of reservation had to do with the lack of understanding of how the democracy worked. A technician summed up the difficulty: 'The grass roots level is lacking. There's a need to foster a greater understanding of the Scott Bader system and of committee work. They expect people elected to do the work without having any experience.'

It seems safe to conclude from this evidence that at the time to which it applies, namely the end of the 1980s, either a) Scott Bader's democratic and other supposedly worker-friendly institutions were not working all that well, or b) that a significant minority of its employees wished – perhaps for other reasons – to send out a message to that effect. For the 1990s, what I take as evidence for a similar discontent comes from what was said or written by three successive holders of the chair of Scott Bader's trustee body: Roger Hadley, Jennifer Wates and Rob Paton.

The context of Roger Hadley's remarks which were made to the Commonwealth's quarterly meeting on 20 February 1995, and were fully reported in the March issue of the *Reactor*, give them a special weight. He spoke in his then capacity as chairman of the trustees, but with an extra authority on top of that. For the company's accountants, as he told the meeting, were about to declare an 'overall loss', as opposed to an operating loss, for 1994, one which had resulted from 'the planned provision for the voluntary redundancy scheme'. Because of this impending declaration of loss, as Professor Hadley reminded his audience, the trustees were *'empowered to take action under the Articles of Association of Scott Bader Company Ltd (Article 14b)* [emphasis added]'.

What I want to highlight from Professor Hadley's speech of 20 February 1995 is a passage which follows a full acknowledgement of the objective factors which lie behind the overall loss.

> We [viz. the trustees] appreciate the special difficulties created in 1994 by the drastic and unexpected increase in raw material prices. Nevertheless we believe that if the company had been operating more effectively as a cohesive organisation with a stronger sense of common purpose, realising its natural advantages as a common ownership firm, it might have weathered the storm more easily and emerged in better shape than it finds itself today.

'Operating more effectively as a cohesive organisation ... realising its natural advantages as a common ownership firm' – this language surely tells us that, in the view of Professor Hadley and his fellow trustees, Scott Bader's supposedly worker-friendly institutions were not working all that well in the mid-1990s. In other words his diagnosis then was for practical purposes identical with what had emerged from his sample survey of employee attitudes in 1989.

Jennifer Wates took over the chair of the trustee body from Roger Hadley. That was in the same year, 1995, as her predecessor's speech to Commonwealth members from which I have just quoted. She retired from the position and said goodbye to Scott Bader in 1997. But by then she had spent a total of 12 years as a trustee. Moreover, she had in the 1970s been the prime mover behind a project which may reasonably be described as a 'transition to common ownership' – to something in fact called *Common-work* – in an agricultural and craft business previously owned by the Wates family in Kent. So she had a fairly long stint of exposure to Scott Bader at Wollaston and some invaluable direct experience of common ownership in practice in her own backyard. Given that background, the valedictory statement which she made when she finally said goodbye, and which was published in the *Reactor* July 1997, deserves rather special attention. She begins by recalling her response to a question put to her by Peter Mattli about what she could contribute if she was invited to join the trustee body and accepted the invitation:

> I said then that I wanted to make sure that you valued yourselves enough; and still believe that you need to realise how important you are to the outside world. ... Perhaps if you all realised more clearly that you are at the forefront of the movement to make business more moral and humane for the 21st century, and thereby to create a better future – perhaps then there would be more incentive for you all to work at developing the Scott Bader experiment. And if you did so I believe you could operate more efficiently, and harness everyone's potential in a more dynamic enterprise.
>
> So it is a disappointment to me that you haven't progressed further over these years, and I apologise for whatever I have failed to do to help. To me, the main problem seems to be not that you have rather cumbersome structures – though this is true – but that you haven't developed the processes and procedures of working together in practical ways. When the processes don't work, this breeds mistrust and creates a vicious spiral.

I don't wish to labour the same point excessively, but I must also refer to a long article which Rob Paton, who took over the chair of the trustee body from Jennifer Wates, contributed to the same issue of the *Reactor,* July 1997, from which I have just quoted. He wrote that 'the near unanimous views of members with long experience of the Commonwealth's ups and downs pointed to low morale and an unprecedented lack of confidence in the institutions of the Commonwealth.'

TOWARDS AN UNDERSTANDING OF THE EMPLOYEE ATTITUDES EVIDENCE

'We are our own most forceful critics.' That was the first response of Denise Sayer, who took over as Commonwealth secretary when Mick Jones retired in 1998, when I asked her about this evidence, from the 1980s and 1990s, about the not wholly positive attitudes of its UK employees to Scott Bader. And that was also the first comment of many others with whom I raised the issue in Wollaston. It offers at least a first step towards a just assessment of the evidence. Sympathetic outsiders are also surely bound to comment that Scott Bader's openness about all this is a mark of corporate maturity and perhaps, at some level, of an underlying confidence.

A second point which tells in the same direction – viz. as some mitigation of this evidence of negative employee attitudes – is that similar evidence has surfaced quite widely over the years among those employed in other businesses in which conventional capitalist owners have been 'seen off'. In some ways, the closest and most persuasive parallel is with the shop-floor discontent which was a conspicuous feature of the experience of the great German optical business, Carl Zeiss, in the 1980s. During that decade the Zeiss equivalent of Scott Bader's Community Council took the management of the business to a German industrial tribunal no less than three times, and won on each occasion. I have already suggested that by the criterion of ownership arrangements this famous optical undertaking is probably Scott Bader's closest corporate relative. For that reason it may be that we should actually *expect* that similar conditions may quite well result in similar discontents.

What's more there is widespread evidence, especially in America, that adversarial attitudes between shop floor and management tend to 'snap back' in businesses which have become employee-owned whether by using the tax assisted mechanism of an Employee Share Ownership Plan (an ESOP) or in other ways. In the late 1980s and 1990s there were notable cases of this happening in two large employee-owned steel companies, Weirton Steel in West Virginia and Republic Steel in Ohio. More recently there has been evidence of the same thing at the Chicago-based United Airlines. It is probably not too much to say that except in cases where rather special conditions apply, industrial relations – and therefore job satisfaction – are typically more problematic than not in employee-owned businesses. The research evidence further suggests that this is especially so when the going in the market becomes less easy, when there is not much profit to share and employee earnings are not much better than flat. As we already know the going for Scott Bader became notably tougher from the end of the 1970s onwards – as it did for those two American steel companies within a few years of their having become employee-owned.

Research studies suggest that there are only two types of employee ownership in today's world which may be expected *not* to experience systematically or at least seriously problematic industrial relations. One is where final decisions on big issues, and consequently business leadership, lie with the elected representatives of the workforce but in which professional managers are responsible for the normal tasks of management. The best examples of undertakings of this kind at the start of the 21st century are a) in the Mondragon co-operative group in the Basque Provinces of Spain, and b) among the old workers co-ops in Italy and France, and perhaps vestigially in the UK, and c) among other more recently established workers co-ops elsewhere, especially in America. These arrangements may be differently described. But their key feature is that the professional managers are accountable to, and can fairly easily be sacked by, an elected body which functions as a supervisory board.

The other type of contemporary employee ownership which seems to avoid having recurrently problematic industrial relations is best exemplified by the John Lewis Partnership (JLP). There, with one qualification, both final decisions and day-to-day management functions are the prerogative of professional managers. It is true that the professional managers at JLP are accountable to a mainly democratic representative body and may at any time be required to defend their actions in front of it. It is also true that the mainly democratic representative body has the ultimate power to remove the chief executive by a weighted majority vote. On the other hand, though there is nothing at JLP directly comparable to a supervisory board, its professional managers seem to enjoy a notably unproblematic legitimacy.

It is not easy, and I suspect it may not be possible, to analyse the complex balance of power which has evolved at Scott Bader so that it can be classified alongside either the John Lewis management-accountability model, or the supervisory board workers co-op model of successful non-capitalist business ownership in today's world. If that is so, it may give us a clue to the source of the not wholly positive employee attitudes at Wollaston that we have been considering. Maybe we should expect, in these circumstances, that industrial relations and employee satisfaction at Wollaston will be systematically problematic. I have already quoted an insider's view that this state of affairs makes for 'creative friction'. I have also already quoted a second insider's view is that the representative arrangements which have evolved at Scott Bader are 'dysfunctional'. More explicitly, he argues that election as an office holder in one of the business's representative institutions often tends to

result in the adoption of unreasonably ideological rather than pragmatic attitudes. I cannot resist referring to the local description of the
elected shop stewards at America's Weirton Steel when that business
was employee-owned in the 1980s and 1990s. They were known as the
'grievance men'.

So the proper initial response by outsider friends of Scott Bader to
evidence of the negative attitudes of some of its employees might be
that that is to be expected. It occurs widely when the traditional
authority of conventional capitalism – whether of the state or private
shareholders – is extinguished. One might add that a psychological
probability may also be involved: that in exercises like employee attitude surveys, 'free spirits' will tend to overstate their criticisms. In
England at any rate that has surely been the tendency of 'Village
Hampdens' since Wat Tyler and even earlier.

A second line of response is that in judging Scott Bader we should be
at least as much interested in the business and Commonwealth record
as in the findings of attitude surveys. We can then point to some notable
successes and above all to the series of voluntary redundancy programmes, starting from 1979, which seem to have taken much of the
sting out of job losses. From the fact that each of the three main programmes has been oversubscribed one might even argue that all or even
more than all of the sting has been taken out.

Perhaps too, as Brian Elgood has suggested, the greater 1990s
emphasis on customer satisfaction needs may count in the same direction and eventually deliver improved results in the shape of increases in
value added. That will happen if the financial benefits of that new
emphasis come to exceed its financial costs. That is something which, if
it happens, is bound to take time. The payback on a new customer
service centre may well take longer than that on a new set of polymer
reactors.

Moreover if we are looking at the business record rather than attitude surveys there is some evidence of improved performance starting
from the mid-1990s. This evidence, as we saw in the narrative 1990s
chapter, includes the successful savings programme of 1995. Most
recently, as discussed earlier in this chapter, there has also been the outcome of Andrew Gunn's working party on wage determination, with
its shift of emphasis to more of a link between wage increases and
improved individual performance. There is no need to go over this evidence in any detail a second time. But it all seems to reflect a greater
concern by the working community to achieve better results.

All the same, both inside the working community and among its friends outside there is a recurrent and – sometimes almost deafening – murmur that Scott Bader 'ought to be doing better'. I have already in this chapter quoted three successive trustee chairmen to that effect. Perhaps the most specific piece of concrete evidence is that the 'continuous improvement programme' formally launched by the company board and recorded in the Traxton/Reeves diary in 1992, and partially revived by the savings programme in 1995, had been discontinued well before the end of the decade.

We will clearly have to come back to these questions once more in the final chapter.

12

Wollaston: The 150 Years to 2001, and Scott Bader's Relations with the (Local) Community

Wollaston was evidently a working village with very few gentry.
David Hall, 'Wollaston, Portrait of a Village', p 244

POPULATION, EMPLOYMENT AND OCCUPATIONS

In his dry but invaluable and well-researched study, *Wollaston, Portrait of a Village* (The Wollaston Society, 1977), David Hall goes back, at the start of his final chapter, to the period 'after the ice ages [when the] ... Nene valley was left with a variety of soils, many of them well-drained, fertile, and suitable for agricultural settlement'. The Nene river is the principal waterway running through the Wollaston area of Northamptonshire, eventually spilling into the Wash. But my main point here has to do not with Hall's final chapter but the one before, which is headed 'Industry', where he writes: 'The census of 1851 is convenient for an in-depth study of the Wollaston population and occupations.'

It clearly makes sense for us to take that as our starting point and, with every necessary acknowledgement, to quote Hall's opening summary of what that census tells us about Wollaston, just 100 years before the life of the Scott Bader Commonwealth began:

> The total population was 1,261 plus 2 unknown people sleeping in a barn. There were 280 families living in 264 houses, with 6 empty houses and no new ones being built. ... A total of 645 persons worked and there were 603 housewives and children etc. ... The chief occupations are lace-making, boot and shoe, and farm work.

David Hall then summarises the 1851 occupational data in a table:

OCCUPATION	NUMBER	PERCENT OF POP.	PERCENT OF WORKING POP.
Agriculture	140	11.1	21.3
Lace	158	12.5	24.0
Shoemaking	157	12.5	23.9
Other	203	16.2	30.9
Wives, Children etc	603	47.8	——
Total	1,261		

As it had done since the first ever decennial census in 1801 – when the recorded number was 761 – Wollaston's population increased steadily, if only gradually, from 1851 down to the outbreak of the First World War. The only exception was a slight decline in the 1860s. By 1911 the figure had climbed to 2,449, but over the next 50 years each successive census number is lower then the one before. The depressions of the interwar period are presumably the main explanation, though those killed in the First World War, between 1914 and 1918, may also have been a factor. In any event the 1911 number was not exceeded until 1971. The three final census records of the 20th century show a renewal of the pre-1914 upward trend:

Wollaston Census Numbers 1971–91

1971	2,710
1981	2,932
1991	2,982

But that is to anticipate. In the Commonwealth's foundation year, 1951, Wollaston's population at 2,069 was nearly 20% below what it had been before the First World War. And the downward trend only began to be reversed in the 1960s. Apart from an on-going drift to the larger towns, the main post-Second World War driver of the Wollaston numbers was almost certainly its boot and shoe industry. On the other hand, if Scott Bader had not arrived in 1940, the decline of numbers in the 1950s would no doubt have been sharper and the recovery of the 1960s that much less.

In any event David Hall is in no doubt about the overriding importance for Wollaston of the boot and shoe industry for most of the 100-year period, from the 1851 census to the formation of the Commonwealth, and indeed on into the 1970s. He writes (p 237):

During the latter part of the [19th] century, boot and shoe work became the dominant industry, and remains so today. ... The number of manufacturers and shoe agents increases rapidly from 1866 to a maximum of 19 in 1924. Messrs Griggs [about whom more later] have absorbed many of the smaller firms but have retained their employees. One of the earliest factories was that of Pratt Walker in Thrift Street, built in 1883. Wollaston produced 5,000 pairs of boots a week in 1891.

We may take Messrs Philips Bros as a case study ... There was some initial trading at Ringstead, and then the Wollaston firm was set up as a new independent private operation in 1902. The first premises were in South St ... As was usual at that time most of the employees worked at home in small workshops at the bottom of their gardens. The firm moved to its Park Street site in 1915, when about 90 people were employed, including the home workers. A limited company was formed in 1916 ... The firm was taken over by Messrs Griggs in 1972 at which time between 12,000 and 14,000 pairs of boots per week were made. Messrs Griggs still use the Philips Bros Company name for part of their business.

David Hall, as we have seen, counted 19 shoe 'manufacturers and agents' in 1924, having compiled his statistics from a series of local directories. By 'shoe agents', elsewhere also called 'contractors', he means middlemen who put out materials to cottage shoemakers and then buy back the finished articles for selling on. That number had declined to 14 by 1936, but then seems to have stabilised. As we shall see later, the expansion of Griggs did not really get underway until the 1960s. In any event, in his Wollaston-focused dissertation *Breaking with Tradition,* G. E. Stockwell tells us that 'there were at least 12 aggressive [shoemaking] competitors in the village after the war'. More of Mr Stockwell and his dissertation when we come on to the R. Griggs story in a moment. But my point here is about the astonishing number of independent shoemakers who survived in Wollaston into the post-war period. This tells us that, however measured, these were quite small undertakings with an average workforce number of not much more than 40 and quite likely less.

We can also, I think, reasonably suppose that the 'social distance' between the manufacturer masters and the shoemaking men was quite modest. In this respect a shoe manufacturer in Wollaston in 1950 was very different from a steel manufacturer in Sheffield at the same date. What we are talking about in Wollaston must surely be *small masters.* That judgement is clearly in line with David Hall's opinion which I adopted as the epigraph for this chapter: 'Wollaston was evidently a working village with very few gentry.'

To put the same point rather differently, it seems safe to conclude that very few if any of those who owned and managed Wollaston's shoemaking businesses had graduated to the status of gentry, at least not by the 1950s. Using language which is now perhaps a little old-fashioned, we might say that the 'working' character of Wollaston at this time was essentially artisanal and that many of those who had risen to management positions in the village shoe trade had started their working lives 'on the tools'.

THE DISSENTING CHAPELS AND THE RETAIL CO-OP

I suspect that my hypothesis of Wollaston's essentially artisanal character as a 'working village' in the years down to 1951 – and indeed beyond – is reinforced by the local strength of two institutions in the village which appear to have stood the test of time. It is true that in one case its origins go back to the 18th century and even before. But both unquestionably flourished – and probably also passed through their zenith – over the years when traditional shoemaking was the dominant economic activity in Wollaston. I refer to the Nonconformist congregations, each with its own separate chapel, and to the retail co-operative society and its various stores.

The tower and spire of St Mary's Anglican church stand out on the Wollaston skyline from whichever compass point you look at the village. Notwithstanding the absence of hard evidence, it must be a racing certainty that very few artisanal shoemakers or members of their families will ever have been members of that congregation. We know from David Hall that during the 18th century no less than three Nonconformist congregations started their lives in the village and have endured. These are the Congregationalists, the Baptists, and the Methodists. David Hall provides some excellent historical background:

Nonconformity has a long history in Northamptonshire, beginning with the Lollards at the end of the 14th century. After the Reformation, Puritanism spread, and it was at All Saints Northampton that the statements of faith known as 'Prophecyings' or 'Exercises of the Ministers' were made in 1571. Music was forbidden, except the singing of psalms by the congregation, and sermons took a more prominent part.

Thereafter, in fact about a century later, it seems to have been the Congregationalists among these Dissenting Christian groups who got a head start in Wollaston. David Hall (p 187) cites evidence from Amy Wichell's *Annals of Wollaston* (3rd edition, 1930) to the effect that John Bunyan, no less, 'obtained permission for Congregationalists to hold religious meetings in Wollaston in the latter part of the 17th century'. Bedford, Bunyan's place of birth and the town of his imprisonment and main ministry, is less than 15 miles from Wollaston. The main tradition suggests that the author of *The Pilgrim's Progress* was a Baptist, but perhaps the distinctions between the various Nonconformist sects mattered less in the 17th century than later. In any event, we get onto firmer ground when David Hall tells us (p 187) that 'a chapel was built in 1752', though 'an organised congregation and regular minister were not set up until 1788'.

It seems in fact that if we assign primacy in Wollaston by the date at which a regular place of worship was first established, then the Baptists were somewhat ahead of the Congregationalists. At Wollaston, Hall tells us (p 190), 'there was a church in 1735 affiliated to the old Baptist meeting at Rushden ... [It] was in the London road near the former Marquis of Granby public house.' However, it seems that this Baptist place of worship in Wollaston was short-lived. Hall tells us that it was closed in 1750 'and converted into a bath house'. It seems that the first permanent Baptist Chapel in Wollaston was built only in 1835.

Finally about the Methodists, Hall tells us (p 189) that a first chapel 'was built about 1812' and that the 'present chapel was built in 1840'.

In other words, by the middle of the 19th century and before the census of 1851, each of England's three main Nonconformist Christian sects had permanent chapels and regular congregations in Wollaston. Furthermore, if the Methodist numbers are anything to go by, attendance was rather good. Hall tells that at the Methodist chapel in 1851 'the attendance was 192 in the morning and 109 in the evening'. Even if we assume that all those who attended in the evening were doing so for the second time in one day, these are surprisingly high numbers in a total population of less than 1,300 and with three competing chapels. What don't seem to have survived are the statistics of chapel attendance by the Congregationalists and the Baptists on a typical Sunday in the same year. Just possibly, at least in the case of the Baptists, the numbers might be even higher than those of the Methodists.

No doubt, like much else that has changed, chapel attendance will have declined in the 100 years between the census of 1851 and the foundation of the Scott Bader Commonwealth. All the same it seems as certain as anything can be that widespread chapel attendance in Wollaston's artisanal working village must have had a notable impact on the moral and ethical sense of the local people. The main source of such political ideas as they entertained will have been the teachings of Wesley and the New Testament rather than Marx.

As a contemporary footnote to this discussion of the importance of Wollaston's Dissenting chapels in the 19th century, it is worth reporting that all three chapel buildings, of the Baptists, the Methodists and the Congregationalists, have survived into the 21st century, even if the oldest, that of the Congregationalists, was converted into the Wollaston museum in the 1980s. In the case of the Baptists and Methodists, their congregations also survive, the Baptists in perhaps surprising strength. According to Austin Shelton, a local Wollaston man who served his electrician's apprenticeship at Scott Bader and continued working there until his retirement in the late 1990s, the Baptist congregation still numbered 'about 100' in 2001. About Mr Shelton I should only add that his career at Scott Bader was – and indeed still is – notable for the high offices to which he has been elected. He served more than once as an elected director on the company board, he was three times chairman of the CBoM, and in 2001 he was elected to be one of the company's three external trustees.

Austin Shelton and his wife Marie are very much Wollaston locals. The propensity of these same locals to become members of the retail Co-operative movement when it first arrived in Wollaston seems to reflect the same values which explain the strength of the Dissenting chapel tradition. David Hall (p 241) supplies a thumbnail sketch:

The Co-operative movement has been active in Wollaston for over a century. Officially titled the Wollaston Industrial and Provident Society Ltd, the 'Co-op' was founded in 1876 ... Detailed records go back to 1884 when there were 109 members. Only groceries were sold at first, then a bakehouse was built in 1883 and a butcher's shop in 1886. Coal business was introduced in 1887 and milk in 1917 ... Furniture and hardware began in 1922 and confectionery in the same year.

Trade prospered, there being 527 members in 1900 and a turnover of £15,574; by 1926 the figures were 1,258 and £53,184. Branch shops were opened at Bozeat in 1914 and Grendon in 1918.

Census numbers for 1921 and 1931 show almost identical population totals on either side of 2,340. No doubt some members lived outside the village. Nevertheless the 1926 membership of 1,258 is truly astonishing. It is surely good evidence that the soil of Wollaston was particularly receptive to the seed which the Co-operative Pioneers had first planted in Rochdale in the 1840s.

Like most of the smaller retail co-operative societies, the Wollaston store gave up its independence in the 1980s. According to Marie Shelton, that happened in 1981 when the business was taken over by the East Northants Co-operative Society. However, those who live in the village have assured me that it still dominates the grocery trade at the start of the new century. Brian Elgood has a pleasing memory of its relative prosperity, compared with that of the Royal Arsenal Society in London, when he came to work at Scott Bader in the 1960s. In London the 'divi' on the family's purchases had typically been no more than one penny in the pound. At the Wollaston store in the year of his arrival it was one shilling and nine pence; and the locals were sadly recalling the days when it had been half a crown.

THREE INDIGENOUS WOLLASTON BUSINESSES: NPS SHOES, THE R. GRIGGS GROUP, AND TRYLON

NPS Shoes was registered as a production co-operative in 1881 and had been in continuous business since then. It had already reached its 60th trading year when Scott Bader arrived in Wollaston in 1940, and its 70th birthday coincided with the formation of the Commonwealth in 1951. As we shall see, it is senior by at least a generation to the R. Griggs Group. As for Trylon, it is a child of Scott Bader and its trading dates essentially from no earlier than 1966. Nevertheless, it had reached a respectable age for a small business by the end of the 20th century.

It is insufficiently known that when the Rochdale Pioneers started their consumer co-operative store in the 1840s, their main goal was not consumer co-operation but co-operative production. Nor is it widely known that: a) They actually succeeded in starting a co-operative production venture: a cotton mill; b) The mill was outstandingly successful, so much so that it came under pressure to expand; c) In the process of expansion, having been poorly advised about finance and voting rules, the original co-operative shareholders lost control to conventional outside investors.

I mention this piece of co-operative production history partly to underline the achievement of NPS Shoes in Wollaston. Readers need to know that NPS stands for Northamptonshire Productive Society. Its most striking achievement is that, after 120 years of continuous business history, it is the oldest of Britain's surviving production co-ops and one of less than half a dozen which date from the last two decades of the 19th century. That was the period of the great, and in many ways unrepeated, early flowering of these essentially artisanal ventures in the UK.

To have survived as a co-operative business for 120 years is in fact something of a *double* triumph by NPS Shoes. On the one hand it has succeeded in weathering more than a century of increasingly tough trading conditions. The environment in its markets got progressively more competitive from the end of the Second World War, even more so from the 1960s when NPS lost its semi-privileged supplier status to the consumer co-ops, and above all in recent times with the coming of the single world market. But secondly, and unlike some others in many of these old production co-ops, its members have resisted the temptation to sell out to a third party. There is an anomalous and perverse incentive in British co-operative law: in the event of a liquidation and the sale of the business, but only in those circumstances, co-operative shareholders may receive the full market value of their shares. In all other circumstances their shares must be sold back at no more than their nominal value. The second achievement of the NPS membership is to have resisted the temptation to sell out. Using Dr Schumacher's language, we might say that each successive generation of NPS members has chosen to extinguish the ownership of the business by not agreeing to sell. An arrangement imposed on the Commonwealth by its founders has been voluntarily adopted by the NPS membership over a series of working generations.

How did a group of artisan Wollaston shoemakers manage to start the business in the first place? In his *Co-operative Production* (Oxford, 1894) Benjamin Jones (p 403) tells a remarkable story. Its starting point is the employment of the future NPS members by Wollaston's agents or 'contractors' in the shoe trade, small businessmen who were also in many cases the owners of local grocery stores. The 1870s, as we already know, had seen the opening of Wollaston's retail co-op store. The prospective NPS members were among the villagers who chose to take their custom to it. Whereupon the contractors owning private grocery stores, upon whom the employment of prospective NPS members depended, gave notice that these artisans would be offered no more work if they continued to buy at the co-op. The rest of the story involves an extraordinary chance. About this time, some of these shoe-makers happened to meet Benjamin Jones – the author of the book from which I am drawing this story – at the nearby opening of a new CWS warehouse. Let Benjamin Jones tell us what happened next:

> I recommended them to dispense with their employers and start a society to employ themselves. They were willing to do this but saw difficulties in getting capital and getting a contract from the Government. By the help of friends connected with the Central Board and the Guild of Co-operators but principally through the pertinacity of the men themselves the society was formed and sufficient capital secured; and a contract large enough to last for twelve months was for the first time obtained from the British Government by a body of working men.

The going for NPS shoes started to get progressively tougher after the Co-op's 70th birthday, and from the foundation of the Scott Bader Commonwealth in 1951. That first government contract had given them a good send-off and was indeed renewed for a few years. Moreover during each of the two world wars NPS switched its production capacity to making army boots. But for most of the 70 years between 1871 and 1951 they relied for their market very largely upon the co-operative movement's consumer stores. From the early 1950s onwards both that market and the degree of the preferential access to it of NPS Shoes started to decline.

However it is not too much to say that their luck started to turn again in the 1960s when, under licence first from the Wollaston Vulcanising Company (WVC), in which they were initially themselves minority shareholders, and subsequently from R. Griggs, they started to manufacture the increasingly famous Dr Martens boots and shoes. The UK patents from the German inventors to manufacture and sell an entirely new air-cushioned sole for use in Dr Martens boots and shoes had initially been purchased by WVC in a negotiation in which William Griggs, by then the chief executive of the Griggs Group, played an initiating and dominant role. Later, the Griggs group bought out the minority shareholders in WVC and held the Dr Martens licence in its own right and by itself.

Some account of WVC is needed. There seems to be no doubt at all that the initiative behind this venture, as well as for the subsequent deal with the German inventors of Dr Martens air-cushioned soles, came from the Griggs Group and from William Griggs in particular. On the other hand there does seem to be some doubt about its corporate status. It is referred to more than once in the sources as a *co-operative* but also as the Wollaston Vulcanising Company Ltd. However that may be, there seems no doubt that together with NPS and at least one other Wollaston shoe manufacturer, G. W. & R. Shelton – and possibly more – Griggs set up the Wollaston Vulcanising Company as some kind of corporate joint venture in the early 1950s. There is no space to describe the new, hot moulding, technology for making footwear soles, which the joint venture introduced into Wollaston village. It is enough to make just two points: first that the new technology was the source of substantial improvements in productivity; and second that the whole episode demonstrates the readiness of the R. Griggs management, and to a lesser extent of G. W. & R. Shelton, and NPS Shoes – and perhaps some other Wollaston shoemakers – to try out new technology and to take risks.

But, as I have said, it was not until the 1960s that the fortunes of NPS Shoes really started to turn upwards, following the acquisition by WVC of the Dr Martens patent from Germany. It seems that for up to three decades – from the mid-1960s to the early 1990s – close to 100% of NPS's productive capacity was devoted to making and selling Dr Martens footwear under licence: from WVC in the first place and later, once the minority partners in that joint venture had been bought out, from the Griggs Group. It is, incidentally, a proud claim by NPS Shoes that the first actual Dr Martens boot had its welts sewn on its premises on that red-letter day in Wollaston's history, 1 April 1960.

In any event, the co-op's workforce and membership expanded and a total of 68 was recorded in a department of industry publication in 1973. By the middle 1980s, when the present general manager, Mr Barry Dunkely, took up his appointment, it had climbed to over 80. Since then it has declined and the number was just 43 when this was written in 2001. Though the co-op has made air-cushion technology its own, it has not been licensed to sell Dr Martens and has not used the Dr Martens brand name for the last dozen years.

Indeed, from the beginning of the 1990s and, to offset declining sales of its own 'air-cushioned but not branded' footwear, it started to build up its output and sales of more traditional boots and shoes with more ordinary leather soles. But the competition has since become such that in the late 1990s it was forced to buy in its uppers from an Indian manufacturer in the Punjab. All the same, and in ways partly similar to those of Scott Bader, it has survived, and has survived as a very small player in a very large global market. In the meantime all the other competing Wollaston shoe manufacturers – of which, as the Stockwell dissertation told us, there were as many as 12 as late as 1950 – had either been absorbed into what had by then become the R. Griggs Group, or folded.

THE R. GRIGGS GROUP

Whether by the measure of increased employment or of increased value added, there can be no doubt at all that the R. Griggs Group, rather than Scott Bader, was the great business success story of Wollaston village over the second half of the 20th century, that is over the first 50 years of the Scott Bader Commonwealth. The business performance of the group may well also have been superior to that of any other manufacturer of boots and shoes in the UK over the same period. Some key statistics of business growth were set out in the second paragraph of a group profile published in 1998:

> Today as the millennium approaches, Griggs Group factories, from producing a few thousand pairs a month in 1960 and employing less than 100 people, are making and selling Dr Martens footwear at a rate of one million pairs a month. The global workforce now stands at nearly 4,000 people.

As we have seen, the commercial part of Scott Bader's post-war business success came from the lead it managed to grab in the manufacture and sale of the new 'wonder material', glass-reinforced plastics (GRP). Using similar shorthand language we can now reasonably say that the post-1960 commercial success of the Griggs Group came from the lead which it managed to grab in the manufacture and sale, not of a new 'wonder material' but of a new 'wonder boot', Dr Martens. The parallel is neither complete not exact. But the overlap is sufficiently striking to be worth putting here up front at the start of this brief Griggs Group story.

What's more, the sources of the commercial success in the two cases suggest similar questions about their business future. Especially when it is protected by patents, a lead in the manufacture and sale of a new material or product can provide a real comparative advantage for many years and perhaps for as long or longer than the protection afforded during their lives by the patents. And that protection may well be reinforced where the patent is associated with a brand, like Crystic in the case of Scott Bader's 'wonder material' and Dr Martens in the case of the Griggs Group's 'wonder boot'. But the initial advantage cannot presumably be sustained for ever. So in the case of both Scott Bader and Griggs – and of course of other businesses which are similarly positioned – the big question for their business future can be easily identified: how sustainable is their business success? About Scott Bader we already know that by a number of measures – for example profit measured as a percent of sales – its commercial success became progressively more squeezed from the middle 1970s onwards. About the Griggs Group we should already flag up a cautionary point. Both sales in the UK and employment worldwide were significantly lower in the year 2000 than they had been in 1998. A growing public taste for trainers is said to be the main explanation.

But that is to anticipate. We need to go back here to the experience of the Griggs business before the launch by it in the UK of Dr Martens footwear, a brand of boots and shoes defined technically by their 'air-cushioned soles'. It is certainly true that the development and success of this business could not have been achieved without the technology of the 'air-cushioned sole' and without the patent protection which gained the group a head start in the manufacture and sale of Dr Martens boots and shoes. On the other hand, as we shall see, that may not be the most eye-catching or important feature of the whole story. Apart from the quite astonishing scale of the build-up and sale of this new branded footwear, which has already been highlighted, other notable features of the story are:

1 The securing of national brand recognition with relatively modest advertising and marketing expenditures.
2 The retention of the ownership of the business in the private hands of the Griggs family.
3 The group's somewhat unorthodox business philosophy.

Many of those who have been the owners of a pair of Dr Martens boots – and some like the writer who have not (yet) been – will know the date on which the first in what is now a series of many millions was manufactured. It was 1 April 1960 and has become widely known, because it was at once, and from then on into the 21st century, adopted as the brand name 1460.

As we have seen, monthly footwear production by the Griggs Group at that time – that is after Wollaston Vulcanising company had already been in operation for some years – was still in single digit thousands of pairs and numbers employed were below 100. So the scale of the undertaking was still genuinely small at the kick off. By the end of the century, to repeat once more, the Griggs Group employment world wide was not far short of 4,000 and monthly footwear production was around one million pairs. That is the scale of the production and sales increase achieved by Griggs following the introduction of the Dr Martens brand. Admittedly the speed of the increase was much slower in the earlier years and leapt forward only in the 1990s, with exports jumping from 14.8% of output in 1990 to 75% in 1996. Small wonder that AirWair, which had by then become the group's export division, was a recipient of the Queen's Award in both 1993 and in 1997. More of all this Dr Martens build-up in a moment. But here we need to turn back for a little pre-history: to the period before 1 April 1960.

William Griggs has already been mentioned as the chief executive of the family business starting from 1950, and as the prime mover behind first WVC in the early 1950s and then of the deal between the latter and the German owners of the 'air-cushioned soles' which became a key feature of the Dr Martens boots and shoes. He was in fact a member of the third generation of Griggs family shoemakers in Wollaston. He and his brothers, Ray and Colin, had inherited the ownership of the business from their father Reginald and their grandfather Benjamin in 1950. Perhaps because an original shoemaking partnership in Wollaston which had involved Benjamin had later been forced to close, the family company when it was eventually formed in 1911 was named R. Griggs Ltd, after Reginald, and not either B. Griggs, after Benjamin, or B. Griggs and Son. According to an important local source (the 'double bill' dissertation *Breaking with Tradition* by G. E. Stockwell which deals with both Griggs and Scott Bader), R. Griggs Ltd became the R. Griggs Group in 1918. What seems certain is that at the time of writing, in early 2001, the business had been the R. Griggs Group for many years.

But now back to William Griggs. He was undoubtedly the entrepreneur and in large measure the architect of the near £250m annual sales business which Griggs had become by the late 1990s. For he it was, as we have seen, who initiated both the WVC and the deal over the air-cushioned sole patents negotiated in 1959 with their German owners. Later it was he who led the acquisition in the 1960s and 1970s of all the other surviving boot and shoe manufacturers in Wollaston – barring just one: NPS Shoes. And he also led other important acquisitions outside Wollaston.

According to David Hall in his *Wollaston, Portrait of a Village*, the group offered to continue employing all those who had been working for the Wollaston shoe manufacturers which it absorbed.

Shoe manufacturing businesses acquired by the Griggs Group, 1960–90

INSIDE WOLLASTON	ELSEWHERE
Septimus Rivett	Luther Austin Co
Humphrey & Smart	John Pick & Co
Denton & Stuart	Sunday Shoes
Bayes Bros	Desborough Shoes Co
Phillips Brothers	Kids & Co
G. W. & R. Shelton	M. & F. Jinks
	Tower Boot

We need to ask what drove William Griggs to have a go at breaking with tradition in the 1950s and to initiate first the WVC project in the early years of the decade and then the deal with the German inventors of the Dr Martens air-cushioned soles in 1959. The 'tradition' in this case was, of course, the making of boots and shoes by the traditional hand methods, including in particular the fixing of leather soles to leather uppers by the age-old techniques of hand-nailing and/or hand-riveting. The Stockwell dissertation has a valuable discussion of this question:

> In the 1950s Bill and his brothers ... were the third generation ... to inherit the business and ... [found] that after 50 years ... there was little or no growth to show for it. To complicate the situation there were obvious problems imminent. There were at least twelve aggressive competitors in Wollaston alone, and a threat to the whole industry in the offing from G.B. Briton's 'TUF' working boot. This was highly competitive, had a vulcanised rubber sole, and was manufactured using a production technique which gave vastly higher output rates than traditional methods. It was Bill's reaction to this threat and his decisive action that set the firm on the road to recovery and success as he came up with a counter to the 'TUF' competition ... [the] Wollaston Vulcanising Company was set up.

... The project was successful in meeting the TUF competition from G. B. Britton but this was not enough for Bill Griggs who, with his vision and business acumen, saw it only as a reactionary move and not the pace-setting one which he considered to be required.

It is at this point in the R. Griggs saga that what was to become the Dr Martens boot makes its first appearance, even if still off-stage. I can do no better than reproduce what the Stockwell dissertation has to say:

> During the 1950s Doctors Maertens and Funck were experimenting in Germany with air-cushioned soles. They came up with a form of construction based on putting sponge rubber between the outer sole and insole of footwear that made shoes 'easy on the feet'.
>
> Initially the idea was used in women's shoes. Production and sales were good in Germany but Maertens and Funck saw the need for collaboration with other manufacturers in other countries. The next move really was revolutionary, for Bill learned that Dr Maertens desired to license UK production and he decided 'to go for it !' At this point the attitude of the British companies seems to have been more that of sticking in a rut than maintaining tradition. They saw the product as a 'short-lived gimmick' ...Two manufacturers who had the opportunity to take up the agency rejected it.

Readers are of course entirely free to speculate about what might have happened if one of those two other manufacturers had in fact chosen to take up the agency. But what mattered – for Wollaston as well as for the R. Griggs business – was what actually happened. It would be an exaggeration, but perhaps a pardonable one, to say that from the moment Bill Griggs had secured the agency it was a straight run through to the £250m business at the end 1990s. To make the brand acceptable in the UK market it was probably necessary to anglicise the name of Maertens to Martens. To have called the brand *Dr* Martens (with the street-friendly abbreviation 'Doc' ready to hand) – as opposed to say, just *Martens* – was surely a piece of marketing genius. And much the same applies to the decision to brand the first boot which went into production by the date of its debut as 1460.

Was there a link between the soles made by the WVC technology and that used to manufacture Dr Martens footwear with their air-cushioned soles? According to the Stockwell dissertation, the answer is 'yes and no'. In contrast to leather soles, both are examples of what are called in the trade 'unit soles'. These according to Stockwell may be made in one of two ways:

1. Vulcanisation by heat and pressure starting with a specific portion of material called a blank. This was placed in an open
mould, melted and then squeezed into shape using very high
pressure. Rubber is the basic material.
2. Conventional injection moulding. Once again heat and high
pressures are required but in this case it is heat-liquefied material which is injected into closed moulds. The usual material is
PVC (polyvinyl chloride), from which the Dr Martens sole is
made.

And yet ... unlike what is true about Scott Bader and its initial world lead in the new post-war 'wonder material' of Glass Reinforced Plastics (GRP), it would be a mistake to put too much emphasis in the Griggs case on the technology behind its new Dr Martens 'wonder boot' in the 1960s and later decades. It is true that the protection of the air-cushion technology patented from Germany was a necessary condition for the Griggs Group's commercial success in developing a market for Dr Martens footwear. But the scale of that success, especially in its later stages and in the explosion of exports in the 1990s, is a marketing and essentially a 'brand recognition' rather than a technology phenomenon and success story. Apart from anything else the original patents from Germany had only a limited life span. For many years now shoe manufacturers anywhere and everywhere have been free to put boots and shoes with air-cushioned soles on to the market. But none have enjoyed a success remotely comparable to the R. Griggs Group with its Dr Martens.

In the beginning, in the early 1960s, Dr Martens boots were aimed mainly at industrial markets. But then something happened. The company literature explains what it was, namely a 'totally unexpected growth in business generated by the exploding British youth culture'. The same Griggs source goes on:

It was an explosion which rocked the establishment of the day and
signalled the birth, particularly in Britain and Northern Europe,
and later in North America, of a disaffected even anarchic youth
movement which was essentially anti-establishment. With music
and fashion the natural means of communication, Dr Martens
quickly found itself recognised as the 'official' uniform of the

aggressively macho, young urban male. It's a street cred that per-
sists to this day: from the Mods of the 60s to the Skinhead bovver
boots of the 70s, through to the Punks, Indie Kids and Grunge
looks of the 80s and 90s. The late 80s also saw the emergence of a
huge market for girls' footwear as the Dr Martens look became a
'must' fashion accessory.

Future historians of the British shoe industry as well as of
Wollaston will surely see what happened to the domestic sales of Dr
Martens footwear in the 25 years from the middle 1960s to the end of
the 1980s as having resulted from a most unusual conjunction
between a rather unconventional new product (the Dr Martens boot)
and a male youth culture which was hungry for something of just that
kind. Clearly the R. Griggs Group was not responsible for creating
that new youth culture. But through a mixture of good luck and what
the Stockwell dissertation calls the 'vision and business acumen' of Bill
Griggs, it found itself sitting on a 'wonder fashion product' or
'wonder boot' which the new culture demanded: the Dr Martens boot,
soon to become the 'bovver boot' to the boy teenagers and young men
of that time. Fairly soon afterwards – though it may not be politically
correct to voice this opinion – the young women and teenage girls said
in effect that they would like their own Dr Martens boot too. And
from Wollaston the R. Griggs Group was able to meet this second
demand challenge.

For those readers, like the writer, with no pre-Dr Martens acquaintance with the word 'bovver' in the phrase 'bovver boots', clarification
is offered by the group on a poster in its new, 1990s flagship store in
London's Covent Garden: 'Bovver boots is taken from the slang
euphemism for bother, as Skins would often go out looking for bother.'

There cannot be many examples in the British market similar to Dr
Martens boots, of branded fashion products which so largely 'sold
themselves', without the need for advertising, because of their response
to a new demand by the youth culture. That seems to have been what
drove the expansion of sales until Griggs launched a new priority tar-
geting of export and, especially, US markets at the end of the 1980s.
Here is how the same company profile document from which I quoted
earlier describes what then happened:

> Little or no brand marketing had been done at this stage [up to
> 1990] except by a few of the larger independent wholesale
> customers. By 1993 Griggs, through its AirWair Ltd Sales and

Marketing Division, had begun the process of replacing these wholesalers, largely UK-based, with a structured international distributor network working on a coherent single-market strategy. The network was crucial to the development of the brand and that year the group made its first major move towards changing brand perceptions. It was dubbed within AirWair as the 'Way of Life for feet' and began the process of fundamentally extending the range in order to broaden the appeal of the brand, and presenting it to the trade in specific well-designed categories.

Though I haven't access to statistics which would demonstrate the point, I suspect that a majority of the owners of private companies which enjoy business and financial success on the scale of that achieved by the R. Griggs Group in the last 40 years of the 20th century have chosen to sell shares to the Stock Exchange. But that has not happened in the case of the R. Griggs Group. In his dissertation G. E. Stockwell puts the point with some force. On the basis, evidently, of a discussion with Max, Bill Griggs's son and successor as chief executive, he writes: 'Consolidation of the group's gains through a public flotation had been considered as a possibility but never adopted. The reason was that losing personal independence for the sake of profit was not attractive.'

The Stockwell dissertation goes on to quote from a paper written by Bill Griggs in 1978 to explain more fully the thinking behind this policy:

> We prefer not to have to please outside shareholders. We prefer not to be inhibited by financial wizards. We prefer to read the *Sun* rather than the *Financial Times*. We prefer to be a collection of small companies. We prefer to be small and to think we're beautiful.

We may remember David Hall's claim about what happened to employees working for the Wollaston boot and shoe manufacturers acquired by the Griggs Group in the 1960s and 1970s: that all were offered new jobs. This sort of evidence suggests an employee-friendly business. On the other hand, whether surprisingly or otherwise, I have seen no reference to schemes for sharing profits with employees. On the other hand again, the group's jealous commitment to business independence is very strikingly similar to the same commitment, even if achieved in different ways, at Scott Bader.

As has been said before, the same main question about their future arises in the case of each of Wollaston's two main businesses at the start of the new century. Is their success sustainable? In relation to Scott Bader that question will be addressed among others in the next and final chapter. About the Griggs Group there is the cautionary evidence which I cited earlier about a decline in output and sales which began to become apparent at the end of the 1990s. Comparing the rate of annual production at its peak in 1998 with the numbers for early 2001, there was a decline of about one-third: from about 240,000 to 160,000 pairs per week. Pessimists will no doubt want to remind us of the fickleness of fashion. Dr Martens have had an astonishingly good run. Can it really continue much longer? Optimists will point to the way that sales are holding up well in the US where the brand has plenty of space before it reaches anything like the market penetration that has been achieved in Britain. That was in any case the line taken by Mr Stephen Griggs when we discussed the future prospects of the business in his Wollaston office in early 2001. Stephen is a member of the family's fifth generation of shoe manufacturers. He took over the chairmanship of the group from his father Max in 1994.

Despite the similarities between the R. Griggs Group and Scott Bader which I have chosen to stress, there is one huge difference which is going to become apparent soon, probably in the next few years or even earlier. Scott Bader is anchored to Wollaston in the way that the Griggs Group is not. Already the bulk of the latter's production has been shifted to its large and relatively new factory in the neighbouring and slightly larger village of Irthlingborough. The head office will surely follow in the not too distant future. The Griggs family interest in the new Irthlingborough football stadium and the team – Rushden and Diamonds – will pull in the same direction. Indeed given the team's notable success in gaining admission to the Football League in the first week of May 2001, it is likely to become that much stronger.

TRYLON

The Trylon Catalogue 2000/1 tells us this about its age and corporate nature: 'established over 50 years ago Trylon is a Common Ownership Workers Co-op where every worker is a co-owner and therefore has a vital interest in giving you the best service possible.' How does that square with what was written earlier in this chapter, namely that it is a business which has 'essentially' been trading since just 1966? The short answer is that both statements are strictly true. A brief word of explanation is, however, clearly required.

We have to go back to the 21st birthdays of those two first cousins, Godric Bader and Brian Parkyn, which both fell in 1944. They received identical presents from Ernest Bader: a gold watch and half the share capital (50 x £1 shares each) in a £100 private company. The name Trylon was suggested by Ernest's nephew. At that time of his life he had a rather special attachment to the number three. The new synthetic fibre Nylon had lately been invented and brought to market. Trylon was a word which combined both references.

The logic of this second Ernest Bader gift to the two first cousins was in some ways open-ended. No one knew what was going to happen after the war, which still had a year or more to run. In Ernest's opinion the two young men might or might not choose to work for Scott Bader after it. If not, they might choose to set up a new business together. Even if they chose to accept invitations to work for Scott Bader, which both of course did, having a second corporate entity, as it were in the family's pocket, might always prove useful.

It *did* prove useful, if only marginally at first, though it was pressed into service more then once to take on tasks which Scott Bader itself was prevented from undertaking. But then in 1966 it effectively went into business on its own account. Susanna Hoe discusses that at some length (pp 186–91), associates its timing with the stepping down by Ernest from the chairmanship of Scott Bader, and identifies its first agenda as the commercial development of polyester resins to make arts and craft products. Ernest put £5,000 of his own money into the venture but was unable to persuade Scott Bader to add some more.

Two years of loss-making and somewhat unfocused business activity ended with the fortunate acceptance by Roger Sawtell of the job of Trylon's manager in 1968. Roger has already appeared in this story as an ally of Ernest in the opposition to the Strand Glassfibre acquisition 10 years later. I called him there a 'small is beautiful' fundamentalist. Before embracing common ownership, and other ideas of Ernest Bader, he had held senior management positions in the steel industry in Sheffield. That qualified him to manage Trylon.

After what must have been an unsettling false start trying to market and lay 'marble-lookalike flooring' made of polyester resins, Roger had a brainwave. He steered Trylon into the manufacture and sale, mainly to schools, both of small canoes made of GRP and of the moulds to make those canoes. Later there was a concentration on making and selling just the moulds, leaving the schools themselves to make many canoes out of each mould. Eight years later, in 1974, Trylon, according to Roger, had become 'a small employee-owned co-operative with 15 working members [and] was the largest maker of canoe moulds not only in the UK but also in Europe'. Roger himself then decided to resign. He was succeeded as manager by Michael Angerson, who stayed in that post for 23 years.

But the making and selling of GRP canoe moulds to schools and other voluntary sector bodies was evidently killed off as a business by the growing thickets of anti-pollution rules which mushroomed up from government regulatory bodies in the 1980s and 1990s. So now at the start of the new century, as Roger himself has written, 'Trylon is no longer in the canoe business but continues to supply craft materials to schools, and provides secure employment and fulfilling work to members, without risk of exploitation.'

When Brian Elgood and I visited the business in its old shoemaking premises in Thrift St in 2001, the numbers were down to seven full-time and two part-time employees. But cautious optimism was expressed to the effect that a long decline had been halted and numbers stabilised.

SCOTT BADER, WOLLASTON VILLAGE, AND THE LOCALITY

As I argued at the start of this book, it is jobs and the associated incomes that are overwhelmingly the most important benefit which businesses can offer to the communities and neighbourhoods – and perhaps more exactly in today's world – to the 'travel to work localities' in which they are located. By this criterion Scott Bader's contribution to Wollaston village, and to the travel to work locality in which it falls, has clearly been exemplary. The numbers by themselves are not the only measure. Quality of work, conditions of employment, levels of income, are obviously important too. And so, among the employment conditions, is its continuity. By all these subsidiary tests, as well as by the crude numbers themselves, Scott Bader is entitled to feel reasonably well satisfied with its record of 60 years at Wollaston, that is since its arrival at Wollaston Hall in 1940. It is true that, relative to its competitors in the synthetic resins industry, the incomes and conditions of employment offered by Scott Bader were less good at the end of the century than they had been 25 years before, midway through the Commonwealth's first 50 years. It is also almost certainly true that in at least one decade, the 1980s, and perhaps for several years on each side of it, the number of jobs offered in Wollaston village by the R. Griggs Group was greater than those of Scott Bader. All the same it would be hard to deny that measured by jobs and incomes, by their quality as well as their quantity, Scott Bader's contribution to the Wollaston locality over the 60 years to the end of the twentieth century was very good and probably the best of any other local business.

At least in passing we should note that for most of this period, from 1940 down to the introduction of the national business rate by Mrs Thatcher in the 1980s, businesses made a quite specific and direct tax contribution to their localities, by paying local rates to local authorities. In modern times businesses have not, so far as I know, paid local taxes to village or parish councils. But the county council records in Northampton would surely show that Scott Bader was a key contributor to its finances from 1940 to the middle 1980s.

As for the village of Wollaston itself, we covered in the discussion of the Commonwealth's charitable giving, the early – later discontinued – Scott Bader schemes for the distribution of firewood and food parcels to villagers in need. Scott Bader can I think still claim to be a good parish and locality citizen. It still organises annual pre-Christmas coach outings which are open to all Wollaston pensioners, and not just its own. Within the locality, it contributes to a number of charitable schemes to assist the unemployed and relieve poverty – for example by helping to support workshops in Wellingborough which rebuild furniture for those in special need.

Its efforts to secure continuous reductions in the chemical emissions from its plants into Wollaston Village have been dealt with separately elsewhere.

Susanna Hoe mentions (pp 138–9) the part played by Scott Bader and its founder in the building of a Wollaston village hall. First she explains that 'the business community of Wollaston and Wellingborough was never really to accept him'. And she goes on, 'In 1960 Ernest started an appeal for a village hall. Scott Bader gave £8,000. The nearest and only match was £500 from one of the shoe manufacturers.'

At least up to the 1960s, the cultural differences between the Bader family and Wollaston's shoe manufacturers evidently made meaningful relationships almost impossible. Scott Bader sold plasticisers to Wollaston Vulcanising – to render the PVC for air-cushioned soles soft and flexible – for many years, until it sold its own plasticiser business. But the extent of the cultural chasm is surely well demonstrated by the fact that neither Ernest nor his son Godric ever visited NPS shoes in the 20th century – the oldest production co-operative in the UK.

13

The Commonwealth's First Half Century, and the Quest for a Just Verdict

I confess I am not charmed with the ideal of life held out by those who think that the normal state of human beings is that of struggling to get on; that the trampling, crushing, elbowing and treading on each others heels, which form the existing type of social life, are the most desirable lot of human kind or anything but the disagreeable symptoms of one of the phases of industrial progress. *John Stuart Mill, 'Principles of Political Economy', Routledge & Kegan Paul, 1965, p 754.*

At the risk of offending both Godric and the shades of his two formidable parents, Dora Scott and Ernest Bader, I shall postpone until quite near the end questions about how far the Commonwealth has succeeded in meeting its spiritual and moral goals, or – to put the same point rather differently – in changing the *values* of those who have worked for Scott Bader over the last 50 or so years. Roger Sawtell, in his 'Critical Celebration', uses slightly different and more dramatic language to refer to what I am sure is much the same set of issues. In the context of Ernest Bader's objectives, he writes of the Good/Evil Struggle and refers to both The Kingdom of God and The New Jerusalem. More about all that later.

Instead, using Mill's famous observation as one starting point, and the logic of businesses that have eliminated outside equity capital ownership as the second, I will in a moment plunge straight into what must surely be the first question in most readers' minds: how well or otherwise have its beneficiaries used the gift of the Scott Bader resin business which Ernest and his family presented to the Commonwealth all those years ago? Might well-informed observers have reasonably expected a better performance? As for the criteria for any judgements we might make, I suggest that whatever the importance either of its so-called political task – which has been quite extensively covered earlier in this book – or of Scott Bader's moral and spiritual objectives, any serious assessments should be overwhelmingly based on the performance of the business, measured of course in human as well as more narrowly economic terms. Apart from anything else, if the business cannot be sustained, the political task and the moral and spiritual objectives would go by default.

However, before moving on to discuss the logic of Scott Bader's ownership arrangements, let me remind readers about the successes upon which Ernest Bader might reasonably congratulate himself were he still in a position to make a judgement today. It is especially important to do this so as to make clear that any subsequent criticisms start from a position of the greatest respect and even awe for what Ernest Bader achieved. Within Scott Bader, as opposed to outside it, I would myself highlight four of his successes as having been wholly unproblematic:

1 He gave the position of head of the new polyester laboratory to a nephew who was still not out of his 20s, and was rewarded for that boldness when SB was thereby enabled to gain a critical lead in the manufacture and sale of GRP (Glass Reinforced Plastics).

2 By an act of the most far-sighted beneficence, however worldly or otherworldly its motivation, he passed the ownership of the business to a second entity, the Commonwealth, and thereby gave Scott Bader a protection against takeover which had already, when this was written, stood the test of time for just over 50 years.

3 He set in motion an evolutionary process within the business of moving power and authority, away from himself, his family and appointed top managers, and to a pair of democratic bodies accountable to all the Commonwealth members. As a result civilised, democratically acceptable and apparently sustainable solutions have been found by those who have worked at SB since 1951 to two of the most critical and problematic industrial relations issues of conventional business, whether private or state-owned: the problem of final responsibility for industrial discipline, and the problem of de-manning in the face of reductions in demand.

4 By eliminating the outside ownership of equity capital he conferred on the business which he handed over to the Commonwealth a potentially substantial comparative advantage.

In the outside world, beyond the business itself and beyond Wollaston and its locality, Ernest Bader and those who worked with him, both inside and outside SB, can also claim to have been among the promoters of at least one set of enduring and linked contributions which were briefly noted in an earlier chapter but which must not be forgotten in this summary:

5 The creation of the Industrial Common Ownership Movement (ICOM).
6 The creation of Industrial Common Ownership Finance (ICOF).
7 The enactment by Parliament of the Industrial Common Ownership Act in 1976.

That seems to me to be a most impressive list of successes to attribute in part to the founder of SB and in part to those who have worked in it. And I haven't even mentioned the local jobs and incomes which had been associated with Scott Bader – to the great benefit of Wollaston and its neighbourhood – for over 60 years when this was written. As we shall see later, I do have one or perhaps *one and a half* serious questions about the Scott Bader business and its sustainability into the 21st century. But I can not reasonably raise them before proper tribute has been paid to what has undoubtedly been achieved.

Leaving on one side for later discussion the spiritual and 'value-changing' achievements of Scott Bader, I move on next to the second of my two starting points: the logic of businesses which have eliminated outside equity capital ownership. My premise, if I may repeat a point which has already figured in my list of the founder's achievements, is that there is potentially a significant comparative advantage to be derived from that. It is true – and I must immediately concede – that there is nothing automatic at all about the conversion of that potential comparative advantage into reality. From Robert Owen to Tony Benn, business history, heaven knows, is littered with examples of the failure of production co-operatives and similar ventures. Still, with an obvious proviso about other things needing to be equal, those calamities should not blind us to the potential advantages. Moreover, research work in recent years has thrown a good deal of light on what structures and what policies are likely to work more and what less well.

Two different sources of the comparative advantage which businesses owned in this way may potentially enjoy need to be distinguished. The first source is simply the absence of any claims by outside equity owners upon the value added of the business. At least in theory, the resulting potential advantage can be almost arithmetically estimated. For example, in a business environment where profits average, say, 25% of value added and where one-third of profits are typically paid out in dividends, the potential comparative advantage from this source will be just over 8%.

Put crudely but adequately, the second source of a potential comparative advantage is the prospective improvement in motivation – or reduced alienation – which may be expected to come about when people are working only for themselves and not for either faraway absentee shareholders or the state. Once again, however, I must emphasise that there is nothing automatic about the emergence of a comparative advantage from this second source. The empirical evidence all points in the same direction: that an advantage from this second source is not going to materialise unless specific programmes are adopted to foster it. Moreover, the empirical evidence suggests an even more cautionary point: that for a number of reasons – of which the frustration of unrealistic expectations and survival of class antagonisms may be among the most important – the removal of outside equity capital, and its replacement by, say, common or trustee or co-operative ownership, may generate negative rather than positive results. In those situations, the new forms of supposedly more worker-friendly ownership arrangements may turn out *not* to be the source of comparative advantage at all, but just the opposite. There are far too many examples of that having happened to dismiss them as isolated examples of bad luck. It seems also to be true that neither the idealism nor the practical business experience of the founders of ventures of this kind offer any certain protection against disaster. The failure of Robert Owen's experiments at New Harmony in Indiana during the 1820s – and indeed the near complete lack of success of his similar co-operative experiments elsewhere – surely tells us that. In part no doubt because of fundamentalist beliefs in either state socialism or conventional private capitalism, some indeed have argued that 'alternative' ventures of this kind have an inescapable propensity to fail.

If only to avoid the charge of suppressing parts of the evidence which are unfavourable to my case, I must flag up the failures in the record and the inferences that have been drawn from them. But having done so I must repeat my own premise: that 'alternative' and 'worker-friendly' business organisations and ownership arrangements from which outside equity capital has been eliminated carry with them potentially significant comparative advantages. So one main question which has to be asked before any verdict can be reached about its experience is whether or not Scott Bader has succeeded in making that potential a reality.

And that brings us on to my other starting point: the critical response by England's great liberal thinker of the Victorian age, John Stuart Mill, to a world in which everyone is struggling to get on. It comes in the sixth chapter of the fourth book of his *Principles of Political Economy*, a chapter to which he gives the title 'Of the Stationary State'. Whether surprisingly or otherwise, Mill expresses some confidence that we shall reach such a state sooner rather than later. In the meantime he leaves his readers in no doubt about his feelings for the state in which we now find ourselves.

A HYPOTHESIS: SB HAS APPLIED ITS COMPARATIVE ADVANTAGE SUBSTANTIALLY TO EMPLOYEE WELFARE

But I do not plan for a moment to use Mill's sentiments in these matters as a platform for a discussion about a possibly very different and stationary economic future in the medium or long term. Instead I want to use it to clarify the various different ways – or combinations of ways – in which any significant comparative business advantage resulting from the end of outside equity ownership may be applied. Specifically I want to suggest that it might be substantially applied *not* to Mill's 'struggle to get on'; but instead, or anyway in part, to improve employee welfare. Translating Mill's phrase into more contemporary language, what I am suggesting is that at least over the second 25 years of the Commonwealth's life, Scott Bader has applied a substantial part of its comparative advantage *not* to achieving higher rates of growth in the productivity of its labour but to improvements in employee welfare.

I am not claiming for one moment that there have been no increases in labour productivity at Wollaston over the last 25 years. The three schemes of voluntary redundancy over those 25 years tell us that. Instead what I am claiming, or rather suggesting as a hypothesis, is that that productivity growth could have been that much stronger if it had been addressed by other means as well as by de-manning, and if less of the company's comparative advantage had been devoted to improvements in employee welfare.

Let me at once introduce two disclaimers about this hypothesis. The first is that it is far from being original. Indeed it is more or less exactly what you would expect to figure prominently in a standard critique of worker-friendly businesses from the standpoint of conventional private capitalism. The underlying thought is, of course, that 'feckless' labour cannot be expected to do otherwise than to favour its own welfare even to the point at which the future of the business becomes less secure. My second disclaimer is that though it seems to be supported by an 'overview' of the data, I doubt whether it can be demonstrated in fully persuasive detail.

The best readily available statistical evidence to support my hypothesis comes from the comparative data which we reviewed at the end of the first chapter. That seemed to show that there was a sharp decline in Scott Bader's business performance compared with those of its competitors as between its average results for the six-year period 1971 to 1976 and the latest available data, namely for 1998. There is no need to reproduce all that comparative data over again. For our purposes here a single pair of comparisons will make the point. By the measure of profits per employee, and for the six years 1971–6, Scott Bader had the highest average score within the group of five firms with which its results were being compared: in three out of the six years, it came first; it came second once and third twice. The relevant measure used in the 1998 comparison is not quite the same. It is the ratio of pay to value added; and the identity of the firms with which Scott Bader's score was being compared is also different. In a much larger sample of firms, what Andrew Gunn has found is that 'Scott Bader's ratio of pay to value added' was the fourth highest. About the same set of comparative statistics for 1998, Andrew found that Scott Bader's sales per person were 'close to the lower quartile'.

This comparison between Scott Bader's performance relative to some other chemicals and plastics in the first half of the1970s and in 1998 is far from perfect. On the other hand, the downhill direction of Scott Bader's financial performance relative to its competitors over this period is supported by looking at its own numbers by themselves. By the measures of both profit margins on sales and of return on capital employed, the company's results in the 1980s were less good than those in the 1970s and those in the 1990s than the 1980s. Moreover, there is an entirely persuasive explanation of why there was downward pressure on profits: competition in the markets for Scott Bader's main products, its polyester resins, was getting tougher year by year. To clinch, finally, the case I am trying to make, I must point out that ever since he became head of finance at Wollaston in the early 1980s, Andrew Gunn has been warning his fellow Commonwealth members about what was happening; and telling them that a continuing increase in the percentage of value added taken out in the form of higher employment compensation – whether in higher wages or higher company pension costs or anything else – would become unsustainable sooner or later.

So I take it that my hypothesis about Commonwealth members

having tended at least since the second half of the 1970s to give a high priority to improvements in their own welfare is not going to be seriously challenged. To those who will judge that to have been short-sighted there are a number of answers. The most general one is surely a version of what Mill might have argued, given the sentiments expressed in our epigraph. In the absence of any need to pay out dividends, the toughest 'Mill-based' answer would be that Commonwealth members may reasonably ignore low levels of profit and high allocations of value added to employment costs, so long as the sustainability of the business does not become at risk. No one at Wollaston whom I have spoken to while writing this book believes that such a risk is around the next corner or indeed the next but one or even two. But what if, against the odds, if turned out to be? In that case Commonwealth members would rightly take comfort from those earlier occasions when the Wollaston working community has accepted the need for schemes of voluntary redundancy. And they would remind sceptical outsiders of the ringing affirmation by Roger Scott, the Community Council's chairman over the years around the turn of the century and when this book was being written. I quoted it as the epigraph of an earlier chapter. It is right that I should do so again here.

> Our Community will not see the Scott Bader enterprise fail with the loss of all our livelihoods as well as our (and the founder's) aspirations to show an alternative way of doing business.

SECOND HALF OF THE 1990S: SOME MORE POSITIVE EVIDENCE

Though they would in some sense have only themselves to rely on if they were ever called upon by Roger Scott to respond to a challenge, Commonwealth members can point to some more positive evidence, making for greater sustainability, which began to emerge from the second half of the 1990s. Some of that has already been covered in chapter 9. For example, as a result of the extended discussions on pay and related issues in 2000 and 2001, there was a real prospect, when this was being written, of a shift in the balance of annual wage and salary adjustments: to make them more sensitive to individual employee performance.

There is more positive evidence too in the Postscript which has been added at the end of chapter 9 to take account of what has happened since Ian Henderson retired as chief executive in September 1999, and Allan Bell took over. What might turn out to be of special significance is the feedback, highlighted in that Postscript, from recent customer surveys. It almost seems as if Scott Bader, or anyway the consequences of its commitment to the long term, is coming to be loved more by its customers than by Commonwealth members. Finally, notwithstanding the only rather partial success of schemes for performance improvement in the 1990s – both the supposedly on-going scheme introduced by the company board in 1992, and Ian Henderson's rather different and more ad hoc 1995 scheme – the early years of the new century seem likely to be good ones for mobilising widespread support behind effective schemes of continuous improvement.

This has not been an area of conspicuous success at Scott Bader over the last 50 years. Some, like Roger Hadley, have explained this relative failure by an initial hostility on the part of Ernest Bader, followed by something like an instinctive lack of enthusiasm by top management since then. On the other hand, there were some signs at Wollaston during the writing of this book that those attitudes may be changing. That, if it happens, will not be before time: in schemes which should be a natural for businesses from which outside shareholders have been excluded, Scott Bader has fallen well behind what is already happening in many conventionally owned businesses. But it would also represent a most timely change. Partly because of the now widespread availability of the writings of the great American engineer and post-war tutor of Japan's manufacturing industry, Edwards Deming, knowledge about how to make a sustained success of such schemes is much more readily available in 2001 than it was even in 1991. There are other sources too, as well as the writings of Deming and his followers. To one of them, a book by Christian Schumacher, who belongs to a family greatly honoured at Scott Bader, I shall return at the end.

AN OBVIOUS AIM: TO MAKE LABOUR-FRIENDLY VALUES
YIELD REAL COMMERCIAL ADVANTAGES

I have no serious doubt at all that it is the company's relative failure to introduce productivity-enhancing schemes of employee involvement to match an almost uniquely labour-friendly set of constitutional and related arrangements that substantially explains why it has increasingly tended to disappoint its friends and admirers – though not, I must immediately add, its customers – over the last 25 years. Yes it is true, as readers will hardly need reminding, that in its summary of events for 1992 the Traxton/Reeves diary drily noted: 'Continuous improvement process endorsed by the board.'

Yes it is also true, and again readers must forgive my repetition, that Ian Henderson introduced a rather different scheme to 'squeeze waste out of the system' in connection with the voluntary redundancies of 1994. But it is not too much to say that both had been more or less forgotten by the time this book started to be written in the spring of 2000, and sceptical answers tended to be given to questions about any enduring benefits which may have resulted from them. So far was the idea of organised continuous improvement from having entered the Wollaston culture that it seemed to have dropped out of the language.

We hear much these days about 'accidents waiting to happen'. We don't hear enough about 'potential blessings waiting to be plucked from trees'. But something very like the latter seems to me to be the case in relation to the prospective benefits of well-organised schemes of continuous improvement at Wollaston so long as they are sustained for long enough to become part of the culture. They would make a splendid matching fit with the company's existing employee welfare arrangements.

What of the objection that to introduce such schemes would offend against people's natural hostility to pressures of the 'rat race' expressed so eloquently by John Stuart Mill in the epigraph? My answer, and more importantly the answer of those who know in detail about these schemes and have direct experience of them, is 'not at all'. The Americans have invented a cliché phrase to describe what happens in the workplace when changes are introduced in work practices as a result of continuous improvement schemes. People work better not because they are working 'faster' as part of a general speed-up. They work better because they work 'smarter', and they are enabled to do that because of improved working practices which they themselves have largely invented and thus largely own. It is perhaps regrettable that 'working smarter' should have become a cliché. But there is no doubt at all that that has been the typical outcome of unnumbered schemes of continuous improvement which, starting from Deming's work in Japan, have now spread all over the Western world and indeed elsewhere.

Roger Hadley drew quite explicit attention to the absence of any such schemes of employee involvement when he was working full time at Scott Bader in the 1960s. He made the same point in his joint 1995 article with Maurice Goldsmith from which I quoted earlier. And I believe it may well have been in his mind when he made his unusually important speech as chairman of the trustees to a general meeting of Commonwealth members in February 1995. I have already quoted from that too.

In this context readers may also sensibly recall the disappointment expressed by Jennifer Wates in her valedictory contribution to the *Reactor* after twelve years of association with Scott Bader as a trustee, and the suggestion she made about its possible source: 'So it is a disappointment to me that you haven't progressed further over these years and I apologise for whatever I have failed to do to help.'

And she then went on to suggest why perhaps it was that Scott Bader's progress had not gone further: 'You haven't developed the processes and procedures of working together in practical ways.'

It is true that Jennifer Wates does not explicitly identify schemes for continuous improvement as the needed 'processes and procedures of working together in practical ways'. But anyone familiar with these schemes will confirm that they offer an almost uncannily exact fit with what Jennifer Wates believed, after 12 years of experience, Scott Bader needed most. They offer that fit partly because they depend on managers and non-managers working together. They offer it too because they are essentially 'processes and procedures' and perhaps above all because they are neither theoretical exercises nor indeed just calls for socks to be pulled up, but fundamentally practical.

It is worth saying that Jennifer Wates's expression of 'disappointment' at Scott Bader's lack of 'progress' is quite frequently the response of sympathetic outsiders who become involved with businesses like Scott Bader from the ownership of which external equity has been excluded. Moreover it is perhaps an especially frequent response when the ownership change has happened through the beneficence of the former owners. In its crudest and most naïve form the premise behind that response is that, with the seeing off of private outside capital, the growth of labour productivity should move automatically into overdrive. By contrast, the real virtue of Jennifer Wates's response is her clear perception that nothing of that kind will happen in the absence of 'processes and procedures of working together in practical ways'.

I wrote earlier that I had one or one and a half questions about Scott Bader's record. This is the one of those one and a half questions. It may be expressed in various more of less specific ways. Most specifically, it may be expressed as the question of whether Scott Bader has ever really committed itself to schemes of continuous improvement. More generally, we may ask whether Scott Bader knew what it was doing when it repeatedly failed to implement proposals, especially from the late Roger Hadley and others over many years, for much greater shop-floor involvement in the workplace. Most generally, perhaps, we may ask whether Scott Bader has ever seriously attempted to unlock the knowledge and enthusiasm of its workforce as perhaps its single most important resource when it comes to the promotion of productivity improvement.

So that it is the one question I have about Scott Bader's record over the first 50 years of the Commonwealth. What about the half question? It relates to the issue of where final responsibility for decisions about the business is located. As we have seen, when those decisions are of the very highest importance and consequence – as for example about successive schemes for voluntary redundancy – they have, anyway from the end of the 1970s to the start of the 21st century – been taken by a vote of Commonwealth members in general meeting. On the other hand, below the level of those 'supreme importance' issues and in relation particularly to decisions about pay and conditions, it seems that 'management prerogatives' normally prevail and that the role of Alan Green's 'democratic bodies' goes no further than the contribution of 'influential input'. My half question is whether Scott Bader is served well by these arrangements. Some have talked about the 'creative friction' or 'creative ambiguity' which these arrangements generate. Well maybe. I do no more than flag the matter as a 'half question' and one to which, incidentally, there is more than one possible answer.

THE SURVIVAL OF A (RELATIVELY) SMALL BUSINESS IN A WORLD OF GIANTS

Towards the end of the 1990s, Ian Henderson put a rhetorical question – expecting the answer 'no' – to Professor Jack Quarter, a Canadian specialist in employee ownership. The question was, 'Can you name any other business which has survived and is competing in the international market for polyester resins and emulsion polymers with total workforce numbers which are closer to 600 than 1,000?' Neither Professor Quarter nor, so far as I know, anyone else has managed to come up with the name of a company in these markets which could remotely match the smallness of Scott Bader's workforce size.

I hope adequate credit has been given to Scott Bader – in this case its democratic institutions as much as its management – for its success in finding an acceptable way to slim down its workforce size with schemes of voluntary redundancy. But equally, as we know, ever since the pioneering acquisition of Artrite Resins in the far-off days of 1968 when Godric still held both top posts, there has been a recurring need to take over businesses operating in the markets into which Scott Bader sells its core products, and above all its polyester resins. In effect, and with the 1980s only excepted, there were enduring acquisitions of polyester businesses in every decade from the 1960s to the 1990s. One of them, that of Strand Glassfibre in 1978, was indeed seen by two people well placed at that time to make good judgements – Ralph Woolf and Brian Parkyn – as having been necessary if the business was to survive at all. Scott Bader, and in this case mainly its management, deserve great credit for the skill with which these takeovers were managed. And where, as in the case of Strand Glassfibre, what was taken over was not just a technology and a customer list but a going concern, both Scott Bader's management and that of the acquired business deserve credit for a successful subsequent integration exercise.

In the record of these acquisitions, the one which didn't endure and was for other reasons a special case was, of course, SRL on Merseyside in the first half of the 1980s. It was a special case at least in part because, according to the then chief executive, Ralph Woolf, it was a takeover motivated by social rather than economic considerations, namely to try to save jobs in an area of high unemployment. The whole story was told in considerable detail by one of the chief actors in it. There is no good reason to repeat that here. However it is worth recalling that while Scott Bader spent over £1m of its own money in its efforts to turn the business round, that expenditure had all been recovered, and more so, well before the end of the decade. It was recovered by contributions made to the Wollaston business by various SRL customer lists and technologies. As readers will recall, the venture ended with a closure and with roughly 100 compulsory redundancies. On the other hand, the compensation terms offered to and accepted by those who then lost their jobs were in line with those which had applied in the two voluntary redundancy schemes at Wollaston a few years before. Brian Elgood in fact argues persuasively that for the SRL workforce the whole Scott Bader episode was the 'least worst outcome' for them, once Unilever, SRL's previous owner, had decided to put the business on the market. Arguably there was also some intellectual gain. For whatever else is true about it, the experience demonstrated that there was little short of a chasm between the traditional union-mediated industrial relations on Merseyside and those which had evolved within a fundamentally co-determinational framework in Wollaston.

For the rest we should recall that all these acquisitions, except in part perhaps that of SRL, were driven by the need to sustain employment and the company's research base in Wollaston, and do so without getting so large that the principle of 'small is beautiful' became totally and manifestly abandoned. We should recall too that the same driver and the same logic which explain the core product and especially the polyester acquisitions also explain Scott Bader's moves into and out of subsidiary products and its development and sale of new ones: for example its move into and then out of plasticisers, and in the case of alkyds its successive moves, into and out of and then again into these speciality polymers. Finally we need to recognise a vital and continuing contribution by the Wollaston research and development department in the shape of modifications to existing products to meet customers' evolving needs. A good example is what has been done to modify gel-coats, especially for the marine market.

In concluding this summary of the business history of Scott Bader (reviewed at length in the earlier narrative chapters), we need to remember that from the middle 1970s onwards competition in the company's main markets became progressively tougher and margins progressively tighter. In the late 1970s and 1980s the company was able to survive and protect its future by using voluntary redundancy to boost its productivity. In the 1990s what seems to have ensured survival was not a single strategy but a number of them: the acquisition of international subsidiaries together with a hugely increased emphasis on customer service; limited de-manning and some check on the previously inexorable rise in the proportion of value added devoted to employment costs. Can the same formulas continue to ensure the survival of the business in the future?

THE NEED FOR NEW MEASURES, ADDED TO ALREADY WELL-TRIED ONES, TO SAFEGUARD SB IN THE 2100S

As we have seen in the Postscript to chapter 9, Scott Bader had already, during the year 2000, defined a new main strategy for the first decade of the new era. At the centre of that strategy is a co-ordinated focus on the polyester markets of mainland Europe, that is, of markets in the newly opening up post-communist countries of Eastern Europe and the former Soviet Union, as well as those in Western Europe which have been supplied from Wollaston and Amiens since the end of the 1960s. The key new piece in this strategy is perhaps the Chromos business in Zagreb, the capital of Croatia, which Scott Bader has effectively controlled since the end of 1999. The new focus has already been strengthened by policies which have begun to treat the three manufacturing and supply bases in Europe – Wollaston, Amiens and now Zagreb – as if they were one. There are special hopes about the polyester market's growth prospects in the countries of Eastern Europe, including successor states to the old Yugoslavia, in Russia and in the Ukraine. The distribution centre and warehouse facilities which Scott Bader acquired in Prague in 1998 have been built up with these growth prospects especially in mind.

However those readers who have come with me thus far will not be surprised by the first main conclusion which I draw from this final summary chapter. It is that Scott Bader will need additional new measures, as well as this new market focus, and its now well-tried and economically successful emphasis on customer service, if there is to be real confidence in the company's ability to survive over the Commonwealth's second 50 years. Readers will not be surprised by what I think is perhaps most needed: a programme of continuous improvement aimed at putting a permanent squeeze on any waste in the system, and given sufficiently strong emphasis for at least as long as it takes to become part of company culture.

I see this need for new measures to strengthen confidence in the company's future sustainability as stemming from the second as well as the first of the two factors in Roger Scott's epigraph to chapter 11. Of course it is a matter of safeguarding the livelihoods of Commonwealth members and their families. But it is also a matter of the continuing need to demonstrate that there are alternative ways of doing business and not just those of conventional private capitalism. It is true that Scott Bader is far from being alone in this second respect. It is also true, or so it can be fairly persuasively argued, that businesses other than Scott Bader are having as much or even more success in making this demonstration, where success is defined both by business and working community values. Nevertheless such is the fame of Scott Bader and so close is its identification with alternative ways of doing business – to use Roger Scott's phrase once again – that it will be a huge calamity if it fails to survive.

THE NEED FOR NEW RESEARCH TO CONFIRM THE QUALITY OF LIFE BENEFITS OF THE COMMONWEALTH

But as well as the need for new measures designed to strengthen Scott Bader as a business, there is a real need for a piece of systematic, well-designed and objective research to establish the quality of life benefits which those who work at Scott Bader for significant periods of time are believed to enjoy. The research is perhaps especially needed in Scott Bader's case because of the rather patchy response elicited by a long series of employee attitude surveys going back to the 1960s. It is true that in her interviews for the 50-year oral history project, Tracy Smeathers has elicited some really positive anecdotal evidence. But more objective evidence is needed. Andrew Gunn has suggested what could well be an excellent starting point: a look at the comparative longevity of Scott Bader pensioners. A recent study is said to have shown that clergymen in the Church of England are typically living on for two or three years beyond their lay counterparts. It would be good to be able to confirm that the same is true of those who retire from Scott Bader after, say, twenty years' service.

SPIRITUAL OBJECTIVES, CHANGING VALUES AND GOD IN WORK

As indicated at the start of this final chapter, I have left to the end a discussion of the spiritual objectives which both the founder and his son Godric have hoped that the Commonwealth might achieve. However, I should make clear at once that I am not myself really competent to discuss these objectives in their own spiritual terms. I feel more at home if the language of the discussion is more in terms of changing values. As readers will remember there was a long and well-attended series of workshops on Scott Bader Values, chaired by Canon Frank Scuffham in the 1980s. They were described at some length in chapter 7. Their main outcomes were presented in that chapter as being two: an agreed list of seven Scott Bader Values, of which the first three were: Universal Love, Love of Neighbour, and Peace; and secondly a move away from putting the word 'ownership' at the centre of the functions of the Commonwealth and its members, and the substitution of the word 'trusteeship'.

Then in the 1990s, with leading roles played by Jennifer Wates, then chairman of the trustees, and Ian Henderson, then managing director, the question of values was revisited at an all-day workshop attended by participants from Scott Bader's four institutional bodies. In this second case the main outcome was a pair of two agreed 'statements': a 'mission statement' and a behaviour statement. These were reproduced in chapter 8.

My own view is that, taken together with the various and successive constitutional documents, these explorations of Scott Bader Values have had two enduring legacies:

1 A civilised, well-mannered and fundamentally 'democratic if necessarily unequal' relationship between Commonwealth members who are and are not managers.
2 A commitment to ethical business standards in the company's relationship with its customers and suppliers.

From the feedback coming from recent customer surveys, there can be no doubt at all that the second is the source of real business advantage for Scott Bader. This point was already noted in the Postscript to chapter 9. But it is so important that it is right to repeat it here. It is as if there was an advantage to those football teams that imposed on themselves a total self-denying ordinance in relation to foul play.

On the other hand, when the Founder spoke of 'spiritual objectives' for Scott Bader, or anyway for the Commonwealth, and when Godric and people like Roger Sawtell continue to do so at the start of the 21st century, it seems clear that what they have in mind is something rather different. Roger has given some indication of what that is in a short paper of reflection about Trylon as it was when he retired from the position of its chief executive in 1974:

> Commercially it was a success but I was dissatisfied with myself because it had not become a 'church', an expression of the Gospel, a city built on a hill which cannot be hidden. Some members were active Christians, others were nominal or agnostic and we were not really living up to our (viz. Trylon's) preamble regarding the spiritual nature of men and women. All we had was a carol service at Christmas and even that was discontinued in due course.

I suspect that – perhaps with a few changes, a reference to Gandhi here and to Dr Schumacher there – Godric might well express similar feelings of dissatisfaction about Scott Bader. I need hardly say that I have every possible respect for the sincerity of those feelings. But they seem to me to betray a deficient grasp of the reality principle. Yes, as I suggested in the discussion on voluntary redundancy in chapter 5, it may be possible to achieve objectives of the kind wished for by Roger and Godric if what you are taking about is a mainly religious – and probably residential – institution like an Israeli kibbutz or a Gandhi-inspired ashram where the personnel are essentially a self-selected band of brothers and sisters. But it appears simply not to be possible, anyway in today's world, when what you are dealing with are non-residential businesses like Scott Bader and Trylon and with the lads and lasses who are working there because they have responded to advertisements about employment openings.

On the other hand, if we are talking about *God in Work,* in the sense used by Fritz Schumacher's son, Christian, as the title of his recent book about how to improve workplace performance, that is an entirely different matter. What Christian Schumacher prescribes has now apparently proved itself successful time and again in businesses large and small, up and down the country. His prescriptions are based on the hypothesis that what workers need is a set of tasks which can be related to the successive functions of planning, implementation and assessment. Schumacher derives these in turn from the three persons of the Trinity. On the basis of his track record there is every reason to believe that he could make an outstanding contribution to improving performance at Wollaston. I should make it clear that he does not require that his clients must sign the Thirty-nine Articles, or even believe in the doctrine of the Trinity.

As noted in the first sentence of this book, appearance and the reality behind it are often rather different. Who would have thought that it would be possible to think about the Trinity and come up with what is now a well-tried approach to improved working practice? But then Scott Bader itself is a source of continuous paradox. One of the more striking reflections collected by Tracy Smeathers in her oral history project was from a former blue-collar pensioner in Wollaston who told her that, in his own eyes as well as those of his family and neighbours, the experience of a lifetime's work with Scott Bader had turned him into a mini-capitalist. He was not complaining. But was it what either Ernest or Godric Bader had hoped for on his behalf? Well, maybe it was. After all in Ernest's words which I have already quoted: 'Taking the long view the original purpose of forming the Commonwealth was to raise employees to the status of RESPONSIBLE OWNERS.' Would that be possible without building up a modest capital?

Some Personal Memories and Reflections

ALAN GREEN *retired on 31 December 2000 at the age of 60. He was twice a member of the Community Council, being its elected Chairman on both occasions. He was then invited by the Council to be its Chair for a number of years. Whilst Chair he was also a Trustee. He served as an Appointed Director on the Board of Scott Bader Company Limited. He was an Elected Director of Scott Bader Commonwealth Limited on four occasions, serving as its Chair for a number of years. All these positions were held at the same time as fulfilling his role as a chemist in the Production Area at Wollaston. All holders of elected positions within Scott Bader are expected to fulfil their normal operational duties as far as possible and, with the exception of the Elected Directors to the Board of Scott Bader Company Limited, are unpaid.*

When I put forward the name of Robert Oakeshott as chronicler of the birth and first 50 years of the life of The Scott Bader Commonwealth Limited, little did I think I would be asked to pen my reflections of my working life with Scott Bader. Having read the draft manuscript of this book, I am relieved that my expectations – fuelled by my knowledge of Robert, the evidence of his past work and his renowned commitment to employee ownership – have been largely met.

You may wonder at my qualification to draw a conclusion from a work such as this. For the greater part of my working life I have been an employee of Scott Bader Company Limited – thirty-seven years in all. I joined the company as an industrial chemist and spent the majority of my very happy years in lower middle management working in the Production Area at Wollaston. However, this in no way qualifies me to add my words to those of Robert. It is the thirty-four years I spent as a member of the symbiotic company, The Scott Bader Commonwealth Limited, that enables me to do so. As a member of the Commonwealth I was able to be part of this history and, in my elected offices, to be one of the architects of the organisation as it is today.

Scott Bader, both Commonwealth and Company, are living organisms reacting and developing to the events of the world around them. In the early days the Commonwealth was a beacon for better industrial practice, stability of employment, pensions for all employees and fair wages paid, even when overcome by sickness or on holiday. When I joined Scott Bader in 1964 it was primarily in the business of 'employing people' to manufacture and sell a product. This changed over the years, as Robert so ably reports, with the voluntary redundancies. As the years unfolded, the Commonwealth redirected its energies, continually remaining true to its founding philosophy of involving employees at all levels in the governance of the total enterprise, sharing their wealth with the less fortunate and telling others of the benefits of this way of working.

Robert has said a little about Scott Bader's impact on the local economy and referred to those national organisations, ICOM and ICOF, whose early days were supported by Scott Bader and drew strength from having a viable example of an alternative to conventional industrial practice. However, as a past Chairman of the Commonwealth, I take greater satisfaction for our social successes – our support for Geoffrey Williams, the round-the-world yachtsman, who came to us with the concept for an Ocean Youth Club; for a fledgling Intermediate Technology group who wished to publish and distribute a catalogue featuring farming tools for third world rural economies; and the support for Dr Halley Stott, now aged 92, who founded the Valley Trust in South Africa, believing that education, clean water and healthy diet was the way to combat disease. These are just a few of the many initiatives that the Scott Bader Commonwealth supported in their infancy.

My greatest disappointment was the failure of the Commonwealth, over a long period of time, to extend Commonwealth membership to those working in overseas group companies, particularly in France. For many years, as a member of the Commonwealth and as an occasional leader in its ruling body, I have, together with others, campaigned to extend the concept of industrial democracy to all employees of Scott Bader wherever they might be. However, the ruling body of Scott Bader Commonwealth Limited has no executive power in the Operating Company and has to rely on the goodwill, dedication and commitment of members in senior management positions in Scott Bader Company Limited, to implement Commonwealth Policy. It was only in the latter half of the 1990s that the Group Managing Director, Ian Henderson, took up the challenge, agreeing that the extension of Commonwealth Membership must be one of the tenets of Group Operating Policy and this has been continued by his successor, Allan Bell, the current Group

Managing Director. Towards the end of the year 2000, the Commonwealth Board of Management was finally able to grant membership to colleagues in France and South Africa and employees in other group companies expected to become members soon.

Robert deals extensively with the acquisition of Strand Glassfibre Limited. However, it was the admission of the employees of this company to Commonwealth Membership that breathed new life into Scott Bader and shook the complacency that was building up in the Commonwealth of the early 1980s and it is certain that the advent of a global membership will repeat that process. The Scott Bader Organisation of the twenty-first century will never again be primarily an employer of people with a saleable product but it must always be an organisation with demanding principles or it will not be the Scott Bader founded upon the beliefs and dreams of Ernest Bader, family and friends.

JOHN LEYLAND *joined Scott Bader in 1954 as Company Secretary and went on to become Finance Director from which role he retired in 1981.*

My attention was first attracted to Scott Bader by an advertisement for the Company Secretary in the Quaker journal *The Friend* in 1954. At that time I was working with a firm of chartered accountants in the City and I had quite a formidable interview with Ernest Bader, Dora Bader and Godric at the London sales office of Scott Bader which at that time was in Kingsway. I remember thinking that the London office was quite an impressive set-up. (But later shown to be uneconomical and expensive to maintain.)

I have just found a file of correspondence I had with Ernest Bader over the two or three months following the interview. I discovered quite early on his tremendous thoroughness and eye for detail. There were thirteen letters from him and a number of visits to Wollaston, before he clinched my appointment. I had to comment on the latest Company accounts, give a view on the Company investment plans and answer a four-page questionnaire on an article by an economist (and I still retain a copy of my five foolscap pages in reply). I wondered if he was really looking for a social economist rather than a Company Secretary!

My first letter was from the then Personnel Officer, Gwen Veal, and what a powerful personality she was in the firm at that time and what a great help she was to me in those early days, battling from time to time with both Ernest and Dora, and particularly with the Assistant Secretary, Betty Turner, who ruled, with her sister Alice, the Accounts offices with a rod or iron. The girls had to say 'Permission please to go to the lavatory, Miss Turner'! Betty Turner didn't trust me an inch, even allocating one of her male clerks, Roland Ferris, Bernard Ferris's brother, as my personal secretary.

My wife Barbara and I moved house from London to Wellingborough. I recall the car we had at the time, a 1928 Brooklands Riley, very sporty but no room for any luggage and just a year older than Barbara. I think it was considered a bit disreputable to be parked outside the back of the Hall! But at least two of the Directors approved; as it was joined by Brian Parkyn's 1934 Lagonda and Godric Bader's Bristol.

My reason for making my 'career' move was quite a positive one. As a Quaker and conscientious objector I had spent five of the war years with the Friends Ambulance Unit in China, going out through India and up the Burma Road into West China. We were mostly doing medical transport work, having converted our trucks to run on charcoal. Being half way through my accountancy training, I soon got stuck looking after the Unit accounts. After the war I finished my training in the City, but soon wearied of auditing company accounts and particularly helping already rich individuals to avoid Income Tax.

So the possibility of joining a firm like Scott Bader was quite exciting, especially as I had been given a copy of the employees' handbook *New Life in Industry*. I think I was nostalgically looking for a working community not dissimilar to the FAU in China where we were completely autonomous and democratic and appointed our 'officers' at our annual general meeting to run the Unit for the next year.

I think I might quote a couple of small paragraphs from the Introduction to the July 1955 second edition of *New Life in Industry*. It gives some flavour of the organisation that I was expecting to be joining and to which I hoped to make some contribution.

As a creative and production association of men and women, irrespective of class, race, nationality or religion, we have bound ourselves together in a bond of friendship and service to one another.

We believe that our purpose is not only to work hard for our living, but also that an atmosphere of joy and freedom, based on self-discipline, is essential if our corporate life is to be really worthwhile.

Utopia of course and I suppose I was naïve to think it would be otherwise. Because it wasn't like those two paragraphs at all, and in the 27 years that followed of my time at Scott Bader I think I was swept along with the idea that maybe, possibly, *sometime* there would develop a community that might have a few of those attributes.

I had a particularly hard time three years after joining the firm, when Barbara died leaving me with our two daughters aged three and one. Barbara had been such a help in enabling me to face many of the surprisingly awkward situations that cropped up in the Company in my early years, even to a decision whether or not I should stay at Scott Bader. Suddenly I was utterly on my own. But struggling on with my job turned out to be a great healer. Though I cannot recall that I was given much support from the community.

My personal aim over the years had never been to help establish a Utopia. But just to get a bit further towards a democratic way of running the Company which truly reflected the fact that we were all meant to be 'owners'.

I have to be careful, in looking back, to be constructive in my comments. It would be so easy to be destructive. Because most of my memory is of a constant battle with Ernest.

I had my job to do in the business of course and this in the main I found enjoyable and satisfying. Apart from being Secretary to the Board of Directors, there was a lot to do in modifying the internal accounting systems with the basic aim on my part to try to get quicker and more accurate finance reporting to the executives and the Board to allow informed decisions to be made. I particularly concentrated on added value, trying to show as reasonably as possible the detailed profit on every sale we made so that the totalling of these detailed sales gave us our total profits. It was these totalled figures that I used to present our financial results to employees at our quarterly meetings. And I like to think that most members in the Company felt that they were continually informed of where we stood from quarter to quarter. I felt strongly that knowledge was power and most members in the firm were desperately short of the confidence to exert their power within the various organs of democratic control.

I also know that the question of power was very much misunderstood. Apart from this periodic finance reporting very little was done in the firm to teach employees to be good members, and by good I mean effective members. It seems to me now, and I know it has been said over and over again, that one of the mistakes Ernest Bader constantly made was to believe that the act of giving away his shares to the Commonwealth would vitalise everyone in the firm to becoming hardworking committed Commonwealth members and workers. But no one was going to be harangued into perfection; they should have been trusted more and no one was trusted.

I kept a file over the years of most of the communications I had personally with Ernest, first when he was Chairman and Managing Director, then as Chairman and latterly as Founder President up to his death at 91, just about the time I retired. This bulky file also contains copies of his effusive output to all members of the community and its various management organs. What a heap it has amounted to – God's gift to Rank Xerox as someone once said! I still have it.

It makes me weep that the charisma and energy that went into this output generated such little response from those it was meant to reach. This was because it was mainly criticism and vituperation and it never addressed the vital interface between the Commonwealth members and the community.

There is some strong indication that members might have been more committed if at some point they had had to make an individual contribution towards their share in the Commonwealth. But I never remember that it was ever debated. The subject was anathema. (One of the papers in my file is a long memorandum from the leaders of a Commonwealth company receiving loans from ICOF, in which they said they were debating changes to their set-up along these lines). Across my copy of the memo which I had shown to Ernest he has forcefully written 'All this can be foreseen to happen to *Godless people!*' and this was his only response.

But despite all the heartache I had a happy and fulfilling time at Scott Bader. The Board was always looking for new ideas and bringing in outside help to try and make progress. I feel privileged to have been on the inside and part of the decision-making groups that employed this 'outside help'. One met such fascinating people. The first that comes to mind is Fritz Schumacher as a Trustee and as a Board Director. Then the other first Trustees – Mary Stocks, Bob Edwards and Eleanor Barnes. Then Fred Blum and Roger Hadley and the shaking up they gave us in order to produce their book. The Hay-MSL consultants hammering out a pay and remuneration policy; Bruce

Reed, a behavioural consultant, getting the Board to think through its decision making. And there were the personalities of the Company that were brought in from outside. To mention a few that impressed me over the years: Managing Directors Nick Broome and Ralph Woolf, Sales Directors Ken Docherty, Paul Russell and Ken Johnson. The commercial and technical know-how of Jack Hand, Willi Schmidt and Cecil Phillips. I learned a lot from all of them. I also remember with gratitude the support we all had from personnel officers, Bryan Janson-Smith, Tony Smythe, Margaret Goddard and from John Anagnostelis as Commonwealth Secretary in tumultuous times. Godric Bader and Brian Parkyn were of course the backbone, holding Ernest at bay, and enabling the Board to keep the Company going.

ROGER SAWTELL *joined Trylon Limited (a common-ownership company) as General Manager in 1967, having previously been Deputy Managing Director of Spear and Jackson Limited. Subsequently Founder Member and Manager of the Daily Bread Co-operative. Adviser, consultant and lecturer on worker co-operatives. Formerly Chairman of the Industrial Common Ownership Movement, Industrial Common Ownership Finance and Trustees of Traidcraft, and Board Member of the Co-operative Development Agency.*

> To maintain the Christian quality in the world of business ... without pretension or hypocrisy, was the great achievement of these extraordinary people. *G. M. Trevelyan, describing early Quakers, 'English Social History' (Longmans, 1942), p 267.*

Any friendship with Ernest Bader tended to be a stormy relationship and ours was no exception. We agreed, differed, reunited, over sixteen years and remained friends until the day he died. Ernest's very last outing, in February 1982, was to visit Daily Bread's co-operative in Northampton, where I worked from 1980 to 1995. He gave us his blessing and told us to be the new Jerusalem. Ernest's dominant concern was the struggle between good and evil, both in himself and in the amazing business he founded and then gave away. His writing was an incoherent mishmash of trusteeship, philosophy, vegetarianism, Christian faith, pacifism and sometimes a few other 'isms' thrown in for good measure, but his actions spoke louder than his words. The Scott Bader Commonwealth was to earth the vision and be a model of quality and life at work.

Scott Bader has succeeded well in demonstrating that employee-ownership can be economically viable in a medium-size capital-intensive industry, whereas most employee-owned enterprises are in smaller, labour-intensive markets. But the effort needed to achieve this economic task in the last quarter of the 20th century allowed little surplus energy for participation in the good/evil struggle. The pass was sold in the early 1970s when the 1961 Constitution clause not to grow to more than 250 people was abandoned. Larger was to be more beautiful. More conventional entrepreneur observers, who thought Ernest and his Commonwealth were slightly mad but not bad, rubbed their hands with glee; Scott Bader was 'going for growth', they had fallen for the age-old formula and the employee-owners would soon be tied with golden handcuffs

Growth required new management expertise and so the 7:1 salary differential, a Quaker witness in a greedy world, was also abandoned and a Chief Executive recruited from conventional industry, then another and then a third, all from outside and with no experience of employee-ownership nor of the Quaker philosophy which had underpinned the early development of Scott Bader. They concurred – who can blame them? – that growth was the only option. Others in the social justice debate took a different view and 1,000 small independent producer co-operatives emerged in the 1970s and networked with each other in accordance with co-operative principles. But, regrettably, Scott Bader took little part in this national debate as they were fully occupied with their own economic survival and prosperity.

A Quaker meeting has no hierarchy and all members are expected to take part in decision-making. Thus it might be expected that a business influenced by Quaker philosophy would have a high level of participation. Not so. A truly employee-owned enterprise cannot have subsidiaries with widely differing democratic responsibilities, but by year 2000 Scott Bader had as many employees overseas as at Wollaston and the former played little or no part in policy-making. Even at home, decision-making appeared to be dominated by management without much involvement of non-management people, whose judgement in the good/evil debate is equally valid with that of managers.

In summary, Scott Bader have achieved exemplary wages, pensions and security, in the same league as Marks & Spencer, but have not contributed much in matters of quality of life at work and participation in decision-making. Plenty of bread and a few circuses, but not much more. We wait in hope for this century.

ROGER SCOTT *joined Scott Bader in 1967. He is Information Manager, has been an elected member of the Company Board and is Chairman of the Community Council.*

How can we assess the achievement of Scott Bader since 1951 when there are so few true comparisons?

One company that does compare is the American Cast Iron Pipe Company (ACIPCO) which too was given by its founder to his employees. This company is still in existence and is regularly quoted by *Fortune* Magazine as being one of the top US companies. Its website declares it to be a company very concerned for the welfare and concerns of its employees. But here the parallels end: early in its common ownership life its management usurped control from the employees and had all the members of its employee representative body ejected from the company by security guards. What they have now is an employee body that acts purely as an advisory body to management. Their Founder's intent was thwarted, but the key difference between ACIPCO and Scott Bader is that the latter has a written Constitution. The lack of such a Constitution prevented the ACIPCO employees' rights from being upheld in law.

It is not surprising then that the Scott Bader leadership's successive attempts to modify the Constitution have been met always with suspicion and usually with opposition. ACIPCO's history is not widely known within Scott Bader but there is the genuine fear that in changing the Constitution some measure of employee participation may be lost.

During the common ownership years the crude yes/no vote measure of management confidence at the Annual General Meeting has been refined to continual influence upon management through the employee-elected representatives serving on the Company Board, the Commonwealth Board and the Community Council.

Those at the very top of the management pyramid, the company Directors, know that their position is directly dependent upon employee approval. Those further down the management chain are appointed by managers and may forget for whom they are ultimately working. Some ambitious managers may well be tempted to indulge in normal company pursuits of politics and empire building to further their personal careers rather than act in the best interests of all the employees. In these and other circumstances those elected to represent the whole must firstly be true representatives i.e. not pursuing a personal agenda, and secondly must find considerable strength of character in order to resist sometimes quite focused personal pressure.

The one community body that has risen consistently in employee standing in the last decade is the Community Council. It is perhaps no coincidence that all its recent Chairmen, before appointment, had either reached the end of their career paths or had been close to retirement. I do not wish to infer from this that they were frustrated and bitter, rather that they have been able to assert objective independence.

The future for Scott Bader can only be optimised if both managers and employee representatives do work together for the common goal. It is much easier to adopt the 'us and them' mentality where games are played, the winners gain brownie points and the losers take the blame. These activities only win Pyrrhic victories. The real and difficult challenge (because it is so often counter to human nature) is for all components of the company to work together to secure the future. This is the only way to generate true wealth in common.

AUSTIN SHELTON *worked for 24 years within the Engineering Department at Wollaston before retiring in 1999. During this period he has served, at different times, as a member of the Trustees, the Commonwealth Board of Management, the Company Board and the Community Council. He has also served as Chairman of both the Commonwealth Board of Management and the Community Council. He was appointed as a Nominated Trustee in 2001, and is currently Chairman of Trustees.*

It was during the late 1940s, as a boy, that I first came into contact with Ernest Bader. He was paying a visit to my father one evening, seeking advice and asking for the use of bee-keeping equipment – Ernest had decided to keep bees in the Hall grounds.

Some 24 years later, by then married to Marie and with three small children, I was to join his Company as a member of the engineering staff. I belonged to Wollaston Baptist church and was determined to try to live out in practice the Christian principles to which I was committed; so joining Scott Bader, which was founded on these principles, seemed to me the right way forward. I was to find that the majority of workers did not necessarily have a personal commitment to these same values, but the Company was so formed that guidelines were written into the Constitution and were to be followed. Whilst Ernest was alive his overwhelming presence and influence ensured that the community was constantly reminded of the principles upon which his Company was founded, and of the need to practise them.

I spent 24 very happy years at Scott Bader, forming lifelong friendships from comradeship enjoyed within the Engineering Group. During this time I was also given the opportunity to serve on several of the representative bodies and, for this experience, I shall always be grateful to my fellow workers. There were difficulties involved in serving on these bodies, mainly because of time spent in meetings, which meant leaving the engineering work that I had been employed to do. Conflict could be overcome, provided the local management were supportive of the Scott Bader system – which of course should have been the case, but was not always so. In general I had good support from management and in return gave a considerable amount of my free time to the representative roles.

The installation of new plant equipment to improve the quality of our products, and work in energy-saving projects, was very rewarding, but working within the representative bodies to meet and deal with the continuing problems and challenges which confront all businesses was for me the most rewarding of all. The many hours we spent as a Council considering and reporting to management the community's views regarding the first voluntary redundancy programme proved a lengthy process, but in my opinion the end result was a very fair one to all concerned.

A low point came one Saturday morning when chairing a Commonwealth Meeting. In the presence of some 15 Trade Union shop stewards from Synthetic Resins Limited in Speke, which Scott Bader had acquired, I was required to ask the 200 members present if this plant should be closed down. After much debate it was agreed by members that Speke should be closed.

I have been witness to many difficult decisions which the Company has had to make over the years, but believe, because the values and principles which Ernest built into it have been respected and followed, Scott Bader has moved forward in a positive, successful and exemplary way, and has arrived at this milestone of 50 years as a unique Common Ownership Company.

At this point in the journey, leadership through management and the representative bodies has an enormous responsibility to stand firm and remain faithful to the Founder's wishes, despite being faced at times with seemingly insurmountable problems.

If Ernest's gift is to continue to be a shining light in what has sadly become a very dark world, we might do well to remember his writing in *The Times* of January 1973, when he said:

> Possession of material things is the essence of the human drama on this earth. The whole of history is the story of our endless squabbles over the distribution of worldly goods, and this conflict is going to be fought out to the last man on earth unless we change and put human values before material values, of our own free will, from the heart, and not by compulsion.

Afterword: Godric Bader's Reflections

Humanity is now going through its final examination as to whether it can qualify for its universe function and thereby qualify for continuance on board the planet. Whether humanity will pass its final exams for such a future is dependent on you and me. *Buckminster Fuller*

> The future starts tomorrow – building it begins today.
> *Northern Friends Peace Board*

INTRODUCTION

I appreciate being invited to write an afterword of my comments and memories prompted by the author's history of The Scott Bader Commonwealth. It is a mammoth task to write up a complicated history of 50 years and I admire Robert for taking on such a formidable task. I believed my thoughts would be easy to pen. This is not so. After deliberating I concluded that this is because Robert remained in his professionally correct journalist mode all the way through. I respect this hard-earned and highly skilled attribute, but allied to where I felt he is coming from, this results in a history that, rather than illustrate it, fails to reflect the depth of purpose of the revolutionary shift to a Commonwealth company in 1951.

The establishment of the Commonwealth was designed to be different in many ways. First it is primarily concerned with people and not profits. So, of course, 'labour cost per employee' is 'high'. Low productivity growth is less important than high personal growth. It is just not possible to compare the working patterns of Scott Bader with any other, as comparison cannot be between similar parameters. And to take issue with Robert on the subject of employee attitude surveys, to my knowledge none of them have asked 'Is this the best place you have worked?' – it is quite possible to be 'seriously unhappy' with your work, but still say it is the 'best' you have experienced! Many people who have left the company say 'You don't know how lucky you are.'

I had believed Robert's narrative would come from the long view that is necessary to understand and see the Commonwealth not only in the light of industrial history, but especially in the awareness (and preferably his awareness) that our entire world has entered a turbulent period of fundamental transformation similar to the time we moved out of the Middle Ages. We who are living through it are only beginning to grasp the extent and meaning of the tectonic shift with whole continents of thought and massive economic re-structuring acting on us locally and globally. *The role of business in making this a positive transformation is absolutely crucial, as business is now the 'most powerful institution on our planet'.* I believe we acted intuitively in 1951 with a structure which could move towards this imperative.

Writing from such an awareness would put the work and purpose of Scott Bader's attempt at transformation, and therefore its history, into its true context and perspective. It seems that Scott Bader is also still largely unaware of its intended destiny as it has not become apparent to Robert during his researches, although he must have read Fred Blum's writings and those of our 1985 Commonwealth Lecturer, James Robertson, for instance his *Agenda for the 21st Century*.

Fred Blum talked about this coming transformation, but in his time only prophetically, and believed the Commonwealth was beginning to live it. He would have been quite excited now to find, though still only slowly evolving, but repeatedly appearing in diverse areas around the world, that what Ernest and the other Founders of the Commonwealth 50 years ago were initiating was being acknowledged more widely, and even seen as essential. I have just read a *Financial Times* article (Richard Donkin, 2 May 2001, p xiv) commenting upon the 'corporate mugging' that occurred at a top managerial Hay Group conference in Florence. It says that 'The protestors who braved the water cannon at Davos ... represent only the most active and extreme fringe of a groundswell of concern' with predatory capitalism. Peter Senge reminded the conference that this concern 'may well reach to the top of our corporations'. As we now know after Seattle, Montreal, Nice, Prague, London and, most recently, Genoa, it must be doing so, though the 10,000 people from 117 different countries who came together quietly and constructively in Porto Allegre, Brazil, only made the front page of *Positive News*. It appears this developing groundswell has nonetheless moved even the *Financial Times* as they intend to introduce an ethical FTSE – FTSE4good!

Robert says we are dealing with 'ordinary' people in Scott Bader, not social reformers. This is true – our 1950s handbook entitled *New Life in Industry* was dedicated to 'Tom, Dick and Harry' (to which my mother added in the second edition 'Not forgetting Harriet') 'and all who tread the daily path of labour', but fortunately we also had at that time a few social activists wanting to use their business skills for social change, notably John Leyland, who was attracted by our handbook which had compelling illustrations by the radical artist Arthur Wragg. I remember too we did expect, rather naïvely, that all Commonwealth Members would soon become social reformers. Yet I find, often at an unconscious level, many of those who work in Scott Bader know the direction is right and *are* aware some fundamental change happened and continues to develop. Flashes of realisation break out and appear here and there, saying 'yes, we want change'. Of the many consultants that have worked with Scott Bader all have noted there *is* a different culture and atmosphere. One, Professor Moss-Jones of the Open University, brought in by Jim O'Brien to work up our Learning Centre, later said to me that there was an 'unconscious persistence' in the company, of a transforming presence – that there was a 'new reforming story' around somewhere trying to break out.

For the record I would like to mention we had previously had leading consultants from the Tavistock Institute such as A. A. K. Rice, predating Bruce Reed, and there were others later who all helped to clarify our purpose. This led to Brian Elgood heading a Community Development department comprising the Commonwealth Secretary John Anagnostelis, the Personnel Manager, and two or three assistants with job enlargement skills, with the support of Dr Roger Hadley, who was then an external Director.

Transformation, the jargon words being 'a paradigm shift', as opposed to simply 'change', is very different and not easy to describe. Its very nature starts from what is not conscious. My experience is that it is often sensed better by 'factory level' workers than professional or managerial people. They feel it in their guts, they are aware of the 'dream', and they get the idea; unfortunately Robert was only able to talk to a few of them. One, coming to us in the early 60s, who had travelled round the world with the Army, even states that when he came to Scott Bader he thought he 'had landed in Heaven'. Others are aware that our whole Western techno-economic system is not compatible with a viable future for human society on our planet Earth, and work for change where they can, whilst keeping the company viable as a private collective capitalist activity. It would be good to have seen interviews of these people, especially those who stood for the democratic bodies, and an account of the Community Council development down the years, although this would make a book in its own right.

Schumacher's family told me they could not understand why he regularly travelled to some minuscule company in the sticks of Northamptonshire, when he was in demand as an economic advisor to many governments around the world. Schumacher understood. Why did we attract very significant figures to give our Commonwealth lectures? Robert gives little space to these. To omit the importance and historic significance at the time of such people and worry about how many tons of this or that product we produced is really to miss the wood for the trees.

Willis Harman, to whom I am enormously indebted for developing my beliefs and whom I quoted when I chaired our 40th Anniversary Commonwealth Lecture, said 'Business has to adopt a new tradition which it has never had throughout the entire history of capitalism...as the most powerful institution on the planet it has to take responsibility for the whole. Every decision that is made, every action that is taken, has to be viewed in the light of that responsibility ... it is about investing ourselves in a task of historic proportions. Some will be called to this task, others will not.'

I consider we were called in 1951.

Robert's book starts well, is excellent on leading figures who influenced Ernest's early thinking, but misses out on later ones, e.g. Professor Wilken, J. P. Narayan, Vinoba Bhave, Lord McLeod, Canon Collins, Fred Blum, and fellow thinkers in the US, India and Europe. It has plenty of factual details, but as it does not really grasp the longer-term fundamental aim of the Commonwealth and all that it is entrusted to do, I have felt the need to redress the balance in these comments, a privilege, surely, if not a precedent. So far I feel to do so adequately would entail rewriting the whole background to the approach the book has taken. I am deeply troubled that there is so little written to show that there *is* a difference between Employee Ownership and being Trustees, discharging a Covenant to build a fundamental paradigm shift beyond our present industrial structure. Schumacher sees this when he writes about Scott Bader in *Small Is Beautiful*, '... Scott Bader ... demonstrates that the transformation of ownership is merely, so to speak, an enabling act: it is a necessary but not a sufficient condition for the attainment of higher aims.' Later he says 'everyone in Scott Bader has the opportunity to raise themselves to a higher level of humanity'. Cleghorn, in his PhD thesis, understands this very clearly and Willis Harman saw the Commonwealth as a forerunner of the 'new paradigm in business'.

WHERE I COME IN

The problem is to find some principle of justice upon which human association for the production of wealth can be found. *R. H. Tawney*

None of us are born into similar circumstances. In reflecting on mine I realise how exceptional they were. I cannot expect others to feel about the company as I do – but maybe in reviewing some of them you will find clues and experiences which you can understand, and which may help and support this paradigm shift I think the Commonwealth was born to achieve and demonstrate.

In 1940 our Kingsway offices were bombed, but luckily we could move to a lower floor as ours were only partly damaged. Our family home in the Thames estuary was hit by an anti-aircraft shell, and the East End factory stores and laboratory were exposed to firebombs, fortunately missing the celluloid and nitro cotton. Our garden was littered with shrapnel from the anti-aircraft at night and bits and pieces from daily dogfights, and one night Ernest only just missed driving us into a bomb crater. So we evacuated to Wollaston. In the quieter countryside Ernest felt the world could not go on like this. Violence must be overcome. This was *his* war. He began to understand that he was inflicting on others those very demands that had led him to start his own company: he had been determined to be responsible for himself and not to remain a 'wage-slave' or industrial 'cannon fodder'. He decided to restructure his company so that human values, essentially Christian, but rooted in all world religions, could find their place and be lived out. These aspirations would offer a way forward from economic violence, power struggles and money-acquisitive society. Robert writes sensitively on some of these, as does Susanna Hoe, getting to the roots of Ernest's social concerns. For me, having worked in hospitals for the Friends Ambulance Unit as a conscientious objector, I wanted to contribute to a better world and, sensing there was to be a social purpose beyond the normal industrial environment, I gave up thinking of a medical career and made the decision to officially join Scott Bader in 1947. I had come to believe that service, not private gain, should be the motive of all work.

Evacuating to Wollaston Hall, living with blackout and rationing, with London office staff sleeping on the top floor and working in the offices below, already demanded co-operation, which I had experience of in the Friends Ambulance Unit. We were 'all in it together'. Building a better Britain was the dynamic, and bringing new work to the village was a social good, as was the formulation of wartime resin substitutes and later new and technically advanced, exciting, useful products.

I hoped Susanna Hoe, in her excellent biography, would uncover even further than she did why this motive developed in Ernest and I find Robert identifies the main influences very well, but not the trigger. The underlying cause and, in my view, the primary motive, was the Second World War – resulting in the commitment to create structures and relationships that would develop a less violent society; that would, in 'Quakerspeak', 'take away the occasion for war'; and I felt this is not appreciated enough with either writer. Of course after 1945 building a 'Brave New World' was in the air. Ernest had followed me in joining the Quakers, and intuited that violence lay at a very deep level in society and humanity had to evolve to survive. The seeds of violence lay within the structures of the capitalist work system, and how we have to earn our living. He understood how easy it was, as an employer, to exploit people; how more capital gave him more means and the power of economic dictation in the way he was running his company, how the system encouraged personal greed and how greed between nations leads to war. (Cleghorn sees the connection between economic greed and war very clearly, and finds John Eagan of The American Cast Iron Pipe Co. similarly persuaded in the 1920s.) Ernest read widely and agreed with Pope Pius XI when he said 'dead matter goes out of the factory improved, but men go out degraded'. We had also been moved by the Minute of Social Testimony drafted by Quakers at their 1944 Annual Meeting in London, and this took their seminal 1918 'Eight Points for a True Social Order' further. It read:

> Deep in each human soul lies the seed of the eternal divine life ... Its flowering to the glory of God is the aim and purpose of man's being ... To all men [the resources of the world] are given, to all men in common ownership they belong, and although these resources may be administered by particular individuals, groups or nations, any system which limits their availability for all men and women, regardless of colour and creed, is hindering Christian fellowship and the divine order ... No man is a 'hand' to be kept in or thrown out of the economic life of the community as suits

the need of any system. The community is a system wherein each man and woman should find a place of significant service and creative living. All are members, all share in the duty and should enjoy the right of helping to determine its policies, whether political or economic, industrial or social. For its foundations rest on a democracy based on the brotherhood of man and drawing its reality from the Fatherhood of God.

So, after endless work and discussions, two restructuring attempts, and the 1948 strike, we finally founded the Commonwealth in 1951. But then we were wisely told by Hubert Munroe, our QC at that time, 'Gentlemen, I must remind you that the invitation cards to the funeral of capitalism have not yet been issued', but we soldiered on (a good pacifist phrase!) and had to wait quite a few years before Ted Heath talked publicly of the 'unacceptable face of capitalism'.

The Commonwealth were entrusted with the running of the Company. Most financial and all commercial decisions were expected to be made, and were made, by management, but the Members always have ultimate responsibility, exercised in General Meeting. Although such action is not often taken it was agreed that major decisions are at least ratified, if not made, this way, notably of course any redeployment of major company assets. The decision to offer voluntary redundancy instead of an 'across the board' reduction in pay was a case in point, as are currently discussions on governance and of course profit distribution – a regular AGM responsibility. Redundancy, as Robert recounts, was suggested by and accepted by Members, not imposed by management. In fact nothing can be imposed, the structure demands consensus decisions – a democratic requirement which has not always been honoured by senior management; but neither have Members always had the courage to challenge decisions, even when they had elected representation. This has, not infrequently, caused concern to Members. I recall a difficult one when the closure of SRL was proposed that illustrates the pain we all had. Emotions ran so high that one fitter refused to go to the meeting in the Commonwealth Centre. He said he knew SRL had to go if Scott Bader was to survive but he could not go and vote another man, even up North, out of a job.

At this stage it is worth quoting a couple of paragraphs of Stephen Cleghorn's thesis (one of a number written about us of which Roger Hadley's was probably the first and best researched as he had worked with us). It is entitled *This work of justice: the search for moral common*

ground in the authority relations of work. It compares an in-depth study
of The American Cast Iron Pipe Company and our Commonwealth,
and I consider it exhibits the best understanding of the purposes of the
Commonwealth that I have read so far. He states (p 361): 'While the
forces of convergence towards managerial domination have been
detected at the Commonwealth, any significant change in structures to
accommodate a more overtly managerial organisation would require
the active agreement of a majority of members of the Commonwealth
and the Trustees' (quoting Hadley & Goldsmith, 1994). He goes on,
'The constitution of the Commonwealth thus protects against the dominance of managerial interpretations of what Ernest Bader wanted to
create. It could almost be considered a kind of "sacred" text available
to all members of the organisation, by which all members have a fundamental right to interpret how the organisation ought to be governed.'
And on page 360, 'Most significantly, *the constitution of the Commonwealth does not allow the corporate values to be interpreted only by
those holding power (managers or directors), but puts this interpretation
equally into the hands of the workers themselves* [italics original].'

Readers should also note that the final paragraph of Cleghorn's
abstract says: 'The success of the Commonwealth in converting its
founder's religious values into practical and democratic authority relations is compared to ACIPCO's failure to do the same. The question of
"can moral common ground between workers and managers be found?"
is answered affirmatively, but only if the firm does the "cultural work"
necessary and *constitutes* as a "third element" between management and
labour the cultural values it identifies as most important.' Translated,
this means if the Commonwealth is to succeed a good learning centre is
imperative. This is made abundantly clear in the Constitution, which I
repeatedly tried to get action on from the Commonwealth Board. It is
their primary and executive responsibility and clearly spelt out in
Articles 38 to 41.

FURTHER ENDEAVOURS IN THE SOCIAL TASK

Gandhi sought a corrective to the mere exploitation of capitalism and
its pursuit of wealth, through his concept of Trusteeship. *Anthony Copley*

The Company grew with American 'know-how' obtained by John Hand
in 1945, and developed by others, as Robert describes well. I became
MD in 1957 and Chairman in 1966. In 1978 I was invited (for the first

time outside SB) to lead a small seminar I had entitled 'Common Ownership – An Effective Means for Social Innovation' at the prestigious
European Management Symposium in Davos (now the even more prestigious World Economic Forum and behind the questionable WTO).
1978 was a large conference, even then guarded by police with guns and
dogs, with diverse and eminent people from Fred Hoyle, the astronomer,
to the Dutch PM; and there was even ski-ing between sessions! I had
friendly support from Hamish McRae, the financial journalist, and his
wife Frances Cairncross, and to my surprise was invited by an LSE professor to a follow-up conference in Italy. Here I first crossed swords with
Robert Oakeshott who was then promoting the Mondragon approach
after his problems with Sunderlandia, a postwar building project which
our Commonwealth Development Fund had supported, and which
looked as if it might have developed a better company structure than
ours. My general approach at the Conference was seen as over-ideolog-
ical and Scott Bader a 'one-off' experiment, although I had support from
Christian Schumacher and his wife Diana and a few others.

In Davos I had referred to Scott Bader's No 1 Certificate of the Industrial Common Ownership Act of 1976. This, I claimed for the first time,
gave us official recognition as an advanced and innovative company
where capital was invested democratically with the workforce, instead
of being used to exploit the workforce for its own ends – its dividends –
and was the way to a better industrial world. (Spedan Lewis was cred-
ited with saying 'Money should be used by men instead of men being
used by money' although I believe the statement is not in the John
Lewis Partnership papers and is possibly a lot earlier – maybe Marx?)
More importantly I claimed that common ownership 'fostered co-operation to create a space [I learnt later that the sociologists call it a 'force
field'] in which men can be free and so grow to become responsible, creative and productive' – so a better company results. I remember in
Davos complaining to Charles Levinson, Secretary of the International
Union of Chemical Workers, that it was going too slowly. He said 'OK,
it must be difficult, Godric, but please keep it going, it's the only place
we can point to that's really trying!'

Although I 'retired' in 1979 I still act as 'Ambassador' for Scott
Bader and for Common Trusteeship in general. Robert has always been
very generous in what he has written about me, particularly in this case.
I attend, within a budget, what I consider to be forward-thinking
conferences, and try to encourage others to look at better structures
than capitalism and go beyond employee ownership. As has been said,

'employee ownership' is only a first step and often misfires, like National Freight for example, or at best stops at collective capitalism. I gave a paper in Toronto at a 'Quality of Working Life' Conference in 1981 (and, always keen to plug our products, was able to point out of the window to our 'wonder material' Crystic resin used on the top of the Toronto Tower, then the highest in the world). And in 1983 I gave a paper to the Business History Unit at the LSE (and could then mention the extensive use of Crystic resin on the BT Mondial building on the Thames, not far away, nearly opposite the Festival Hall, and still in good condition). This paper was developed and printed in 1986 in the 100th celebratory issue of the Long Range Planning Society journal and used the words Common Trusteeship for the first time in print. It later became a pamphlet, produced by Scott Bader, called *Putting People First* and was translated into French, principally through support from Brian Elgood, for the benefit of our French companies and at Continental conferences. When Charles Handy (an external Director here for three years) read it, he said it was looking at the Company through rose-coloured specs, but when you read his current books you will find, I believe and hope, that he learnt a few things from us, including the need for working communities and managers having to learn 'to surrender some power and take risks with people' (*The Empty Raincoat*).

Scott Bader is described in many books and theses – for example the Cranfield case study; the OU's unit on management structures (their case study on our common ownership was screened regularly by BBC2 for over two years); *Small Is Beautiful*; Fred Blum's books; BBC TV and radio, The British Council (in seven different languages), articles in Malta, the Philippines, Australia and Canada, ITV and recently CNN, and higher degree theses, including Cleghorn whose work is, in my eyes, the most fundamental and relevant on problems of moral authority. A US professor once stated that there must be more academics who had referred to and written about us than we had people in our Company! A recent writer on economics in the Philippines, Maximo Indolos, after describing the Commonwealth's fundamental purposes, ends his book with this perceptive paragraph:

> There is no surer way of guaranteeing the destruction of the Earth than the maintenance of economic systems that are constantly compelled to waste massive amounts of resources in the unending and futile effort to get them out of deflationary gaps, recessions, and mass unemployment.

My 50+ years' experience has increasingly led me to believe the Commonwealth *is* about a paradigm shift, an attempt at redeeming our Western economic system, and represents all global issues and should become the transforming ethic of the 21st century. I do see our attempt in Wollaston tries to address the task for 'business to realise its crucial role' in the present turbulent world, as urged on by the World Business Academy (WBA), following the words of its co-founder, Willis Harman.

Over the years I have found that the leading edge of change has moved from ICOM/ICOF, ESOPs, and allied organisations, towards the work, for instance, of the WBA, New Economics Foundation, Servant Leadership, Social Venture Network Europe (SVNE) and European Baha'i Business Forum (EBBF). The latter demonstrates the application of spiritual values in advance of present Quaker work, applying essential values for the transformation of business to create the better world we need, and is creating great interest on the Continent and in Eastern Europe.

When I stepped down from the Managing Director's position it was in the belief that someone else should be trained to take my place, as I had done for Ernest. This should have been Cecil Phillips, but this did not work out and we had to look outside The Commonwealth and Nick Broome came in. I had the same hope, as well as feeling 'burnt out', for 'retiring' from the Chairman's position, but similar circumstances applied. I had asked Fritz Schumacher to follow me, but sadly he died before he could be formally approved. I still feel my proposal about Chairmen, given to Susanna Hoe (p 203), should be a way forward – and not just in Scott Bader. It read: 'I hope there won't be any need to project into the body of one person the role of company chairman, to carry the image and purpose, in essence, the responsibility for it. I would hope that there might be at least two – or maybe an on-going group – that are able to take it in turns.'

As Honorary Life President I am privileged to advise where and when I can, and to try to influence trends when they seem to be departing from the original purpose, i.e. supporting the recent Agenda for Action 'initiated by the external Trustees' – an attempt to remind the Commonwealth and create awareness of the importance of Constitutional requirements. The 'Family Power' which Robert assumes to have continued until my retirement was always something of a myth, although I have been rightly accused of not using what power I had more resolutely. Even Ernest had to accept the Commonwealth decisions, and the Hay pay system was installed against my wishes. All that is a problem of a democratic structure. It can often fall to a not so well informed majority decision, sometimes at the lowest level of understanding. For democracy to work there has to be a well-informed, involved and committed body of members, and I know the present Commonwealth Office is working hard to this end but they still badly need a better resourced Learning Centre. 'More of this later' as Robert would say!

However, there are now some highly instructive and worthwhile words in the latest Commonwealth pamphlet, *The History of a Future*, (which I neither influenced nor was responsible for), '… the structure of the organisation … is about involvement and participation at all levels. It is also about a diffusion of power so that no … group … becomes a 'power centre' to the possible detriment of the others.' Robert does not seem able to accept that this is what we are trying to do. He finds 'creative friction', 'dysfunctional bodies' and 'a mix that is neither one thing nor the other' but does not point out our original fundamental endeavours, of a constructive, integrated balance of responsible authority for and on behalf of the Scott Bader community. This means management are expected to manage, but out of service, as Servant Leaders appointed by Members, and ultimately accountable to them. To quote again from Tawney who many decades ago prophetically saw the problem the Commonwealth has with change, with mindsets.

> It is obvious, indeed, that no change of system or machinery can avert those causes of social malaise which consist in the egotism, greed, or quarrelsomeness of human nature. What it can do is to create an environment in which those are not the qualities which are encouraged. It cannot secure that men live up to their principles. What it can do is to establish their social order upon principles to which, if they please, they can live up and not live down. It cannot control their actions. It can offer them an end on which to fix their minds. And, as their minds are, so in the long run and with exceptions, their practical activity will be.

More hints for establishing a good learning process in the company.

SOME OF THE PEOPLE OF SCOTT BADER

In a world of massive social problems at all scales and in all directions and especially issues around the role of business, the ongoing development of Scott Bader is hugely important. It does not need me to say that there are many observers of the Company throughout the world. *John Moss-Jones*

When I was invited to write this afterword, my initial response was to think of people and incidents triggered by Robert's words, which kept impinging on my consciousness. I can clearly remember sitting, with my sister, in the back of the car during the 1930s and hearing my father in front say to my mother 'I'm fed up with the business. I'm going to sell it.' How nearly was the Commonwealth lost!

When it became apparent that we would need to move from London, everyone was involved in the search for new premises. Courtney Bryson, then Chief Chemist, who was touring the countryside on his bicycle, found Wollaston Hall, after seeing it advertised in Bedford. Later I remember walking across the fields with him to Farndish, to watch him enlarge his excellent photographs, taken with a Leica camera, many of which were hung in the London Salon of Photography. He was a member of the Alpine Club, and took me rock climbing in Wales. He also regaled me with tales of a colloid conference in Cambridge – this was the apogee of sophisticated high-tech science – and accelerated my interest in physical chemistry.

My father was a bewildering mixture of charm, bombast, bully, altruist, perfectionist, intuition, intelligence, impetuosity and tough love. He was seen on the front lawn wagging his finger at Eddie Lancaster as if he had committed a cardinal sin. When questioned what it had all been about Eddie replied that Ernest had found a weed! I was on the receiving end many times; once I found the tub from outside the front door on my desk, with a furious note, headed 'sledgehammer communication', saying that the state of the dead cyprus bush in the tub was indicative of the moral decay of the company. He would jump from loving father to power-demanding tyrant alarmingly fast, once stating that 'I made you, so I can destroy you'. He did not like 'yes' men, but he hated to be thwarted. When a senior Commonwealth Member's behaviour displeased him he told him that as he, Ernest, entered the pearly gates he would tell St Peter that no way was such a Member to be allowed in!

Robert has asked for 'empirical research' to back up the claims of the Commonwealth to be a better place to work. I would say that a company which enables a young man with no self-esteem to transform himself into a man who now helps those suffering from depression, and who gave his sabbatical payment to the local children's home so that they could enjoy the holiday he never experienced, cannot be said to have failed. No one can fail to notice how responsibility for running the Commonwealth has developed Members far beyond what could have been expected in a 'normal' environment.

Robert claims that it was idealism which led Ernest to believe he could create a Christian environment. I think he has *just* missed the point, and has confused spirituality with overly religious Christianity. Certainly Ernest felt that he had a duty to encourage spirituality and the only way he knew was Christianity. The Scott Bader Commonwealth was intended as an environment in which people could grow, particularly spiritually, but certainly holistically, in this secular age, in their relationship with each other and in their work. This was particularly evident when Fred Blum decided to take Holy Orders after working with Scott Bader, but it is manifest in much more subtle and invisible ways amongst Members, who consider their fellow workers, their environment and helping others. They used to take firewood and food parcels to old people in the village, directed by the village nurse, and still work out of hours to help meet local needs, as well as with the Commonwealth charitable work. Again this is not an 'objective statistic', but it is true of many people who work here, and particularly those who have experienced other employments.

Ernest and Dora were essentially 'seekers'. Although their personal beliefs were fundamentally Christian (though not of an Establishment kind), they would agree with Fritz Schumacher: 'The Buddhist point of view takes the function of work to be three-fold: to give a man a chance to utilise and develop his faculties; to enable him to overcome his egocentredness by joining with other people in a common task; and to bring forth the goods and services needed for a becoming existence.' To concentrate only on the last of these (as so many mainstream companies do) results in materialism.

A 'COMMON TRUSTEESHIP' COMPANY

The idea that there is a sacred trust between mankind and our Creator, under which we accept Stewardship for the Earth has been an important feature of most of our religions and spiritual thought throughout the ages.
Prince Charles's Reith Lecture

When Ernest and Brian Parkyn decided on the name 'The Scott Bader COMMONWEALTH' they had in mind 'wealth in common' or 'Common Weal'. With the advent of the British Commonwealth this term has perhaps become misunderstood as has the term Common Ownership. The core essence of Scott Bader is our Common Trusteeship – being 'Trustees-in-Common' is a good phrase.

Trusteeship is not just 'ethics'. It is an attempt to develop, to live and to propagate 'the principle of justice upon which human association for the production of wealth can be found'. I've deliberately used the word 'propagate' as it is a living system we're talking about. The need to do so is even more urgent than in Tawney's day. Of course now we know production also has to be sustainable and fairly distributed, and justice must be extended to our environment, ourselves and our neighbours, providing good overall quality of life. I hope in the future we will be able to be solve our problems of maintaining a profitable business when so much of our output is dependent on non-renewable materials, and escalating costs, by using biomass, through biotechnology – mainly sunlight – to obtain our raw materials and our energy.

Robert rightly praises a shoemaking co-operative in our village. There are many excellent ones, but I recall a co-operative where individual shareholder-workers tended to sell their shares to buy the family a fridge/car/etc. This frustrated any possibility of participation or Common Trusteeship – a current ESOP problem and another reason why we chose not to have individual shares.

Gandhi's thinking is highly relevant to our major current problems. His vision of Trusteeship is, I am convinced, the only viable way forward. It has to be the transforming ethic of the 21st century. Industry is the engine of our economic life and the dominant activity on our planet, but is at present creating a casino economy. Clearly our economic ways have to change and money has to be issued without interest and debt. The true 'business of business' to my mind is to have a system to produce common wealth. The stakeholder inclusive Company concept is good but is only a beginning. Wacker Chemie and Dutch State Mines for example have integrated the responsibility for the environment into their management and both are developing life sciences for sustaining their future and realise a vital stakeholder is our earth. This shows that companies are moving to be inclusive of other responsibilities than profit, but not yet into a paradigm shift and are being moved by outside pressure and not inner conviction. The purpose of Scott Bader is to set an example of Trusteeship through conviction.

Trusteeship may be more difficult to explain, but George Goyder and Brian Parkyn (who gave brilliant Commonwealth Lectures in 1976 and 1991) had supported such a development. The Commonwealth owns Scott Bader and its subsidiaries but it is not financial ownership. Fritz Schumacher says ownership has been 'extinguished' and replaced by responsibility for 'power over a bundle of assets'. It is not unlike 'stewardship' in our local Methodist church, where Trustees are responsible to the church members for the buildings and the function of their church – although to my mind 'stewardship' connotes too much of a static state and is more suited to 'not for profit organisations'.

Fundamentally Prince Charles is right, we hold our planet in trust. We must become trustees for the Earth's resources, and the assets that we make, convert, or use from those resources. Now we are realising we must be joint trustees with Nature – we have discovered that there are limits to our exploitation, domination and, more noticeably, pollution. My hope is that it will increasingly be seen that it is crucially vital that Scott Bader develops as a true example of these principles, and demonstrates that it is part of trusteeship to respect, husband and recycle resources. Fritz Schumacher was horrified to find that the world is using finite fossil fuels as income. They are capital assets, and as such should be used to build a sustainable economy. This is a basic economic principle. Forty years ago, well ahead of its time, our code required us to be economic with the earth's resources. Now it should require us to recycle them – like Nature where there is no waste – and follow 'The Natural Step' of Karl-Henrik Robert.

Industry has to start the change – Scott Bader has set a mini-example. Warwick University Business School's MBA on Corporate Citizenship, the New Academy of Business in Bristol and 'the triple bottom line' are advancing, but too slowly. The ethic of the Cadbury rules and various ISOs are gradually being used by businesses as they find it essential to their probity to be accountable to, and aware of, their effect on society, and the planet, and make these claims as good PR in their company reports to maintain new investment.

In 1977 I visited The Trusteeship Foundation in Bombay. Some Indians claim that an owner could hold his company in trust. Maybe they can, as responsible people hold their ethical investments in trust, e.g. for wind power. Some people such as Jeff Gates, a writer, lawyer, and lecturer, who promoted US ESOPS, believe individual nationwide shareholding would bring a better society. Employee ownership or current Indian type trusteeship are only alternative shareholding models, not full democratic trusteeship. Professor Wilken of Freiburg University, a very important figure in Ernest's life, wrote about individual shareholding being a sham in his sadly ignored book *The Liberation of Capital*, which Ernest financed through his excellent stamp collection, which I took to Switzerland to sell for him. Wilken said 'the [wider] allocation ... of capital ownership ... neither frees [the worker] from the wage system nor develops any social outlook in his psyche. If anything it would make him as materially-minded as the private capitalist...' and *that widespread share-ownership could be seen as a way of avoiding the necessary social restructuring.*

I would like to see legislation enacted so that when a company gets to a certain size it should become a trust and have a licence to operate for the common good and to serve society. George Goyder talked along these lines in 1976 in Wollaston. I am afraid the new Company Act presently being drafted will neither legislate for real change, nor even restrain the 'carpet baggers' and 'dawn raiders' of our mutual and other companies. It is interesting to recall that in Portugal it used to be the king's privilege and responsibility to control and licence industry according to the county's need. Courtney Bryson had to get a licence from Dr Salazar to make resins when he went there in the 1940s. Many ways forward have been discussed and formulated but one of the clearest was that of David Spreckley of Landsman Caravans, who developed draft Company laws and legislative procedure for the Liberal Party in the 1960s. The Commonwealth was mentioned in the Party handbook as a model. He wanted something, he said, practical and legally binding for their manifesto. Yet maybe there is some truth in what Professor Ota Sik, previously deputy PM of Czechoslovakia, an early Commonwealth lecturer in 1973, told me – 'Your approach is only for artists, poets and musicians.' I often now think this was quite a compliment because if we are to be a human race, live holistically, not be visionless automatons, we need structures that can appeal to our spirits.

A LEARNING PROCESS

We need a nobler economics that is not afraid to discuss spirit and conscience, moral purpose and the meaning of life, an economics that aims to educate and elevate people.   *Fritz Schumacher*

Community in the workplace is not some airy-fairy, impossible ideal. It does require considerably more sustained psychospiritual exertion from top management on down than does 'business as usual' ... [but] it will also make most work, from top management down, ultimately more satisfying and fulfilling, more creative and productive, more profitable and cost effective.   *Scott Peck*

I have found any fundamental behavioural change (in our case, an explicit and an abiding covenant to work to create a just industrial order) has to be rooted in and driven by personal conviction and experience. Professor Fred Blum's book about us called *Work and Community, the Quest for a New Social Order*, written in 1968, had these words:

> ... many people who hear about the Scott Bader Commonwealth become intrigued; something is stirred in them and they know in their heart that something significant is going on. They also sense that more demands are made on people than industry does in general; the Commonwealth demands more maturity, it calls for personal change besides change of organisation and it requires the ability to give up false power, status and values to realise true relationships.

If people are motivated only by obedient, or – more usually – expedient, responses to regulation, or incentives such as wearing the company tie, or a mission statement, let alone share option bonuses or political correctness, it is inevitably only a temporary development and we need to change mindsets to enable the realisation of 'higher cultural codes', to quote Cleghorn.

We should always remember the whole of the company is a learning organisation, which is why a properly funded Learning Centre is so essential for focusing such work, and not just for surfing the Internet! As far back as 1968 Fred Blum thought it so important that he said it should be a formal Institute, and 33 years later this vital need is not yet a reality. I remember a Canadian professor from McGill University visiting us who said we should stop 'paying out to charity'. We needed the money ourselves to educate us to the vital importance of our purpose in the world – for 'so few of us appeared to know'.

In chapter 9 Robert has spoken of the 'duty... to strive for personal and collective transformation' and then asked 'to what?' He would not have needed to ask this question if Articles 38–41 (which have been in place since 1951) had been met. They clearly require resources to be discharged to honour the requirements of training staff to be better Commonwealth Members. (He actually answers himself with the quote from Jennifer Wates in chapter 10 – '... to make business more moral and humane for the 21st century'.) But is it really necessary to spell it out again? Surely no one would wish for a transformation to anything but a better world, person, society – whatever. He has also stressed (and I entirely agree with him) the need to provide a programme of continuous improvement – this is exactly what the Articles were there to achieve. There was also to be the opportunity for continuous *personal* holistic improvement, the chance for individuals to fulfil their potential in the Commonwealth with both learning *and* training, and provision of links to other organisations like the Co-operative Research Department at the OU, or work at Cranfield and Northampton. All of these are in our area, let alone contacts with other advancing companies and social reformers, made easy via the Internet. There is so much we can learn from each other in making a better world. The Commonwealth aim was – and I hope yet will be – to engender enthusiasm and speed a process of individual and synergistic group company development. I think this is a world away from Robert's description of a 'Godric ideological centre' – don't we want to be better people and live better lives? It should become a College – an advanced adult school – open to all who want a better industrial society. (There is a 1960 proposed model in my office.) There have been proposals for it to be linked to a university, or to the Tavistock Institute. The obvious links to establish now would be with the Schumacher College and The New Academy of Business. I know from Satish Kumar, the director, that Shell and other leading companies are sending managers to Schumacher College to raise their awareness. The college teaches, among other good things, that capital is not only a quantity but a quality, whether financial or the Earth's resources.

Stephen Cleghorn, in his thesis, states that greater democracy in the workplace 'requires structures of democratic learning…and structures which check and balance the tendency of any human organisations which hoard power'. It is necessary to counter the threat that Scott Bader could revert to 'prevailing norms' through apathy, fear, or career-hungry management. In my 1983 AGM report I said 'To fail to give our hearts and our sustained co-operation is, in our Commonwealth, tantamount to withdrawing our labour.' This message is tacitly present in the struggle in training given to prospective employees and to update members, but needs to be more overtly understood, if – as I come to describe in the next pages – signing on for Membership *is* a covenantal relationship.

Unfortunately it is, as yet, not well understood in Scott Bader (let alone outside) that the urgent role of business towards positive transformation is critical for a viable future for our children and the planet. Scott Bader is here to set an example, and it should be proud of what has been achieved. But it must consolidate and build on its progress, not just sit back and rest on its laurels. And it is not a radical example simply for ideological reasons alone, but to have a stronger and fundamentally more efficient and viable Company because it has purposes that will drive and sustain it in the 21st century. Let us all remember, *ideals are the engines of progress.*

ON BEING TRUSTEES AND HAVING A COVENANT

Trusteeship...means faithfully and confidently taking responsibility for not only material assets, but also for social values, human skills, and administration of rightful and creative culture for the benefit of others now and in coming generations.   *Godric Bader in 'Gandhi and the Contemporary World'*

Robert does not make clear the origins of the Trustees. They were not retained to 'ease the pain', but to keep alive the Covenant between the Founders and the Commonwealth. Their role is to remind the Commonwealth Board in particular of their increased responsibilities, since the Trustees handed over responsibility for confirmation of the appointment of Company Directors to the Community Council and responsibility for philosophical oversight to the Commonwealth Board. They act as Guardians. The Commonwealth Board clearly has Executive responsibility for Commonwealth Membership, for updating the code, and formulating new guidelines when necessary. Trustees may act should these become watered down or, worse, ignored; may mediate when normal grievance procedures fail, and to ensure that remedial action is taken should Constitutional breaches occur or when the company viability is in danger. The Founders believed that committed outsiders in particular could stand back and see a wider picture than was perhaps possible from inside the organisation, and there were internal Trustees as well for balance. Charles Handy said they were 'remembrancers' (which is why the last group of Trustees put together the 'Agenda for Action', which unhappily was ignored by management, and sidelined to the extent that Robert does not even mention it).

It is vital to understand what was meant by the original Covenant given to the Commonwealth. I wish to take this opportunity to clarify the nature of the Covenant undertaken by Members, which the Trustees have ultimate responsibility to keep alive.

Daniel J. Elazar has beautifully defined my understanding of this Covenant, quoted in Doug Gwyn's book *The Covenant Crucified*. This is vital to understanding the Commonwealth and clarifies the nature of the responsibility for the 'power over a bundle of assets' characterised by Fritz Schumacher when the shares were handed over.

A covenant is a morally-informed agreement or pact between

people or parties having an independent and sufficiently equal status, based upon voluntary consent and established by mutual oaths or promises witnessed by the relevant higher authority. A covenant provides for joint action or obligation to achieve defined ends (limited or comprehensive) under conditions of mutual respect which protect the individual integrities of all parties to it. Every covenant involves consenting, promising and agreeing. Most are meant to be of unlimited duration, if not perpetual.

This describes the basic meaning of the Commonwealth certificate all Members sign on their acceptance by the Commonwealth Board

Doug goes on to say that 'covenant allows for continuing evolution of institutional structures and laws, as long as the essential quality of relationship is maintained'. This, to my mind, sums up the nature of the continuing evolution expected when members sign on as Commonwealth Members. It has both moral grounding, and in the relationship it is intended to create becomes a binding force in our relationships with each other.

He explains that a covenant is chosen freely, 'binding us to a cause beyond ourselves'. We can be contracted to many covenants according to our particular interests. But 'True covenant is predicated on a transcendent authority.' This is the spiritual element which Robert finds it hard to understand or accept, but which gives Scott Bader a transcendental purpose, and makes it a truly 'different' place to work.

The book goes further to say that covenanted communities have been 'the bellwether of an imminent cultural transformation', which is what the Commonwealth was intended to be – a covenanted community responding to the forces which require fundamental change in the way our economic life operates. I know this has been felt and experienced in the Commonwealth.

CONCLUSION

We are now married to the world but we keep acting as though we are on a first date. *Newt Gingrich, Republican Speaker of US House of Representatives*

Business as the most powerful institution on the planet must come into balance and take responsibility for the whole. *Willis Harman*

Most people believe Scott Bader has three main tasks: (1) working to maintain a profitable business, (2) keeping abreast of and achieving technical innovation whilst (3) trying to maintain motivation for creating a better industrial society. Unfortunately this is the order in which it is normally seen, but I think this is the wrong way round. The Commonwealth purpose is not a bolt on at the end. It is the fundamental drive to achieve the 'economic' and 'technical tasks' necessary to stay in business, noted in the work of Bruce Reed, which he said we have to keep in balance. It is abundantly clear that the ultimate purpose – the *raison d'être* – is one of social obligation, The Commonwealth is not only here to serve our society and do good work, but also to develop society. Its aim is to serve the public good and consider future generations – even if this is not sufficiently realised. This is the reason it was registered as a charity.

Nevertheless I believe the Commonwealth is answering Tawney's question of how to find 'some principle of justice upon which human association for the production and distribution of wealth can be founded'. And it is struggling to take 'responsibility for the whole', to respond to Willis Harman, and also to demonstrate true 'stakeholder' responsibility to meet the current elementary demands. It was described by one of the speakers at the 50th Anniversary celebration on 28 April as 'a prime example to our politicians at the present time, of the kind of company the UK requires'. So, whilst the Commonwealth treats people as whole persons, and holds itself in Trusteeship – as we should all hold our world – it cannot, on its own, transform the global socio-economic order, although this is the ultimate covenantal commitment. Hopefully the current protests against global capitalism – referred to by George Monbiot in the *Guardian Weekly* of 26 July as 'numerically the largest protest movement in the history of the world' – though relatively still marginal, may be seen in the light of the words with which David Jenkins (when Bishop of Durham and scion of the Establishment) ended his Commonwealth Lecture in 1987. He quoted our 1951 Preamble: 'We recall that social progress has always had its roots in the activities of a small minority retaining faith in the face of overwhelming opposition.'

So the Commonwealth, with responsibility for its 'bundle of assets', must continue to lead, teach and motivate its members with its dynamic covenantal ethic. This means employees learning that when they are accepted as Members they sign a certificate that registers them as Trustees in law of the company through the Commonwealth. They are responsible for developing the company for their livelihood – a contractual relationship – and signing into the Commonwealth – a commitment that is a covenantal one – to use their work to literally change the world.

List of Commonwealth Members
1951 to 2001

[BY YEAR OF ACCEPTANCE INTO MEMBERSHIP]

1951

A. Adomenas
C. Allsop
Syd Andrews
Bert Austin
Edward Austin
Dora Bader
Ernest Bader
Godric Bader
Heinz Bader
Ramsay Bader
J. Bailey
Peter Bailey
Jim Barnett
Sid Barrett
Pam Barrick
Reg Barrick
Thomas Bayes
Jim Beaufoy
V. Bennett
A. Bialacki
Betty Blundell
B. Blunsom
P. Boller
Jim Bone
Sidney Bonham
Cyril Brawn
Maurice Brawn
Bob Bridgeford
Arthur Brown
Graham Brown
J. Burgess
Ernie Byrne

Eileen Candy
G. M. Carpenter
Charlie Catlin
M. Chambers
G. Church
Ron Clarke
H. E. Coombes
A. E. Cooper
Arthur Cross
W. Currell
Robert Dallas
Doris Debbage
Joe Dipper
Aubrey Drage
Sidney Dudley
L. J. Edwards
Tommy Elliott
Jon Emms
Bob English
Bernard Ferris
Rowland Ferris
Jim Fisher
Bert Fothergill
M. Frost
C. E. Garrard
Louis Gierszewski
Eric Golbourn
Dorothy Grant
Geoffrey Green
Harry Green
Ken Haigh
Frank Hall
M. Harper

Albert Hart
Frank Hart
Doreen Hatch
Jim Hathaway
Bill Hicks
Ted Holloway
M. Hooton
Albert Hughes
N. Jagelman
J. James
Dr Alfred Kraus
Joseph Kubacki
Alan Lack
Jill Layram
B. Legiec
Dr Adolf Lendle
George Lester
Percy Lissimore
John Litchfield
Tony Lovell
Frank Luck
June Luck
Harry Manston
B. Maslackiewicz
Len Maycock
Rudolf Meier
J. Meredith
Leonard Mills
E. Mobbs
Dorothy Moore
William Moore
Ron Munday
Ted Nicholls

Owen Nutt
Ruth Nutt
Brian Oliver
C. Olney
Gilbert Palmer
Brian Parkyn
Bernard Partridge
Joan Partridge
Denis Patchett
W. Pell
Fred Pettitt
Alfred Phillips
Sidney Polaine
R. Preston
D. I. Prichard
Oliver Rance
Reginald Rice
Dennis Riddle
Agnes Robertson
H. Robinson
Bob Russell
Edith Sayer
J. Sikora
Harry Smart
Bob Smith
Evelyn Smith
Ron Smith
Bert Speight
Sylvia Speight
Arthur Spriggs
Mrs A. Spriggs
Reginald Stanford
Albert Steel
Grace Steele
M. Stork
Janet Stormer
Douglas Sturman
Rex Swindall
Hedley Thompson
Kathleen Timpson
Brian Tivey
Norma Tompkins
Vic Tompkins

Alice Turner
Betty Turner
Sid Underwood
John Upcraft
Tom Warboys
Rita Ward
J. Wathan
Edward White
Don Wildman
Joe Wodzenski
C. Wood
Aggie Woodhams
Percy Wyman
E. Zuczek
1952
Mavis Austin
Joan Barnett
Kenneth Busby
Georgina Dean
Dennis Durkin
Edith Gerber
Jill Knight
Tom Marsh
Anita Mason
Marjorie Moore
Z. Niedowoz
Brian Parker
Thomas Pettit
Audrey Raven
Barbara Rodgers
Joyce Rudd
Clifford Sharp
Francziszene Skrzycki
Joe Sullivan
Rita Tall
Gwen Veal
Vic Wheeler
Alf Woodhams
1953
William Cherry
Dr Albert Cutter
Jack Edwards
George Gee

Colin Hackney
John Hand
Charles Hulbert
M. Lack
J. Lewis
Mr Los
G. Lozuish
Claude Smart
Mrs Steel
Charles Woodhouse
1954
Brian Chambers
Mr Chapman-Purchas
Doreen Cox
Eric Drage
Mr V. Drage
Michael King Beer
Jack Sparrow
Eric Stockwell
Colin Wells
1955
B. Bigley
Joseph Brunton
G. Butler
W. Crampton
Kenneth Docherty
Patricia Earl
J. Fitzmaurice
P. Foulger
John Kirbyshire
John Leyland
Philip Minor
Jack Parker
Charles Parkin
J. Michael K.
   Rowntree
J. Rudd
Mike Seamark
John Thornton
W. Tuson
Cecil Whitney
1956
Stanley Anstis

Kenneth Boyce
Eddie Clarke
Michael Gosbell
Joan Hipsey
Arthur Holmes
Eric Palmer
Oliver Rudd
William Wyant
1957
Lorna Archer
S. Augusti
Charles Avery
Brian Boardman
Whitfield Braithwaite
Sidney Cleaver
A. Downing
Gordon Hart
Stephen
    Hollingshead
Ivor Jones
Audrey Mitchell
Hedley Munns
Robert Parrish
J. Pratt
Stan Rawlings
B. Sebastian
Donald Smith
Holly Trotman
Philip Turner
1958
Roy Burrell
Frederick Perkins
John Shave
1959
Peter Clegg
John Hunt
W. Inwood
Douglas Kempster
Graham Langford
Norman Parkinson
Alan Reed
Robert Shelton
Albert Ward

Thomas Wildman
J. Wilson
1960
Jack Angwin
Raymond Annies
Kathleen Bone
Clarence Busby
Leslie Carrington
John Catlin
Alfred Crisp
Frederick Edwards
John Edwards
Peter Ellis
Bert Foard
B. Jenkinson
Roy Line
Bob Nye
Ernest Ostwald
Gordon Pentelow
Ken Perritt
William Prentice
Seaford Romain
Garnet Sebastian
Stan Silsby
Bert Smith
Gloria Ward
David Woodford
Janet York
1961
John Benfield
Peter Berrill
Wendy Church
Dennis Clarke
Charles Corke
Maureen Crouch
Joan Down
Margaret Hornby
James Jarvis
Sean Karley
Anthony Kirby
Mick Kiziak
Jack Knightley
Geoffrey Moxley

Joseph Osborne
Patrick Pennell
John Raymond
J. Richardson
Maureen Webb
1962
Keith Driver
Roy Freeman
J. Holdsworth
Robert Smith
1963
Michael Angwin
Arthur Barnes
Michael Barnes
Philip Barrett
John Bax
Joan Bird
Richard Busby
Brian Carney
Graham Clarke
Joan Cox
Newman Darnell
Derek Dawson
George Dent
Bob Edwards
Keith Edwards
Wendy Edwards
Albert Frost
Brian Hickman
Vincent Homer
John Howlett
Kenneth Johnson
Michael Jones
Robert Kilsby
Stefan Kocikowski
John Layton
C. Lett
Keith Lett
Martyn Line
Brian Love
Brian Lymn
Peter Mattli
Janet Odell

Bob Parker
Benjamin Parry
Harold Rogers
Paul Russell
Dr Willi Schmidt
Fritz Schumacher
Jan Snijder
Mary Stocks
Geoffrey Swailes
John Tebbutt
Michael Traxton
Irene Weed
1964
Paul Asbery
Anthony Bayes
Sydney Blundell
John Bounds
Eamonn Burke
Peter Dismore
Peter Dzydza
Michael Fitton
Norman Gennis
Albert Henry
David Higham
Richard Holman
Frank Jones
P. Lynham
John McIlroy
Myron Pawluk
Kenneth Payne
Cecil Phillips
Dr John Powell
John Reynolds
Dennis Rogers
Anthony Rose
Barry Sauntson
Arthur Seymour
D. Sharp
Kenneth Skinner
Patricia Tubby
Michael White
Arthur Whitehouse
Jutta Wyman

1965
Reginald Beard
Clive Childs
Susan Deacon
Sidney Dobbs
Brian Elgood
Eric Foster
Thomas Furman
Alan Green
Jack Haywood
William Mayes
Rupert McBride
Clement McLeod
David Mullen
Anthony Page
Peter Scales
Elstead Smith
Archie Stewart
Peter Sunderland
Michael Taylor
Kathleen Tebbutt
Michael Walker
1966
Arthur Allen
John Anagnostelis
Roy Bigg
Graham Clayson
Michael Dean
Harry Drage
Robert Lovell
Elbert McLeod
Anthony Mitchell
Robert Munn
Peter Richards
Norman Rogers
John Umfreville
Robert Ward
Samuel Whyte
1967
Christopher Betney
Gordon Brown
Gladys Gale
Robert Harris

Kelvin James
Ian Knight
Eddie Lancaster
Martin Maule
John Murphy
Colin Skidmore
Michael Summerfield
1968
Stephen Adkins
Heather Beard
Jack Beaty
Alan Brealey
Michael Campbell
Arthur Cole
Roy Collymore
Douglas Gooch
Kathy Green
David Lovell
Ron Peacock
Keith Richardson
Henry Shrouder
Nicholas Swailes
Kenneth Wright
1969
Kenneth Carter
Stuart Chirnside
Alan Cockshott
Brian Coles
Allen Earl
Stuart Fearon
Eric Goodfellow
Thomas Hall
Brian Horne
Eric Hughes
Colin Johnson
Stephen Johnson
Peter Knight
Jim Lane
Donald Parker
Colin Parr
Keith Plummer
David Ralley
Eddie Smith

John Steel Snr
Tony Sutton
Raymond Swepson
1970
Albert Armstrong
Roy Holland
Stephen Hosler
Geoffrey Jackson
Michael Lucy
Bill Lussignea
Dick Matthews
Eddie Murphy
Mick Mykytiuk
Kenneth Parvin
Stanley Puk
John Rowley
Brian Sellars
Vernon Silsby
John Thomason
David Townsend
1971
Derek Bedford
Trevor Brannan
Nicholas Broome
Cavan Browne
Gus Franze
Leslie Fuller
Geoffrey Goodall
Dr Roger Hadley
Samuel Hall
David Mansell
Alfred Maycock
John Mayhew
Terry Prentice
Rosalind Rice
Alan Saddleton
Ken Sansom
Roger Scott
Canon Frank Scuffham
Tad Sroka
Marilyn Stapleton
Roy Tobin
David Walding

Eric Woods
1972
Patricia Blackwell
Barry Bonham
Ron Brown
Albert Crisp
Ray Cumberpatch
Gill Dilley
Pam Fuller
Ivor Jones
Frank Lowe
Vivienne Marriott
Les Pitcher
Edna Richards
Christine Riddle
Paul Sinfield
1973
Rex Austin
Phil Ball
Eleanor Barnes
Stephen Burns
Peter Costello
Sally Hewitt
Doreen Hillier
Margaret Jobson
Simon King
Eileen Minney
Trevor Osborne
Ruby Palmer
Graham Robinson
Bob Rowe
Bob Smailes
Keith Taylor
Lynda Taylor
Malcolm Waters
Sheila Wyant
1974
Dianne Angwin
Paul Armstrong
Brian Besant
Mick Broe
Joan Butler
Prof Peter Forrester

John Francolini
Peggy Hewitt
John Hoddle
Patrick Keehan
Nora Kehoe
Pat Knight
Jill Luck
Peter Lymn
Ron Mardling
Roger Miles
Nihad Mustafa
Charles O'Keefe
Josephine Palmer
James Paxton
Arthur Piggott
Chris Pink
Anita Renicks
Bridget Ringrose
Annabeth Robb
Edwin Sinclair
Cheryl Stroz
Bill Susouns
Les Taylor
Mike Truman
Alan Wheeler
1975
Brian Bateman
Jim Batty
Ellen Carter
Cecilia Davis
Vic Hope
Alan Law
Ian McDonald
Sue Minor
John Percival
Suzanne Spencer-Cox
Phil Webb
1976
John Abbott
Dr Ian Alexander
Eddie Blenco
Harold Brown
Diana Coulson

Ted Endersby
Eileen Gilbert
Richard Hollowell
Daphne Hunt
Herbie Joyce
June Kirbyshire
Brian Lewicki
Jim McCourt
Betty McIlroy
Terence Page
Dom Ponzi
Edwin Porter
Tony Powell
John Pratt
Gwynne Probert
Paul Rantle
Haydn Salter
Austin Shelton
Kenneth Smart
Bernard Smith
Gregory Smith
John Steel Jnr
James Strangward
Tony Tite
Maurice Toyer
Brian White
Peter York
1977
Dennis Bates
Roland Brawn
David Burditt
Robert Cass
Keith Cheasman
Noel Cox
Joe DiFabbio
Elisha Dubar
Bill Edwards
Noreen Elderton
Rose Ellis
Carol Giles
John Goring
Martin Harding
Bryan Janson-Smith

Les King
Leyland King
David Mawby
Tony Millman
Dr Les Norwood
Frederick Redden
Lambert Sebastian
David Seear
Peter Vass
Ralph Woolf
1978
Trevor Bailey
Keith Barnes
Colin Beck
Brian Blaine
Alan Bull
Stephen Bush
Roly Butler
John Connelly
Alan Cotter
Melvyn Cottey
Greta Cox
Anthony Davy
Betty Kilsby
Colleen Neunzer
Mick Nunley
Richard Panther
Sonia Stephenson
Gordon Thompson
Roy Tilley
Janis Trembecki
Bernard Walker
1979
Lilian Clipstone-
    Roome
Lesley Day
John Hunter
Pauline Kellett
Bob Martin
Jean Osborne
Steve Perkins
Eileen Reed
Jane Silsby

Don Smith
Julie Smith
John Thompson
1980
Michael Edgecombe
Dave Everitt
Dennis Hamer
Julie Hutson
Pat Kilsby
Elizabeth Masters
Nigel Rogers
Mick Skinner
Barbara Smith
Delma Sutton
Oliver Tynan
Glynis Vorley
Gillian Whittemore
Pat Wilby
Frank Wildman
1981
Alan Anderson
Tony Campbell
Graham Charles
Roy Close
Bob Dickens
Peter Doe
Linda Eady
Colin Easton
Doug Flower
Malcolm Gadsby
Allan Hawking
Doug Kenmore
Chris King
Terry Marks
Peter Moultrie
Mick Norman
Jean Norton
Keith Reeves
Stuart Reeves
Michael H. Rowntree
Bashir Sheikh
George Skinner
Jonathan Smith

Pat Timoney
Chris Tucker
Gary Usher
Wayne Wilkinson
1982
David Abbott
Bill Bashford
Charles Bate
Susan Beenham
John Bethray
Singh Bhangra
Frederick Body
Denise Braines
Peter Bretherton
Fred Brown
Kevin Byles
Peter Cheshire
Derek Clark
Carol Connelly
Frank Cook
Philip Crouch
Rita Cunnold
Derek Dennis
Helen Dollimore
Mike Edwards
Terry Fewell
Peter Ganfield
Joan Gardiner
Barry Golden
Dr Maurice Goldsmith
Laurence Hacker
Chris Hall
Kathy Heath
Paul Hewitt
Geoffrey Hodshon
Mike Holden
Malcolm Hope
David Hopkins
Elena Hopkins
Merve Hopkins
Derek Horner
Anna Houghton
Carol Jolley

Tony Jolley
Patrick Kelway
Peter Larkin
Bob Leeson
Kelvin Line
Stephanie Line
Edward Loughman
Robin Mason
Kevin McNevin
Alvind Mehta
Ian Milne
Angela Moffatt
Lesley Patmore
Dilip Rathod
Tony Rees
Peter Senior
Steve Shepherd
Stan Sibcy
Cliff Skey
Doug Steele
Jeffrey Taylor
David Tonkinson
John Toyer
Mossy Waters
Tony Wicks
Christopher
   Wilkinson
Tony Willis
Colin Wood
1983
Tony Allen
Christine Bailey
Philip Baxendale
Albert Bell
Steve Bickmore
Michael Bourne
Michael Brain
Kay Connelly
Billy Cook
Peter Dedman
Kathryn Green
Prof Charles Handy
Brian Hill

Steven Larwood
Stephen Malley
Peter Nash
Fred Osborne
Terry Panther
Steven Pinnock
Iain Prentice
Steven Rigby
Brian Smart
Roger Snedker
Martin Taylor
Keith Thomas
John Walsh
Sue Webb
Albert Wrighting
1984
Cathy Calder
Trevor Daeffler
Mick Drage
Jenny Gadsby
Ruth Gumery
Ray Hutcheon
Mike Jiggins
Andrea Lightfoot
Vivienne Lovell
Mike Mason
Alec Norrie
Vic Penn
John Shaw
Norma Skerratt
Brian Taylor
Sally Tomlin
1985
Martin Bignall
Wendy Gregory
Andrew Gunn
Dick Lawson
Joanne Mulvey
Stuart Ovens
Pete Poulson
Ray Smart
June Starmer
Jackie Taylor

Barry Tomlin
Dennis Toms
Jenifer Waites
Sandra West
1986
Phillip Aries
Reg Bailey
Lester Bowman
Paul Brenchley
Serena Handcock
David Headland
Ed Posey
Mark Potter
Len Smith
Terry Strickland
Paul Sullivan
Keith Turpin
Roy Wilkinson
1987
Godfrey Bland
James Brown
David Cobbold
Thomas Cook
Alan Crout
Sheila Duffy
Rod Fry
Gillian Hartshorn
Dennis Lee
David Mead
Vreni Schumacher
David Taylor
Carol Walker
Bob Watt
Melanie Wright-
  Simmons
1988
Tony Boddington
Elizabeth Holton
Roman Mikolajewicz
Ray Mitchell
Jonathan Payne
Richard Sharp
Malcolm Tate

1989
Sheila Bonham
Susan Carter
Michael Chester
Margaret Cook
Kevin Lawson
Gary Le Normand
Angela Meager
Jim O'Brien
Lynn Theobald
1990
Greg Ainge
Sue Ardern
Sandra Bridgman
Louise Brown
Ian Henderson
John Keith
John McMurray
Judy Povey
Eileen Scott
David Shatford
Tracy Smeathers
Janet Souster
Valerie Summers
Anita Thorne
Alan White
Jon Wiles
Kevin Williamson
David York
1991
John Abraham
Allan Bell
Valerie Busby
Dr Arshad Chaudhry
Dr Simon Clarke
Elizabeth Clegg
Brian Drage
Geoff Fairbrass
Robert Freer
Robert Garner
Roger Greenacre
Andrew Horton
Dennis King

John Knibbs
Michael Lee
Ray Lilly
Rachel Little
John Mackay
Julie Palmer
David Rice
Margaret Roberts
Denise Sayer
Donald Sevier
Arne Strand
John Wojakowski
1992
Eric Barker
Hayley Cobbold
Geoff Fleming
Gloria Letch
Mike Lewis
Vanessa Lloyd
Dean Lockwood
Sharon Lucas
Jennifer McMahon
Pankaj Patel
Tanya Pearson
Nicholas Pincott
Helen Plowe
June Reilly
Lloyd Tee
Rod Varley
Anthony Wood
1993
Ros Ager
Samantha Barry
Stephen Cave
Darren Coniff
Mark Cooper
Sharon Durrant
Julie Elford
Ronald Gilder
James Glachan
Paul Glyn
Paula Gray
James Harris

Paul Harvey
Boyd Horton
Neil Kegg
Mark Lane
Jacqueline Long
Roy Mayhew
Andrew Moore
Dean Nicholls
Johanna Nichols
Jonathan Oldroyd
Simon Parsons
Robert Savage
Malcolm Smith
Andrew Thomas
1994
Richard Aldridge
John Barclay
Stephen Bell
Suzanne Berry
Paul Elder
Hugh Fenton
Anthony Gardner
John Horne
Peter Kelby
Robert Marsden
Dr John Nixon
Gill Nott
Peter Spriggs
Mark Sweetman
Paul Thacker
1995
Timothy Cheetham
Paul Chipperton
Darren Cox
Neil Gray
Gerry Lappin
Richard Lia
Zara Lloyd
Joseph McKeever
Kathryn McLean
Derek Muir
Kevin Olds
Julian Ord-Hume

Nigel Probert
Warren Robins
Charles Scott
Clive Williams
1996
Sarah Carter
Jennifer Griffin
Stephen James
Victoria Kenyon
Marie Lawson
Graeme Manley
Susan McDonald
Carole McKenzie
Lesley Morgan
Phillip Noble
Rob Paton
Damian Rice
Ray Sheath
John Whittenbury
1997
Robert French
Justin Herrin
Mark Hill
Katie Holt
Jenni Hyde
Jeff Legg
Colin McCarthy
Stuart McLachlan
Anthony Mills
Jamie Newell
Fabio Paladino
Laura Parish
Sailesh Patel
Martin Pearson
Alan Powell
Prof Janette Rutterford
Philip Scott
Michelle Sharman
Steve Sheppard
Tony Sibcy
Andrew Silsby
Caroline Tapp
Jamie Wilkinson

1998
Christopher Berry
Helen Bowman
Bala Cheramparambil
Anthony Clarke
Ellie Cole
James Connell
Rachel Earis
William Fitzgibbons
Robin Healey
Duncan Howland
Gary Jacobs
Francis Jenkinson
David Johnson
Stephen Jones
Dr Bill Lees
Martin Line
Murtaza Makda
Darren Matthews
Richard Meikle
Andrew Murray
Sean Palmer
John Phillips
John Pike
Hilary Pinder
Benjamin Rumbelow
Terry Smart
Charles Sparrow
Mark Stanion
Barry Taylor
Sioban Tobin
Paul Treverton
Daniel Waters
Ian Wilson-Benn
1999
Stephen Brady
Martin Brickland
David Brown
Rikki Bryant
David Cartwright
Malcolm Forsyth
Melody Hales
Steven Hales

Richard Hirst
Scott Inman
Derek Jewkes
Daniel Kelsall
Ifan Lewis
Victoria McCabe
Isobel Mohammed
David Nicholson
Christopher Oram
David Pike
Martin Raymer
William Rees
Kirsty Rhodes
Guy Richards
Ahmed Senouci
Pat Silburn
Gurmaj Singh
Jon Stepeney
Duncan Stewart
Robert Stewart
Susan Upcraft
Christopher Walsh
Melanie White

2000
Adrian Adams
Jean-Marc Bain
Yves Balliere
Darren Brailsford
Rebecca Chambers
Andrew Cotter
Jeffery Davis
Mark Dawson
Jean-René Feron
Christopher Goodall
Keith Grace
Peter Hedley

Richard Hesketh
John Kemp
Carol Kennedy
Michelle Maille
Steven Mason
Didier Mathon
Bjorn Neidert
David Nicholson
Bruce Penn
Jean-Claude Poret
David Rossouw
Neil Runagall
Roger Thevenon
Michael Webb

2001
Mohamed Ameur
Ian Andrews
Didier Benoit
Cecile Bogaczynski
J. P. Bonte
David Boothe
Didier Boulet
Richard Breen
Christian Caulier
Francine De Oliveira
Marielle Delommez
Phillipe Dembicki
Christian Deneux
Serge Depoorter
Karan Kumar Dhawan
Nathalie Fearon
Jean Marc Ferran
Marie-Françoise
    Fontroubade
Christine Galland
Laurent Gapenne

Annie Genty
Louis-Hubert Guilloux
Steven James
Lysiane Langlet
Monique Leclere
Benjamin Leeson
Roger Louey
Stephen May
Stephen Mayhew
Juliette Menetrier
Badrudeen Mohamed-
    Yunis
Laurence Neveu
Edouard Noe
Stephane Nuguyen
Eric Orlandi
Nicholas Padfield
Christian Petit
F. Pinan
Gilles Piquion
Veronique Roche
Herve Selin
Dale Shaw
Aftab Sheikh
Julian Sisley
Mark Stephenson
Marie Terrizzi
Julien Tocut
Joel Trevin
Guy Trompette
Erika Williams
David Wilson
Leigh Woodward
Martine Wrotecki

Select Bibliography

Auerbach, Felix, trans. Paul Siegfried and Frederick Cheshire, *The Zeiss Works and the Carl-Zeiss-Stiftung in Jena: Their Scientific, Technical, and Sociological Development and Importance Described*, London, Marshall Brookes and Chalkley, 1904.

Blasi, Joseph and Kruse, Douglas, *The New Owners: The Mass Emergence of Employee Ownership in Public Companies, and What it Means to American Business*, New York, HarperCollins, 1991.

Blum, Fred, *Work and Community – The Scott Bader Commonwealth and the Quest for a New Social Order*, Routledge and Kegan Paul, 1968.

Bradley, Keith and Estrin, Saul, *Does Employee Ownership Improve Company Performance?*, London, Partnership Research, 1988.

Cleghorn, James Stephen, *This Work of Justice: The Search for Moral Common Ground in the Authority Relations of Work (The Cases of the American Cast Iron Pipe Co and the Scott Bader Company Compared)*, Ph.D thesis, Emory University, Atlanta, 1995.

Cole, G. D. H., *A Century of Co-operation*, London, Allen & Unwin for the Co-operative Union, 1947.

Dore, Ronald, *Taking Japan Seriously*, London, Athlone Press, 1987.

Earle, John, *The Italian Co-operative Movement: A Portrait of the Lega Nazionale delle Co-operative e Mutue*, London, Allen & Unwin, 1986.

Ellerman, David, *The Democratic Worker Owned Firm*, Boston, Unwin Hyman, 1990.

Gates, Jeff, *The Ownership Solution: Towards a Shared Capitalism for the Twenty-First Century*, Harmondsworth, Penguin Books, 1998.

Goyder, George, *The Future of Private Enterprise*, Oxford, Basil Blackwell, 1951.

——, *The Responsible Company*, Oxford, Basil Blackwell, 1961.

Hadley, Roger, *Participation and Common Ownership: A Study in Employee Participation in a Common Ownership Firm*, Ph.D. Dissertation, University of London, 1971.

Hoe, Susanna, *The Man Who Gave His Company Away: A Biography of Ernest Bader, Founder of The Scott Bader Commonwealth*, London, Heinemann, 1978.

Kelso, Lewis O., and Adler, Mortimer J., *The Capitalist Manifesto*, New

York, Random House, 1958; reprinted, Westport, Connecticut, Greenwood Press, 1975.

Lewis, John Spedan, *Fairer Shares*, London, Staple Press, 1954.

——, *Partnership for All*, London, Kerr-Cross, 1948.

Liebenstein, Harvey, *Beyond Economic Man*, Harvard, 1980.

Meade, James, *Agathatopia, The Economics of Partnership*, Aberdeen University Press, 1989.

Oakeshott, Robert, *Jobs & Fairness: The Logic and Experience of Employee Ownership*, Norwich, Michael Russell, 2000.

——, *The Case for Workers Co-ops*, Routledge and Kegan Paul, 1978; 2nd ed., Macmillan, 1990.

Parkyn, Brian, *Democracy, Accountability, and Participation in Industry*, MCB Publications, 1979.

——, *Polyesters Vol 2: Unsaturated Polyesters*, Iliffe Books, 1967.

Partnership Research Ltd (PRL) [later Job Ownership Research (JOR)], Case Studies commissioned and published by PRL, London:

Workers as Entrepreneurs: Two Striking Success Stories from Italy, 1990

The Carl-Zeiss-Stiftung: Its First Hundred Years of Impersonal Ownership, 1990

World Leaders in Low Voltage Cables and Luncheon Vouchers: A Study of Two Outstanding Industrial Co-operatives in France, 1992

A Tale of Two Bus Companies, 1992

The Potential of Employee Ownership for Listed Companies: The Case of Polaroid, 1994

The United Steelworkers of America & Employee Ownership: An Exemplary Contribution to the Preservation of Jobs and Improved Performance, 1994

Co-operatives in Community Care: A Multiple Case Study, 1994

New Employee Ownership Challenges for Traditional Craftsmen at Herend, 1995

Majority Employee Ownership at United Airlines: Big Wins for Both Jobs & Investors, 1996

Quarter, Jack, *Beyond the Bottom Line: Socially Innovative Business Owners*, Westport, Connecticut, Quorum Books, 2000.

Schumacher, Christian, *God in Work: Discovering the Divine Pattern for Work in the New Millennium*, Oxford, Lion Publishing, 1998.

Schumacher, E. F., *Small Is Beautiful*, London, Blond and Briggs, 1973.

Sorensen, The Revd Lord (Reginald), 'A Backbencher's Pilgrimage', unpublished autobiography, available in House of Lords records.

Vienney, Claude, *L'Economie du Secteur Co-operatif Français*, Paris, Editions Cujas, 1966.

Weitzman, Martin, *The Share Economy*, Harvard, 1990.

Wellock, Wilfred, *Off the Beaten Track; Adventures in the Art of Living*

(Foreword by Jayaprakash Narayan), Bombay, Sarvodaya Pranchuralaya, 1961.

——, *Gandhi as a Social Revolutionary*, Birmingham, pamphlet, 1949

Whyte, W. F. and K. K., *Making Mondragon*, Cornell, 1988.

Wilken Folkert, *The Liberation of Work: The Elimination of Strikes and Strife in Industry through Associative Organisation of Enterprise* (Foreword by E. F. Schumacher), London, Routledge & Kegan Paul, 1969.

——, trans. David Green, *The Liberation of Capital*, London, George Allen & Unwin, 1982.

ERNEST BADER COMMON OWNERSHIP LECTURES 1973–8

1972, *The Politics of Revolution*, Professor Harvey Wheeler (Not truly in the series, but perhaps a prototype)

1973, Professor Ota Sik

1974, *Peace and Cooperation*, Professor Adam Curle

1975, *Partnership Not Participation*, Sir Bernard Miller

1976, *The End of Economic Man*, George Goyder CBE

1977, *The End of an Era Calls for New Departures*, Christian Schumacher

1978, *Innovative Technologies for a Future Society*, Carl-Goran Heden

SCOTT BADER COMMON OWNERSHIP LECTURES 1983–2000

1983, *Industry and the Chief End of Man*, Dr Magnus Pyke

1984, *The Practice and Experience of the Mondragon Basque Cooperatives*, Josu Irigoien

1985, *Work, Money and the New Economics*, James Robertson

1986, *Industrial Partnership: Utopia or Necessity?*, Professor Branko Horvat

1987, *Common Wealth, Common Ownership, Common Confusion*, Rt Rev David E. Jenkins, Bishop of Durham

1988, *Who is Really to Blame?*, Dr Jose Lutzenberger

1990, *The Challenge of Conflict and Concord*, Dr. Ivan Ravel

1991, *The Challenge of Conflict and Concord*, Brian Parkyn

1994, Seminar: *Common Ownership in the 1990s*,
    Common Ownership, Co-Operatives and Corporate Governance, Stuart Bell MP
    A View from the Co-operative Sector, Roger Jones
    Does Employee Ownership Improve Performance?, Nigel Mason

1997, *Beyond Tomorrow's Company*, Mark Goyder

Index